The
Toy and Game
Inventor's Handbook

The
Toy and Game Inventor's Handbook

Richard C. Levy and
Ronald O. Weingartner

ALPHA

A member of Penguin Group (USA) Inc.

International Standard Book Number: 1-59257-062-3
Library of Congress Catalog Card Number: 2003104300

05 04 03   8 7 6 5 4 3 2 1

Interpretation of the printing code: The rightmost number of the first series of numbers is the year of the book's printing; the rightmost number of the second series of numbers is the number of the book's printing. For example, a printing code of 03-1 shows that the first printing occurred in 2003.

Printed in the United States of America

Most Alpha books are available at special quantity discounts for bulk purchases for sales promotions, premiums, fund-raising, or educational use. Special books, or book excerpts, can also be created to fit specific needs.

For details, write: Special Markets; Alpha Books, 375 Hudson Street, New York, NY 10014.

About the Cover: It is fitting that a book about independent toy inventors, and the opportunities to license their concepts, have on its cover one of the most unique and successful independent inventor submissions ever licensed and marketed worldwide, Furby.
Mark Pesce, founding Chair of the Interactive Media Program at USC called animatronic Furby, "the best example of a new class of toys."
Furby ® & © 2003 Hasbro, Inc. Used with permission.

Publisher: *Marie Butler-Knight*
Product Manager: *Phil Kitchel*
Senior Managing Editor: *Jennifer Chisholm*
Senior Acquisitions Editor: *Mike Sanders*
Production Editor: *Billy Fields*
Copy Editor: *Krista Hansing*
Cover/Book Designer: *Trina Wurst*
Creative Director: *Robin Lasek*
Indexer: *Aamir Burki*
Layout/Proofreading: *Megan Douglass, Becky Harmon*

To Sheryl, the center of my universe, and Bettie, our shooting star. RCL

To lovable Leslie Lawrence, sons Tyler and Tom, and grandsons Tommy and James, all winners in my game of life. ROW

Contents

Preface

In 1990, we co-authored *Inside Santa's Workshop*. Like this book, it was written first and foremost as a tribute to the talented men and women who form what is popularly known in the toy industry as the "inventing community." These seasoned, innovative, exclusive, full-time gifted professional inventors *cum* designers, *cum* engineers, *cum* developers, *cum* marketers, *cum* shtikmeisters satisfy the voracious American appetite for toys and games—and their best creations often find their way around the world.

The American toy market was a $13 billion business in 1990, according to what was then the Toy Manufacturers of America (TMA). Thirteen years later, so much has changed in and about our industry. The American toy market is now a more than $30 billion business (in 2002 this included $10.3 billion in video game revenue) and the TMA has morphed into the Toy Industry Association (TIA).

In 1990, there were scores more independent toy companies than today. Toys R Us was the dominant toy retailer and Wal-Mart was just emerging from an Arkansas dream. Today companies such as Amtoy, Azrak-Hamway, Buddy L, Cap Toys, Coleco, Fisher-Price, Fundimension, Galoob, Games Gang, Ideal, International Games, Irwin, Knickerbocker, Kenner, LJN, Matchbox, Mego, Milton Bradley, Nasta, OddzOn, Parker Brothers, Playtime, Playskool Schaper, Tiger Electronics, Tonka, ToyMax, Trendmaster, Tyco, Western Publishing, and Worlds of Wonder have either been acquired or were unable to survive. And Wal-Mart has overtaken Toys R Us as the biggest U.S. toy retailer.

These independent "idea people" work outside the confines of any single toy or game manufacturer, yet rely totally on the remaining companies to take their creations to market. As a group, they survive on their ability to generate the sparks for new forms, fantasies, and fun that often turn up on children's Christmas lists.

We use the terms *inventor*, *developer*, and *creator* interchangeably, as does the industry, to signify one or more of the independent creative forces behind a product, usually a signatory to the agreement between inventor (licensor) and manufacturer (licensee), and, as such, a participant in any advances and royalty income.

We make no attempt to recognize co-inventing credits, for this would be impossible, as anyone familiar with the business knows. Throughout our book, you may notice that two or more inventors often take credit for the same product. This is normal in a business where many diverse and specialized talents are required to bring an idea from the embryonic stage to the retail stage. It was never our aim to attempt to pinpoint which associate or partner was responsible for a particular key idea, or the contribution and/or enhancement that caused a concept to be licensed by a manufacturer. The process of innovation is never easy to analyze. Perhaps Paul Saffo, a research fellow with the Menlo Park, California-based Institute for the Future, put it best when he told *Newsweek* that trying to understand innovation is like shoveling smoke.

When we use the term *toy market*, we mean to encompass all categories, such as games, dolls, action figures, ride-ons, pre-school, infant, and so forth. The same is true when we call someone a *toy inventor*; that is, he or she could be a creator of a wide range of playthings and gaming devices.

We interchange the terms *marketer* and *manufacturer* when referring to companies. This is because in today's industry, more companies are, in fact, performing marketing functions and relying on off-shore sources for production. There are fewer industry members today that are manufacturers in the traditional sense.

By focusing on the independent inventor, it is not our intent to imply that there is any lack of creativity or inventiveness at the corporate level. On the contrary, many outstanding concepts come from in-house. And the contributions made by corporate research-and-development and marketing executives to outside submissions can often make the difference between success and failure.

It also should be noted that many of today's most accomplished and respected independents came from the corporate ranks. Conversely, inventors have been known to seek refuge in the security of the companies. But without the work of the inventing community, the industry as we know it simply would not exist.

Through our combined experiences in product development and marketing, we are aware that cross-pollination and synergism of many forces produce ultimate success. Product development to eventual retail sale is a delicate, complex, and serpentine chain of egos, events, whims, technologies, designs, and marketing skills. If any link were to break, an entire project could flag. In the end, the whole is more powerful than any of its individual parts.

The professional inventors mentioned in our book fully understand that it is one thing to have an idea; another thing to design and engineer an idea; another thing to polish, package, promote, and position an idea; and yet another thing to negotiate the sale of a product to the retail trade. They know—luck being a given—that it takes teamwork to make anything happen. It is rare when one person has an idea, proto-types it without assistance, shows it to a manufacturer, and walks away alone with the deal. If you scratch beneath the headlines of any product introduction, there is always a cast of characters and technical people, as certain as the credit crawl that follows every movie.

We made every effort to interview as many independent inventors, agents, corpo-rate executives, and industry observers as possible. Some of those contacted did not wish to participate. Hey, inventors can be quirky. Others missed our deadlines. We cross-checked our lists of professional inventors with numerous corporate vice presi-dents of R&D and marketing in an attempt not to overlook any prolific concept sources. No doubt we missed some people, and for this we apologize. Nonetheless, the story of our book would not change.

We made every effort to include as many current, full time, professional inventors as possible in the highly visible profile section. But, our publisher gave us tight specs and we did not have unlimited space. In fact, we had to remove many pages—enough for a second book—from our completed manuscript. This was the most painful part of this project. Some inventors we were unable to profile are quoted throughout the book, and we appreciate their time and interest in our work. Omissions were uninten-tional. An inventor we missed may be as talented and productive a product source as the contributors who opened their minds and workshops to us.

We intentionally focused on American inventors, but fully recognize and applaud the contributions of our many creative colleagues in England, continental Europe, Israel, Japan, China, and other nations around the world. We certainly recognize that toy inventing is a global industry, and the majority of participants interviewed by us keep their passports at the ready.

We, alas, also had to dramatically reduce the amount material used from the in-ventor questionnaires. But what we picked up was left in the inventor's own editorial style. We also accepted less than complete questionnaires, if someone did not have the time or desire to answer every question. The answers indeed chronicle, in their own words, who these inventors are, what they have done, and what they dream of doing. Aspiring first-time inventors with interest in toys and games should find the thoughts of these experienced professionals as inspiring as they are informative.

We included a listing of TIA-member companies that welcome outside submissions. We did our best to canvass the industry and reach out to as many companies as possible. We were faced here, too, with space restrictions. There were some companies, frankly to our surprise, that accept outside submissions but did not want to be included. We honored their wish, or simply stopped calling, reading their lack of response as no interest. This information should be particularly helpful to first-time inventors, since the list shows where they and their ideas are welcome versus those companies that have policies against viewing unsolicited new concepts from wannabes.

We really enjoyed creating the industry dictionary we call Talk the Talk. After all, if you're reading this preface, you must enjoy playthings, and we tried to be a bit playful in our approach to the subject matter.

Just as in any business, toy executives change jobs and affiliations. All executives are credited with the positions held at the time they were interviewed. The fact that they may not be at the same company when you read this book in no way diminishes the knowledge imparted by them.

The Toy and Game Inventor's Handbook provides insights to the selection and development of new product concepts and how the creative forces inside and outside a company mesh. These are intended to provide a roadmap to those inventors hoping to license a toy or game idea to a marketer. It is our hope that the book will intrigue, inform, entertain, and turn over a rock or two for even the most seasoned toy industry veteran. We blended our words and interviews into a flavor that we feel accurately reflects the industry and its personalities. We have stocked it with a wide-ranging and colorful cast of characters, a bit of hyperbole, a dash of dreams, the crackle of the irresistible fire of imagination, inspiring and exciting stories of success, and the hard troubling realities of one of the toughest businesses.

In the end, we hope you enjoy this read, use a lot of yellow highlighter, and continue to dream of creating the next megahit toy or game.

RCL
ROW

Introduction

The toy industry has always been inextricably tied to the year-end gift-giving season. Understandably so, since the success of business has long been measured by 4Q results. Three-quarters of the year can be sluggish, but if the December rush hits with desired impact, the year's sales goals are saved!

Retailers can hardly wait to clear away October orange and get out the red, green, and silver to put shoppers into the spirit of holiday shopping. Even the weatherman is brought into the plan. A cold fall with early flakes has long been viewed by toy industry execs that the meteorological gods are looking favorably at a long buying season. Warm weather gets blamed for keeping shoppers out of malls and is not welcomed by industry observers.

Television networks start to advertise holiday specials even before the candy corn is gone. Commercials blare with greater frequency about hot, new toys. Little consumers start thinking about "being good," lest the delivery to their chimneys be sparse. While they're thinking about the toys they will unwrap, industry executives watch daily store results at a time they know is make or break.

Some 85 years ago, we came very close to not having a Christmas—the Grinch nearly got away with the holiday, childrens' letters to the North Pole stood a chance of going unanswered, stockings could have gone unfilled. Santa almost didn't show.

In 1917, the United States had entered World War I. The U.S. Council for National Defense, called by one news service "a committee of bureaucratic Scrooges," proposed an embargo on the purchase and sale of Christmas gifts as a way to conserve the nation's resources and direct the economy toward the war effort. Toys were looked at as a frivolity. Uncle Sam threatened to close Santa's workshops.

Empty stockings? Broken hearts? Disappointed children? Not if the toy industry could prevent it! A.C. Gilbert, inventor of the Erector Set and then-president of the one-year-old trade association the Toy Manufacturers of America, went to the nation's capital accompanied by a delegation of fellow toy makers, prepared to do battle on behalf of their industry and America's kids. Fortified with an assortment of product, they set out to persuade the men on the Council that most toys would not sap the war effort of raw materials or manpower.

According to a report in the *Boston Post*, Gilbert and his colleagues at first were so intimidated by the dignified atmosphere of the Council's offices and the serious demeanor of its members that they stashed their toy samples behind a couch. However, Gilbert went on to present a powerful argument for the importance of toys in building national pride and readiness among American youth. Perhaps recalling the dreams of their own past holiday joys, it didn't take long for the Council to reverse its position.

A toy inventor had saved Christmas! As the *Boston Post* reported, from the moment the toy representatives opened their bags of samples, "the Secretaries were boys again. Secretary [of the Navy] Daniels was as pleased with an Ives submarine as he could be with a new destroyer …. 'Toys appeal to the heart of every one of us, no matter how old we are,' said another Cabinet member. And it was because they did … that the boys and girls of the United States are going to awake this Christmas morning upon a day as merry as Christmases in the past."

That was then, but the dreams are forever strong. Switch to a December 22, any year. The Christmas shopping countdown is in the final digits. Colorful roto-sections in extra-heavy newspapers announce red-tag specials, early-bird sales, and slashed prices on goods for all ages. Mailboxes have been stuffed with slick mail-order catalogs, and TV commercials have become kid-directed. Storefront billboards scream super savings on sophisticated do-all playthings; 21st-century abracadabra, electronic toys and games; and the latest whirling, screaming gizmos.

To children, the next few days are filled with great anticipation. Besieged moms and dads—and *their* moms and dads—make last-minute plans, selections, and purchases to build the pyramid of gifts that will surround the tree. They know their tasks and rush wildly to complete them on time. With the accompaniment of booming holiday Muzak, millions of Christmas-smitten parents play out the role of the plump, scarlet-and-fur-clad, all-knowing, ever-giving, eternally beloved holiday cherub known as Santa Claus.

It is December 22, any year. Cars are double-parked and idling in fire lanes at suburban malls. The sprawling, multi-tiered bazaars are resplendent with a near-endless array of gewgaws, bric-a-brac, curios, and vitals. Mountains of merchandise stand ready to satisfy the seasonal spirit of consumer generosity. After all, if the retailers and marketers don't make it now, their year will be dubbed "a loser".

In the middle of each of these mind- and eye-boggling winter fairylands, at the end of all mall avenues, is the epicenter of holiday fantasy, the huge, candy-cane throne. Artificial gingerbread cutouts and twinkling gumdrop lights line pathways to the red-and-white perch befitting only the most revered royalty. Among papier-mâché elves and bridled, plastic reindeer is an endless procession of youngsters anxious for a brief chat with the celebrity of the season.

Each child delivers a message with varying degrees of confidence, but with consistent intent. Every youthful visitor enumerates a lengthy list of most desired playthings. And as the children chatter to their bearded listener, adoring parents strain to overhear the desires and dreams. It may be the Santa figure who probes, questions, and teases to learn the prized toys and games. But it will be up to the loving onlookers to see that their children's hopes of the season are delivered.

It is December 22, any year. The season of buying may be all around, but inside a business office an independent toy inventor works with his or her design team finishing a product prototype. Their hopes are that the new product will be in demand not 48 hours from now, but a full year or two into the future.

The center of attention is a novel idea, the prototype of which is targeted as a real product for debut at the annual American International Toy Fair in New York City. The inventor isn't waiting for Santa's elves to create this exciting new toy opportunity. The plan is to license it to a toy company and, with the right marketing, land high on children's "I want" lists at some future Christmas.

The inventor has alerted an established network of toy-industry contacts that the labors may yield the next Barbie. Or maybe the next Furby, an animatronic marvel with seemingly the intelligence and speech of many toddler owners. NYC appointments are set with executives at Hasbro and Mattel and recorded into a Palm Pilot.

No bell-ringers, twinkling lights, or mistletoe will interfere in this inventor's tasks. The inventor turns aside the hype of the season, and even though he or she is part kid and part industrial designer, he or she is also a marketer who operates in Santa's real workshop: the mass market toy industry. Santa's real helpers are on the job far longer than the final two weeks in December. Every day, year after year, the inventors and developers behind Santa's bounty are on the job. Their genius is being tested constantly; their creations are in demand by toy companies not just at year's end, but all year long.

Santa's toys are born in the workshops of real people who have committed their talents to originating the next megahit toy. In the kiddie world, Santa may get credit for the sugar plums, but in the adult world, highly talented entrepreneurial people compete to create the hot-selling plums. *The Toy and Game Inventor's Handbook* is their story and a book filled with what it takes to join the community of Santa's unsung helpers.

Acknowledgments

As authors of a book of this nature, we are essentially investigative reporters, heavily dependent on the cooperation, assistance, recall, and time of many people. During the course of our 3½ month full-court press to meet our deadlines, we contacted no less than 100 professional toy and game inventors, and more than 75 key executives, educators, patent counsels, and industry observers.

People responded to us from their offices and homes, through e-mail, via fax, and mobile phones from cars, trains, and planes. Some folks worked with us while on holiday, here and overseas, to answer our seemingly unending stream of questions, compose quotes, write up recollections, and fill out questionnaires to help craft what we hope is the most informative toy and game inventor handbook ever published. A few people were virtually carpet-bombed with e-mails as our work ratcheted up. Everyone's warm reception, patience, interest, hospitality, generosity, and friendship helped to make this project enjoyable, enlightening, and one we will both fondly remember always.

The people and companies we contacted that did not wish to cooperate can be counted on one hand. What became abundantly clear was that the busiest people, and the most committed, got back to us the quickest. They understood this was a meaningful project to us, and we hope to the industry, and wanted to contribute.

Some specific people who merit special designation are: Bang Zoom: Steve Fink; Endless Games: Kevin McNulty; Estes-Cox, Inc.: Barry Tunick; Fisher-Price: Stan Clutton; Hasbro: David Berko; Rich Berne; Wayne Charness; Nichole Cook; David Dubosky; Judy Flathers; Michael Gray; Alan G. Hassenfeld; Mike Hirtle; Darlene Horan; Sheila Kilday; Richard J. Maddocks; Sandy Marks; Cathy Meredith; Mark Morris; Marc Rosenberg; Sandy Schelhase; Dale Siswick; Helen Van Tassel; George Volanakis; E. David Wilson; Mattel: Jamie Filipeli, Phil Jackson, Tor Sirset, and Judy Willis; Patch Products: Peggy Brown; Pressman: Susan Adamo Baumbach; Jim Pressman, David Shapiro; Racing Champions: Jeff Jones; Radica: Jeff Conrad, Pat Feeley; S.R.M.: Bruce Bennett; Stephen Mickelberg; SpinMaster Toys: Ben Varadi; Team Concepts: George Propsom; Uncle Milton Industries: Frank Adler, Eric Poesch; University Games: Bob Moog; USAopoly: John Davis, Maggie Matthews.

At F.I.T.: Judy Ellis and Jennifer Rice. Otis: Martin Caveza and Jennifer Lizzio. Prudential Securities: Dave Capin.

At Glenbrook Middle School: Annette King and Thoma Miller for opening their classrooms to get a read from ninety game playing students on what's doin' today!

At the TIA, the organization at the epicenter of the industry, thanks to Thomas Conley for his quote, and to Diana Cardinale for her quick responses to our frequent requests for updated figures and fact checks.

Special thanks to the following friends for editorial contributions above and beyond the call of duty: David Berko, Tom Dusenberry, Marc Rosenberg, Joel Seidman, and Stewart Sims; and to Arlene and Norman Fabricant for the Vermont Group photo.

George Harvill, president of Greentree Information Service, put in countless hours searching the patents that fill these pages, and many more that did not make the cut.

Thanks to Mike Sanders, our acquisitions editor, who championed our proposal, and made this book happen; we appreciate his wise counsel, contributions, and confidence. Phil Kitchel, our developmental editor, who helped organize this body of work to make it even more reader-friendly; Krista Hansing, our copy editor, for her probing and polishing; Trina Wurst, our designer, for her artistic touches; and to (Wild) Billy Fields, an awesome production editor who worked with us on edits right down to the last nanosecond before the book was released to the printer.

Richard Thanks ...

To my co-author, Ron, thanks for the idea that gave birth to this project back in 1989. It has been a pleasure to collaborate with you again. You can now hit Fast-Forward on the control panel of your life.

To Sheryl, my beloved and gifted wife, thanks for your unwavering support as I flew through yet another editorial Danzig Corridor. To Bettie (a.k.a Buckie); as always, you bring me great joy and pride. I love you muchisimo and then some.

To super-savvy Michael Ross, Malcolm Hall (fairdinkum, ridgy-didge, dinky-di friend down under), Haig der Marderosian (wherever you are), and all my associates and corporate partners o'er the years, y'all rock. And, as always, The Beck Rules!—RCL

Ronald Thanks ...

I am delighted to have co-authored this book with you, Richard. As a top "go-to" guy in the inventing community, your boundless energy, enthusiasm, perseverance, and experiences make any creative undertaking possible. For all you have done, my sense is that your best is yet to come!

To my wife, Leslie, thanks for finding time beyond running your marketing firm to assist my side of the project at crucial times. And sons Tom and Tyler, your frequent participation in kitchen research and playtime has kept me wired to reality.

I have been fortunate to have worked with most of the creatives and execs whose contributions to the industry in general and this book specifically are incalculable. Thank you all.—ROW

Wanna Play a Game?

Question-and-answer (Q&A) trivia is one of the most popular forms of commercial gameplay—on virtually any conceivable subject. So, we created our own version of it just for this book. We just couldn't resist weaving in important (and not-so-important) industry trivia in the form of a game you can play.

Interspersed throughout the pages of this book are 100 trivia questions designed to challenge your factual knowledge, stimulate your inquisitive mind, and appeal to your playful nature.

Answer all 100 questions. The answers are in Appendix D, on page 472. We also created a highly unscientific and totally arbitrary scoring system that appears on page 471 so you can see how you would rate against a hypothetical cross-section of industry figures.

We hope you enjoy playing as you read and suggest you bookmark the questions as you answer each question. You should get a laugh or two from this special toy and game Q&A challenge, learn some interesting industry facts, and maybe even gain a high score.

Here are some sample questions:

Toy Trivia

I. Which state is home to the greatest number of professional toy and game inventors?

a. New York

b. Florida

c. California

Toy Trivia

II. The site of the International Toy Center at 200 Fifth Avenue, New York City, was once _____.

a. farmland

b. a NY/NY Port Authority garage

c. NYPD headquarters

Toy Trivia

III. Name the original Rock'em Sock'em robots.

a. Red Rocker and Blue Bomber

b. Red Fred and Billy Blue

c. Saultarus and Umgluk

Toy Trivia

IIII. Tiny Tears came with her own _____.

a. Kleenex

b. make-up case

c. purse

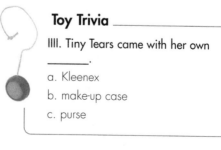

Answers: C; A; A; A

Chapter 1

Ideas R Us: Names in the Game

"The elixir of our industry is creativity. Whether from independent inventors or internal magic, this is a life force which must be nurtured forever ...."

—Alan G. Hassenfeld, chairman and CEO, Hasbro, Inc.

Let's play Ask and Answer. You have 20 seconds.

Ask: Which toy and game companies conceived the following products?

25 Words or Less
ABC Dancer Elmo
Adverteasing
Aerobie
Aggravation
Air Rebound
Air Trigger
Alphie
Amazing Ally
Ants in the Pants
Axis and Allies
Babbles to Books
Baby All Gone
Baby Check Up
Baby Face
Baby Go Bloom
Baby Grows
Baby Kiss and
  Giggles
Baby Secrets
Bad Eggs Bunch
Barbie Says
Barney Banjo
Barrel of Monkeys
Basket Blaster
Battling Tops
Bead Blast Barbie
Bead 'N Beauty
  Barbie
Beanie Babies
Bed Bugs
Bible Trivia
Boggle
Boglins
Bop-It

Bottle Cap Cars
Bubba
Bug Truck
Bumble Ball
Bump 'n Go R/C
Buzz Blitzer
Cabbage Patch Kids
Candy Land
Cap Blastin' Hot
  Wheels
Careers
Catch Phrase
Chicken Limbo
Chicken Soup for the
  Soul: The Game
Clue
Color Me Cuties
Come to Me Blue
Computer Warriors
Connect Four
Cootie
Cotton Candy
  Machine
Counting Eggs
Crayola
Cricket
Digger the Dog
Disney Uno
Diva Starz
Dizzy Dryer
Doh-Nutters
Dolly Surprise
Don't Break the Ice
Don't Spill the Beans
Doodle Bear

Dr. Drill 'n' Fill
Dragon Strike
Dress 'n Dazzle
Dune Machine
Dynamite Shack
E-Doodle
Elmo's Bubble
  Trumpet
Encore!
Etch-a-Sketch
Family Reunion
Farm Families
Fashion Avenue Kitty
  & Puppy
Fireball Island
Floam
Funnoodle
Furby
Furby Baby
Game of Life
Game of the States
GEM
Geni
GI Joe
Giga Pets
Giggle Wiggle
Girl Talk
Glo Friends
Gnip Gnop
Go for Broke
Go Go Worms
Go to the Head of
  the Class
Goofin' Around with
  Goofy

Guess Who
Guesstures
Gurgling Baby
Gurlz
Guzzlers
Halloween Glow
  Barbie
HammerHead R/C
Hands Down
Handy Dandy
  Notebook
Harry Potter Chapter
  Games
Hi-Ho! Cherry-O!
Hilarium
Hit Clips
Hot Lixx
Hot Potato
Hungry, Hungry
  Hippos
Husker Do
Jenga
Jungle Hunt
Lincoln Logs
Lite Brite
Karaoke Mickey
Kasey the Kinderbot
Katie Kiss & Giggles
Kerplunk
Kissums
Kissy Doll
Klixx
Koosh
Lazer Attack
Little Lost Socks

Little Lullabyes
Little Sparklin' Clouds
Magic Hat
Magic Love Ball
Magic Works
Magical Pets Barbie
Magnetic Poetry
Major Morgan
Malarky
Manhattan Game
Mechanix
Men Are from Mars, Women Are from Venus: The Game
Merlin
Micro Machines
Mighty Mo
Mille Bornes
Mindtrap
Miracle Moves Baby
Monopoly
Monster Mash Play Doh
Mouse in the House
Mouse Trap
Mr. Bucket
Mr. Machine
Mr. Potato Head
Music 2 Go
My Size Barbie
Mystery Date
Mystery Mirror Puzzle
Name Dropper
NBA Finals Game
Nerf
Nitro Dozer R/C

Noteability
Oodles
Oops & Downs
Operation
Othello
Ouija
Out of Context
Outburst
Payday
Pente
Perfection
Phase 10
Pictionary
Pivot Pool
Pocket Kite
Pokemon
Polly Pocket
Pose Me Pets
Pound Puppies
Pretty Cut and Grow
Psycho R/C
Puffalumps
Punch Lines
Puppy Check Up
Puppy Racers
Puppy Surprise
Push 'n Roar
PXL-2000
QuizWiz
Raggedy Ann
Rap Master Mike
Razzle
Read My Lips
Ready-Steady Ride-O
Risk
Robo Wheels
Robot Play Doh
Roll Over Rover

ROM: The Space Knight
Route 66: The Game
Rubik's Cube
Rumples
Rush Hour
Scattergories
Scrabble
Scrabble Up
Screamers
Screamin' Kart
Screwy Looey
Scruples
Sea Monkeys
See & Say Winky Says
Shaker Maker
Shark Attack
Shark Bowling
Sharkinator R/C
Shelby
Shining Stars
Shrinky Dinks
Silly Dillies
Silly Putty
Simon
Simpson's Trivia
Sing 'n Snore Ernie
Sit 'n Spin
Sky Dancers
Slinky
Smart Alec
Smoochie Pooch
SNL Trivia
Soft 'n Silly Friends
Song Burst
Sonic Fazer
Sorry

Spin Pops
Spirograph
Split
Spray Effects
Star Rider
Stay Alive
Starbird
Stompers
Stratego
Street Beats Jam Van
Stretch Armstrong
Super Soaker
Sure Putt Golf
Suzy Snapshot
Sweet Secrets
Taboo
Talk Back Crib Mirror
Talking Big Bird
Talking G.I. Joe
Teenage Mutant Ninja Turtles
Tetris
Thinklings
Tick Penz
Tickle Me Elmo!
Time Bomb
Tin Can Alley
Tinkertoys
Tip-it
Top It
Toss Across
TriBond
Trivia Bingo
Trivial Pursuit
Trouble
Trump: The Game
Tubtown

Twister	Vortex	Xtreme Moto-X Cycle
UBI	Water Babies	Yahtzee
Uncle Wiggily	We Did It Dora	Yak Backwards
Ungame	Weebles	Yakity Jack
Uno	Wheels on the Bus	Yakity-Yak Talking Teeth
Upwords	Who's On First	Yo Ball
Vac Man	Win, Lose or Draw	Yomega
Verticross	Wiz-z-zer	Zip 'N Zoom Shannen
ViewMaster	Wrist Racers	

Answer: None.

Each of these products was the brain child of an independent inventor. Many generate big business on a year-to-year basis. Some are money-spinners that sustain companies. These are evergreens. You may not recognize all of them, and not all were blockbusters or even hits. Some came and went faster than a speeding Hot Wheels car. But every product on this list, and countless others that could fill volumes, was licensed from external creatives and commercialized by toy or game companies. Executives in charge of product selection obviously felt there was something special enough about each item, if only the seed of an idea, to commit the human, material, and financial resources of their companies. The products were developed, manufactured, marketed, and sold in hopes that the toy and game gods—and certainly consumers—would smile upon them.

The people who conceived these concepts are not all, as one might expect, lettered engineers and designers. Some are far removed from the world of playthings. Many of the men and women behind these products pursued their own careers before signing their first license agreement. Among the professional independent toy inventors interviewed or discussed in this book are a former barber, stock brokers, newspaper editors, a registered nurse, talent agents, artists, data systems programmers, psychologists, marketing MBAs, teachers, social workers, commercial real estate developers, a radio and television announcer, restaurant managers, nonprofit workers, TV producers, advertising executives, a biologist, sales types, an options trader, and even two members of the clergy: a priest and a nun.

Toy Trivia

1. Mattel's Hot Wheels brand marked which anniversary in 2002?

a. Thirtieth

b. Thirty-fifth

c. Fortieth

Donner, Dancer, Dasher, Blitzen, Comet, Cupid, Prancer, Vixen, and, okay, Rudolph!

Everyone knows what these legendary names mean to Santa Claus. Once a year, on a most significant and magical night, Ol' Saint Nick calls on these trusted reindeer to pull his sleigh, laden with toys, to homes of children everywhere.

Breslow, Fabricant, Goldfarb, Hyman, Klitsner, Mass, Meyer, Rudell, and, okay, Wexler!

Few outside the toy industry know what these names mean to the mythical Santa Claus. Throughout the year, these people, and others you will meet in this book, create the toys and games that will be in demand during any Christmas season. There's nary an elf among them, but they represent the great talents who invent the goodies that stuff the stockings, surround the Christmas trees, delight millions of kids—and generated in excess of $30 billion (includes $10.3 billion in video game sales) in retail sales in 2002!

The stories of such inventors as Robert "Steamboat" Fulton, King "Safety Razor" Gillette, Edwin "60-Second Camera" Land, George "Air Brake" Westinghouse, and Clarence "Frozen Food" Birdseye are legend. But few people know much about Jeffrey "Guesstures" Breslow, Norman and Arlene "Dr. Drill 'n' Fill" Fabricant, Marvin "Mr. Machine" Glass, Eddy "Stompers" Goldfarb, Greg "Alphie" Hyman, Dan "Bop It" Klitsner, Larry "Boglins" Mass, Steve "Silly 6 Pins" Meyer, Elliot "Upwords" Rudell, and Howard "Connect Four" Wexler.

4-11

Over 7,000 toy and related industry professionals subscribe to *The Bloom Report* for up-to-date news and views. The Internet-based, weekly newsletter was founded and is operated by Phil Bloom, a 40-year veteran of the retail toy industry. Learn more about *The Bloom Report* and subscribe. It's free! Go to www.thebloomreport.com.

What Makes Them Special?

Like marquee inventors Alexander Graham Bell, Marie Curie, Rudolf Diesel, George Washington Carver, Thomas Alva Edison, Ole Evinrude, and Guglielmo Marconi, toy inventors share a sense of adventure, contentiousness with the status quo, and courage to continually meet new challenges head on. They know that there is no future in believing something cannot be accomplished. The future is in making it happen. They spend much of their lives as a minority of one, on the edge, pushing the envelope and, of course, dreaming. Sure, lots of people dream, but toy creators spend time with their dreams. As Edgar Allan Poe once observed, those who dream by day are cognizant of many things that escape those who dream only by night.

The pros do easily what others find difficult. The most inventive do what others have never done. These product developers can make people fall in love with their creations before they exist. They can fan burning ideas into flames that illuminate. And like all artists, they speak to the human capacity for amusement and amazement.

The imaginations of professional toy and game inventors are fired not only by compensation and commendation, but as much or more by curiosity and challenge. They are people to whom the elves still whisper. They operate in a kind of never-never land where pumpkins turn into coaches and mice into horses, where cows jump over moons and dishes run away with spoons. Their talents are special creative gifts broadened by the acquisition of business experience.

"The toy industry is filled with characters, and everyone has a story about their favorite vendor or customer. But the success, the innovation, and the personality of the industry is best exemplified by the independent inventor," says Bob Moog, president and co-founder of University Games.

"In this age of corporate and bureaucratic obsession, the creative inventor serves as a constant reminder that the business is about finding fun for kids and playing Santa Claus to America," Moog opines.

George Propsom, director of product development at Team Concepts, says companies primarily focus on marketing and producing product, while inventors focus on supplying ideas. "In most cases, we in the industry are too busy doing the day-to-day issues it takes to get a product to market," Propsom says. "We do not have the time to devote to developing concepts, tracking trends, or even frequent communication with consumers."

He goes on to say that inventors have a backlog of ideas that may not have been right at the time they were developed. "Inventors are the people who know what products have been done in the past and by whom. They are on the outside and see things differently than we do from the inside. They will often show ideas that they think will help expand a company from its existing lines into new areas—areas that we would never think of."

Mike Hirtle, vice president for R&D, product acquisition, and inventor relations at the Hasbro Games, says, "To the best of my knowledge, the toy and game industry is unique in all the world in how it relies on the professional inventor community for virtually all of its truly innovative concepts. In the automotive, aerospace, pharmaceutical, electronic, housewares, and just about every other industry, innovation comes from big internal R&D organizations. For toys and games, the source of innovation is separate. As a result, an interesting symbiotic relationship has developed between the manufacturers and this cadre of creative professionals. At Hasbro Games, we are dedicated to 'incentivizing' the professional inventors to think about games a lot and to think about Hasbro first."

In a letter inviting select professional inventors to its 2003 New York Toy Fair Inventor Night, Spinmaster wrote, in part, "It's your products and concepts that keep the wheels turning here."

411 Keep up-to-date on the toy industry, its products, and the movers and the shakers with the industry's magazine of record, *Playthings*. Subscribe by writing to 345 Hudson Street, New York, NY 10014. Phone: 212-519-7200. Website: www.playthings.com. Publisher: Andrea Morris.

The Right Stuff

Few outside the industry understand the requirements for excelling at toy and game inventing. When you need to fix a foreign sports car, build a house, play a professional sport, cure an illness, or program a computer, you call an expert. But people everywhere seem to think they're capable of developing toys and games. Yet just as some jobs require a highly skilled mechanic, carpenter, athlete, physician, or computer programmer, it takes a person experienced in toy and game development to create new playthings.

In this highly specialized profession, you get no edge simply by having once been a child or by being the father or mother of one. Nor does dating or marrying a professional toy or game creator give one claim to this esoteric ability or talent. Only in the seasoned professional are creativity and imagination guided and tempered by hard business instincts and historical perspective. Toy inventing isn't brain surgery, but it is far from child's play.

Pros in the inventing business are not so much *rational* animals in the Aristotelian sense as *doing* animals, agents of action who see variation as the raw material of evolution and nonconformity as acceptable. They think in degrees and believe in taking their own chances, not those of others. They seek opportunities, not guarantees. This group of self-actualizing, "you ain't seen nothing yet" artists live to experience what Ralph Waldo Emerson called the "delicious awakenings of the higher powers."

The most successful toy inventors believe that thinking is a form of doing. If creative thinking is an important prerequisite to their profession, initiative and strong motivation to *do something* with their ideas are also vital. Nine out of 10 professional inventors surveyed for this book gave highest ratings to both creativity and initiative or strong motivation as key attributes for success.

The Chosen Few

Every year, thousands of would-be inventors submit ideas to toy companies in hopes of licensing them. Jamie Filipeli, director of inventor relations at Mattel, reports that her department receives 3,000 outside submissions annually. Jaime's team is comprised of one manager, three senior outside resource administrators, an administrative assistant, and a department aide. Mattel has 165 staff toy designers, and it still looks to the independents. John Handy, Mattel's senior vice president of design, told the *Los Angeles Times* that the company gets 20 percent of its products through outside inventors.

Hasbro also operates in the 3,000 zone, as does Spinmaster Toys. Cadaco sees 500 submissions a year, DSI Toys reviews circa 300, Educational Insights 300, 4Kidz 100, Duncan Toys 50, and on and on it goes, company after company.

Note that Hasbro and Mattel work only with known professional inventing sources or through agents with whom they have established relationships. Our research shows that approximately 125-150 professional toy and game inventors in the United States are "recognized" by the likes of Hasbro, Mattel, and other marketers. These people have both the "know-how" and the "know-who." Within this group, between 25 and 30 inventors are recognized as "long-ball hitters"—perennial originators of hot-selling products.

Toy Trivia

2. Formed from the Danish words "leg godt," what does "LEGO" mean?

a. "Play well"

b. "Toy god"

c. "Build it"

According to the Toy Industry Association, the industry trade association, 6,000 to 7,000 new playthings are introduced at the annual American International Toy Fair in New York City. Interesting fact: Fifty percent of these items may have disappeared by the following Christmas. The professional inventors profiled in this book average about 75 to 85 original concepts each year. If this is the case, this group of inventors alone could generate almost 100 percent of the product introduced by the industry each year.

We Are Family

Professional inventors are amazingly close-knit. Toy and game manufacturers refer to the group as "the inventing community," the people whose packages containing new ideas are never returned unopened with boilerplate rejection letters—at least not often!

Their previous credits give them access to the highest levels of corporate management, and an appointment to show a new product is just a phone call or e-mail away. Why? Because manufacturers count on these pros to fill idea pipelines with innovative, well-executed, fresh products year after year. The industry thrives on those ideas, and the pros deliver!

There is a trust and respect between these outside idea sources and corporate executives. Exchanges on concepts are valued and confidential. Most inventors maintain active relationships, both business and personal, with key corporate contacts. In many cases, if inventors cannot make it to a manufacturer's headquarters, the company will dispatch executives to inventors' offices, studios, workshops, and homes. The executives know that the time and money spent dealing with these inventors can bring their company its next runaway best-seller and surpass even the highest sales goals.

Weekend in Vermont: A Tradition

While Hasbro and Mattel are arch rivals, in the greatest tradition of American enterprise, professional toy and game inventors are, for the most part, friendly toward one another. They may compete for treasured slots in annual toy lines, but many rely on each other to stay up-to-date on the latest industry goings-on.

An excellent example is the so-called Vermont Group. Every autumn for the past 10 years, a group of about 30 inventors takes over a country inn in Vermont for a long weekend of camaraderie, game playing, and trading of war stories about companies, people, and current affairs in the industry. In some cases, new ideas originate while walking through villages and woodlands, antiquing, biking, and otherwise enjoying each other's company.

The Vermont Group was organized by John and Nancy Hall. John is a former senior vice president of R&D at Playskool. Nancy is a book packager. It was Nancy who planned the initial event and selected the invitees; it was actually an outgrowth of a dinner she hosted in New York City each year after Toy Fair for a group of women friends who were inventors or inventors' wives. Over the years, this group expanded to include husbands, extended from dinner to a weekend, and then ultimately grew in numbers until there was literally "no more room in the inn." People make the annual pilgrimage to the Green Mountain State from far away places like California; Florida; and even London, England.

Vermont Group
From L-R, back: Greg Lambert, Richard C. Levy, Sid Tepper, Larry Mass, Steve Schwartz,
Greg Hyman, Larry Bernstein, Carolyn Bernstein, Robert Schwartzman, Michael Satten,
Sabra Satten, Cath Kay, Rob Kay, Marcy Hyman, Honey Schwartz; front: Chris Taylor,
Terry Mass, Arlene Fabricant, Elliot Rudell, Norman Fabricant, John Hall, Sheryl Levy,
Karen Lambert, Nancy Hall, Carol Taylor, Robyn Rudell, Helen Tepper.

Elvenbasch

Another example of the cooperative spirit that permeates the inventing community occurred in the Twin Cities in the late 1980s. Some clever Minnesota-based inventors organized their own toy fair as a way of attracting manufacturers to their area.

"After the 1987 New York Toy Fair, Tony Miller and I were brainstorming ways to get toy manufacturers to visit Minneapolis/St. Paul," mused inventor Tim Moodie of the Moodie Consulting Group. "They were traveling regularly to New York, Los Angeles, and Chicago. We wanted them to add Minneapolis.

"We came up with the idea of calling ourselves the Uneasy Alliance of Northern Toy Inventors, and Tony coined the event Elvenbasch," Moodie fondly recalled. The term was derived from *elven* (elves) and *basch* (bash or party).

The original group had 19 mostly Minnesota-based toy creators, including Andrew Berton, Scott Crosbie, Charlie and Maria Girsch, Clem Hedeen (an import from Wisconsin), Mike and Lyn Marra, Tony Miller, Tim Moodie, and Rick Polk.

"Maybe you've heard of Elvenbasch, the traditional Nordic festival of the Toy Elves, up here near the North Pole," read the original invitation to companies. "Every year, after cleaning up the mess that Santa left, all the elves celebrate the thaw, the end of hibernation and the taking down of igloos. As the first leaves appear and bird calls fill the air, we elves invite our friends, the toy company executives, to come and join the celebration of Spring and New Toy Ideas."

Perhaps this whimsical approach was overstating the weather conditions of Minneapolis and St. Paul, but it was effective in getting the companies to visit inventors in another location than the usual stops. In the first three years of the event, Rick Polk of Leisure Design & Development said that Elvenbasch turned Minneapolis into a minihub for toy inventors. Today a caller to any one Elvenbasch elf will get a fully scheduled itinerary to see all the Twin City inventors who are ready to show concepts.

Toy Trivia

3. The Canadian couple that invented Yahtzee did it traveling in which mode of transportation?

a. Rolls-Royce

b. Yacht

c. Piper Cub

More Than Just a Hobby

Toy and game inventors are in the full-time, 24/7 business of conceiving, defining, formulating, and pitching ideas. Inventors for this industry cannot work in an isolated laboratory: They can't afford to be caught with their trends down. They originate ideas for a market that is constantly seeking the new playthings that make it a multibillion-dollar annual business.

There Is No Substitute for Hard Work

The best and the brightest inventors do their homework. They know the history of playthings. They know their product. They know the markets. They know the manufacturers. They know their way around Hong Kong and other Far Eastern destinations. They know costing. They know the odds. They know how to sell product visions. Most of all, they know it isn't easy. And as much as luck plays a factor in the business of originating new toys and games, the pros leave nothing to chance. They train hard and, like top prizefighters, when they get knocked down, they're up at the count of eight and back in the fight.

In fact, Jesse Horowitz, a New York City inventor, applies Zen philosophies associated with traditional karate to cope with the heavy dose of rejection common in the idea business. Says Horowitz, "We learn to have and maintain a nonquitting attitude. *Nana korobi ya oki* literally means 'Get knocked down seven times, get up eight.' I've altered that to the independent invention business to mean 'Get knocked down 2,000 times, get up 2,001.'"

Far more than creativity, sweeping visions, and model-making skills separates the pros from thousands of amateurs and second-tier designers and developers. The major asset full-time professionals possess (emphasis on full-time) is a profound understanding of and feel for the toy industry as a business: its personalities, the realities of its marketplace, and the changing needs of the consumer and the trade. The pros are also sensitive to lead times, buying and selling cycles, tool and die costs, margins, play value, packaging, telegenics, perceived values, nichemanship, focus testing, and the internal evaluation process. They understand and appreciate the powerful and changing forces behind every detail of product evolution and execution, and the unfortunately frequent rejections.

The pros are accustomed to seeing UPS, Federal Express, Airborne, and DHL trucks gridlocked in their driveways delivering rejected submissions. They know that rejection is part of the game and that new concepts rarely sell the first time out. They don't take rejection personally. It's part of the business. It's part of the game. And it's why one of their most important traits is raw perseverance. They're like the salesperson who drives the extra miles at 4:15 P.M.; the actor auditioning for the hundredth time; and the writer facing a keyboard every day, turning out 25 pages to get 2 or 3 usable passages. Professional toy inventors don't quit on their dreams, and they often love the ideas in their closets just as much as the ones on retail shelves.

Many inventors like to say that the glamour of the industry drives them more than the money. But the pros also know the financial rewards a hit item can produce. The professional toy inventor is a self-employed owner and operator of a business—one that runs on profits and chases the big return.

A lot of inventors, but far from all, are professionally trained to generate ideas. They are graphic artists and designers who can illustrate and sketch. They are industrial designers and model-makers who can dimensionalize and sculpt ideas. They are mechanical engineers who can mock up and schematize ideas. They are electronics experts bringing state-of-the-art microelectronics to toyland. But not all have "golden hands." Many of the most successful are innovative thinkers and marketers with a keen sense of product and pop culture.

The Full Glass

In describing the late Marvin Glass, perhaps the most celebrated independent developer of toys and games the industry has seen to date, Jeffrey Breslow says, "Marvin wasn't necessarily hands-on, but he was very creative, very stimulating, and very imaginative. He didn't have the skills and dexterity to make something, per se, but he certainly had the vision and imagination for concepts." Mel Taft, whose career in the industry spans over 50 years and who has seen countless new toys and games from hundreds of inventors, characterized Glass as a "true product genius mixed with vision and showmanship."

Writer John Michlig, who has done research on Glass, writes in an e-mail to an author: "There's a great quote from Marvin Glass when asked if he listens to kids when creating toys. Something to the effect of: 'That's the worst thing you can do. Kids don't know what the hell they want. I tell them what they want.'"

> **Toy Trivia**
>
> 4. As a child, Leslie Scott, originator of Jenga, lived in Africa and learned to speak Swahili. Jenga is a Swahili word for what?
>
> a. "To build"
>
> b. "Tall tree"
>
> c. "Giraffe"

Inventors on Inventors

It is interesting that when asked to define what they do for the industry, many inventors tend to sound very much alike:

"We are people who recognize unfilled needs in the toy and game marketplace and have the vision and skill to create something of value to fulfill those needs," says Paul Lapidus, inventor of the Star Wars X-Wing Flight Simulator (Hasbro).

Independent inventor and agent Michael Marra, who brought 1313 Dead End Drive to Hasbro Games, says that inventors "provide the toy industry with all the home runs and grand slams."

Inventors deliver "true novelty and invention rather than window dressing on old ideas," says Larry Mass, inventor of Ballzerko (Hasbro).

Elliot Rudell, inventor of Weebles (Playskool/Hasbro), feels that the inventors provide a "freshness of global thinking." He adds that they also have "motivation to dare to think outside of anyone's box, with the sober understanding that along with the uncertainty and volatility of the toy business in general, and the inventor in particular, they also have the freedom to fail or succeed."

Where Do They Get Their Ideas?

The anatomy of an inventor's inspiration and creativity is complex. Ideas can come to an inventor anywhere at any time. The best products come through observation, a walk through a shopping center, an amusement park, a gaming arcade, or a hardware store. Maybe the inspiration comes during a relaxing afternoon at the movies, while paging through magazines, while scanning newspapers, or while watching television. Perhaps it is just watching kids kicking stones, a can, or the cat.

Rudell sometimes gains inspiration through prayer. "Several major ideas have just been given to me," he says. And the late Mike Ferris, whose Mickey Mouse Telephone for AT&T was the first personalization of a Bell box, got ideas "usually from skuszoos of past failures."

Howard Wexler, who has been inventing for over three decades, says it's a common misconception that inventors walk around and, like magic, an idea is born. "For me, what works is thinking about an area or general plaything that I would like to invent. I believe that subconsciously what I have loaded into my mind eventuates into a specific invention."

Asked what sparks an original idea, Adam Wolff of Excel Development Group says that if he knew, he'd bottle it.

Life on the Edge

Most full-time independent developers receive no weekly paychecks and no paid vacations, sick days, or coffee breaks. Financial rewards, when they arrive, come in the form of advances and royalties. Advances come with a signed agreement; royalties, if any, come after the close of each calendar quarter, and not always on time.

The fear of financial insecurity and rejection that hinders the casual inventor gives birth to wisdom and creativity in the full-time professional. The pros have the security provided only by their wits, drive, instincts, and whichever products are currently being marketed and bought by a "prove-it-to-me" trade and demanded by fickle consumers. A career in toy inventing is not for the faint of heart.

Independent toy developers have deserted traditional thought and structured work for spontaneity and unrestricted creative license. They ask, "Why not?" and "What if?" Whether market-pulled or technology-pushed, their highly intellectual work is not a pursuit, but a passion.

These men and women stay fresh and up-to-date, but their minds are always reaching into the future and back to the past for inspiration. In fact, for all intents and purposes, there is no "now." Although independent developers compete with each other and against internal company R&D groups, everyone is betting on and working toward the product introductions of the future.

The most talented independents combine knowledge of what's happening with their own concepts, flights of fancy, and fascination with the odd and extravagant deviations of the human experience. They are always on duty and alert for clues and impressions, with a notepad or tape recorder at hand.

Charlie Phillips, self-proclaimed futurist and inventor of Advance to Boardwalk (Parker Bros.) and Spy Web (Parker Bros.) feels strongly that products have to be a real turn-on to kids to stand out in all the entertainment choices. "Most kids today are tech heads from all the computers and electronics around," says Philips. He goes on to say that what you invent for them has to be "hip and cool" if you expect it to be successful in their world.

Toy Trivia

5. The Crayola brand name is recognized by what percentage of Americans?

a. 75 percent

b. 99 percent

c. 85 percent

Toy inventors are people who, like little Susan in the classic holiday film *Miracle on 34th Street*, keep on believing even when common sense tells them not to. And that extra ounce of believing can make the difference between success and failure. No matter how seasoned and businesslike today's professional toy inventors are, they—like Pinocchio's kindly old wood-carver, Geppetto—also feel a sense of magic when they see someone embrace their ideas or see something special created by a competitor.

Over his 55-year career in the toy industry, A. Eddy Goldfarb has been awarded 300 patents and has developed a host of successful toys and product lines, among them Stompers, Busy Biddy, Shark Bowling, Quiz Whiz, the Baby Beans doll, and Milky the Cow for such toy companies as Aurora, Coleco, Hasbro, Mattel, Pressman, and Tomy. Oh, and let's not forget to mention Yakity-Yak: The Talking Teeth (yes, the wind-up ones).

Eddy invented his first toys while at sea, serving during World War II in the U.S. Navy as a submariner. After the war, he established and continues to maintain his successful toy-invention business, A. Eddy & Martin Goldfarb and Associates, LLC. He says emphatically, "Before originating an abundance of great ideas, one needs a keen sense of what's in vogue, a sense of humor, and a strong stomach."

Belinda Recio, inventor of the game Alien Autopsy (DaMert), says "A toy inventor is an artist whose medium is ideas." Bill Dohrmann, a central corporate figure at Parker Brothers behind the naming and introduction of Nerf, says that the independent inventor is "an integral and indispensable segment of the industry—symbiosis at its best!"

"It takes a lot of fortitude, ... a lot of drive, ... steadfastness, and the ability to recover from rejection after rejection after rejection," says Howard Wexler. "Talent must be there, but it takes perseverance ... and luck, too. You could have talent and perseverance and not get anywhere if your timing is wrong."

Charlie Girsch and his wife, Maria, own and operate Creativity Central. They report licensing over 200 concepts worldwide in 3 decades. Charlie has said that he reflects on the words of two "contemporary philosophers" when he thinks about what it takes to make it as a professional inventor in the toy industry. The first is Bud Grant, former coach of the Minnesota Vikings, who said, "You work and practice hard so in case the ball bounces your way on Sunday, you'll know what to do with it." The other is Ronald McDonald, who says, "Keep your eyes on the fries."

Putting Dreams into Action

The power to create resides in mastering the process of transition from the "I've got an idea" stage to the "Look at my idea" stage. Idleness destroys inventiveness. Hence, professional toy and game developers must be self-starters by nature. They must be as can-do as the kids for whom they invent. They may slow down for a speed bump, but no obstacle can completely stop them or a great concept.

Dr. Erno Rubik was once asked how young children were able to solve his puzzle cube in no time flat and adults could not. Responded the Hungarian professor, "Because no one ever told the child it could not be done."

The pros know that creating toys is serious business. It is big business. It can be a cutthroat business. It is also a very risky business. It's part fun house and part chamber of horrors. Too many amateur inventors think that if they sell one product—voilà!— a cash cow is born that's destined to become another Cabbage Patch or Trivial Pursuit franchise. No way. More often than not, the inventor is told, "Your ideas will not pass 'Go.' Do not collect $200." Experienced independents know not to celebrate when a contract is signed or a product is optioned for a cash advance. They may be told after months of internal development that the trade doesn't like it. Products are subjected to numerous and critical manufacturer line reviews (a.k.a "shoot-outs") that go on right up until Toy Fair.

Although the pace has accelerated in recent years, toy development remains essentially a filtering process. Items are in one day, out the next. New concepts are constantly flowing into review, and with thousands of proposals each year—not to mention concepts generated by their own internal R&D groups—manufacturers' priorities change and products get dropped, often in spite of substantial corporate financial commitments. At any time, a chief executive may say to his team, "If I told you that one product had to be cut, which one would it be?" Everything is on a life-support system until it can survive on its own at retail—where it might be a "stiff," languishing on the shelves, rejected by the ultimate judge: the consumer. Every toy inventor has experienced the axing of a concept or the dropping of a product or, worse yet, a line of products. The pros learn to live with the reality of high product burnout. As Murphy's first corollary goes, "Nothing is as easy as it looks." And Murphy's second corollary says, "Everything takes longer than you think."

There's No Easy Money …

It is a misconception that there is an easy dollar to be made developing and licensing a product to toy manufacturers. In an industry with legends of instant millionaires such as Dr. Erno Rubik (Rubik's Cube), Xavier Roberts (Cabbage Patch Kids), and Robert Angel (Pictionary), very few inventors actually make a lot of money. Most independent toy and game developers grind it out on a day-to-day basis. Only the strong survive. In this way, it is on a par with the most highly competitive businesses. "Even when you're doing well, there are days when you are so down because it is rejection after rejection. One day you have 15 concepts out; the next day you have 3," muses Mike Satten, inventor of the Hot Wheels Car-Go Carrier (Mattel). But would he rather be doing something else? "Oh, please, no way."

Toy Trivia

6. Which is the oldest American toy company?

a. Mattel

b. Pressman

c. Tootsietoy

17

Losers far outnumber winners. No manufacturer is exempt from failure. No inventor is exempt from licensing a concept that stiffs. The rejection rate for inventor game submissions is reported to be 99 percent; and of the games that make it to retail, most last no longer than a year or two. Toys have about the same rate and life span, says Hasbro's David Berko, senior vice president for product acquisition.

Now you see them, now you don't. Here are some memorable losers:

- The Dr. Laura Game (Hasbro)
- Elvis UNO (Mattel)
- National Inquirer game (Tyco)
- Computer Warriors (Mattel)
- E Brain (DSI)
- Speed Wrench (Tyco)
- Don't Free Freddie (Spin Master)
- P.O.D.S. (Playmates)
- Biker Mice from Mars (Galoob)
- And one of the biggest bombs, The Baby Jesus doll (Ideal)

The Baby Jesus did not sell, but because of its religious significance, retailers refused to mark it down. Ideal had to take back most of its production run. The dolls were subsequently given away to the company's factory workers.

... And It's Not Getting Any Easier!

Although the toy market is lucrative for some inventors, the number of major companies marketing product is declining. Mergers have consolidated former competitors into larger corporate entities. Bankruptcies have stripped many brand names from retail shelves. This has resulted in fewer companies buying ideas from professional inventors. Many ex-R&D staffers at dissolved companies gravitate toward independent inventing either as "associates," as competitive startup product sources, or as broker/agents, using their industry connections to jump-start new careers.

Game diva Cathy Rondeau, inventor of Encore (Endless Games) and countless other games, says that consolidation has been the greatest change in the past 10 years. "It has been tough just keeping track of contacts and maintaining relations as people shift within the industry frequently. All of this is a distraction from inventing."

Elliot Rudell agrees that while the industry is not necessarily shrinking in dollar size, it is shrinking in placement opportunities. He adds that when something does get placed and meets with some success, the licensee is very much inclined to expand it and wring as much out of the concept as possible. "We are seeing this with our KICK DIS puck at Estes. And it held true for our radio-controlled track sets with multiple extensions at Fisher-Price," Rudell says. "But the downside is that the targets are moving faster and they are fewer and farther between. To get someone behind a new concept with great enthusiasm is daunting. And with acquisition of other companies being an acceptable means of corporate growth, a rejection by one company now becomes a rejection by many companies, since there is (logically and with good reason) communication within divisions of each conglomerate. So what one might have shown Hasbro and Playskool and Kenner and Tiger in the past, now gets one showing. Suggestion: Make it a great showing."

When asked to characterize the climate for selling ideas, pro Benjamin Kinberg, inventor of Handy Dandy Notebook (Mattel), said, "Very simply, there are fewer people and fewer companies with whom to do business. As some toy companies become larger, their procedures become more complex with more people involved in the selection process. Should one member in the selection chain fail to sign off on a new product, that product is effectively killed."

Driven by the Market, Not by Inventors

Hasbro and Mattel are so large that they are not interested in $1 million or $2 million products anymore: They need items that will generate, at a minimum, $10 million and up. For such companies to make a commitment and develop an advertising program around a product, it must be a very special product capable of performing at rapid turnover with consumers in the marketplace.

Entertainment licensing is another force that is reducing opportunities for independent inventors. Rather than acquire a unique invention and build interest in that feature through advertising and promotion, toy and game marketers are applying character licenses to products to drive interest with consumers. Some marketing MBAs, who base decisions more on their Excel sheets than their "gut," feel it is a no-brainer to go with an entertainment license already known to the public rather than cast their lot with an unknown product that needs heavy promotion to customers. (Perhaps they forget about the high cost of guarantees to the entertainment licensors.) This often means that an inventor must share a reduced royalty to cover the cost of the license.

Even worse for an inventor is when his or her product loses out entirely to an internally developed item that, since there is no double royalty, covers more of the license expense. Character licensing on toys and games is covered in Chapter 11.

"The potential damage to inventor licensing from brand licensing is enormous," says Harvey Lepselter, senior vice president of R&D and Marketing for Babies 'n Things, who started in the business over 30 years ago working for Louis Marx. "Brand licensing allows toy companies a 'safe' opportunity to buy known properties and place them on 'safe' toy products in hopes of creating less risky products, at a lesser expense."

But in attempting to guarantee success, the big companies are sacrificing novelty. How many of the classic toys and games are tied to entertainment licenses? Lepselter says. "In reality, brand licenses (unless you are the master licensee) typically do not produce the excitement and volume business as compared to successful inventor licensed product. Two remarkable examples of inventor licensed product that went atomic are Cabbage Patch Kids and Furby."

But in the short run, there is this temptation. "Inventor licensing generally requires television advertising to make the product known and successful, while brand licensing is pre-promoted by the licensor," Lepselter says.

"There is no creative marketing anymore, it's all cookie-cutter, by the numbers," moans Tim Moodie, inventor of many games such as Chicken Soup for the Soul (Cardinal). "The big companies should have a portion of their marketing budgets dedicated to 'hare-brained schemes.' Dedicate 10 percent of each year's budget to reaching emerging markets or exploring unique distribution channels. An example is Starbucks selling the game Cranium. Quite frankly, it's the reason they (the companies) don't grow. They are too busy doing *business as usual* to realize that *business as unusual* is the way to grow." And few executives want to bet their bonuses on an unknown product.

John Michlig, a chronicler of the modern toy industry, observes that the paradigm under which toy developers and inventors create playthings and then hand the finished product to a marketing department to promote and sell was turned on its head back in the 1970s. "GI Joe, for instance, began life in the early '60s as a completely new type of boy's toy in which the Hasbro salesmen had little faith. No matter: Company president Merrill Hassenfeld and his creative director, Don Levine, would educate, motivate, and direct their sales and marketing force based on their belief in the product. That was the way things worked."

Michlig went on to say, "By the middle '70s, however, the marketing department began calling the shots. It was Merrill Hassenfeld's son, Stephen, in fact, who recognized that a product's appearance and performance in its TV commercial was more important than its shelf appeal. Stephen basically reversed Hasbro's product-development scheme: GI Joe's vehicles, for example, were molded in yellow plastic because the marketing department mandated the color as best for color TV commercials. And it worked. Kids saw that Mobile Support Vehicle in action on their living room RCA (television) and had to have it."

Michlig says that this flip-flop was devastating to many "old school" toy guys. It was so untenable and harmful to some that they actually left Hasbro rather than cede power and answer to the marketing department. This happened at many companies that followed the same path. Today marketing has completely displaced R&D as the decision-making corporate entity at the major toy companies. And independent inventors are even farther out in the cold.

Another threat to inventors is the flood of imported toys and games, greater now than ever in our nation's history. The TIA estimates that 80 percent of the toys (including video games) sold in the United States are manufactured in whole or in part overseas. In 2002, the United States imported $17 billion worth of toys (excluding video games), of which $12.22 billion represented toys produced in China, according to the TIA. The more entrepreneurial developers are forming alliances with foreign manufacturers to merge their inventiveness and connections with sources of supply. They then are able to approach U.S. marketers not only with unique concepts, but also with the product completely manufactured.

The sales of video games continues to attract kids over age 8. New gaming platforms and a wide range of game titles with new technology offer increasingly sophisticated game play. These products all eat up consumer dollars that might otherwise be spent on conventional games and playthings like R/C cars, handheld games, and other electronic fireworks.

Toy Trivia

7. Since 1959, more than ___ Barbie dolls and members of the Barbie family have been sold in more than ____ countries worldwide.

a. 1 billion; 140

b. 500 million; 200

c. 2 billion; 225

The aforementioned notwithstanding, market share is controlled and expanded one way only: through the introduction of fresh, exciting, imaginative product. So the professional inventor with something truly special *always* has an edge. There's always room for a super item, especially when the manufacturers want to make leadership moves.

Surviving Toyland: Outwit, Outplay, Outlast

It takes a special talent to survive in an industry like this that's ever-changing, faddish, transitory, sometimes whimsical, sometimes volatile.

Among the most special talents are Jeffrey Breslow and his recently retired partners Howard Morrison and Rouben Terzian. In 1967, when the trio joined the legendary Marvin Glass, they began a more than 30-year collaboration that has led to the creation and design of some of the industry's most successful toy and game products. In 1988, BMT and Associates was formed to continue their tradition of excellence. Their best-selling products include Mighty Max, Fashion Polly, Trump: The Game, Guesstures, Brain Warp, California Roller Baby, Real Talking Bubba, Uno Attack, My Size Barbie, Kasey Cartwheel, Jennie Gymnast, Hot Wheels Fireball, and many more.

A little over a decade ago, 30-year industry veteran Bill Dohrmann, a former senior vice president of global R&D at Hasbro Games, said, "I would be frightened to death if I was put into a room and told, 'Look, here's some capital, be a toy inventor.' It's a terribly tough thing. You can make a lot of money. You can get very rich in this business. But it's like going to Hollywood, working in the car wash and hoping you're going to be the next Tom Cruise. Inventors own a decaying asset. A product goes in and two years later, if they sit still and go to sleep, it's gone. Unless you build up a list of perennials, which is very hard to do, you gotta push the rock up the mountain every year." Retired from Hasbro since November 1998, today Dohrmann owns and operates Idea Development, LLC, an invention and idea representation business. (Guess he wasn't *that* frightened.)

Toy Trivia

8. The Spin Pop was invented by four ____.

a. postal workers
b. real estate agents
c. dentists

Some years it's a great living, some years it's a good living, and some years there is no income—but the pros never give up.

"Through good times and bad, you learn and grow, and so do your dreams," says Randi Altschul, inventor of The Simpson's Game (Cardinal). After a background in martial arts, Randi has licensed over 200 products, but too often, times can be bad. Alan

Amron, a 30-year veteran and holder of 28 patents, recalls almost giving up on his dream to become an inventor when he lost a patent litigation that was "all in (his) favor, due to hometown lawyers lying and cheating to win for their big corporate client."

Ned Strongin, former dean of the New York City inventing community by virtue of his 40 years in the industry, didn't dream about doing something—he just did it. Strongin lists Connect Four (Hasbro) and Giggle Wiggle (Hasbro) among his over 50 licenses.

Greg Hyman, inventor of Thinklings (Mattel), took off a couple of years early in his inventing career "to get a real job." Then it was all sail, no anchor for this prolific inventor of over 88 licensed toys and games. Cathy Rondeau, inventor of over 50 licensed products, explains that she has taken breaks here and there to recharge. "It's a roller coaster at times, so now and then I like to chill in the teacups."

Bruce Lund, a former biologist, licensor of over 100 products, once almost threw in his magic markers. But then, he says, he changed his mind, put his shoulder to the wagon, and kept on pushing: "The rest was in God's hands." But perhaps Ralph Baer, who was the first to suggest incorporating a game into a television set in 1951, and the holder of 50 U.S. patents and 100 more worldwide, sums it up best when asked if he ever thought of giving up on his dream to be an inventor: "Heck, no. How can you stop breathing?"

It *Can* Happen!

So why do it? With all those drawbacks and dangers, what keeps an independent inventor at it? First, independents experience what few outside the artistic community do: freedom. Personal freedom and, if they get lucky, financial freedom. Freedom provides not safety so much as opportunities, the most satisfying of which is the opportunity to use their talents. Second, while their careers are fraught with pitfalls, they can also make a fortune if the right products are a hit.

When asked if he had earned a million dollars in the toy business, inventor Eddy Goldfarb told *Parade* magazine, "Actually, it's closer to several million."

"My goal was to make $50,000 a year and stay home with my kids; anything after that is gravy," Cathy Rondeau told a reporter in an interview for *48 Hours*. "How's it going?" she was asked. "Lots of gravy," she responded.

Robert Schwartzman, went from working for a nonprofit consulting firm to inventing. He reports that 3 of his 85 licensed products have sold over a million units each: Barney Banjo (Hasbro), Dancin' Debbi (Mattel), and Hot Wheels Power Launchers (Mattel).

Toy inventing gives Mark Setteducati, an inventor and a performing magician who created the hugely successful Magic Works line for Milton Bradley/Hasbro, "the freedom to do whatever I want when I wake up every day." He continues, "By licensing inventions to toy companies, I have royalties coming in and am making money when I sleep."

Robert Angel, a Seattle waiter, did it with Pictionary after he licensed his self-published game to The Games Gang. Pictionary has sold millions of sets worldwide since 1986, spawning its own industry. The game has earned classic status.

Cleveland, Georgia, artist Xavier Roberts did it with his megahit Cabbage Patch Kids. Some estimates put sales of the homely, latex-faced dolls at over 80 million units sold. Canadians Scott Abbott, a sports editor for the *Canadian Press*, and Chris Haney, a photo editor at the *Montreal Gazette*, created Trivial Pursuit and then enlisted the help of brother John Haney, an ex-hockey player, and Ed Werner, an ex-hockey player turned lawyer. Their first production run of 1,100 games sold out in Canada.

They did a second production run of 20,000 games and said that even if these games had sold through, they would have barely broken even. Its first showing at New York Toy Fair was in 1982. Selchow & Righter, the game's original U.S. manufacturer, sold 22 million sets at retail prices ranging as high as $40. Since 1982, Trivial Pursuit has sold more than 70 million games worldwide, and the story of its origin was immortalized in the Canadian Broadcasting Corporation's made-for-television movie *Breaking All the Rules*. Trivial Pursuit has since been acquired by Hasbro. At a reported astronomical royalty of 15.7 percent (the industry average is 5 percent), each co-inventor made a personal fortune.

Erno Rubik, a creative Hungarian professor of interior design at a Budapest arts academy, saw his Rubik's Cube go atomic. The deceptively innocent-looking 2¼-inch puzzle, with more than 43 quintillion possible combinations but only 1 true solution, became such a craze that it made the inventor a household name and one of his country's wealthiest individuals.

411

Don't miss *Inventor's Digest*, billed as America's only inventor magazine. Published since 1985, it delivers information by the shovel load. Publisher Joanne Hayes-Rines, the first lady of the independent inventing community, is on the front lines of the intellectual property wars, working to protect the rights of the small inventor. Subscribe by calling 1-800-838-8808. Visit the magazine website at www.inventorsdigest.com.

Toy Trivia

9. Which of these women does not participate in the Hasbro product acquisition process?

a. Darlene Horan

b. Leslie Lawrence

c. Judy Flathers

Pound Puppies made their designer, Mike Bowling, a factory worker at the Ford Motor Company near Cincinnati for 17 years, a multimillionaire. What began as a Christmas present to his wife has sold more than 200 million units in 52 countries since he signed the product with Tonka Toys in 1984. The Puppies were named "#1 New Toy Introduction of 1985." Today, Pound Puppies are licensed to Jakks Pacific, Inc.

Larry Jones, president of Cal R&D, says he has fathered over 1,700 products in the last 30 years, including Cricket (Playmates), one of the first interactive dolls. At its height, Cal R&D employed over 50 designers, engineers, sculptors, and support staff, Jones says. "The toy business has more turnover than any business. But I think it probably still is and always will be one of the best opportunities for entrepreneurs."

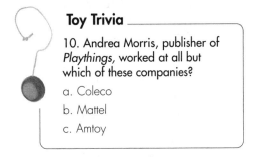

Toy Trivia

10. Andrea Morris, publisher of *Playthings*, worked at all but which of these companies?

a. Coleco

b. Mattel

c. Amtoy

The Butcher, the Baker, the Candlestick Maker

Such an unconventional profession as that of the toy inventor requires faith and belief in oneself. Like their ideas, these men and women are naturals, people whose entry into the fluid and egalitarian business of toy and game development just happened at the appropriate time through a variety of circumstances rarely planned, but that in retrospect seem predestined. In that retrospect, it may be true that some successful inventors might not have gained admission to the inventing community today, with its high expectations and demanding criteria.

Judy Blau wrote and illustrated the children's book *The Bagel Baker of Mulliner Lane* for McGraw-Hill in 1976. As a result of the publicity and licensing of the characters from the book into children's apparel and home furnishings, a toy manufacturer called her to ask whether she would consider designing toy concepts. "I gave it a try and sold my first plush concepts," explains Blau, now the president of J. Hope Designs, Ltd. "I then discovered that two talented electronic toy inventors lived in my neighborhood [Greg Hyman and Larry Greenberg], and we got together. With their help and encouragement and introductions, I found myself working both independently and with other inventors." Blau is now the inventor of Sweetie Pops (Playskool) and holds 10 patents, 20 trademarks, and over 100 copyrights.

Elliot Rudell, president of Rudell Design, a prolific innovator, and the holder of some 60 patents, says he got into the inventing business through the most basic of drives: "I needed to eat."

"After college, I worked as a talent agent for four years and then went on to get my Master's in business," explains David Vogel of Vogel Applied Technologies Corp. in New York City, whose most successful products include Barbie Holiday Dance Musical (Mr. Christmas). "The MBA helped me land a job at Kiddesigns, where I worked in product development for two years. After that I worked for an inventor group for two years before opening my own office."

"The first toy I sold was myself to Marvin Glass in 1967," jokes Chicago-based inventor Jeffrey Breslow. "I had to convince him that I could design and invent games. That was the hardest job, getting through the door at Marvin Glass & Associates."

"I started in the toy business coming out of school as a designer with Child Guidance before moving on to Knickerbocker Toys," says Mike Satten. "I was in the middle of the best job I ever had when Knickerbocker was sold to Hasbro and suddenly I found myself unemployed." He landed at Determined Productions, a San Francisco manufacturer of plush and gift items. The company's president, Connie Boucher, permitted him to do his own products as long as they were noncompetitive with her company.

In 1957, 10-year-old Greg Hyman issued a hand-printed flyer to the third and fourth graders at his New Rochelle, New York, elementary school. His journey to the North Pole was not direct. Greg Hyman was an electronics engineer doing readouts, lockouts, buzzers, and bells for Ron Greenberg Productions in New York City, a company that specialized in TV game shows. Then one day he backed into the game industry in partnership with Greenberg's brother, Larry (a.k.a. "The Colonel"). A special sound-effects device he had designed for a pilot show became, through a series of serendipitous events, a toy called Major Morgan (Playskool). Hyman/Greenberg also hit with Alphie and Alphie II (Playskool), a child's first electronic learning toy.

A Force of One or More

Professional toy and game inventors understand that ingenuity is just a first step, not an end in itself. Inventors need help. It often takes teamwork to create a concept that is salable to a manufacturer. Few inventors work alone. Garry Donner, inventor of Don't Go to Jail (Parker/Hasbro Games), says, "You can no longer work alone. You need to be an expert in too many areas."

Greg Hyman's "Learn to Invent" flier.

It is not unusual for the more prolific developers to find themselves working simultaneously on projects that require expertise in areas ranging from gearing, hydraulics, levers, and electricity to plastics, fabrics, refractors, and microelectronics. It is also common to see the highly technical developer join forces with a sculptor, an illustrator, or a gaming theorist. A marketer who smells an opportunity may seek a developer (and associates) to make a concept come alive. In the toy and game inventing business, it is a daily survival skill to know how and to know who: "Whatever it takes" is the rule.

"I think there is a wonderful brotherhood between inventors, and I am talking about successful people, because they realize how difficult this business is …. I wish very well for any of my fellow inventors," says Howard Wexler.

"I think it is very hard to invent successfully in a vacuum," notes Greg Hyman. He believes that even when you can build a model to describe a great concept, you still need input from other sources because it is hard to be objective about your own creation. This airing of the concept, he explains, may take the form of a partnership with another professional developer.

A lack of experience in one area, however, should never be a reason for an idea to go undeveloped. The pros will merge talents at the drop of a marble, the tick of a timer, or the roll of a die. They understand the big picture. They know that there is always a need for good product, and a hit generates enough reward for everyone. This is why a single product often has several parents; it is truly the creation of multiple talents.

The objective is to get points on the scoreboard and, more important, dollars on the royalty statements. Touchdowns are desired, but field goals are equally valuable. A shared spotlight is better than no spotlight. To give just a few of many examples, the headline inventors of such megahits as Cabbage Patch Kids, Furby, Pictionary, Pound Puppies, Scattergories, and SuperSoaker shared portions of their lucrative royalties with others—without whose assistance, either financially or creatively, their items might never have come to market.

The Anonymous Elves

Professional toy and game inventors can walk up and down the aisles of a toy store and tell you who invented what, as if the products were books with authors' names emblazoned across their covers. A stroll through Toys R Us has Julie Ellman's Mr. Potato Head (Hasbro) merchandised not too far from Norman and Arlene Fabricant's Dr. Drill 'n' Fill (Playskool). Bob Jeffway's Diva Starz (Mattel) is in the doll area. In the game section, Mike Marra's WWF Trivia (Cardinal) is near Fred Kroll's Hungry Hungry Hippos (Hasbro), Brian Hersch's Taboo (Hasbro), Robert Angels's Thinkblot (Mattel), Martin Goldfarb's Spiderman (Pressman), and David Yearick's TriBond (Patch). Reuben Klamer's Game of Life (Hasbro) is a few giant steps from Jeffrey Breslow's Guesstures (Hasbro) and Gunther Degen's Scattergories (Hasbro). Hanging on the wall nearby are offerings such as Dan Klitsner's Bop-It (Hasbro) and Ron Mager's Light Wars (Tiger). Eddy Goldfarb's Bubble Gun (Hasbro) has become a staple for spring and summer.

Of all creative endeavors, perhaps the one in which individual achievement is least recognized is toy invention. This is an odd phenomenon because toys and games touch us all from our earliest days and make as great an impression as other forms of popular entertainment. From a commercial standpoint, some toys and games earn more money than best-selling books, records, or films. A few toy developers collect royalties that put them in the same league as rock stars, athletes, movie idols, and TV celebrities.

Books are bought for their authors, not publishing houses; records for recording artists, not labels; and feature films for actors, not production companies. Though there are no popularly known "stars" billed on toys and games, there is a known group of professional inventors on whom manufacturers rely for the blockbusters of the toy shelves.

In an industry that says product is king, independent inventors are about as close to the throne as anyone. Executives are unanimous in their praise for and appreciation of the independent developer. In surveying the industry for this book, we found that executives at the highest levels know the value of outside professional developers, and that, *ipso facto*, the most successful manufacturers license the greatest number of concepts from this valued resource. When looking for significant sales dollars from new products each year, corporate officers go looking for the latest ideas from the pros.

"The inventors have been and remain the lifeblood of our success," says E. David Wilson, president of Hasbro Games, the man at the helm of the world's largest game company. "We are very proud of our strong working relationship with the inventing community, and we make every effort to make them feel part of our family. We work very hard at this."

"We all know that the next Spin Pop is out there, waiting in the back pocket of some toy inventor—maybe even a rookie. We just need them to find us and make an intelligent presentation," says Alan Dorfman, president of Basic Fun, which markets about 175 product SKUs.

"The more prepared the submitter is, the more seriously we will take them. Our industry is starving for innovation, and often it takes unbiased thinking to be innovative," Dorfman concludes. "When you live every day with toys and toy development, and see what is accepted by the retail community, your vision gets clouded by what you are familiar with and what you know is and is not selling. The independent inventor occasionally offers the breath of fresh air that shakes us out of the routine."

"Toyland would be a much duller place without the independent inventor," said Standard & Poor's toy-industry analyst Paul Valentine. "When you go down the list and look at the megahits that have emerged in the past 10 years, lines that have done more than $50 million each, they are primarily coming from the independent inventor, with the exception of licensed properties."

The colossal sweep of the independents' genius, the web of interlinking ideas that they spin, and their varied artistic gifts weave a plexus of unsurpassed product and business opportunities for manufacturers who buy their concepts.

Forty-two-year industry veteran Mike Meyers, a former senior vice president of R&D at Milton Bradley/Hasbro Games and a founder and board member of specialty game publisher Winning Moves (US), says, "The main reason for external inventing has to do with economics and mathematics. The outside inventor is free until you pay royalties. The company doesn't pay a thing for failure, only for success. Such a deal."

When Meyers was asked where Milton Bradley would be today without the input of the independent inventing community, he answered, "Well, first of all you begin by rattling off a bunch of products that are our classics, that have sustained this company: Candy Land, The Game of Life, Chutes and Ladders, Operation, Yahtzee, Mouse Trap, Twister, Electronic Battleship, Taboo, Simon, Upwords, to name a few. What do you have left? When you take a look at a list like that, that's very impressive. It's the backbone of the company. These items all came from the outside."

Toy Trivia

11. Which item was carried into space on Apollo?

a. Silly Putty

b. Play-Doh

c. Friendly Plastic

Howard Bollinger, former senior vice president of advanced concepts at Kenner and Hasbro, who is now developing product and consulting, maintains that independents are important because they "bring a keen awareness of how to put things together in such a way that it gives kids goose bumps .... They mix current awareness with a lot of traditional things, stir the pot, and visualize what will happen. They can always feel the magic. They've never had the kid programmed out of them."

The Outside Advantage

Tony Miller, vice president of Hot Wheels Design at Mattel, finds that most toy companies focus on what they are accustomed to doing, which can lead to only a limited number of conclusions. The outside inventor, he says, is coming from beyond internal management and marketing parameters, which leads to ideas that would be totally unpredictable. "The main value of the outside inventor to the company is to produce the wild card," Miller notes.

Miller was at Tonka as the vice president of R&D when the Pound Puppy concept came through the door. Tonka, a maker of steel trucks, would never of its own volition have decided to make a line of stuffed dogs, he explains. But Mike Bowling, the man who brought stuffed dogs to Tonka, put something on the table that looked like a solid business opportunity for the company. Low investment. Fresh idea. A track record in some foreign markets. "In its best year, our Pound Puppies did $140 million, which was more than all the company's other business combined," Miller recalls.

Bill Dohrmann remembers the time in 1969 when he was Parker Brothers' director of marketing and product development, and a couple of men from Minneapolis walked through his door with what he describes as "a sort of beer-drinking game where you put a little net up in your living room and bounced around a ball cut from foam."

He wondered why anyone would bring a novelty ball to Parker Brothers, a manufacturer of board games. (It had first been shown to Milton Bradley and rejected.) "We must have been way down the line, because as the inventor of Milton Bradley's hit game Twister, Reynolds Guyer had access to every company," he figured. Upon seeing the foam ball, Dohrmann recalls saying to himself, "My God, that's it, the world's first indoor ball. I even wrote that line down, and it wound up on the first package of what would become Nerf." According to Dohrmann, Nerf became a $25- to $30-million-a-year category for Parker after the item's introduction in 1970. Today Nerf is licensed to Hasbro.

Mel Taft, a former senior vice president of R&D at Milton Bradley, recalls that in 1978, a Boston consulting firm had made strong recommendations for electronics to be brought into his game line. Co-author and inventor Richard C. Levy and his partner, Scott Dankman, brought in an exciting electronic space craft, conceived and engineered by their partner, Bryan McCoy. It was called StarBird. Taft says, "Even though we were a board game company, to hear the roaring effects of the jet engines and feel the power in your hand, it was the answer to the consultant's charge. I 'flew' it to our president's office, and Jim Shea gave an immediate approval." Starbird arrived at the East Long-meadow facility after Thanksgiving 1977, and it debuted at the New York Toy Fair two months later. And over a million flew off retail shelves.

Corporate executives know that there is no limit to how far the imaginations of professional independent inventors can stretch, nor a boundary to their efforts, discoveries, or successes. Just when it might seem impossible to top the current crop of magical playthings, a new cycle for the coming year brings inventors with even more innovative products. These inventors are vital to companies in an industry that, like large businesses everywhere, requires its employees to do something as a form of thinking more than allowing time for thinking as a form of doing.

The independent inventors see it as their birthright to be different. They tinker with the abstract and impose design upon experience. The best and brightest have a multivalued orientation; a fresh, schooled, and inquiring eye; and a sophisticated innocence that permits them to have one foot in childhood and one foot in the corporate world. Toy manufacturers benefit by getting independent toy and game inventors to provide what amounts to speculative external research and development. On a continuing basis, the inventing community provides an endless array of innovative product concepts, unencumbered by corporate dogma. Furthermore, the passion that independent professionals bring with their submissions often stimulates internal corporate creativity. In return, ideally, the outside developers receive what every artist seeks: an audience for their work and a rich patron who can afford to buy and *commercialize* it to the artist's advantage.

In September 2002, in a confidential 2004 Wish List (yes, toy companies work well into the future) sent to its stable of independent inventors, Fisher-Price concluded, "We value the creativity and ingenuity that you bring to our brands."

Mel Taft, today a member of the board of directors at Radica, says that independent inventors contribute more than 50 percent of the good ideas companies market and 75 percent or more of the big hits.

Frank Adler, executive vice president of sales and marketing at Uncle Milton Industries, manufacturer of the Ant Farm, offers a motto: "Know your product, know their business." Frank hardly sees professional inventors as ants, but like ants they are social, live in a community, are amazingly strong and resilient, and get the job done. "The pro inventor understands that a manufacturer has different categories and subniches within those categories where they're trying to increase market share," Adler says. "In addition, the manufacturer has definable strengths and weaknesses. It's important for the inventor to take all of this into consideration in order to present product that will fit with the marketing direction the company is pursuing. When an inventor does his homework on our company and understands our challenges in the marketplace, my level of confidence rises significantly and leads me to believe this is someone we can work with long term."

"I believe the independent inventors play the part of a 'think tank' as they conceptualize new product concepts," says Dale Siswick, senior vice president of R&D at Hasbro Games. "Unquestionably, a great deal of thinking is required in the initial ideation phase sorting out the 'maybes' from the 'dead ends.' This is time-consuming and can be somewhat challenging for a large company to regularly undertake, as its focus is generally on the development process at hand."

"You naturally want to do as much development inside as possible when you have an R&D staff," says David R. Berko, senior vice president for product acquisition at Hasbro. But he feels that the outside people serve the industry well because they're generally off in their own corner of the world thinking differently from the rest of the business in the mainstream. Adds Berko, "The home runs in this business have been things that weren't done yesterday—like small creatures that speak Furbish."

Says Bill Ritchie, president of Binary Arts, "Independent inventors and their ideas are what keep my company fresh to the market. Because of the way the system works, I get to look at all the ideas I want for free and select only the concepts that truly fit Binary Arts' mission. Then we all profit according to how well our customers like what we've done. It's a great system that works for everybody involved."

For years there has been running debate at the corporate level regarding how much pure R&D a company can afford to fund. While a few of the larger companies operate advanced planning groups—designers and engineers charged with consulting crystal balls and dreaming up way-out concepts for two to five years into the future—most find it more profitable to depend upon the pros for left-field concepts. Creative staffs within R&D departments are assigned instead to engineer and design outside products, as well as to extend existing product lines or licensed character merchandise.

Mike Meyers, a former senior vice president of R&D at Hasbro Games, says that using internal staff or external sources is a numbers game. He had X amount of staff time to develop 30 or more internally generated products a year as well as redevelop other ideas from outside sources. He saw from the outside in excess of 2,000 opportunities annually. The talents of his staff were brought into hundreds of those ideas. But, he remarked, his staff was left with little time for pure invention. "To invent, you need time to fail," Meyers said, and they really didn't have the luxury to fail very often.

Meyers also noted, "The outside concept really has the advantage because with the inside one, you have the option of waiting. The outside product is looked at with much more intensity. There's always that paranoia that you'll make a mistake and turn down something great. With the inside product, if you don't do it, you can't make a mistake. It might have been great, but who knows?"

Independent inventors have choices, whereas corporate employees, no matter how creative, do not. No one dictates how the independents should look at something, or when and if they should work on something. They are not burdened by corporate standard operating procedures.

"Without having any people devoted to inventing new games in-house, Pressman relies on the independent inventor to generate ideas for both our licensed and nonlicensed games," says Susan Adamo Baumbach, vice president of R&D. "If I could be 20 places at once, I think I would choose to be in the 20 backyards of the best toy and game inventors in the world. That way, when I hear them say, 'This is a *great* concept,' I could be sure to be the first one to see it!"

An executive who mines ideas from the inventing community, speaking on the condition of anonymity, suggests that a great line could be put together year in and year out using about 10 inventing groups. He added, "You keep the field broad as much for public relations as anything, and, of course, there is always the remote possibility that a big winner will come from a distant star."

The Amateur Disadvantage

Outside inventors are divided into two categories—the professionals (the known quantity) and the amateurs (the unknown quantity). When toy executives talk about the value of the independent inventing community, they refer to the full-time professionals whom they can rely upon and work with, day in and day out, to create innovative products. On the other hand, manufacturers receive thousands and thousands of unsolicited ideas every year from amateur inventors. Most companies, especially the larger ones, return packages unopened if the sending party is not on a list of known inventors.

"The main problem I have with amateur submissions is that they're rarely fresh. They are usually the reinvention of some wheel that has been seen 10 times in the history of the industry, or not sufficiently novel to warrant a big company making a serious investment in it," explains Tony Miller of Mattel. Years ago, he said he had actually been shown a stick and hoop by two so-called inventors who apparently thought the world was waiting for another stick and hoop.

Mike Hirtle, vice president of R&D, product acquisition, and inventor relations at Hasbro Games, says, "The best guys don't leave anything to chance. Their ideas are executed in a 'looks-like, works-like' sample that is so professional that it will survive not only the first screening by the R&D guy who can see past the quality of the sample, but in each of the successive presentations. These are the meetings that have to happen with the marketing staff, the sales organization, senior management, and everyone else involved with endorsing a product before a contract is actually written. The top inventors usually execute those samples so that they look great and knock everybody out."

Another indictment against amateur inventors is that they do not understand how things are marketed, manufactured, or prototyped, or what they cost to make. All are important factors in the decision process and must be understood to make sense of the marketers' final position on an idea. Woody Browne, who has held senior marketing positions at various toy companies, in addition to currently consulting on licensing opportunities, echoed this sentiment in an interview. He said that even when amateurs have a great idea, they never think about the business side, such as how to market the product or what it's going to cost to produce. When Brown was at Tyco, his colleague Michael Lyden explained that some people come in, put a product on the desk, and wait for a reaction. He said it's almost like a con game; they want the company to get so excited that it will do the market research, costing, and other exercises that the inventor should have done. "Or they'll bring you something and you'll say, 'Can we contract with you to develop this?' and they say, 'Well, no, I don't know how to do it.'"

Peggy Brown, vice president of R&D at Patch Products, concurs. "The overwhelming majority of concepts from first-time inventors are noncommercial; that is, they have already been done. They are based upon themes that are outdated or inappropriate, or they are designed in such a way that they are impossible to manufacture for a marketable price." A former independent inventor herself, Brown adds that most companies are not willing to shoulder the liability of meeting with amateur inventors. "Companies have been burned by too many lawsuits."

411 Published periodically from toy fairs around the world, don't miss The Kroll Report. Read news and commentary as reported by the legendary Fred Kroll, whose credits include creation of Trouble (Kohner/MB). In 2003, he attended his sixty-fifth NY Toy Fair. Log onto The Kroll Report directly at http://personal.mia.bellsouth.net/mia/u/n/unclfred/index.html.

Mixed Attitudes

While almost every promotional toy company works with the professional inventing community, a few vary in their use of the pros. Small companies that sell unpromoted products such as plastic beach pails and what the industry calls "plastic-by-the-pound" usually do not buy designs from independents. Their lines are so basic and profit margins are so thin that products will not support a royalty load. Staff engineers and designers or offshore sources create their lines on a nonroyalty basis.

At one time, Mattel had a reputation for not making outside developers feel welcome. Even among the best and most successful pros, it was known as a difficult penetration. According to several former Mattel executives, much of this attitude came from in-house design managers who felt that their people could do anything better than the inventing community. It is not hard to see where the company got its confidence, with powerful lines like Barbie and Hot Wheels. The company expanded its own design staff rather than relying on inventors. This attitude has dramatically changed in recent years and Mattel now reaches out to professional inventors.

Toy Trivia

12. On July 4, 1956, Uncle Milton had his idea for the Ant Farm. What is his last name?

a. Levy

b. Leroy

c. Levine

No Growth, No Glory

Perhaps a manufacturer can survive without the contribution made by inventors, but there will be no growth, and growth is evidence of life. Manufacturers tend to get stuck on plateaus, and only explosive products can move them to a higher level. Sales records indisputably support that much of such product emanates from the creatives in the independent inventing community.

Without Santa Claus, Christmas would be just another holiday. Without professional independent toy and game inventors, a toy and game manufacturer would be just another injection molder or marketer. It is indeed the creative input from the inventing community that breathes life into both the Yule season and the product supplied to marketers. Few people exhibit a greater diversity of skills or touch more lives with their work than the inventors who fuel the industry workshops with the toys we adults know don't come from Santa Claus.

Fun Facts

- ◆ The game of parcheesi was first played in India. The English call it Ludo.
- ◆ Ideal produced the first Shirley Temple dolls in 1934, after the four-year old child actress won the country's heart with her performance in the feature film *Stand Up and Cheer* (Fox). The dolls were sculpted by Bernard Lipfert, perhaps the most prolific sculpture of American dolls.
- ◆ A fresco found in the ruins of Pompeii show two men playing what appears to be an early version of backgammon. Above their heads are two inscriptions: "I've won," and "It's not a three, it's a two."

Chapter 2

Maple Seeds to Microchips: A History of Playthings

"In an industry such as ours that thrives on innovation, the need for new product ideas is constant; independent inventors are an important source for these ideas that will become tomorrow's playthings. A good toy with child appeal and play value, whether it is created by the novice toy developer or professional designer, will always get to market."

—Thomas Conley, president,
Toy Industry Association, Inc.

A History of Toy Invention

On the Eighth Day, he created the toy inventor ....

Okay, so we may not be able to trace modern-day inventors back to divine origins, but we do find evidence of playthings dating back to antiquity. Given that, we can only surmise that some individuals toiled, if not for royalties, then to exercise their imaginative talents to create things for amusement and play.

Toy inventors have therefore played an important role in children's lives since the dawn of humanity. Through toys, children learn about themselves and the world around them. Toys are the tools of play, prompting the earliest curiosity, exercising physical skills, and opening what Lewis Carroll called "eyes of wonder." Toys make up a miniature world that never quite relinquishes its hold on our imagination.

The very first toys may have been the playful inventions of Mother Nature. In addition to the stick and the stone, the maple seed no doubt amused the ancestors of today's consumers, spinning like helicopter blades as it fell from trees. The rotary motion of the seed's descent, virtually unique in the plant kingdom, has been captured in spring-loaded plastic flying toys today. Indeed, many ancient amusements have stood the test of time and in some form still occupy space on retail shelves. Some may now be inexpensive novelties; others have been spruced up with decoration or microelectronics that let them light, talk, or vibrate. Kids today may be sophisticated consumers with high expectations—but they're also still kids and are still playing with toy concepts lingering from the past.

In this brief history of venerable playthings, reference is made to the number of companies still supplying such product as shown in the 2003 *Playthings Buyers Guide*. For the toy inventor, these marketers are potential licensees of new ideas that update old classics through the addition of a new function or design that makes the variants salable today. Charlie Phillips, inventor of Advance to Boardwalk (Parker Bros.) says, "It wouldn't surprise me to hear that some toy inventors are poking around museums and history books for sparks to new ideas. We look for inspiration in many places. No reason a fresh look at something old wouldn't yield a clue to a version of a classic that could be new again ... with the right spin."

The More Things Change, the More They Stay the Same

Few examples of prehistoric toys or games have been found by archeologists. However, it's a good bet that some Stone Age inventor drew pots, rings, and gullies in the dirt with his heels; pressed his knuckles to the ground; took aim with his favorite "game stone"; and challenged his friends to the first known contest of Ringer. It has been reported that marbles were unearthed in the Egyptian pyramids and in North American Indian burial mounds. Evidence reveals that a young Roman boy named Octavian (history buffs will know him as Emperor Augustus) played games using nuts as marbles.

Today marbles are made of glass, plastic, or wood. Some are molded in clear half-spheres with inserted objects visible when the halves are fused as one. Other uniquely colored agates have become collectibles. How consumers play with marbles may have changed, but they nonetheless remain, by definition, marbles. Seventeen manufacturers of marbles are listed in the 2003 *Playthings Buyers Guide*.

411

To obtain the latest copy of the *Playthings Buyers Guide*, call 212-519-7342. This invaluable resource contains listings of trade associations, products, trademarks, licensors, licensed properties, manufacturer reps, suppliers, designers, and inventors.

Toy Trivia

13. E. David Wilson, president, Hasbro Games, is a passionate fan of which college football team?

a. Michigan Wolverines

b. Notre Dame Fighting Irish

c. Florida State Seminoles

Another age-old toy can be traced back to primitive man's quest for food. The yo-yo originated when hunters sat in trees and threw small rocks at animals below. With a vine wrapped around it, the stone could be retrieved instantly for another try. Today there are highly decorated versions, some with LEDs for night play and others with high-performance clutch mechanisms to make "walking the dog" easier; one of these is Mike Caffrey's Yomega. Forty-three manufacturers of yo-yos are listed in the 2003 *Playthings Buyers Guide*.

Like the yo-yo, the slingshot obviously originated as a primitive hunting weapon. It was the progenitor to the sling David used to kill the Philistine warrior Goliath. Roman armies and other warriors through the sixteenth century carried this handheld catapult as a device for inflicting bodily harm on enemies. Five manufacturers of sling shots are listed in the 2003 *Playthings Buyers Guide*.

In the third millennium B.C.E., archaeologists tell us that young boys played army with terra-cotta toy soldiers and girls cradled wooden dolls. Here we see the genesis of Larry Reiner's G.I. Joe (Hasbro) and Ruth Handler's Barbie (Mattel), both inventors of blessed memory. Egyptian graves have yielded balls; crude pull toys; hollow whistles crafted from baked clay; rattles in the shapes of birds, fish, and animals; jointed puppets; dolls hand-painted in vibrant hues; and whip tops.

The top is often mentioned in classical literature. It is found in Aristophanes' *The Birds* (1461)—"You get the idea. I'm busy as a top."—and Homer's Iliad (XIV.413)—"… reels like a top staggering to its last turnings."

There are 54 manufacturers of balls, 26 of pull toys, 23 of whistles, 19 of rattles, 44 of hand puppets, several pages of dolls, and 33 of tops listed in the 2003 *Playthings Buyers Guide.*

In the glitzy Caesar's Palaces of Las Vegas and Atlantic City, one instrument of gaming madness is a set of two small cubes called dice. At Caesar's original palace, Romans tossed knucklebones (the ankle bones of sheep), thought to be the first dice. Today dice are a requisite part of many games of chance, be it Yahtzee or Liar's Dice or board games in which dice determine movement of players pawns. Inventors like Fred Kroll have come up with electronic dice displays. However, such efforts at improvements just do not give the same sensory pleasure of "rattlin' dem bones," not to mention the escalated costs for such devices. Twenty-eight manufacturers of dice are listed in the 2003 *Playthings Buyers Guide.*

Greek pottery has lively examples of children playing with hoops, hobby horses, balls, and airborne disks. The basic idea of today's classic flying toy, the Frisbee, invented by California building inspector Fred Morrison and introduced by Wham-O in 1958, can be traced back to Greece. Five manufacturers of hoops, 13 of rocking horses, and 47 of things that fly are listed in the 2003 *Playthings Buyers Guide.*

Roman and Greek children were offered dolls at the altar of a god or goddess to symbolize a ceremonial loss of childhood. Unlike today's high-fashion, coiffured, and anatomically sculpted dolls, these were mostly made of wood or clay, though some were carved from bone or ivory.

The remains of board games have been found in the ruins of Ur, one of the world's oldest known cities (circa 3500 B.C.E.), in the ancient region of Sumer (now southeastern Iraq). Hand-carved wooden game boards, inlaid with gold and ivory, were found near the stone coffin of the Egyptian boy-king Tut, who died in 1339 B.C.E. These wooden boards were for the ancient game Senat, an early form of backgammon.

There is some debate over which is the oldest board game that is still being played. To find this answer, we went to game guru Michael Gray, Hasbro Games' senior director for product development. He reports that early versions of Mancala (Mankala'h) were found in Memphis (Egypt) in limestone and at Thebes on roofing slabs, dating around 1400 B.C.E., according to *Bell's Book of Board and Table Games* (1960). Other versions were found at Karnak and Luxor. Boards have been found in Arabia dating from before the time of Muhammad, and the followers of the prophet carried variations of the game to the countries influenced by their culture. Go (or Wei-ch'i, pronounced "Way Key") is first mentioned in Chinese writings from Honan about 625 B.C.E. According to Bell, Confucius advised the idle rich to play Wei-ch'i rather than allow their minds to stagnate. According to tradition, the game was taken to Japan in 735 A.D by the Lord Kibi. It looks like Mankala'h may be older than Wei-ch'i, Mike concludes.

Here at home, EPA inspectors are rumored to have found the remains of poor-selling board games in landfills near the facilities of some U.S. game producers. One hundred nineteen manufacturers of board games and 23 manufacturers of backgammon games are listed in the 2003 *Playthings Buyers Guide*.

The history of toy and game development is as rich in the East as in the West. The Far East is the birthplace of many popular modern games. Very casual observation of thirteenth-century Chinese paintings suggests a depiction of toy inventors, with the figures holding satchels of prototypes in one hand and unsigned contracts in the other. Experts estimate that dominoes probably was invented in China and introduced in Europe in the 1300s. Playing cards are said to have originated in China, where paper was invented, circa A.D. 800. It is unknown how they arrived in Europe, but they appeared in Italy by the late 1200s. Before the printing press, all cards were hand-painted. Forty manufacturers of dominoes and 90 producers of playing cards are listed in the 2003 *Playthings Buyers Guide*.

No one is positive about the origins of carving jointed wooden snakes, animals with nodding heads (could these have been the first Bobble Heads?), and weighted tumbler dolls (were Elliot Rudell's Weebles a descendant?), but they, too, may have come from China. Kites, perhaps the oldest form of aircraft, first flew in China about 3,000 years ago. During the Han Dynasty (200 B.C.E. to A.D. 200), inventive Chinese military designers lashed bamboo shoots to kites. As the kites soared above the enemy, the harsh whistling sound made by the wind passing through the shoots instilled fear and panic into opponents, causing them to flee. (An ancestor of David Fuhrer's Vortex Screamer football?) Twenty-four manufacturers of kites are listed in the 2003 *Playthings Buyers Guide*.

The Hacky-Sack footbag, still being kicked around by today's youth, is based on a "football" kicking game invented in 2597 B.C.E. by the Chinese emperor Hwang Ti.

Called Kemari, the game consisted of kicking a leather ball filled with hair. Hacky-Sack was invented by John Stalberger and Michael Marshall and was licensed to Wham-O in 1983. Their original game was called Hack the Sack.

Historians believe that chess originated in India around A.D. 600. A war game, it is unique among the classic games in that each piece has a rank, paralleling India's caste system. The popularity of chess first spread to Persia and then to neighboring countries via warring Arabs. In the Middle Ages, chess became popular in Europe, brought to Spain by Muslim invaders, and was reportedly seen being played as far north as Scandinavia. Over the years, many inventors have tried to improve on chess, but none has been able to break the enduring appeal of this strategy game. Forty-six manufacturers of chess sets are listed in the 2003 *Playthings Buyers Guide*.

In the Dark Ages and the Middle Ages, people continued to play with clay marbles, rattles, hobbyhorses, toy soldiers, weapons, stilts, bubble pipes, puppets, and dolls. In contrast to the Far East, very little is known about European toys developed during this era. However, historians tell us that children of the poor played with simple folk toys made from scraps of wood and cloth. Sixteen manufacturers of toy soldiers, a lone maker of stilts, and 28 companies making bubble products are listed in the 2003 *Playthings Buyers Guide*.

Children born into royalty, on the other hand, received dramatically costumed and detailed dolls with full wardrobes (early relatives of Ken and Barbie?) and miniature weapons, as well as replicas of men-at-arms in full battle armor. Few European medieval clay dolls and toy horses and knights survived. Evidence remains merely in old pictorial sources and written documents.

Toy Trivia

14. There are approximately 5,000 fibers in each 1 of these balls.

a. Super Ball
b. Koosh Ball
c. Nerf Ball

We do know that Nuremberg, a prosperous market and cultural center at the crossroads of many trade routes, became (and still is) the hub of Germany's toy industry. What better setting than near the rugged Black Forest region, location of many German legends and fairy tales? Nuremberg was home in the fifteenth century to toymaker guilds, the first known professional associations of toy inventors.

Today this city hosts the annual Nuremberg Toy Fair, Europe's largest toy industry trade event, which ranks in importance with the American International Toy Fair in New York City. Toy professionals flock to Nuremberg in their unending pursuit of fresh ideas and foreign licensees. At the 1959 Nuremberg Fair, for example, The Ohio

Art Company found and licensed the rights to produce Etch-a-Sketch. Spirograph was created by Dennis Fischer, an Englishman. He took it to Nuremberg in 1965, where Kenner licensed rights to manufacture and market it in the United States. More than 30 million Spirographs have been sold to date.

Tiddlywinks was an English pub game, in the tradition of darts, that originated during the late 1800s. Its name comes from "tiddly wink," which is English slang for an unlicensed pub.

In 1746, jumping jacks were the most popular toy in France. Then a government official, convinced that pregnant women who saw the toy's twisted limbs would risk giving birth to deformed babies, banned them.

France was also the setting for perhaps the first toy craze. In 1747, French playwright and librettist Paul Jules Barbier wrote,

In Paris some toys have been devised called puppets .... These little figures represent Harlequin and Scaramouch, or else bakers, shepherds, and shepherdesses. These ridiculous things have taken the fancy of Parisian society to such an extent that one cannot go into any house without finding them dangling from every mantelpiece. They are being bought to give to women and girls, and the craze has reached such a pitch that this New Year all the shops are full of them ....

It was Barbier who first observed that toys can assume fad proportions and become ingrained in the culture. Certainly, many toy executives continue to hold this thought today as they seek ideas they hope will spawn megahits.

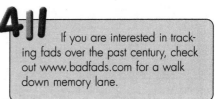

If you are interested in tracking fads over the past century, check out www.badfads.com for a walk down memory lane.

No doubt somewhere an inventor or two has plans to cast one of these ancient forms in some new polymer on some new high-speed machine with some new chromatic finish that will be merchandised in some new style. With an inventor directing all this freshness at an ancient concept, can the result be anything but innovative? After all, isn't the quest of new what the industry is all about?

Explorer Discovers the American Toy Market

Long before Christopher Columbus reached the North American continent in 1492, Native Americans had made a wide assortment of toys and games. Among the favorites were toy animals carved from wood and bone, whip tops, bow-and-arrow target games, lacrosse, and cat's cradle. Pick-Up Sticks has been traced to Native Americans, who played it with straws of wheat. They reportedly passed it on to English settlers at the time when the United States was comprised of 13 colonies. The Pawnees invented an infant toy similar to today's Fisher-Price Play-Gym. Mothers hung rattle balls and spinning wooden gripper hoops on a center axis over their babies' cribs to stimulate the infants' hand-eye coordination. Could it be that Fisher-Price, long regarded as an innovator of infant and preschool toys, was also an astute observer of history?

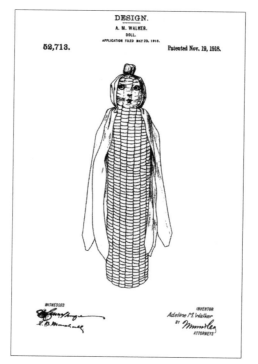

Corn Cob Doll
Patented November 1918
U.S. Patent 52,713

As pioneers opened America's frontier from the Appalachian Mountains to the Pacific Ocean, few new toys or games were developed, perhaps because children had little free time. They worked alongside their parents to ensure the survival of the community. Nevertheless, they improvised play and adopted many Native American toys and games. Dolls were fashioned from corncobs, no doubt the inspiration for A. M. Walker's doll

(U.S. Patent 52,713, issued November 19, 1918). Rawhide strips were rolled up to form balls. (Could this have been the progenitor of the Koosh Ball?) Whistles were carved from tree branches. Dried kernels were often used as game markers.

The Beginning of the American Toy Industry

The first toy shops appeared in New England as Puritan prohibitions began to ease in the early eighteenth century, some 100 years after the Pilgrims came ashore at Plymouth Rock. By the early 1800s, the Industrial Revolution had spread to North America. Industry began to overtake agriculture. By the end of the century, the United States was the largest and most competitive industrial nation in the world.

The toy industry kept pace with mechanization, and in 1783, after the Revolutionary War, the first companies began to produce individual playthings in quantity. From being the creations of home tinkerers making handmade wooden wagons, sleds, kites, and other amusements, toys became the products of large-scale manufacturing firms.

On April 10, 1790, President George Washington signed the country's first patent bill. For the first time, the inherent right of an inventor to profit from his or her invention was recognized by law. Previously, privileges granted to an inventor were dependent upon the prerogative of a monarch or a special act of a legislature. As Secretary of State, Thomas Jefferson (known to have invented a toy or two himself) was, in effect, the first administrator of the American patent system. Clara Barton, founder of the American Red Cross, served as the first female clerk in the U.S. Patent Office.

The Tower Shop, later renamed the Tower Toy Company, was perhaps the first American toy-manufacturing business. Organized in the late 1830s by William S. Tower of South Hingham, Massachusetts, a carpenter who made wooden toys, the company was originally a cooperative guild of craftsmen representing different skills. By pooling their talents, they were able to create a wide range of items, including doll furniture, toy tools, and toy boats, mostly of wood. In 1878, the enterprise was successful enough to exhibit its toys at the Exposition Universelle Internationale in Paris.

Toy Trivia

15. Lincoln Logs were designed and developed in 1916 by the son of whom?

a. Babe Ruth

b. Buckminster Fuller

c. Frank Lloyd Wright

At about this same time, the Crandall family, originally of Hopkinton, Massachusetts, began toymaking with at least 11 members from 2 branches of the family involved in inventing and producing toys from about 1830 to 1929. They held several hundred patents, among them those for the spring rocking horse, the velocipede, nesting blocks, and interlocking building blocks.

Children's Play Becomes Adults' Work

In 1860, Milton Bradley, then 24 years old, established the Milton Bradley Publishing and Lithography Company in Springfield, Massachusetts. However, financial problems began to plague the printer before a year was up. Looking for innovative products to keep his presses rolling, Bradley decided to diversify by inventing and marketing a game entitled The Checkered Game of Life. This game was eventually retired, but in 1959, MB's senior management needed a commemorative game for the company's one hundredth anniversary. They hired California independent toy inventor Reuben Klamer, who saw the original Checkered Game of Life in the company's archives. He participated in the redesign of it, and in 1960 the "new" Game of Life was introduced.

Searching for another success, Bradley began to consider outside game submissions, thus initiating the company's long relationship with independent inventors. Today's game inventors can thank Bradley's early dependence on outside ideas for opening opportunities with major manufacturers.

In 1888, Jeanne P. Clarke sold Politics and the Race for the Presidency to Milton Bradley and became the first woman to license a game to the company. The firm then bought a board game called Eckha, a combination of chess and checkers, from a Harvard mathematics professor, and it became one of the most popular games of the late 1800s. Dr. Thomas Hill, a former Harvard president and pastor of a Unitarian church in Maine, licensed a board game called Kerion.

Across the Commonwealth in Salem, Massachusetts, George S. Parker, an enterprising 16-year-old, took $40 of his $50 life savings and started in 1883 what would become one of America's largest game publishers. The entrepreneurial lad literally bet his last dollar on a roll of the dice when he opted to publish Banking, a game he had invented. Sales were brisk; he not only got back his investment, but he also made a profit of almost $100. More important, the George S. Parker Company was in business. By 1888, his enterprise was going so well that George was joined by his elder brother Charles, and they renamed the firm Parker Brothers. A third brother, Edwin, joined them a decade later.

The Parker Brothers line featured 29 games in 1888, most of them invented by George Parker. Page after page of the 1892 mail-order catalogs from Marshall Field & Company, Butler Brothers, and Sears, Roebuck & Company show a plethora of Parker Brothers product. In the century since then, Parker Brothers has published more than 1,000 games, many of them world renowned. We all grew up playing classics like Monopoly, Sorry!, Risk, and Clue.

Bradley and Parker games have always mirrored the era in which they were released. In the earliest days, their products were obviously influenced by Puritanism, as in The New Game of Virtue Rewarded, Vice Punished, The Checkered Game of Life, and Happy Days in Old New England. In fact, the oldest known commercial American board game was Mansion of Happiness, a children's path game designed to challenge a player's moral fiber. Published by W. & S. B. Ives Company in 1843, it had a playing field boldly marked with such words as *justice, piety, immodesty,* and *ingratitude.*

Interestingly, when Hasbro bought Milton Bradley and Parker Bros., in 1984 and 1991, respectively, the corporation acquired a collection of blue-chip games that have entertained families for 40 to 50 years. Actually, the aggregate experience in game development, manufacturing, and marketing the two companies brought to Hasbro was 232 years! These two game publishers were combined to form Hasbro Games, which today is a rock-solid powerhouse of profits for its Pawtucket, Rhode Island, parent company.

Novel Materials for Novel Ideas

In the mid-1830s and 1840s, new toy factories were equipped to use any and every kind of material to make toys better—and in more variety. Pull toys and miniature dollhouse furnishings were die-cut from tin. Dolls' heads were made of ceramic in Philadelphia. The use of metal facilitated beautiful and complex shapes and, more important, improved the quality of toys with tougher wheels and more durable gears. Teething rings, dominoes, and bagatelle balls were produced from ivory; rubber from India and what is now Malaysia was used for balls, rattle boxes, and doll heads; and paper was used for playing cards and board games.

The toy industry had grown so much by the mid-1840s that nearly every town, no matter how remote, had an emporium selling toys. In New York, Woolworth's Fancy Store advertised the arrival of popular playthings from Europe in time for Christmas 1844. Locomotives and mechanical toys for children were being promoted in one of the first seasonal toy advertising campaigns.

Although toy and game invention, patenting, and production slowed during the Civil War, manufacturers managed to benefit from the crisis. As might be expected, toy guns became very popular. In 1861, Milton Bradley designed a lightweight kit of popular games for the Union troops. Called Games for the Soldiers, it contained special portable editions of chess, checkers, The Checkered Game of Life, backgammon, and five varieties of dominoes.

But Milton Bradley was not alone in capitalizing on wartime demand. In 1898, as the United States prepared to enter the Spanish-American War, Parker Brothers released such games as Hold the Fort, War in Cuba, The Siege of Havana, and Battle of Manila. Another company published Uncle Sam and the Don, depicting a fistfight in which Uncle Sam decked his foe with a blow to the solar plexus.

At the outbreak of the Civil War, 12 factories reported combined annual sales of under $200,000. By 1900, volume had jumped to more than $4 million reported by 500 companies with retail sales of $20 million, a third from foreign imports.

In 1882, author James Lukin is reported to have observed, "Talk of the march of the intellect, the march of toydom beats it all hollow. I do not believe a modern body would look at such crude creations as delighted the babies 50 years ago …. The really instructive and highly interesting toys of our time, the scientific and mechanical ones [were] a class utterly unknown in olden days." Lukin described the earliest "mechanical" toys of wood and cardboard, powered by fine sand running over a wheel that brought human figures to life, as "rude creations." On the other hand, in the 1880s, *Harper's Bazaar* described "The doll of today … endowed with an interior phonograph, and this enabled to reproduce the human voice." So the inventors of Teddy Ruxpin, the megahit "talking" plush bear of the 1980s, were not so original after all. Toys throw long shadows.

At this point, toward the end of the nineteenth century, toy and game inventors were still independent part-timers or in-house staffers. Except for those inventors who were entrepreneurial enough to establish their own manufacturing companies, no one was making enough money to survive without other income. Independent inventors needed to sustain themselves with alternate livelihoods. And in-house inventors often performed other tasks for the company, such as machine operator or sales clerk, occasionally providing a product idea that was considered worthy enough to bring to market.

Around the turn of the century, however, immigrant toymakers began to make their mark on America. What became known as the Golden Age of Toys saw the introduction of walking and talking dolls, toy pianos that plinked, wind-up clockwork, vehicles

powered by friction motors, gravity gizmos, magnetics, and realistic steam toys,
to name but a few. There was an electri-
fied dollhouse with running water. Newly
discovered scientific principles in optics
were incorporated into toys. A. C. Gilbert
invented the Erector Set. The entrepreneurial spirit had arrived in a thriving toy
business.

Toy Trivia

16. Herb Schaper whittled the first
Cootie out of wood in 1948.
What was his profession?

a. Fisherman

b. Letter carrier

c. Mechanic

The First Megahits

Samuel Leeds Allen owned a successful farm equipment company in New Jersey. Farm
equipment sales being seasonal, he sought to diversify his product line and set out to
develop a sled. Allen tested various designs on a slope at his Ivystone Farm near West-
field and at nearby West Town School, where his daughter Elizabeth and her classmates
field-tested his designs. By combining features of each of his earlier models, called
Phantom, Fleetwing, Ariel, and Fairy Coaster, Allen perfected the first steerable sled
with flexible T-shape runners and a slatted wooden seat. On February 9, 1887, he
applied for a patent for the Flexible Flyer. It was granted on August 23, 1887. For
more than 100 years, Flexible Flyer has been synonymous with winter, snow, and kids.

Beatrice Alexander Behrman, who became known as Madame Alexander, was born
above the first doll hospital in America, which her father, a Russian immigrant, started
in 1885 in New York City. The recurrent scene of tearful little girls bringing their
broken porcelain dolls to the "doctor" left an indelible impression on young Beatrice.
When shipments of European dolls practically ceased during a period of war, Behrman
saw an opportunity to express her artistic talent, while also fulfilling a new need in the
marketplace, by designing her own line of "made in America" dolls in 1923. Each
required an average of two to three weeks for completion, in contrast to Barbie, which
has a gestation period counted in minutes. To date, the Alexander Doll Company has
introduced well over 5,000 different dolls.

The Lionel Manufacturing Company opened for business in 1900. Its founder,
Joshua Lionel Cowen, produced fuses; small, low-voltage motors; and electrical novelties. He also invented the first dry-cell battery. In 1901, the imaginative Cowen put
one of his electric motors in a model railroad car, and the best-loved name in trains
chugged its way into toy history.

Alice Stead Binney conceived the trade name Crayola for her husband Edwin's crayons in 1903. She derived it from the French word *craie* (stick of chalk) and the word *oleaginous* (oily). Research indicates that 65 percent of U.S. children between the ages of 2 and 7 color or draw at least once a day for an average of 27 minutes, mostly using Crayola crayons. More than two billion of them are manufactured each year. If all the regular-size Crayola crayons made in one year were laid end to end on the Equator, they would circle the Earth six times.

Charles Pajeau, a stonemason by trade, invented Tinkertoy in 1913 and sold one million sets the first year. A display in a Grand Central Station window that year caused a massive traffic jam. Since then, more than 100 million Tinkertoy sets have been sold worldwide.

In 1916, John Lloyd Wright was with his father, architect Frank Lloyd Wright, in Tokyo, to observe construction techniques for an "earthquake-proof" hotel, the Imperial Palace. The 24-year-old Wright returned home to Merrill, Wisconsin, and drew up the specifications for a new construction toy that would become Lincoln Logs. Wright was granted a U.S. patent in 1920.

Fred A. Lundahl owned the Moline Pressed Steel Company in Illinois, where he made fenders and other heavy-gauge steel parts for International Harvester Company. As a birthday gift to his son, Buddy, he crafted a realistic, toy-size, working replica of a dump truck from scraps of steel, thereby inventing the first heavy-gauge-steel toy vehicle. It proved so popular with Buddy and the neighborhood kids that, at the suggestion of a friend, Lundahl took it to F.A.O. Schwarz in New York City. He was stunned to receive an order for a carload of his toys. When asked what he intended to call them, his choice was simple: "I'll call them Buddy L Toys."

With the Wright Brothers' first airplane flight in December 1903, the American love affair with speed and motion moved into the wild blue yonder. Toymakers began to foresee and outpace adult reality, as replicas of all sorts of flying machines would anticipate man's greatest adventure, the exploration of space.

One of the first examples of a manufacturer getting caught with its trends down was Kingsbury's introduction of a monoplane in 1924. It collected dust on the shelves because the World War I aces' kids adored biplanes. But Kingsbury learned. After Charles Lindbergh made his historic flight to Paris in 1927, the monoplane was re-decorated to resemble the Spirit of St. Louis, and it sold. After the excitement over the Lone Eagle subsided, it was spray-painted green to resemble the plane used by

Wrong-Way Corrigan on his misadventure to Ireland, and sales soared again. This was indeed an early lesson that some companies today still find difficult to practice. If you give toy consumers what they desire, it will sell. But misread the market with styling, and the products will be nailed to the shelves.

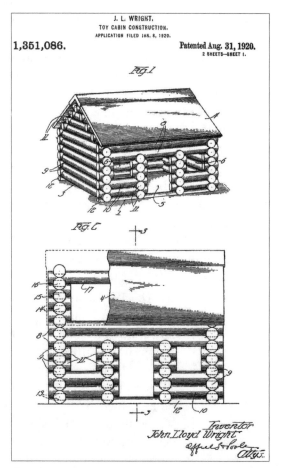

Wright's U.S. patent 1,351,086
Issued on August 31, 1920.

The Rise of Modern Mass Marketing

Then, as today, the more innovative the toys and games are, the more kids want them. Prolific inventors and manufacturers had a hard time keeping the ever-expanding market filled with fresh product. Even nontoy merchants saw the opportunities. Soon dry-goods stores and mail-order houses such as Sears, Roebuck and Montgomery Ward joined other retail outlets in devoting store shelf space and catalog pages to playthings.

The first American Toy Fair took place in New York City in February 1902, when 10 salesmen representing American factories set up exhibits at a lower Manhattan hotel for 4 weeks. They timed their trade show in hopes of catching buyers on their way to and from European buying trips. With the exception of 1945, when the Toy Fair was canceled due to World War II priorities, it has been held annually in New York City since 1934, the same year that the Toy Center Building at 200 Fifth Avenue made its debut as an exhibition site. From 1952 until 1994, it was a 10-day event. Since 1995, the Toy Fair has been shortened in time to an eight-day event, but it expanded to include exhibitors at Javits Center. After the 1983 show, the TMA board of directors voted to change the name from the American Toy Fair to the American International Toy Fair, to reflect its preeminence among the world's toy trade shows. *Note:* The TMA has since morphed into the Toy Industry Association (TIA).

It was also in 1902 that America's love affair with the teddy bear began. For the cuddly critters, it's been a bear market ever since. Americans annually spend hundreds of millions of dollars on them. In 2001, the Vermont Teddy Bear Company alone accounted for $37 million in catalog sales, according to *Entrepreneur* magazine.

Toy Trivia

17. While Eleanor Abbott of San Diego was recuperating from polio in the 1940s, she created this classic game.

a. Candy Land

b. Game of the States

c. Go to the Head of the Class

Toy production in the United States doubled between 1900 and 1910. During the following decade, it soared to even more spectacular heights, experiencing a 500 percent increase due to an almost total disappearance of European imports during World War I. The war was a catalyst to the American toy industry. Designers began creating war toys and war games. Much as it had done for Civil War soldiers, Milton Bradley supplied game kits to General Pershing's American Expeditionary Forces on the battlefields of France.

When Germany got back on an even footing after World War I, it launched an economic invasion of the American toy industry. Lower-priced, quality German toys began to flood the U.S. market. Even the most powerful American manufacturers were affected, and many newer firms were forced out of business.

To stave off this economic scourge, A. C. Gilbert, inventor of the Erector Set and president of the Toy Manufacturers of America, formed a delegation that went to Washington, D.C., in 1921, and successfully lobbied for a 75 percent protective tariff on imported toys and games. This helped smaller manufacturers survive and grow, and it protected the U.S. toy industry until it was strong enough to fend for itself, at which point the tariffs were reduced.

Perhaps the most significant business development of the 1920s did not seem so at the time. This was the founding of Hasbro, Inc., in 1923 in Providence, Rhode Island. Originally called Hassenfeld Brothers (for Henry, Hillel, and Herman), the company began by selling textile remnants and then pencil boxes. In 1943, Henry's son Merrill was named president, and he expanded the product line to include toys. The company accepted ideas and suggestions from customers, family, and independent inventors.

By the end of the 1940s, Hassenfeld Brothers had annual sales of $3 million. Mr. Potato Head, created by indy inventors George Lerner and his partner, Julius "Julie" Ellman, was introduced in the 1950s. The 1960s saw monumental growth with such items as Marvin Glass's Lite Brite and Stan Weston and Larry Reiner's G.I. Joe. The diversity of product lines and aggressive acquisition of other toy companies eventually built Hasbro into the No. 2 industry marketer, with $2.8 billion in sales in 2002.

Mattel was founded in 1942 by Elliot and Ruth Handler, and their partner Harold Mattson. They took scraps of wood from their picture frame business and began making and marketing doll house furniture. See Chapter 3 for details on the start of Mattel and the birth of Barbie. In 2002, Mattel reported $4.89 billion in sales. It is the global leader in toy sales.

The year 1929 brought the stock market crash, and the nation's economy toppled like a house of Bicycle-brand playing cards. Curiously, however, what was to be the worst and longest business slump of modern times did not affect the toy and game industry as adversely as might have been expected. It prospered through the 1930s and did not flatten out until World War II imposed severe material and manpower shortages.

It remains an axiom today that many companies in the industry—game marketers, in particular—do well during economic down cycles. At the height of the Great Depression in 1933, about 13 million Americans were out of work, and many others had only part-time employment. With much idle time and little money to spend on entertainment, Americans stayed home and amused themselves with board games and toys. Some people who did not play for amusement began inventing.

The first millionaire game inventor was Charles B. Darrow, who was awarded U.S. Patent 2,026,082 for Monopoly on December 31, 1935. It became the most successful board game of all time. Introduced during the Great Depression, "Monopoly let people fantasize that they could win in the real estate market," said Robert Barton, George Parker's son-in-law. "It was a godsend. It rescued the business [Parker Brothers], which had come within an inch of disaster." Milton Bradley's Easy Money was another game that enabled players to cut deals and handle thousands in fantasy funds. What people found impossible to achieve in reality, they could fantasize about in their parlors with stacks of toy money.

In East Aurora, New York, on October 1, 1930, Herman G. Fisher and Irving R. Price established Fisher-Price Toys with a $100,000 investment. In 1937, Fisher-Price sold more than two million toys, and the company grew rapidly to keep up with consumer demand. Today F-P, the standard in the infant and preschool markets, has broadened its product base to become a $1.6 billion producer of a highly respected brand of diverse playthings within the Mattel family.

New Babies + New Companies = Burgeoning Business

After World War II, the United States entered a great era of economic growth. Withstanding periods of inflation and recession, more enterprises and people than ever enjoyed prosperity. A new wave of materialism and self-indulgence struck the country. People had money and a compulsive drive to spend it. The baby boom brought a previously unknown commitment to family life and children. And the toy industry experienced unparalleled growth.

The first reference we could find to a prominent toy inventor was in the January 1939 issue of *Mechanix Illustrated* magazine (which sold for 15 cents!). The cover showed a photo of Edward Savage and billed him as America's No. 1 toy inventor who earned $10,000 for a single idea. The cover headline read: "TOY INVENTION! Big Money for Home Workshop Fans."

"Toy invention is a little-worked 'gold mine' for truly inventive craftsmen or home workshop fans. Devise a novel action for a mechanical toy, and toy manufacturers will give you royalties of 3 to 5 percent for permission to make and market the item," Stanley Gerstin wrote. Upon hearing this, inventor Tim Moodie quipped, "There hasn't been a cost-of-living increase for inventors since 1939!"

The Glass House

Marvin Glass opened his design studio in 1941 in a Chicago loft and began a new wave of professionalism in toy invention. By the time of his death in 1974, it had grown to become the finest and most successful industrial design organization in the business. Glass himself had amassed a personal fortune. Known for his showmanship, Glass often carried his toys in boxes handcuffed to his wrist. It was not uncommon for his items to arrive in an armored truck escorted by armed guards. Security at Marvin Glass & Associates was tighter than the controls at many of his clients' R&D departments.

"As much of a showman as he may have been, I firmly believe he was a true genius," says Mel Taft, who began his relationship with Marvin Glass & Associates shortly after Taft joined Milton Bradley in 1950. "Marvin would always put on a good show when unveiling the latest creation. Almost everything he showed had commercial value."

In December 1984, in recognition of his outstanding contributions to the growth and development of the toy industry, Glass was inducted into the newly formed Toy Manufacturers of America (TMA) Hall of Fame. Inducted along with Glass were such toy legends as Herman G. Fisher (Fisher-Price), Louis Marx (Marx Toys), A. C. Gilbert Sr., and Merrill L. Hassenfeld (Hasbro).

Marvin Glass & Associates became a haven for such young inventors as Gordon Barlow, Jeffrey Breslow, Sam Cottone, John Fertig, Ed and Bonnie Fogarty, A. Eddy Goldfarb, Ed Holahan, Wayne Kuna, Bruce Lund, Bert Meyer, Howard Morrison, Sean Mullaney, Steve Rehkemper, and Len Stubenfoll. These creative designers and many others on the Glass staff developed hundreds of successful toy and game products. Some of these Glass graduates remain active inventors today.

Eddy Goldfarb, for example, was one of the first to use plastic, in such designs as his egg-laying hen Busy Biddy, the Merry Go straw, and Yakity-Yak Teeth. Goldfarb observes, "Toys change because of technology. Right after World War II, plastics became a boom industry and opened up whole new possibilities for toys. The companies that didn't get into plastics after the war went out of business."

As the American Plastics Council states on its website, www.plastics.org, "When Alexander Parkes developed the first manmade plastic in the 1860s, he had no idea what an integral role the material would play in our everyday lives." Designers like Goldfarb made sure that plastic would play a role in the world of toys and applied the APC slogan "Plastics Make It Possible" to their concepts. Plastics hit the industry like a ton of LEGO bricks and gave rise to a new family of toys.

Triggered by World War II severe shortages of elements such as brass and aluminum, the U.S. plastics manufacturers got together and unselfishly shared research and development information to fill the gap. New injection-molding facilities were constructed nationwide. New materials, technologies, and techniques to increase production were developed.

Today no designer can remember when there was no plastic for toys. "I can hardly imagine designing toys without plastics and the enhanced possibilities they offer," Maki Papavasilou, a Mattel designer, told *Modern Plastics* magazine.

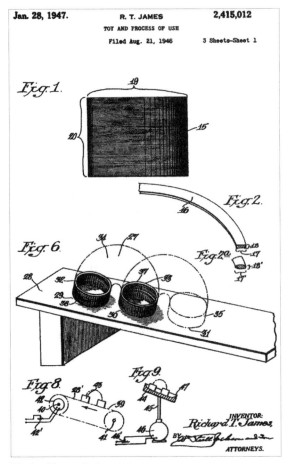

Slinky (James Industries)
Patented January 28, 1947
U.S. Patent 2,415,012

Not all inventors turned to plastics, however. On a tour at sea in 1943, Richard James, a marine engineer, watched a torsion spring fall off a table and bounce around the deck. Back at home, he said to his wife, Betty, "I think I can make a toy go down a flight of stairs." He did. And while the spring was flipping from step to step, Betty went to a dictionary and flipped from page to page to find a name that best fit their novelty. In the "S" section, she found the perfect name: Slinky. As moviegoers know, the Slinky pup in *Toy Story 1* and *2* saved its toy companions in their cinematic adventures. Slinky was awarded U.S. Patent 2,415,012.

A similar creative accident resulting in toy invention occurred to James Wright, an engineer at General Electric's research lab in New Haven, Connecticut. While trying to discover a viable synthetic rubber to aid the war effort in 1945, by mistake he let some boric acid drop into a test tube containing silicone oil. The chemical reaction that took place resulted in a compound that, to Wright's astonishment, had all the qualities of a rubber ball.

Toy Trivia

18. Where has Fisher-Price been headquartered since 1930?

a. East Aurora, NY

b. Hudson, NY

c. Paradox Lake, NY

No one at GE had any interest in this unique compound. Enter Peter Hodgson, an enterprising but unemployed ad man. After seeing the material at a party, he borrowed $147 and bought the production rights from General Electric. He packaged it in plastic eggs because Easter was coming, and thus did Silly Putty come bouncing into the toy business in 1950. Today, about two million "eggs" of Silly Putty are sold yearly. About as close as anyone will ever get to the perfect toy, it has no moving parts; it just invites children to use their imagination. Flash! His $147 investment grew to an estate worth $140 million at his death.

In the late 1940s, Herb Schaper, a Minneapolis woodcarver of toys who loved to fish, whittled lures. He discovered that one in the shape of a flea captivated the interest not only of fish, but of children. So, in 1948, with $75 in investment capital and one product, Cootie, he started Schaper Toys. In time, Schaper became a multimillionaire. Today Cootie remains in the Hasbro Game line 55 years after its introduction.

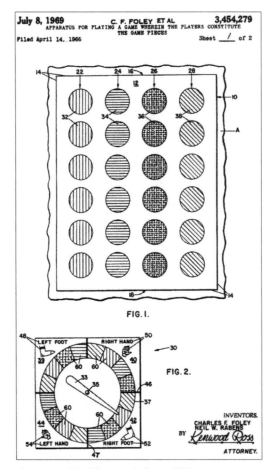

Apparatus For Playing A Game Wherein
The Players Constitute The Game Pieces (Twister)
Patented July 8, 1969
U.S. Patent 3,454,279

While most inventors were working on new playthings for profit, Eleanor Abbott passed long hours recuperating from polio by developing games for younger polio victims. One game, called Candy Land, eliminated the need for reading and counting that most board games required by basing play on matching colors on cards with colors on the game path. The game proved so popular with young players that Abbott submitted it to Milton Bradley in 1949. The rest, as they say, is history. Candy Land has sold more than 40 million copies in its 54-year run with Milton Bradley and Hasbro Games.

In 1966, two Minnesota inventors, Charles "Chuck" F. Foley and Neil W. Rabens, created a whole new approach to board games, one in which the players constitute the game pieces. They were awarded U.S. Patent 3,454,279. After it was assigned by the inventors to Milton Bradley, it was trademarked Twister and went on to become a classic game that is still in production today.

There's No Business Like Show Business

Just as a manufacturing process (plastics) and a promotion strategy (TV commercials) drastically changed the business, so did the practice of linking toys to other forms of entertainment. Manufacturers started slowly with radio tie-ins but later rolled out items mirroring hot properties from TV and movies. The infusion of character or celebrity licensing in toys and games had begun in earnest.

Radio offered the first major media tie-in for toys and games. Broadcast shows of the 1930s, such as Paul Wing's "Spelling Bee" and the question-and-answer favorite "Vox Pop," came to market in boxed versions, as did the first home adult party game based on the broadcast favorite "Fibber McGee and Molly."

As television began its ascent into households across the country, millions of youngsters were able to emulate their small-screen heroes. The Hopalong Cassidy Game, by Milton Bradley in 1955, was one of the first TV tie-in board games. The Mickey Mouse Club, in its Disneyland Game, opened the door for at-home "mouse-keteering" in 1955. A steady stream of television personalities followed on such games as Howdy Doody (1955), Captain Kangaroo (1956), Zorro (1958), Have Gun Will Travel (1959), Mighty Mouse (1960), Looney Tunes (1961), Batman and Robin (1963), Yogi Bear (1964), Flintstones (1965), Man from U.N.C.L.E. (1966), The Monkees (1967), The Brady Bunch (1969), Partridge Family (1971), The Waltons and Happy Days (1974), Charlie's Angels (1976), and The Simpsons (1989). Kid-TV characters like Barney, Big Bird, Blues Clues, Franklin, and Arthur are all over games and toys today.

Game companies used the same successful TV tie-in techniques with adult favorites, especially with quiz shows. Milton Bradley released three versions of The Price Is Right within three or four years of one another in the mid-1970s. Lowell Games had previously issued a home version in 1958, as had MB in 1964. MB reissued the game in 1986. Today the game is marketed by Endless Games, the Hoboken, New

Jersey, board game publishing house founded in 1996 by game mavens Kevin McNulty and Michael Gasser, two of our industry's most savvy characters.

Endless Games spearheaded a retro initiative that has put back in the box a range of early quiz shows, such as Beat the Clock (1950), Concentration (1958), The Newlywed Game (1967), Password (1971), Wheel of Fortune (1975), Family Feud (1977), and others (these dates refer to a show's television debut).

This connection between what is seen on the tube and played in the home is underscored by the success of Pressman's Who Wants to Be a Millionaire game, in which players can fantasize that Regis is actually asking them, "Is that your final answer?" Tiger created electronic versions of the ABC blockbuster quiz show that premiered on August 16, 1999, where it averaged about 29 million viewers per night in the 1999–2000 season. BMT developed the electronic table-top game for Tiger.

Entertainment show licenses were also used on toys in the early 1950s. Rempl marketed Froggy the Gremlin, a mischievous green frog that appeared first in 1954 with Ed McConnel of *Smilin' Ed's Gang* and then with gravel-voiced Andy Devine on *Andy's Gang*. Standard Toykraft introduced the official Winky Dink and Your Magic Television Kit in the 1950s.

In 1956, Ideal marketed a Roy Rogers' toy line comprised of a stagecoach, chuck wagon, and Nellybelle, all with one-piece molded figures. Hartland Plastics introduced Paladin western toys in 1958, Carnell marketed a Bat Masterson cane in 1959, Ideal created The Beverly Hillbillies car in 1963, and Hubley made a Mr. Magoo car in 1961. These are just a few of a tsunami of licensed toy products that came out during this era.

Paralleling the early TV tie-ins were the equally strong influences of movie and book personalities in toys and games with Call Me Lucky: The Bing Crosby Game (1954), Mary Poppins (1964), Flip Your Wig: The Beatles Game (1964), Wizard of Oz (1974), King Kong (1976), Richard Scarry (1976), Star Wars (1977), and E.T. (1981). For under a dollar, kids in the early 1950s could play simple games featuring such cartoon characters as Nancy and Sluggo, Li'l Abner, and Captain and the Kids. Seldom did players realize that the object of play and game action were very similar among these early games, with only the artwork changing to reflect a specific license.

"Licensing gave manufacturers a way to make money using tooling from old toys that would otherwise have no use," explained Andrea Morris, publisher of *Playthings*. "They put a new dress on old molded parts, thus creating new toys for minimal investment."

As toy marketers began to recognize the power of licensed properties, they expanded the use of popular characters to all sorts of product categories. Today the hottest characters appear in various toy forms, from superhero action figures to plush toys, from puzzles to games. And if consumers can't find these media-imprinted toys and games at their local TRU, Wal-Mart, or Target, they're only a click away on the Internet, at Toysrus.com, eBay.com, or a host of others e-tailers. Favorites like Tweety, Sylvester, and SpongeBob SquarePants are waiting! We'll examine this reliance on character licenses from the entertainment world by toy companies in Chapter 11.

Toy Trivia

19. In 1959, the first Barbie doll had all but which of the following accessories?

a. White sunglasses

b. Beach towel

c. Hoop earrings

Electronics: Panning for Gold

If the 1950s and 1960s saw the emergence of character licenses from all forms of media, electronics entered the industry in the late 1970s and 1980s. Marketers' desire to tout playthings featuring solid state electronics forced the pros to raise the sophistication of their latest concepts to utilize new technologies. The infamous cautionary note "Batteries required" became commonplace on toy shelf merchandise as they powered new levels of animation and mobility. The endless capacity of microprocessors and microchips to generate beeps, boops, and blips; visual displays; programmable commands; synthesized sound; and variable play levels brought exciting action possibilities to "high-tech" toy and game designs. During the late 1970s and early 1980s, many toy and game companies altered their longstanding business charters and followed wherever the latest technology took them in a search for "products of the future."

Nolan Bushnell, a creative force destined to play a major role in the electronics business, attempted a commercial version of MIT graduate student Steve Russell's computer game, Spacewar. In 1970, Bushnell soldered the final microcircuits into a game he trademarked as Computer Space. He licensed the manufacturing rights, but the game was unsuccessful in the marketplace. It was too complex.

Bushnell went back to the drawing board to design a simpler game. What he created was a mindless electronic table-tennis game that he dubbed Pong. In 1972, he founded a company called Atari to manufacture and market it as coin-operated table

61

units. The first Pong was installed at Andy Capp's bar in Sunnyvale, California. After only a couple of days, it stopped working. After confirming that the integrated circuits were fine, Bushnell checked the coin box. It was stuffed beyond capacity—so much so that it had short-circuited the game. Gold was soon to flow from the video arcade era.

The home version of video games, however, was born in 1966, when Ralph Baer, a supervising engineer at Sanders Associates in Manchester, New Hampshire, assigned technicians to work on television games. By the first months of 1967, Baer and engineers Bill Harrison and Bill Rusch were playing table tennis and hockey on a 17-inch RCA color set. Sanders licensed its video game technology to Magnavox in 1971, and by the summer of 1972, the Odyssey game system was in production. Odyssey used Mylar overlays taped to the television screen. Each overlay depicted a different game board, such as table tennis, hockey, or football. That first year, 100,000 Odyssey games were sold. By the end of 1967, Baer's team had also invented the first light-gun video games.

During the 1970s and 1980s, much of Baer's work was cooperative product development at Marvin Glass & Associates. Baer invented the circuitry for Milton Bradley's electronic Simon, Ideal's Maniac, Lakeside's Computer Perfection, Kenner's electro-optical Laser Command, and many more toys and games. For more of this extraordinarily talented engineer's career highlights, visit www.ralphbaer.com.

Atari moved beyond coin-operated arcade games into the home market with its model 2600 game console, Video Computer System (VCS), in the mid-1970s. The variety of available games mushroomed. Activision, Epyx, and many other independent companies manufactured game cartridges for use with Atari equipment. The library of "carts" swelled to 1,500 titles in the early 1980s before the trade and the consumers signaled "overload."

Great Expectations from Electronics

In the latter 1970s and early 1980s, as traditional industry marketers such as Milton Bradley, Mattel, and Parker Brothers saw the consumer's love affair with pricey electronic toys and games, they started hiring electronic engineers and ordering microprocessors. They created handheld electronic games, enhanced dedicated tabletop games, and incompatible software cartridges. The emergence of products with electronic sizzle had begun and they have been a part of the industry ever since microchips entered the world of play.

Milton Bradley introduced Comp IV in 1977, a tabletop brain baffler powered by a 9-volt battery (its packaging ran the headline "I Am Programmed to Beat You") and Electronic Battleship, a computerized version of its classic board game. To compete with Electronic Battleship, Parker Brothers produced Code Name: Sector as its own naval battle game in 1977. Mattel came to market concurrently with two pocket-size electronic games, Auto Race and Football. These five very early nonvideo electronic offerings brought in $21 million for their manufacturers, and their success opened the gates to a torrent of playtime gadgetry.

1978: Total toy market $5 billion, including 45 electronic items. Milton Bradley was at the forefront with Simon, a light-and-sound follow-the-leader game, and Star Bird, a realistic-sounding toy aircraft that changed engine effects depending upon its flight attitude. The company shipped over one million Star Birds. Simon went on to capture a major share of the electronic game market and remains on the market 25 years later.

1979: Total toy market $5.5 billion, including 125 electronic items. In 1979, consumers rang up some $800 million in electronic toys at retail. Handheld games represented a sizable proportion of that, with sales of $250 million. Some 20 million microprocessors were used in games, and another 10 million in toys.

Among the year's electronic toy and game highlights were Mattel's electronic Football, reaching sales of one million units, and Milton Bradley's Microvision, a handheld liquid crystal display (LCD) game platform sold with an interchangeable demo game cartridge backed by additional games sold separately. Though crude by today's standards, the Microvision game system invention of California inventor Jay Smith was something of a forerunner to the current popular Nintendo Game Boy.

1980: Total toy market $6.7 billion, and talking toys, too! This was a pivotal year in the electronic toy wars. The first real shakeout took place as buyers were confronted with deciding among the many "me, too" products. Shelves were beginning to bulge with undifferentiated and unrelated electronics. Consumers seemed unable to absorb all the toy and game choices being introduced at record pace. The electronic abracadabra included voice recognition and speech synthesis, features that had never gained popularity with consumers when applied to early toy forms.

1981: A pause, a breath, a sigh. If 1980 was a year when the trade buckled under a flood of electronic SKUs, manufacturers in 1981 reacted with limited numbers of new products. Most notable on a sparse product menu were Atari's innovative Cosmos, the first handheld electronic game that used holography. It made a big splash at the Toy Fair but soon died. Atari's new Video Computer System offered wireless remote controllers. Mattel entered the market with its Intellivision video game system.

1982: Total toy market $9 billion and a cartridge avalanche. Video game sales skyrocketed to $3 billion. The industry sparked to Colecovision, Coleco's new expandable video game system. For the first time, a manufacturer had brought the superior visual excitement and challenge of coin-operated arcade games to the home TV screen. With its "expansion module," Colecovision was able to accept game cartridges from the Atari 2600 VCS, its main competition. Soon Mattel's Intellivision and Atari were making Colecovision games for their own systems. Milton Bradley tried to keep pace with Voice Command video game cartridges tied to the Texas Instruments 99/4A home computer. But the attempt fizzled as the price of the 99/4A plunged and the installed base for TI never reached significant levels.

1983: Cartridges decline; bring on your dolls and trivia. After two years of shakeout in electronic toys, the record sales of video games in 1982 made for a decidedly mixed signal. The dumping and discounting of cartridges eroded the market by $1 billion in 1983, and by the end of 1984, it was a mere 25 percent of 1982 levels.

In a marketplace rife with rumors of the dawn of an immense home personal computer demand, Mattel (with Aquarius and Intellivision II) and Coleco (with Adam) were two toy companies that took the bait.

Coleco's entry was heralded as the first $600 home computer complete with a printer. If consumers were going to use computers to play games and expand into other "edutainment" activities, these two toymakers in the consumer electronics market were well prepared. But whether as a strategic hedge on Adam or merely as a stroke of luck, Coleco licensed for mass distribution the uniquely styled Cabbage Patch Kids. Sales went from $60 million in 1983 to more than $600 million in 1985. In the 1980s, Cabbage Patch became a $2 billion brand, a real American cultural phenomenon. Note: Coleco was founded in 1932 to supply leather products to shoemakers (**Co**nnecticut **Lea**ther **Co**mpany).

Toy Trivia

20. Schaper's 1963 King of the Hill game was played with which type of movers?

a. Marbles

b. Plastic pawns

c. Cardboard standees

Another traditional product phenomenon introduced in 1982 during the electronics shakeout was Trivial Pursuit. This upscale question-and-answer game eventually surpassed the $1 billion mark in worldwide sales, with some 70 million copies sold since its introduction in 1982. Not only did it prove that the consumer would pay a rather high price for a game, but it also broke the hold of video games. People began to return to the parlor and interact without a blipping, beeping video game or TV remote in hand. Game players seemed intent on interacting with each other again through Trivial Pursuit, and they have been doing so for over 20 years. More than 45 variations of TP have been created since its debut.

By 1984, companies that had missed the electronic bandwagon or, at best, had taken a short hitch were being praised for remaining neutral in the tidal wave. The industry seemed to make the collective, conscious decision to let the marketplace unclog the surplus and return to the "basics." Nonelectronic staples were given promotional bumps to rekindle trade interest and remind consumers of longstanding bestsellers. Things were indeed bleak in 1984 as Mattel swiftly dumped its electronics division. In a flip-flop in 1986, Warner Communications sold the Atari home video business back to Nolan Bushnell. Atari Arcade, a separate entity, eventually became part of Midway Games. It became obvious that Coleco could not deliver the quality promised in its inexpensive Adam computer, and Coleco filed for bankruptcy in 1988.

Although there was a cautious shakeout in electronic toys and games in the second half of the 1980s, new designs continued to use microchips as the heart of many lead items. Worlds of Wonder incorporated in March 1985 to manufacture and market Teddy Ruxpin. The bear form may not have been new, but its mouth, nose, and eyes moved to a voice emanating from an internal playback tape deck. It was an animated version of Mego's 1979 hit robot, 2-XL. Worlds of Wonder had another significant hit with Lazer Tag, an interactive, infrared tag game that was high on hundreds of thousands of 1986 Christmas lists.

In 1987, Mattel introduced a new generation of toys under the banner Captain Power that interacted electronically with special television programs. The line of 20 toys, which ranged in price from $30 to $40, was linked to a half-hour Captain Power TV program. Mattel pulled the plug on Captain Power a year later.

Ohio Art's classic Etch-a-Sketch gave birth to the Etch-a-Sketch Animator and the Etch-a-Sketch Animator 2000, high-tech spin-offs that create moving pictures and store them in memory. Independent inventor Andrew Bergman developed the Fisher-Price PXL 2000, a camcorder for eight-year-olds that let kids capture black-and-white video images. Ron Milner's Hot Lixx and Hot Keyz, Tyco Toys' state-of-the-art electronic instruments, delivered perfect music without a single lesson.

From the Ashes: The Next Video Game Wave

If licensing became a hot issue in the 1950s/1960s and electronics boomed in the 1970s/1980s, a strong parallel can be drawn with the place of video games in the 1990s.

The Nintendo Company grew to significant size with the release of NES (Nintendo Entertainment System), Game Boy, Super Nintendo, and the GameCube. This surprising resurgence of video games came from the ashes of efforts by traditional companies like Coleco, Mattel, Milton Bradley, Parker Brothers, and Atari, who made valiant but profitless efforts to control the toy and game software/systems sales in the early market.

However, Nintendo's screen graphics and play-branching possibilities caught the support of consumers (mostly kids age eight and up, with parental funding) and eroded purchase dollars from traditional toys and games. Other giant corporations followed Nintendo into this market segment with their own electronic gaming platforms, including Sony (PlayStation), Sega (Saturn/Genesis/Dreamcast), and Microsoft (Xbox).

But the two largest toy companies would not ignore this latest incursion into their business and formed units to participate in the video game market. Hasbro created Hasbro Interactive (1995), and Mattel established Mattel Interactive shortly thereafter. Neither company showed financial commitment to these new operating divisions and ceased support of these video game ventures. For the most part, however, traditional toy and game companies today have elected to out-license their properties to software producers who create the programs for the major game systems.

The impact and rebirth of video programming in the toy and game market is examined in greater depth in Chapter 12.

Life Goes on for Traditional Products

On the front end of the past 20 years of toy industry launches, we had the influx of technology into new playthings. On the current end—and the nature of today's marketplace—we have game systems and many disparate product categories, all within the galaxy of toys and games. Mixed into that galaxy are the SKUs related to character licenses and SKUs of highly promoted proprietary trademarked names.

But whatever the pedigree, most toys and games have a short existence. Regardless of whether they burst into the consumer's consciousness with a license attached, such as Tickle Me Elmo, or with promotion budgets like Furby, or as merely a utilitarian function to fill out a line, the reality is that toys and games come one year and go a year or two later. The industry indeed does "churn and burn" product lines. There are no more evergreens because the retailers cut the forests down every year, and manufacturers seem unable to influence the situation. Retailers are definitely the gating authority on what gets to consumer awareness since they control shelf space allotted to new toys and games.

The Big Get Bigger: Mergers, Acquisitions, and Departures

As the history of toys and games passed through the late 1800s and early 1900s, many new companies rose to manufacture and supply amusements to a growing population. One hundred years later, when leisure time abounds in most households, the industry has lost most of those early family-owned companies. Many have become tethered to publicly held industry giants Mattel and Hasbro. These acquisitions contribute mightily to the size and revenues these two companies enjoy today.

"The most significant change in our industry in the past 10 years has been consolidation, on both the retail side and the corporate side," observes E. David Wilson, the 32-year industry veteran who heads up Hasbro Games. When asked what the future holds, he quipped, "It will be the survival of the fittest."

To that point, in 1996 Mattel made a surprise move to take over Hasbro, with a $5.2 billion hostile bid. Hasbro got the Rhode Island legislature to throw up legal obstacles and foiled the attempt.

Not all consolidation is bad. Wilson, recalling Hasbro's acquisition of Playskool and Milton Bradley, says, "Clearly this was the most significant acquisition Hasbro has ever made. Milton Bradley has been the profit engine of the corporation, and from 1985 through 1997 we never had a down year." Through Hasbro Games, Hasbro controls roughly 80 percent of the board game business worldwide.

For professional inventors, this merging of companies had a constricting effect on potential licensees. For example, had Hasbro not acquired so many of its competitors—Galoob, Kenner, OddzOn, Cap Toys, Tiger Electronics, Milton Bradley, Playskool, and so on—there would be 11 or 12 more independent companies to view ideas today. Even now with the distinction between toys and games, there are four or five acquisition viewers at Hasbro who will slot new inventor concepts into the marketing plans.

However, inventors may take heart in the annual rise of new companies exhibiting wares at industry trade shows. These new companies may be small and embryonic, but inventors being entrepreneurial spirits will rise to the challenge and help make the small into future giants. Bill Dohrmann substantiates this possibility as he says, "I am invariably encouraged by a visit to Javits every February. I call it the 'primordial soup' of the toy industry. All sorts of innovation and hope are on display, struggling to emerge into the sunlight of success. The industry will always draw entrepreneurs and dreamers for the same reasons that I was drawn to it. And I came to love it!"

Look to the Past, Look to the Future

The toy industry is in the midst of a technology/electronic explosion that burst onto the consumer scene in the late 1970s, dipped a bit, and then came roaring back in the 1990s with new game systems and smaller, cheaper electronics. The pace of change and product expectations is so dramatic that companies and their inventing partners are caught in a high-stakes roll on every product idea. Companies want to shorten development cycles. Inventors want more rapid commitment to their concepts. Retailers want more year-round sales from their toy departments while at the same time reducing the shelf space given to the category. Many of these new pressures come from consumers who want toys and games with more than incremental improvements. Today's sophisticated consumers want more and different fun for the same or fewer dollars.

Toy companies in the past dealt mostly with the inventor as artist, less as scientist and businessman. Though the inventing community does not usually conduct lab research or make quantum discoveries unique to the toy industry, history has shown that inventors' skills often capture technology from other industries and transfer it to toys and games, often at fractional costs. It was done with plastics, it was done with electronics, and it will be done with materials and processes yet unknown.

Toy inventors tether themselves to other industries and adopt new technologies that can be built into new designs of never-before-seen playthings. Today the inventor must bring the total package to the table if he or she expects the company to do the deal.

It's impossible to predict just where the toy industry is headed as it competes for the discretionary entertainment dollars consumers are spending on DVDs, CDs, movie videos, video games, computer software, and other multimedia products. Because of the entrepreneurial nature of the industry, startup companies will always be seeking to dethrone the ruling marketers. At the same time, offshore producers are going direct to retailers with whole lines of packaged goods. Some industry pundits see the movement toward the long-held prediction of a multibillion-dollar marketer selling to one zillion-dollar retailer. Will it be Mattel selling to Wal-Mart or Hasbro selling to TRU?

On the other hand, some see the small start-ups creating the excitement that ignites emerging winners, even at times creating new distribution to augment the traditional retail trade. A good example of this is Starbucks distributing the adult social game Cranium. Through Starbucks, the No. 1 specialty coffee retailer in the United States with about 5,400 coffeehouses, Cranium became the fastest-selling independent board game in history and was named the TIA choice for Game of the Year (2001). It has claimed sales of more than 1.4 million copies through 2002.

Stewart Sims, former senior vice president of Tiger Electronics, an astute industry observer, was asked by a writer to provide a quick-cut overview of the industry—a highlight film, if you will, of what the industry was like around the time he got into it.

- In 1969, the Beatles were still together, Americans were dying in Vietnam, and Elvis was alive.
- Mattel was about a $400 million toy and doll company, and Hasbro had less than $200 million in revenue. There were numerous $100 million plus promotional toy companies.
- There were two dozen important retailers, and Wal-Mart, which incorporated in 1969, was not one of them.
- The PC had not been invented, and nobody in the United States had heard of a company called Nintendo.
- Eight- and nine-year-old girls still played with dolls, and eight- and nine-year-old boys played with action figures, die-cast cars, and slot cars.
- ABC, CBS, and NBC were the only television networks, and the big children's movie was *The Love Bug.*
- Licensing was important, but not as important as a fresh toy concept.
- Products were engineered by the companies that would make them, and many toys, dolls, and games were still manufactured in the United States.
- Electronic toys had not yet been invented. In short, it was a different world.

"In addition to these environmental differences, there was also a fundamental difference in the internal makeup of the industry," Sims goes on to say.

- Most of the toy companies were run by the men and women who had either started the company, were descendants of the founders, or had spent most of their career in the industry.

◆ Similarly, many of the buyers had been part of the start of toy-buying chains or had been toy buyers for years. The result was that they all had an intuitive sense about product and were willing to take chances based upon their instincts. Frequently, these instincts resulted in products and product categories (Barbie, G.I. Joe, Mr. Machine, Mousetrap, Toss Across, LEGO, Star Wars) that went against conventional thinking.

Toy Trivia

22. What word best describes Wooly Willy's personality?

a. Bubbly

b. Magnetic

c. Soft

What has remained constant in this ever-changing industry is the reliance on the professional inventing community. Each year these pros, complemented by a few first-time product sources, provide the annual mix of technologically advanced Wow! with toys offering the simplicity of Mother Nature's maple seed.

Toy inventing and idea licensing remain one of the last great frontiers for the independent inventor as well as the marketer. Together they have built and will continue to build on the $30 billion industry.

Psst! If you have read this far in Chapter 2, you show more than a superficial interest in the history of playthings. To read another chronological record of toys and games, and the origins of many more products than we were able to accommodate in our book, go to the website www.yesterdayland.com and hit the tab marked Toys. It's a gem.

Fun Facts

◆ Eighty feet of wire was used to produce the first Slinky toys.

◆ Two eight-stud LEGO bricks (of the same color) can be combined in 24 different ways. Three eight-stud LEGO bricks can be combined in 1,060 different ways. Six eight-stud LEGO bricks can be combined in 102,981,500 different ways.

◆ Tonka celebrates its 56th birthday in 2003. More than 230 million trucks have been manufactured since 1947. It takes 119,000 pounds of yellow paint and 5.1 million pounds of sheet metal a year to make Tonka trucks and other Tonka vehicles.

Chapter 3

Toy Stories:
Off-the-Chart Winners

"Quite simply, if it were not for the independent inventor, we would not be in business."

—Ben Varadi, executive vice president,
Spin Master Toys

Behind every commercialized toy and game, there is a story about how it was created, developed, and brought to market. The following potpourri of wonderful and inspiring stories covers some classic, some destined to be classic, and some simply pivotal products. We could have given detailed profiles of dozens and dozens of products, but we selected the following for reasons that will hopefully be clear to you. We regret that we couldn't include them all.

Queen of Fashion: Always in the Pink

Ruthie, the youngest of 10 children born to Polish immigrants Jacob and Ida Mosko, had married her penniless high school boyfriend, Elliot Handler, against her parents' wishes. The couple started a company in their garage selling housewares. The business did well, and they expanded in the mid-1940s to include handmade picture frames. Elliot and his partner, Harold Mattson, made the samples. Ruth did the marketing.

Then one day in 1942, Elliot started to create doll furniture with the scraps of wood left over from the frames. They called the sideline enterprise Mattel, combining the letters of their first and last names. It wasn't long until the Handlers bought out their partner and the toy business became more successful than the frames and housewares business.

In 1959, Ruth asked herself, "Why not a plastic fashion doll for girls, and what if we gave it breasts?" She answered her own question with a 5-ounce, 11½-inch, epitome-of-fashion doll that she named after their daughter, Barbie.

Where Ruth got the epiphany that led to the creation of Barbie is subject to some debate. Mattel's official version is that Ruth noticed that out of all her daughter's dolls, Barbie most enjoyed playing with shapely paper dolls, those that she could gussy up in different fashions. In the mid-1950s, the only doll on the U.S. market was a baby doll, with whom little girls pretended to be mommies. But Barbie Handler was doing something quite different. She was pretending to be a hip teenager who got "all dolled up" and went to high school proms and sock hops. Ruth felt that proverbial light bulb go on.

There are also two unofficial versions of Barbie's creation. In his 1996 book *Kid Stuff*, author David Hoffman writes that on a holiday to Vienna, Austria, Ruth saw a display of "sharply dressed" adult dolls in a store. She bought two of them—specifically, Lilli dolls, inspired by a sexy German comic strip character drawn by cartoonist Reinhard Beuthien. Hoffman writes that one was a gift for Handler's daughter, Barbie, and the other one was for her designers at Mattel. "Mattel spent three years creating their own version," he reports.

In his 2000 book *100 Greatest Baby Boomer Toys*, author Mark Rich writes that when sales of the European doll declined, "Lilli happened to be sold to Mattel, who, in 1959, test-marketed and then released a remarkably similar doll with a new name, Barbie."

Whatever the inspiration, in her 1994 autobiography, Ruth said that the philosophy underlying Barbie was that, through the doll, girls could be anything they wanted to be. "Barbie always represented the fact that a woman has choices." In a 1977 interview with *The New York Times*, she said, "Every little girl needed a doll through which to project herself into her dream of her future." She continued, "If she was going to do role playing of what she would be like when she was 16 or 17, it was a little stupid to play with a doll that had a flat chest. So I gave it beautiful breasts."

411 See Barbie and other classic toys on display at Rochester's Strong Museum, which has become the new home of the National Toy Hall of Fame. Strong has replaced A. C. Gilbert's Discovery Village in Salem, Oregon, where the hall had been since 1998. The Strong Museum is located at One Manhattan Square, Rochester, New York 14607; Tel: 585-263-2700. Or, visit it online at www.strongmuseum.org.

Ruth Handler died at age 85 on April 27, 2002, at a hospital in Los Angeles. She was survived by her husband, Elliot, and daughter, Barbie. Ken, her son, had died earlier from a brain tumor.

Barbie has been "in the pink" since she made her debut in 1959. That year, 350,000 dolls were sold. In 1999, Barbie celebrated her fortieth birthday. More than one billion Barbies have been sold. Today the platinum blond plays the starring role in a $2 billion Mattel extravaganza directed by Matt Bousquette, president of Mattel Brands.

Consider these factoids:

- The first Barbie doll sold for $3 in the United States.
- Every second, three Barbie dolls are sold somewhere in the world.
- More than 105 million feet of fabric have gone into producing fashions for Barbie and her friends, making Mattel one of the largest apparel manufacturers in the world. Over one billion fashions have been sold since 1959.
- Placed head to toe, Barbie and her friends sold since 1959 would circle the Earth more than seven times.
- Barbie has had more than 80 careers—everything from a model to a paleontologist to a Desert Storm soldier.

- Barbie dolls are currently marketed in more than 150 nations around the world.
- Barbie has had over 43 pets, including 21 dogs, 12 horses, 3 ponies, 6 cats, a parrot, a chimpanzee, a panda, a lion cub, a giraffe, and a zebra.
- The best-selling Barbie ever was Totally Hair Barbie, with a stream of hair from the top of her head to her toes.
- Barbie has five sisters: Skipper, introduced in 1964; Tutti, a twin introduced in 1966; Stacie, introduced in 1992; Kelly, introduced in 1995; and Krissy, introduced in 1999.
- Barbie's boyfriend, Ken, made his debut two years after Barbie, in 1961. The Ken doll was named after the son of Ruth and Elliot Handler.
- An original 1959 Barbie doll in mint condition has sold for up to $10,000.
- On Barbie's fortieth anniversary, the U.S. Postal Service issued a commemorative stamp with Barbie's image on it. It was issued in El Segundo, California, home of Mattel, and dated September 18, 1999.
- In 2000, the Barbie doll was given a belly button.

A toy buyer for the Broadway Department Store in Los Angeles told *Toys, Hobbies & Crafts* magazine, "Barbie is more than just a doll, it's a system. The others are just dolls; they simply can't beat the system." Pretty good for a gal who can't even stand on her own two feet (they're permanently shaped for high-heeled shoes). And speaking of shoes, Barbie's feet have slipped in and out of more than one billion pairs of them in her fashionable career.

But Mattel's fortune was made not in doll sales. It entered the gates of heaven (pink gates, no doubt) selling Barbie's fashion and nonfashion accessories. That's what generates the money.

Barbie is currently a $2.5-billion-dollar-per-year industry, including licensed products under Barbie Consumer Products. She has never looked prettier, but she grew up last year. My Scene Barbie, introduced for Christmas 2002, traded in ball gowns and bathing suits for skintight low-rise denim jeans, funky platform boots, leather and fauxfur jackets, and belly button–revealing shirts. Her head is larger, too. *The New York Times* described her pouty lips as "slathered with frosted pink lipstick." This is an attempt to tap the so-called "tween" market, girls between 8 and 12 who would rather watch MTV and VH1 than play with dolls.

Barbie was not always universally embraced by the trade. In fact, when the first non-flat-chested doll with rooted Saran hair, earrings, and individually painted red fingernails was introduced, Sears, Roebuck, then the nation's largest toy retailer, didn't order a single one. But even without Sears, after the initial 35,000 dolls hit the market and sold instantly, the love affair with the Barbie doll never flagged.

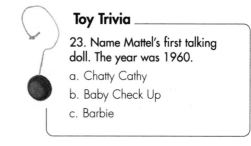

Toy Trivia

23. Name Mattel's first talking doll. The year was 1960.

a. Chatty Cathy
b. Baby Check Up
c. Barbie

The All-American Hero: Articulated Muscle

While the invention of Barbie is clearly attributable to Ruth Handler, 3,000 miles away in Pawtucket, Rhode Island, the origin of G.I. Joe is still the subject of debate.

Inspired by Barbie's tremendous success, executives at Hasbro thought that if girls liked such a highly accessorized fashion doll, maybe boys would like the submission from Stan Weston, then president of Weston Merchandising Corporation, a licensing agency in New York City, and the late Larry Reiner, a career professional. Reiner, a prolific inventor who spent 40 years on the creative side of the industry, died in 2001. His credits include Talking Barney (Hasbro), Dress 'n Dazzle (Tonka), and Silly Story Maker (Mattel).

Writer John Michlig, author of *G.I. Joe: The Complete Story of America's Favorite Man of Action* (Chronicle, 1998), interviewed Reiner and Westin, along with Don Levine, Hasbro's then head of R&D, and G. Wayne Miller, whose book *Toy Wars* (Random House, 1998) includes reporting on the creation of G.I. Joe. Based upon information from these sources and interviews of Reiner by your authors, here is one take on Joe's creation.

"Ideal was going to expand its Tammy doll line to include parents and siblings. Someone suggested making Tammy's father a cop and uncle a fireman," Michlig recounts. "Reiner claimed he suggested putting a soldier in the line to market to boys. When Ideal said no, he went to Weston and augmented an idea Weston had shared with him." Weston's idea was a soldier with accessories. *Note:* Contrary to some accounts, Michlig says Weston is adamant that the then-popular television show *The Lieutenant* had nothing to do with his pitch. Furthermore, the show's title never appears in any follow-up correspondence between Weston and Levine, reports Michlig.

Weston's forte was toy licensing, not design or engineering. He created toys based upon or tied into popular entertainment licenses. Weston went on to create Leisure Concepts, a major licensing company, and is regarded as one of the fathers of the licensing industry.

Michlig continues, "Reiner said, 'Make him articulated and moveable. That's the key.'" Weston and Reiner became 50-50 partners as their ideas meshed into a perfect partnership of creative inspirations.

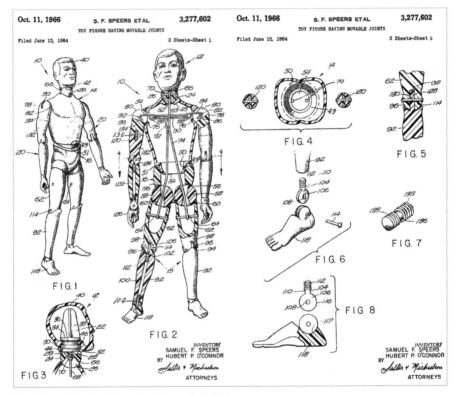

Toy Figure Having Movable Joints (G.I. Joe)
Patented October 11, 1966
U.S. Patent 3,277,602

Reiner told a writer that his idea was stimulated by an articulated, wooden armature in the shape of a human form that he had seen in an art supply shop window. The wooden armatures were used as posing aids for artists.

Weston took Reiner's concept of an articulated military figure straight to Don Levine at Hasbro. He shared Reiner's vision to create a poseable character.

"The real innovation—the actual method of articulating Joe for mass production—was all Hasbro," says Michlig. Their solution was awarded U.S. Patent No. 3,277,602, "Toy Figure Having Movable Joints," on October 11, 1966. The co-inventors are listed as Samuel F. Speers and Hubert O'Connor. They assigned the patent to their employer, Hassenfeld Bros., Inc., a.k.a Hasbro. "One of the most interesting aspects of the story for nontoy people is the fact that Reiner got actual money for a mere idea and didn't have to actually solve any of the problems of making it work," Michlig continues. (It was not uncommon in those days for companies to pay for unproven concepts.)

As reported by Marvin Kaye in his book *A Toy Is Born* (Stein & Day, 1973), the Hasbro staff saw merit in the proposal but was reluctant to link a toy to a television series. "Why should we associate the item with a character that will die when the show goes off, maybe six months from now?" executives asked. How times have changed! Today an action-figure line *would not be launched* without an entertainment tie-in.

But Merrill Hassenfeld's instincts told him there was something exciting about to happen. At the same time, he anticipated great indifference from buyers. "They said that we were trying to make a doll for boys, and everybody knew that boys do not play with dolls," Fredric C. Behling, Hasbro's associate marketing director, told Kaye. "We figured that boys do play with soldiers, but the buyers balked at that, too."

Toy Fair was approaching, Hasbro was heavily—dangerously—invested in G.I. Joe, and there was no deal yet with Weston, who was the point man on the negotiation for himself and Reiner. Hassenfeld sent a memo to Weston, dated December 23, 1963, in which he asked the agent to call after January 1 to set up a date for them to discuss Joe. The first deal offered by Hassenfeld, according to Michlig, who was shown the actual memoranda between Weston and his attorney, Leonard Franklin, proposed that Weston and Reiner wait until Hasbro had earned its multimillion investment and then get a small percentage of net sales, or take a flat-fee buyout immediately.

"The CEO offers them one-half of 1 percent after Hasbro recoups its investment. Weston counters with 3 percent. Hassenfeld goes to 1 percent. The young agent tells the seasoned exec that he'll see him in court," continues Michlig.

Very soon after this impasse, Hassenfeld called Weston to reiterate that G.I. Joe is a huge gamble. He said truthfully that half the trade liked it and half didn't. None-theless, he preferred to own Joe completely, and he offered the partners $75,000. Weston liked round numbers and countered with $100,000. "It's a deal," Merrill said.

As the story goes, a few days later, Hassenfeld called Weston back to suggest $50,000 and 1 percent on all sales after $7 million. Weston thought about it for 24 hours and said thanks, but no thanks. He and Larry split $100,000. Weston thought it was a great deal. He had invested only $52 in military patches and supplies for his presentation, and with the $50,000 he could establish a company. Reiner was also delighted. Had the guys taken the 1 percent, their first payment would have been $150,000 after expenses. Think about what it would have been 50 years out!

At the 1964 New York Toy Fair, in a bold leadership move, Hasbro introduced the line of action figures under the trademark G.I. Joe. There were four characters: Action Soldier, Action Sailor, Action Marine, and Action Pilot. Almost a foot tall and carrying authentic equipment from head to toe, the item had 21 movable parts and was hyped as "America's Movable Fighting Man."

Just as the trade initially was slow to warm up to Mattel's Barbie, toy-store owners were hesitant to join the ranks of G.I. Joe's retail forces. The item contradicted a popular boy's toys principal: "Action figure" or not, it was widely believed that parents would not purchase dolls for their sons—and the trade did not want to invest in such an iffy product. But Hassenfeld stuck to his howitzers, and that first year Hasbro sold more than $30 million worth of G.I. Joes (two million figures) and accessories. To date, Hasbro has sold more than 230 different G.I. Joe action figures and 100 million of his tanks, trucks, and planes.

One of the strangest episodes in the life of Joe (and Barbie) was when a group called the Barbie Liberation Organization bought several hundred electronic Barbie dolls and speech-enabled Joes and swapped their voice boxes, quietly returning them to retail shelves. Imagine the owner's surprise when Barbie screamed "Incoming!" and Joe swooned, "Ken's such a dream."

Toy Trivia

24. Richard James invented this novelty toy in 1943.

a. Super Ball

b. Slinky

c. Silly Putty

411

To receive Cotswold's G.I. Joe collector news and reviews catalogue each month, contact Cotswold Collectibles, 1612 E. Main St./P.O. Box 716 Freeland, WA 98249; Tel: 360-331-5331. Or, visit the website www.gijoeelite.com/f_home.asp.

These Babies Make a Lot Of Beans

He is richer than billionaire Kirk Kerkorian, father of the Las Vegas megaresort.

He is richer than billionaire financier Carl Icahn.

He is richer than billionaire H. Ross Perot, founder of Electronic Data Systems.

He is richer than media magnate Walter Annenberg, creator of *TV Guide*.

He is richer than billionaire investment advisor Charles Schwab.

And, yes, he is richer than billionaire banker David Rockefeller.

His name is H. Ty Warner, the inventor of and marketing genius behind Beanie Babies, under-stuffed, plush bean-bag toy animals. According to the September 13, 2002, Forbes 400, a list that features the 400 richest Americans, number 26 is the Beanie Babies guy. He says he was named after one of the charter members of the Baseball Hall of Fame, Ty Cobb, in which case it should be no surprise that H. Ty Warner hit a grand slam and stole all the bases.

According to a story in the *Chicago Sun Times*, his company, Ty, Inc., a Delaware corporation, earned $700 million in profits in 1998 alone. It was the only time the enigmatic, single Warner publicly disclosed financials for his privately held enterprise— and the only reason he did was to prove that he is the largest toymaker, one-upping the 1998 $538 million in profits earned by his publicly held competitors, Hasbro and Mattel, combined.

Let's consider some top-line facts, all of which are counterintuitive for a major toy company:

- Warner, a college dropout, didn't hire MBAs to come up with a marketing plan. He went with his own spontaneous impressions and entrepreneurial instincts.
- He never built up out-of-control overhead.
- His people keep him *out* of the news, not in it.
- He did not slap entertainment licenses on his toys; he had confidence in great designs, fabrics, and names that he made up himself in the early days.
- He refused to out-license his trademark once Beanie Babies was an established brand, with the exception of the McDonald's promotion, which was the most successful in the fast-food chain's history.
- He refused to sell to the big-box retailers like Wal-Mart, Target, and Toys R Us. Except for Zainy-Brainy, he went with thousands of small gift shops, many of which paid him cash on demand or within 15 days if they had credit, according to *Forbes*.
- He allowed the retailers to figure out how best to merchandise the products. There were no standards.
- He was patient and nurturing, allowing his brand to take root and grow. He never lost focus.

◆ His product was so inexpensive to manufacture that major mass market retailers would likely have dismissed it, saying they'd have to sell too many to reach significant volume to drive promotion.

Last but not least, had an inventor brought this concept to a toy company, most would have probably said, "Are you kidding? Plush has been done. It's all over the place." Warner proved the old adage that so many people today forget or never knew: Product is king.

Little has been written about this reclusive mogul, except that he is extremely generous, donating millions of dollars to charitable causes. It has been reported that Warner's father had been a jewelry salesman before he became a manufacturer's rep for a plush-toy company, which may have been where Warner got his interest in the category. The 59-year-old Chicago entrepreneur, who attended Kalamazoo College, reportedly worked in a variety of jobs during his salad years. After studying drama for just a year, he decided to leave college and head for Los Angeles to become an actor. From all reports, all he did in Hollywood was pump gas and sell cameras door to door.

After returning to Chicago in 1962, he started selling plush animals for Dakin, a San Francisco maker that has since closed its doors. Warner worked for Dakin 18 years, over time reportedly earning more than $100,000 a year. He learned the intricacies of the plush industry, including where to get products designed and made overseas.

Warner took an unconventional approach to sales. He reportedly drove a Rolls-Royce convertible and dressed in fur coats and top hats, frequently carrying a walking stick. He once told *People* magazine, "I figured if I was eccentric-looking in Indiana, people would think, 'What is he selling? Let's look in his case.'"

Ty, Inc., was incorporated in 1986. He launched the company with a $50,000 inheritance from his father's estate, and his life savings. He began selling plush cats imported from Italy. His line of plush grew to include several dozen animals by 1992. Each had a different name. "Kids identify with names," he was quoted as saying.

Toy Trivia

25. Which of the following was not an original Rock'em Sock'em Robot?

a. Red Rocker

b. Blue Bomber

c. Green Machine

It wasn't all smooth sailing. Warner's company survived a jolt in 1990 when the U.S. Consumer Product Safety Commission hit him with a recall. The large Korean-made stuffed animals in question had small red plastic hearts attached to them on the tail or the neck. CPSC said they could easily be pulled off, presenting a choking hazard to children. These stuffed animals had been sold nationwide during 1988 and 1989 for $10 to $20 each.

In 1993, Warner had the idea of manufacturing and marketing small plush animals, inexpensive enough ($5 retail) that kids could afford to buy them with their allowances and small enough that they would fit into little pockets. The Beanie Baby was born. The so-called Original 9 were released: a dog, a platypus, a moose, a bear, a dolphin, a frog, a lobster, a whale, and a pig.

They were not an immediate success; however, in 1996, after the first 11 Beanie Babies were retired, they became collector's items and Warner was off to the races. In 1999, he said his company would cease the manufacture and marketing of Beanie Babies on December 31. There was panic in the collector market! Prices skyrocketed! But on Christmas Eve, the marketing genius showed that he had not lost his touch. Warner came up with a plan to have Beanie Baby fans vote, via the Internet, whether he should stop making Beanie Babies. He charged 50¢ per ballot in an attempt to foil repeat voting. The company said that proceeds would be donated to a pediatric AIDS foundation.

Ty, Inc., never released how many votes were cast. But once they had been tabulated, the company flashed the results on its website: "Newsflash: Beanies Win!"

Warner was criticized for the pay-per-vote and ballyhoo. Some critics said it was just a scheme to reattract interest to Beanie Babies. Industry insiders and observers saw it as a diabolical plan to bring back customers lost to Pokemon.

According to *Forbes*, the eccentric Warner spent $472 million to acquire trophy hotel properties like the Four Seasons in New York City; the Four Seasons in Montecito, near Santa Barbara, California; and the San Ysidro Ranch, also near Santa Barbara, the place where Jacqueline and Jack Kennedy honeymooned.

But running hotels is not the same as selling pellet-filled plush animals like Booties the Cat, Teddy Jade, Bunga Raya Bear, Chocolate the Moose, Side-Kick the Dog, and Hoofer the Horse. The jury is still out on Warner's ability to run hotels. But whatever happens, his life remains plush.

The World Watched the Furby Fly

In 1996, the virtual pet craze swept across Japan like a tsunami. Seeing the popularity of Bandai's Tamagotchi and Tiger's Giga Pets, egg-size gizmos that played out the lives of various animals on liquid crystal screens, David Hampton, an independent inventor living in northern California, had an inspiration for the next generation.

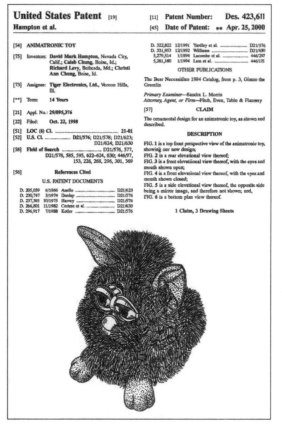

Animatronic Toy (Furby)
Patented April 25, 2000
U.S. Patent D0423611

His vision was to take the virtual pet concept to the next logical level, a three-dimensional robotic friend that would respond, learn, play games, and move while displaying rudimentary artificial intelligence. Furby reacted physically and audibly to changes in light, sound, touch, and physical orientation. There was no on/off switch. The technology was almost invisible. A Furby didn't die, like both the Tamagachi and the Giga Pet; it got bored and went to sleep. It even belched.

An extraordinarily multitalented computer programmer and electronics engineer, Hampton had worked in new business concepts for Mattel a few years before striking out on his own as a consulting engineer and independent inventor. If you remember Q-Bert for the Atari 2600, it was also a Hampton creation.

As the idea came together, Hampton enlisted the assistance of a designer he had met at Mattel, Caleb Chung, to work on the mechanism while he originated Furby's personality traits, language (Furbish), and other unique characteristics that would come to distinguish the item. He also value-engineered its electronic package to hit the magic price point he knew would be required for an approximate $30 retail price, less than one third the cost of Microsoft Corp.'s ActiMates Barney doll.

After two unsuccessful attempts at licensing the concept, Hampton and Chung invited fellow toy inventor Richard C. Levy to join them. Levy, a prolific inventor, brought to their team strong marketing and business capabilities, not to mention close personal and trusted relationships with key industry executives. After meeting with Hampton and Chung in Manhattan Beach, California, during the summer of 1997, Levy agreed to join them and give it his best shot. It became a shot heard 'round the industry.

It was immediately clear to Levy that there was only one company for Furby, and that was Tiger Electronics, an entrepreneurial, innovative family of highly talented, motivated professionals led by two savvy guys who never shied away from challenges and did not make decisions by committee. He knew that they could pull off the impossible.

Reflecting on Tiger, Levy recalled, "It was a serious, energized, close-knit group of distinct personalities; genuine toy people who were never deterred by poor odds and never looked at the clock. They thrived on the leading edge of uncertainty, experimentation, and the exploration of new technologies in the tradition of America's greatest toymakers. While not everything they touched turned to gold, they had a golden gut and the daring to go." Describing Tiger in 1998, *Wired* magazine wrote, "The team at Tiger seems to thrive on beating the odds—they're gamblers at heart."

Levy never thought to take the embryonic concept to giants Hasbro and Mattel. The physical product was not developed enough for acceptance. It was really still a dream. The inventor submission record would have been checked "Inventor to do more work." Even if accepted, these companies would never have made a run for New York Toy Fair 1998, a few short months away. And, ultimately, they would have insisted an entertainment license be applied to it. The name Furby would be replaced by something familiar to consumers, like an animated television or movie character.

Hampton agreed and added that he was sure Hasbro and Mattel would never allow him to become intimately involved with development, programming, and engineering. Having worked at Mattel, he also knew that if there were problems or resistance along the way, or if something came along that was easier to develop, the project would likely be deep-sixed without a second thought.

Levy called Roger Shiffman, the co-founder of Tiger, an executive known for creative entrepreneurship and energy. While they had done only one project together prior to Furby—Tiger had licensed Levy's game, Noteability, a few years earlier—they had a 20-year relationship and were friends.

Toy Trivia

26. Name the largest game publisher in the world.

a. Hasbro
b. Mattel
c. Pressman

Shiffman said that he would make time to see the item while in Los Angeles on September 17. The day before, Roger called Richard to cancel. "I'm sick," he said, hacking into the phone. On top of that, he had to attend a formal dinner that night and wanted to conserve energy for what could be a long evening.

Levy asked if the presentation could be a day or so later, still in LA. Shiffman apologized and explained that he felt so sick, he was going to cut short his trip and fly home the next morning. Knowing that it could take a month or more to pin down the busy executive for a new presentation date, and passionate about the concept, Levy tested their relationship.

"Let me ask you two questions, Roger. First, have I ever wasted your time in all the years I've been pitching product to you?"

"No, of course not," Shiffman responded, without hesitation.

"Are you on your death bed?"

"It's not that bad."

"Then see Furby," Levy beseeched his friend.

"Okay, I'll do it for you," Shiffman responded.

Hampton and Chung went to the hotel suite as scheduled. They showed the model Levy had seen a few weeks earlier, a manually controlled character operated like a hand puppet. It was a tennis ball with eyes that moved when knobs were turned. Shiffman got it immediately. He saw the vision and potential. He called Levy to express his excitement at this ground-breaking concept.

"What's next?" he asked, feeling a bit better.

"How about we come to Chicago to present Furby to Randy and everyone?"

A date was set, and Levy, Hampton, and Chung flew to Chicago to present Furby to senior management. Everyone loved it, but Randy Rissman, Tiger's co-founder and president, was apprehensive. Shiffman knew that Furby could be Tiger's marquee introduction at the New York Toy Fair the following February, but getting the deal done took two more months due to Rissman's travel schedule and concerns, all valid. Nonetheless, in October, everyone started to lay plans for an assault on the New York Toy Fair.

The first bump in the road came very soon after Rissman gave the project a green light. It was November. Furby's mechanism, while extremely innovative, had to be redesigned for mass production. The only elements that survived the redesign were the eyeballs and face plate. At this point, Levy took charge of managing mechanical development from the licensee side and moved it from California to Maryland where he lived. He organized a team of freelance designers, engineers, and prototype makers, including Richard J. Maddocks, a highly skilled design draftsman from Silver Spring, Maryland, and Peter Hall, a design engineer invited from England.

Three thousand miles away, Dave put together his support team to design the electronic hardware and program Furby's brain and personality. Software engineer Wayne Schultz agreed to join Hampton, working from a base in Oregon.

Furby would make it to the Toy Fair, but performing at only 5 percent of its anticipated capability. While the rest of Tiger's line was demonstrated by actors hired specifically for the Toy Fair, Tiger's executive vice president, Stewart Sims, personally did the Furby demos. Sims was intimately familiar with Furby, having been Tiger's most senior point man for the toy's development and marketing.

On the first day of Toy Fair, February 10, 1998, Hasbro announced that it had acquired Tiger for $335 million. That was when Alan Hassenfeld, Hasbro's chairman, saw Furby for the first time. Randy Rissman, Tiger's chairman and co-founder, quipped to Alan that Furby was his bonus for buying Tiger. Though the demonstration prototype exhibited only 5 percent of the functions that would be in the production unit,

Hassenfeld told Randy and Roger that Furby was the coolest toy he had seen in 25 years in the industry.

After meetings with Joseph Chiang and members of his team from Tiger Hong Kong, Dave went home to work on electronics and software. Richard and his team confronted the challenges of making reliable mechanics for the demo models for Tiger's sale's force, at the same time perfecting the mechanism for mass production.

Facing the unforgiving clock and unable to continue without state-of-the-art model-making equipment, Pro/E, and model makers, Richard called Randy for help. By the end of that day, Levy had explained his needs to Hasbro president Al Verrecchia and Charlie Kaberry, vice president of Hasbro's model services. Two days later, Kaberry flew to Maryland for a briefing, accompanied by his colleague Dave Albani. Albani became responsible for try-out tooling and was "borrowed" to tackle the Furby challenge, co-coordinating in-house resources. The baton had been passed.

Maddocks and Hall began working with the Hasbro. The first reference model was completed on April 15, 1998. Levy says Furby never would have been manufactured without Hasbro's unqualified support, talent pool, and state-of-the-art facilities. "They were the white knights who arrived in the nick of time."

"In August of 1998, when we laid out the advertising plan for Furby, we looked at the orders in-house and Randy and Roger allocated a budget of $4.1 million. That had to cover TV for the year," reflected Marc Rosenberg, who at the time was the vice president for public relations and promotions at Tiger Electronics. "More importantly though, we knew PR and promotion had to really carry the day. There was no question that whenever media people saw Furby for the first time, their eyes opened as wide as his. We simply had to translate and ride that excitement in a huge way," Rosenberg continued.

"It started by us agreeing to let *Wired* magazine do a behind-the-scenes look at Furby, once they had decided he was their Toy of the Year. The magazine did a 12-page editorial feature that became our bible to the media. Here was arguably one of the most hip magazines saying for us that Furby had what no other had ever been able to deliver. We used that to open the door with mainstream media whenever we had to. This didn't take very long.

"Within hours of my appearing on the *Today* show with Katie Couric and six Furbys, all interacting, there was a line more than 500 people long waiting to greet the first shipment on October 2, 1998, at FAO Schwarz on Fifth Avenue—an event we had spent $57,000 on, far less than the budgets our competitors would shell out to launch a major new line. From that moment, every time a shipment appeared, whether it be at Toys R Us, Wal-Mart, or wherever, throngs grabbed up more than four million by Christmas that year.

"To keep the momentum going, we knew we had to align the planets with a full-out promotional effort. If I was asked to produce a highlight film, it would include these events: The Cartoon Network stepped up with an unbelievable two-week stunt. Hi-C had our little guy on more than 120 million boxes of their best-selling juice not once, but twice in a year and a half. And McDonald's welcomed Furby with his very own Happy Meal, which fast became the second most popular in their history, right behind Beanie Babies.

"This, coupled with an unbelievable licensing effort, made Furby everyone's darling overnight and assured him a place in toy history."

Reflecting on the PR maven's contributions to Tiger over the years, Roger Shiffman said, "Marc is the greatest showman in the toy industry."

Remarking on his personal experiences with Rosenberg, Levy said, "He can accomplish more with one arm tied behind his back than major toy companies do with entire departments supported by outside agencies. I saw firsthand what Marc and Lana (Simon) did for Furby and other Tiger products."

When Hasbro acquired Tiger Electronics, Rosenberg went on to become senior vice president of marketing and advertising for Hasbro Toys. Shiffman, president and CEO of Tiger, became president of worldwide marketing and brand development at Hasbro. Neither works for Hasbro today.

Furby Factoids

- In 1998, within one week of its release, FAO Schwarz had backorders of 35,000 Furbys.
- In 1999, during the 6 weeks leading up to Christmas, retailers sold 1 Furby every minute, 24 hours a day, 7 days a week.
- In January 1999, the National Security Agency issued a ban on Furby, prohibiting employees from bringing their Furbys to the NSA campus. (It was thought to have a built-in recorder.)
- A National Enquirer headline read, "Fire! Furby Saves Soap Star's Life." Actress Candice Daly of "The Young and the Restless," said that Furby woke her and her boyfriend up from a sleep and saved their lives.

◆ January 1999, hospitals banned Furbys, fearing that medical equipment might be scrambled by the toy's infrared transmitter.

◆ Furby was banned from airplanes and many airports.

◆ In June 1999, Lisa Cantara of Blacksburg, Virginia, said a Furby taught her autistic four-year-old son, C. J., how to refer to himself in speech and increased his vocabulary by at least a half-dozen words.

Toy Trivia

27. Who invented Ideal's Mr. Machine in 1960?

a. Marvin Glass

b. Larry Mass

c. Michael Satten

Still the most complex electromechanical toy ever mass produced, Furby ultimately sold over 40 million units in 52 countries, and in 12 languages.

Unreal Real Estate: Players Never Get Board

Billions of dollars, pesos, schillings, cruzeiros, drachmas, guilders, francs, lire, rupees, rands, kroners, and escudos have been made and lost over it in a few short hours. It has landed people in jail from Argentina to Finland to India to the People's Republic of China. They have been forced into bankruptcy, with no choice but to turn over all of their assets to a hardhearted landlord. People have met, fallen in love, and married over it—and who knows how many arguments it has caused?

It, of course, is Parker Brothers' "Real Estate Trading Game," Monopoly, perhaps the most famous board game the world has ever seen. It has sold well over 200 million copies worldwide. Who could fail to recognize the origin of that familiar imperative, "Pass Go, Collect $200"? Hasbro estimates that an estimated one billion players have "passed Go" since the game's introduction. Since the origination of the game, over six billion little green houses have been "constructed," making Hasbro's East Longmeadow, Massachusetts, manufacturer the largest housing developer in the world. And where else but in Monopoly would going to jail be a welcome respite from an exorbitant rent bill?

Monopoly is marketed in 80 countries and has been translated into 22 languages.

Who invented Monopoly? This is yet another one of those questions that has no sure answer. The creators of this game of games are an amorphous medley of legends. Reliable facts indicate that between 1904 and 1934, a game known as Monopoly was developed. The early board and its components were handmade copies of earlier versions of the game. Though the trademark Monopoly did not appear on any of these iterations, evidence points to it being played in Reading, Pennsylvania, sometime between 1911 and 1917.

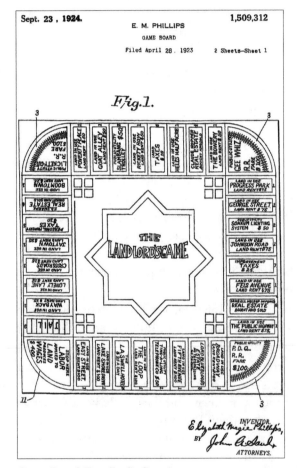

Game Board (Landlord's Game)
Patented September 23, 1924
U.S. Patent 1,509,312

In the early 1920s, Monopoly was reportedly played on the campuses of Princeton, MIT, Smith College, and the University of Pennsylvania. There was commerce in the game as people published copies and sold them among universities. Research by

Dr. Ralph Anspach, a professor of economics at San Francisco State University, and the inventor of Anti-Monopoly, shows the game next in Indianapolis, Indiana, but selling under the name Finance. Evidence shows that the game reached Atlantic City, New Jersey, in the early 1930s, where it took on the resort city's street names, such as Pennsylvania Avenue, Pacific Avenue, and North Carolina Avenue. This is where it is said Charles B. Darrow learned how to play it.

Many chroniclers of the industry attribute the idea to the genius of Darrow, an unemployed heating engineer from Germantown, Pennsylvania. The saga goes that in 1933, during the Great Depression, Darrow came up with the game as a substitute for the entertainment he could not afford while on a visit to nearby Atlantic City, New Jersey.

We say "attribute to" Darrow because game historians have pointed to a woman named Lizzie Magie-Phillips, who created and patented something called The Landlord's Game. Magie-Phillips's board is even reported to have featured a "Go to Jail" space. Phil Orbanes, author of *The Monopoly Companion*, writes, "Strictly speaking, Monopoly got its start the day Elizabeth Magie-Phillips began to sell her Landlord's Game in 1904." Although her game was not a commercial success, Orbanes points out that it did find its way into the economics departments of colleges and that "at one or all of these schools arose the improvements that transformed The Landlord's Game into Monopoly."

Note: It has been alleged that Parker Brothers acquired the rights to Finance, a take on Monopoly by Dan Layman of Indiana, and other games of similar genre, to protect its market position.

However, Darrow sold the game as we know it. He found that it was no easier to sell a game than it is today. In hopes of licensing the game, he took it first to Milton Bradley, which turned him down, and then to Parker Brothers in 1934, but they passed. It took too long to play, the rules were too complicated, and players kept going around and around the board instead of ending up at a final goal. It was rejected by Parker as having "52 fundamental playing errors."

Undeterred, Darrow proceeded on his own to publish and market the product. When reports of the game's success began to reach Parker Brothers, the company reconsidered and licensed the rights early in 1935. But according to Anspach, Robert B.M. Barton, the former president of Parker Brothers, who negotiated with Darrow in 1935, testified in a court case that he did not believe Darrow's claim to inventorship. He said this in spite of U.S. patent No. 2,026,082 issued to Darrow.

The reason Anspach knew so much about the origin of the game is that when he published Anti-Monopoly, he was sued for trademark infringement. He won his case in a 1984 decision by the Supreme Court of the United States against Parker Brothers.

Subsequently, Darrow retired a millionaire at the age of 46. The first inventor to make a million dollars from a game, he became a world traveler and a collector of exotic orchid species.

Game Board Apparatus (Monopoly)
Patented December 31, 1935
U.S. Patent 2,026,082

Monopoly was the biggest thing that had ever hit Parker Brothers. Sales of the game skyrocketed, and by mid-February 1935, the plant was producing 20,000 sets a week, a great number even by today's standards. Before Christmas that first year, so many telegraphed orders poured in that they were filed in oversize laundry baskets and stacked in the hallways. With an ever-increasing backlog of requests, a bookkeeping firm in Boston was summoned to help keep things in order. As Parker Brothers tells the story, the firm's representatives took one look and refused the job, no matter what the price.

Despite the public's initial reaction, the company viewed Monopoly as an adult fad game that would sell for about three years. Certainly, it was too complicated for children. And just as expected, sales soon began to level off. On December 19, 1936, instructions came from George Parker himself to "cease absolutely to make any more boards or utensil boxes .... We will stop making Monopoly against the possibility of a very early slump." But then, as is often the case in the fickle game business, sales went up again and the upward spiral has never stopped.

Tickle Me Mania

"What are you doing here?" Walter Cronkite, the legendary *CBS Evening News* anchor, asked inventor Ron Dubren, as both men made small talk waiting for their segments on the CBS Morning News. Cronkite was there to promote a new book he had written; Dubren was promoting a toy he conceived.

"Have you heard of the toy Tickle Me Elmo?" Dubren asked.

"Sure. My grandkids are asking for it."

"I'm one of its inventors."

"Don't suppose you could get me one?" Cronkite asked, sensing Dubren could be the key to satisfying his grandchildren's wish at the height of the craze.

Dubren couldn't.

Tickle Me Elmo mania swept across America during the Christmas season of 1996. The toy was in such demand that even Ron and his co-inventor, Greg Hyman, had trouble getting one. What was it about this cute, giggling *Sesame Street* Muppet monster that won the hearts of Americans everywhere?

"Tickle him for the first time, and that great giggle already has you laughing out loud," says Dubren, a former research scientist with a Ph.D. in psychology. "Tickle Me Elmo not only appeals to preschoolers; it brings the three-year-old out in kids of all ages. That may be the simple answer to its amazing success, the eager tyke with the joyful laugh makes us all laugh."

Dubren calls what happened Elmo's Law: Anything that could go right, went right. The inspiration came from Ron, who engaged Greg Hyman, one of America's most successful toy inventors, as a partner to help him develop it. Hyman, an electronics wizard, knew how to bring Dubren's idea to life.

Greg and Ron started out with the rough concept of a tickling animal puppet. That core concept evolved into a plush character they named Tickles the Chimp. The essential idea was that of a tickling jag. The more someone tickled the doll, the greater the laughter.

The inventors presented a rough prototype to Tyco Playtime, which at that time did not have the rights to *Sesame Street* plush. Stan Clutton, the company's vice president of marketing and R&D, saw the concept's potential and directed the guys to work with his colleague, Gene Murtha, who anointed Tickles the Chimp, Tickle Me Taz (tied to their Looney Tunes license, the Tazmanian Devil). Greg and Ron licensed their invention to Tyco and it became Tickle Me Taz.

Months later, an amazing thing happened. Tyco wrangled away from Hasbro the plush rights to *Sesame Street* characters. Suddenly Clutton told Murtha to forget Taz and make the concept Tickle Me Elmo. Clutton added. "While we were getting the *Sesame Street* plush rights, we gave up our rights to Looney Tunes. So the product concept would have been without a home in our line had we not gotten *Sesame Street* rights."

And what about the vibration feature? This was not in the inventor prototype. Clutton explains that the vibration element was the result of a preproduction meeting for the commercial shoot. During the meeting, Bob Moehl from the ad agency said that he really liked the product, but since television is a visual medium, it would be much better if it did something visually.

"After that meeting, Marty Scheman, then president of Tyco Preschool, brought in a competitive product that shook, and it was decided that this was the perfect mechanism to represent that out-of-control laughter that was so important to the concept," said Clutton.

Tickle Me Elmo was born.

While the media called it an overnight sensation, the PR campaign had started a year ahead of the toy's retail introduction by systematic cultivation of key print and television media. The toy may have been an overnight sensation, but the public relations campaign devised was so successful that Tyco had trouble keeping up with the demand it generated for the toy.

"We weren't miracle PR workers," Bruce Maguire, CEO of Freeman Public Relations, told *PR News*. "But we did have the foresight to put Elmo into the hands of the right people early on."

"You could tell it was a magical toy, but no one had a clue it would become as big as it became," said Maguire. "We saw it in context with more than 100 other SKUs."

Freeman went after opinion makers first. At the New York Toy Fair, Tyco hosted a breakfast for some 15 carefully chosen media representatives, including reporters from *The New York Times*, the Associated Press, *Playthings*, and *The Toy Book*. This event led to Chris Byrne, editor of *Market Focus: Toys*, taking the doll on NBC's *Today* show. There it wound up in the hands of weatherman Al Roker.

"Obviously, no one could have foreseen the phenomena, but I felt the doll was a real breakthrough in the preschool category," Byrne told *PR News*. "It was the first time in the preschool category an affordable technology had been married to a popular character, and it really stood out as something new and creative." Family Fun named Tickle Me Elmo a winner in its preschool category and ran a story in November 1996.

After assessing the trade reaction to Elmo at the Toy Fair, Tyco Preschool placed its orders at the factory for Christmas 1996—but not for nearly enough product to meet demand the first year.

The PR mavens at Freeman knew that Rosie O'Donnell liked Elmo and often had the Muppet on as a guest. So as soon as samples came off the production line, Rosie was among the first people to get one. As fate would have it, O'Donnell's young son dropped Elmo into a toilet. Rosie made a joke about it and asked for a replacement over the airwaves. When word reached Freeman, they had as many samples as they could get sent to her by messenger. The gesture paid off in a big way. It became a public relations dream.

Toy Trivia

28. Prolific inventor A. Eddy Goldfarb invented all but one of the following items.

a. Shark Attack

b. Stompers

c. Spin Pop

Two days later, the producers called asking for 300 Tickle Me Elmos, one for each member of the studio audience. They devised a "secret word" game. If a guest said the "secret word," each member of the audience would get a Tickle Me Elmo. As the show neared the end, it happened. Suddenly sirens blared as cameras panned across 300 elated people showing off their Elmos.

Then TV lightening struck again. Bryant Gumbel sat with a Elmo on his lap during a segment of *Today*. From there the toy appeared on *Regis and Kathy Lee*. The media feeding frenzy had begun. *USA Today* put a photo of Tickle Me Elmo on the front page of its business section. It became such a pop-culture phenomenon that David Letterman opened one monologue with "Hi, I'm Tickle Me Dave."

Building Blockbusters: Profit from Bricks

People who enjoy crunching numbers have estimated that between 200 million and 300 million children and adults play or have played with LEGO building blocks. Sold in more than 60,000 stores in about 115 countries, the LEGO idea is universal. The company estimates that kids around the world spend about five billion hours a year playing with LEGO blocks.

The world's largest manufacturer of bricks and building elements, LEGO Systems, Inc., has no equal. Approximately 11 billion are produced each year—or enough bricks to circle the globe 14 times and ring up about half a billion dollars in sales. Nearly 100 million homes worldwide have LEGO toys. In the United States, LEGO products can be seen in 50 percent of all households; in Europe, the number is closer to 80 percent. LEGO building bricks were awarded three patents, all somewhat different: U.S. Patent No. 3,034,254, German Patent No. 92863, and U.K. Patent 935308. LEGO Systems now comprises 21 sales companies, 5 manufacturing companies, and 3 tooling shops throughout the world, not to mention theme parks and retail stores, among other enterprises.

LEGOS were created in 1932 in Billund, a Danish hamlet on the Jutland moors, by Ole Kirk Christiansen, a carpenter and joiner who was forced out of work by the Depression. Christiansen named his toys LEGO as a contraction of *leg godt*, which in Danish means "play well." He later discovered that LEGO also has a Latin meaning: "I assemble."

In 1958, the stud-and-tube clutching principle that we know today was patented by Ole's son, Godtfred Kirk Christiansen. As a result, a brick manufactured back in 1958 will fit any element made in 1990. More than 1,200 pieces and elements are fully compatible with each other. The creative possibilities boggle the mind. For example, you can put six 8-stud bricks together in almost 103 million different ways (102,981,500, to be exact).

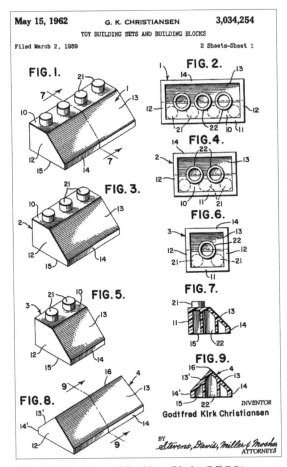

Toy Building Sets and Building Blocks (LEGO)
Patented May 15, 1962
U.S. Patent 3,034,254

It's not very difficult to understand why the plastic bricks are so loved by both parents and children. They fulfill even the most exacting parent's standard for a toy: Kids cannot break them, they're nontoxic, and they have multiple incidental learning values. Above all, LEGOS satisfy three fundamental juvenile proclivities: to construct, to play, and to demolish.

Draw a Card, Picture the Money

"I'll never forget the first time I saw it," Kevin McNulty recalled, referring to Pictionary, the excitement still palpable in his voice 17 years later. "It was fantastic. It even gave me a why-didn't-I-think-of-that moment."

McNulty, who has a "golden gut" for product, was shown the game by Tom McGuire, then West Coast manager for the now defunct Selchow & Righter, the company that brought you Trivial Pursuit. S&R had been one of America's oldest game publishers before it was acquired by Coleco Industries in 1989.

Soon after seeing Pictionary demonstrated in a hotel room in New York City, McNulty joined forces with McGuire, Tom McGrath, Joe Cornacchia (Trivial Pursuit contract printer), Hudson Dobson, and Bill Napier, who had all worked for S&R B.C. (Before Coleco). The guys knew from their Trivial Pursuit experience that the adult game market held huge potential. In hopes that they could make Pictionary the next impact game, they all pitched in money and The Games Gang came to life.

The partners licensed Pictionary, a "charades on paper" game, from its inventor, 28-year-old Seattle waiter Robert Angel, and his partners, accountant Terry Langston and designer Gary Everson.

"We incorporated in October of 1986," McNulty recalled. "Milton Bradley tried to take Pictionary out from under us, but they reneged on their first offer, and we stayed on it and got it." (Sources report that MB was unwilling to pay the royalty rate requested by the inventors, and it backed off.)

McNulty went on to say that Milton Bradley tried to chase them with Win, Lose or Draw. It had a Merv Griffin–produced TV show. "They really came after us. We beat them back, though, because we had filled the pipelines and our game was available. If it had not been, they would have claimed more territory," McNulty continues, sounding like a combat-tested general.

In 1984, Angel self-published the game that contained "some 6,000 usable words" and the rules. When players landed on a color-coded category square (person, place, animal, etc.) they selected from a deck of 500 cards, each featuring 5 words or phrases that had to be drawn against the clock. People liked it—a lot.

This early success in Seattle attracted Tom McGuire, and then Cornacchia flew to Seattle and made a deal for the game rights.

Here are the highlights from that point on, according to Gang member McNulty:

- June to December 1986: 30,000 copies (at $16)
- 1987: 300,000 copies (at $16)
- 1988: 8 million copies (at $16)
- 1989: 4 million copies (at $16)

Pictionary is now licensed to Mattel, having gone from The Games Gang to Western Publishing; then to Hasbro, with its acquisition of Western in 1991; and on to Mattel in 2002. The game reportedly averages one million units per year worldwide.

While U.S. sales have hit a plateau, the major part of revenue comes now from 60 countries overseas. Pictionary is published in 45 different languages.

All Angel wanted when he and his partners did Pictionary was "a nice car at the end." Vroooooooooom!

Toy Trivia

29. The world's oldest recorded game has been played for 7,000 years. Name it.

a. Mancala

b. The Checkered Game of Life

c. Pente

How Do You Like Those Potatoes?

"It's wasteful; a kid shouldn't be playing with food," was the general consensus of most toy executives in the early 1850s to whom independent inventor George Lerner and his associate, Julius "Julie" Ellman, showed their creation, Mr. Potato Head. But Lerner and Ellman knew that kids *did* play with their food, and that was what inspired them to create the toy that was to become the world's most celebrated spud.

It was post–World War II, and the nation's focus was on feeding the war-ravaged countries of the world. Children were told, "Eat everything on your plate. People are starving overseas." The timing was wrong, but that didn't deter these inventors.

Not getting anywhere with toy companies, the inventing duo decided to take their concept to Post cereals. They pitched selling the components (push-pin eyes, ears, noses, mouths, and a body with attached arms and legs) as an in-pack premium for which consumers supplied their own potato. Post liked it and accepted the idea. But the inventors still wanted a toy deal.

At the time, Hasbro was making pencil boxes filled with pencils and school supplies. Then they started adding toys to the contents. This led to designing the boxes as doctor kits, nurse kits, paint sets, and other themes.

George thought their idea would make a nifty extension to the Hasbro line. He set up a meeting with Merril Hassenfeld, president of the Rhode Island company. Lerner's vision for the toy concept was for kids to push the plastic parts into fruits and veggies, creating an endless variety of anthropomorphic friends. Hassenfeld decided to take a chance. Lerner contacted Post and, together with Hasbro, bought back the rights for $2,000. A toy deal was struck.

On April 30, 1952, Mr. Potato Funny Face kit was introduced, but it was not an immediate hit. The first products shipped had parts rattling around in the boxes. Customers thought the toys were broken. To solve this problem, Hasbro inserted a large piece of Styrofoam into the package to hold loose parts. Some consumers complained that the Styrofoam broke down with repeated use, but they were mistakenly using the insert as part of the toy rather than the packaging. The body was born.

The original Mr. Potato Head was redesigned in 1968. He was given a larger body with pieces inserted into a plastic shape rather than the "customer supplied potato." Much of this work was done so the toy would conform to all of the newly established consumer product safety regulations.

Over the next three decades, a variety of Mr. Potato Head products were sold. He was so loved by children that he was expanded into additional toy categories, including puzzles, creative play sets, and electronic hand-held board and video games. The vast popularity of Mr. Potato Head also attracted nontoy companies, which licensed his image and name on apparel, accessories, and novelty items.

Mr. Potato Head, referred to as MPH in Hasbro shorthand, gives the toymaker high-octane sales year after year, and that's pretty good for a dude with no legs. An "I-had-one-of-those classics" toys, Mr. Potato Head turned 50 years old in 2002. MPH grossed $4 million in sales in his 1952 introductory year. Early sales were helped by a then-unique means of product promotion. Mr. Potato Head was the first toy advertised on television. In 1986, the toy was sold outright to Hasbro when George Lerner was 75; Lerner died in 1995. The other member of the original Potato Head group, Julius "Julie" Ellman, continues to invent new toys to this day.

Robert's Rules of Order: Cabbage Patch Orders, That Is

Who will ever forget the Christmas of 1983, when fights broke out at retailers across the country as consumers battled for bragging rights to have their kids "adopt" one of the first Cabbage Patch Kids on the block? America loves a good craze every so many years, and this was a doozy.

At 275 Zayre department stores, 25,000 buyers lined up one Sunday to buy a doll at $17.99 each, in a below-cost sale. A spokesman at the time said, "We sold 60,000 in less than a half hour." At a Zayre store in Wilkes-Barre, Pennsylvania, people pushed through a large plate-glass window. A couple reportedly slept in their car outside a Service Merchandise store in Fishkill, New York, to get one of the first places in line to buy a doll. Someone in Wilmington, Delaware, offered a $100 bribe to a salesperson at Gaylord's Discount Department Store, according to a store manager.

Twenty-five years ago, Xavier Roberts and five of his college buddies opened Babyland General Hospital in Cleveland, Georgia, a town of circa 1,900 inhabitants, to sell a line of soft sculpted, hand-sewn dolls called Little People. The building was an old medical clinic that they converted into a fantasy world containing a hospital, nursery, and adoption center.

The youngest of six children, Xavier lost his dad at age five in a tragic automobile accident. His family struggled to pay the bills. He worked as a carpenter and a textile mill worker to save money for college. Roberts also saw the dolls as a way to pay for his art school education at Truett-McConnell College. His company Original Appala-chian Artworks, Inc., was established.

Using his knowledge of German fabric sculpting combined with quilting techniques, Xavier created the chubby cloth dolls. He called his creations "babies," not dolls, and put no price tags on them. Licensed Patch Nurses at Babyland General Hospital would "deliver" the babies when a gigantic Mother Cabbage went into labor. The LPCs also collected "adoption fees" from prospective parents. Each doll came with an official birth certificate and adoption papers.

In the years B.C. (Before Coleco), sales were made primarily through stands at handicraft shows where Xavier had assistants dressed as nurses. Then in 1980, Roberts was featured on a primetime national television show called *Real People*, and the sales of Little People dolls went ballistic.

In 1982, Xavier reached an agreement with Coleco Industries to mass-produce the dolls. While closely resembling the original Little People designs, the Coleco dolls had molded vinyl heads and were made in China. The name was changed to Cabbage Patch Kids.

In 1983, Coleco was selling around 200,000 dolls per week. Sales went from $60 million in 1983 to more than $600 million in 1985. In the 1980s, Cabbage Patch became a $2 billion brand, a real American cultural phenomenon.

But the company miscalculated the staying power of the craze. It both overexpanded and was unable to deliver on promises for the Adam computer. This may have been the fatal blow. In 1986, sales of Cabbage Patch dolls dropped to $250 million, and the company lost $111 million. In 1987, Coleco lost another $105 million; in 1988, it filed for bankruptcy.

By June 1989, Coleco was going out of business and sold its assets to Hasbro. Hasbro marketed the dolls from then until Mattel took over in 1995, took them in new directions, and actually diluted the charm of the original concept. It added accessories and promotable features such as face painting, teeth brushing, haircut magic, splashing fun, and so forth. Mattel's Snack Time Kid chewed everything, including little girls' hair. Some models had swivel heads. There were smaller dolls with beanie-style bodies. The dolls went mainstream and lost their way as they were ill-advisedly morphed away from Roberts's original unique designs.

In the summer of 2002, the new Cabbage Patch Kids were unveiled at the Toys R Us store in Alpharetta, Georgia, by its native son, Xavier Roberts. Joined by executives of Toys R Us, it was announced that in August 2002, the stores would become the exclusive adoption center for the new generation of one-of-a-kind kids.

> **Toy Trivia**
>
> 30. Inventor Charles B. Darrow reportedly earned over $1 million in royalties from his creation of which game?
>
> a. Monopoly
>
> b. Scrabble
>
> c. Clue

Nothing Trivial About This Game's Success

"They've struck it rich, it now seems clear, by inventing a game called Trivial Pursuit," read the lead sentence in a piece by Toronto's *Globe and Mail* newspaper on January 15, 1983.

Rich is an understatement as Trivial Pursuit celebrated its twentieth anniversary in 2002. Since it was first introduced in Canada in 1982, by co-creators Chris (a.k.a. Horn) Haney and Scott (a.k.a. Scooter) Abbott, the game has racked up sales of more than 70 million copies worldwide in 26 languages and 17 countries.

"I don't care about money," the then–32-year-old Haney told the paper. "We're a bunch of wackos," he continued, "My biggest mistake was quitting school when I was 17. I should have done it when I was 12." Perhaps, but money is no longer an issue. It has not been almost from the beginning of their Trivial Pursuit pursuit.

The game was introduced in the United States in 1983 by Selchow & Righter, the makers of Scrabble; it was under license from Horn & Abbott. Interestingly, the game had been turned down by both Milton Bradley and Parker Brothers—possibly for the same reason. A senior executive at Milton Bradley at that time put it like this: "We were the world's largest game publisher. We knew it all. First, we knew adults didn't play games. We also knew no one would pay $29.95 to $39.99 retail for a game. And, lastly, we said that if people wanted trivia, there were lots of books." Certainly, that executive today would readily admit that those assumptions should have substantiated with hard facts rather than with what the industry calls "isms."

> **411** Don't miss the award-winning website www.drtoy.com, an invaluable resource on playthings and the industry. The site is designed and hosted by Stevanne Auerbach, Ph.D., director of the Institute of Childhood Resources, and was founded in 1975. You'll learn a great deal from the smorgasbord of information she serves up.

This Time, Success Was Simply in the Cards

In 1990, former Boeing employee Peter Adkison founded Renton, Washington–based Wizards of the Coast with the assistance of six friends. After years of struggling, his game company was in need of a breakout product when he met Richard Garfield, by happenstance, through the Internet. Garfield had the solution for Adkison's problem. Solutions were Garfield's specialty. He was, after all, an Ivy League Ph.D. in combinational mathematics. A game aficionado, Garfield began designing his own games at the age of 15. His ideas have since transformed the games industry.

Adkison asked Garfield to design a card game that was fun and portable, and that could be played in under one hour. After working on the game for three months, Garfield presented Wizards of the Coast with the alpha version of the Magic: The Gathering trading card game.

While the game was being tested and readied for release, Garfield began teaching math at Whitman College in Walla Walla, Washington. In 1993, the Magic: The Gathering card game was released to overnight success and critical acclaim. Record-setting sales of 10 million cards in just 6 weeks made it possible for Richard Garfield to pursue his true passion, creating games.

Instead of giving Garfield a royalty deal, Adkison made him an equity partner in Wizards of the Coast and immersed the company in the fantasy card game business. To keep the lights on, the partners awarded stock in Wizards to 200 other people in return for either cash or labor.

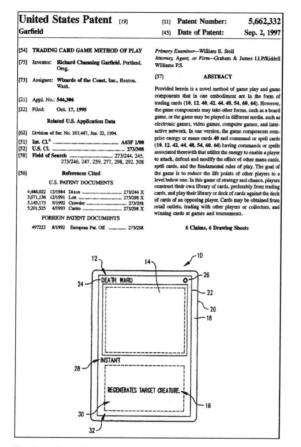

United States Patent [19]

Garfield

[11] Patent Number: 5,662,332
[45] Date of Patent: Sep. 2, 1997

[54] **TRADING CARD GAME METHOD OF PLAY**

[75] Inventor: **Richard Channing Garfield**, Portland, Oreg.

[73] Assignee: **Wizards of the Coast, Inc.**, Renton, Wash.

[21] Appl. No.: **544,306**

[22] Filed: **Oct. 17, 1995**

Related U.S. Application Data

[62] Division of Ser. No. 263,447, Jun. 22, 1994.
[51] Int. Cl.⁶ A63F 1/00
[52] U.S. Cl. 273/308
[58] Field of Search 273/244, 245, 273/246, 247, 259, 277, 298, 292, 308

[56] **References Cited**

U.S. PATENT DOCUMENTS

4,486,022	12/1984	Dixon	273/244 X
5,071,136	12/1991	Lott	273/298 X
5,145,173	9/1992	Crowder	273/298
5,201,525	4/1993	Castro	273/298 X

FOREIGN PATENT DOCUMENTS

497223 8/1992 European Pat. Off. 273/298

Primary Examiner—William E. Stoll
Attorney, Agent, or Firm—Graham & James LLP/Riddell Williams P.S.

[57] **ABSTRACT**

Provided herein is a novel method of game play and game components that in one embodiment are in the form of trading cards (10, 12, 40, 42, 44, 48, 54, 60, 64). However, the game components may take other forms, such as a board game, or the game may be played in different media, such as electronic games, video games, computer games, and interactive network. In one version, the game components comprise energy or mana cards 40 and command or spell cards (10, 12, 42, 44, 48, 54, 60, 64) having commands or spells associated therewith that utilize the energy to enable a player to attack, defend and modify the effect of other mana cards, spell cards, and the fundamental rules of play. The goal of the game is to reduce the life points of other players to a level below one. In this game of strategy and chance, players construct their own library of cards, preferably from trading cards, and play their library or deck of cards against the deck of cards of an opposing player. Cards may be obtained from retail outlets, trading with other players or collectors, and winning cards at games and tournaments.

6 Claims, 6 Drawing Sheets

Trading Card Game Method Of Play (Magic: The Gathering)
Patented September 2, 1997
U.S. Patent 5,662,332

Garfield's game, awarded U.S. Patent 5,662,332, today is the most widely played trading card game, with an estimated 7 million players in 52 countries and more than 100,000 sanctioned tournaments held annually.

In 1999, Garfield's accomplishments in the gaming industry were acknowledged with his induction into the Origins Hall of Fame. The world-famous trading card game he created, Magic: The Gathering, was also welcomed into the Origins Hall of Fame. Today Garfield is continuing to work with Wizards of the Coast to design new

Magic: The Gathering games, including Magic: The Gathering Online, as well as new trading card games, such as the Showdown Sports and new *Star Wars* trading card games. In addition, he is developing original game concepts for a variety of platforms.

In September 1999, Hasbro acquired Wizards of the Coast for more than $325 million. Adkison retired from the company in 2001.

Back to the Future

Our snippets of these toy legends provide a flavor of the industry's past. But what does the future have in store for the industry?

"It will always be bright," suggests toy analyst David Leibowitz. "There will always be a Christmas and there are always going to be children. The children of America aren't going to be denied, and children around the world aren't going to be denied."

Toy Trivia

31. More than how many LEGO bricks have been sold since 1949?

a. 125 billion

b. 250 billion

c. 500 billion

From this bullish forecast, one might conclude that there will always be a Barbie, a G.I. Joe, a "real estate game," electronic friends, and creative blocks. Indeed, inventing pros regularly use their special talents to reinterpret the best of such classic playthings with contemporary flair. With a tweak here and a living hinge there, variants of classic playthings are redesigned to accommodate the tastes of future tykes.

For the toy executives responsible for choosing future hit products, there may be comfort and confidence tying selections to past successes. They know that in the toy market of the 1990s, a fizzle could lead to the financial tremors that shut down powers such as CBS, Coleco, Gabriel, Knickerbocker, Kusan, Lakeside, Mego, Schaper, Selchow & Righter, Skilcraft, LJN, and Ideal.

They know, too, that some of the marketplace fizzles stem from a whole gamut of distractions unknown when the first Barbies, G.I. Joes, and LEGOs reached toyland. Videos, CDs, DVDs, game cartridges, audiocassettes, fashionware, and other nontoy fads are competing for many of the same disposable dollars previously earmarked for toys and games. To maintain and expand their share of those purchase dollars, toy people are looking for all the innovations that technology and inventiveness can deliver in new playthings.

The manufacturing and marketing of toys and games has long been a fast-track business. It is an industry that is contagious, one with a glamour that attracts and holds a core group of "toy people." Key among this group are the independent developers, who know that their best products are yet to come. Once they've been bitten by the bug, few opt to leave the industry. Jack Morrissey, a veteran salesman, relates the inventing bug to the old Roach Motel ad: "Once you check in, you don't check out."

Fun Facts

◆ In 2003, Scrabble celebrates its 55th birthday. One hundred million sets have been sold worldwide, and between one and two million are sold each year in North America. Somewhere over 147,000 words can be used in Scrabble.

◆ John Spilsbury, an Englishman, created the first jigsaw puzzle as a way of teaching kids geography. The year was circa 1760. He painted sheets of wood as maps of global regions. He then cut the wood at national frontier lines, and the first jigsaw puzzle was born.

◆ In December of 1998, the so-called Barbie Liberation Organization swapped electronic voice boxes between Hasbro's "Talking Duke" GI Joe action figure and Mattel's "Teen Talk" Barbie. The group claimed to have altered 300 toys. There was no way to substantiate the claim.

Imagine the child's surprise when her Barbie said "Eat lead, Cobra." And what did the boy think when his GI Joe said, "Let's go shopping,"?

◆ According to Athenaeus, a Greek writer who wrote circa A.D. 200, at the time of the Trojan War, a marble game was popular. In their book, Ancient Inventions, authors Peter James and Nick Thorpe write: "While the hero Odysseus was making his long journey back from Troy, the suitors to his queen, Penelope, played a game against each other: one marble represented the queen; the first to hit it had another turn, and if he succeeded again, then he was first in line to propose to her."

Chapter 4

The Making of a Pro: Getting Started in Toy Invention

"Advancements in technology have made this a very challenging time for toy designers. Robotics, computers, and new materials give us capability to heighten a child's experience with a toy or game. We are training our designers to produce these toys of tomorrow where we will offer new ways for children to explore the world."

—Judy Ellis, founder and chair, Toy Design Program, Fashion Institute of Technology, New York

"Never give up, never grow up."

—Julie Cooper, longtime R&D executive and
then independent toy inventor

"I changed into a grown-up, but I'm really a kid."

—Josh Baskin, played by Tom Hanks in the movie *Big*

These three quotes aptly characterize what it takes to be a toy inventor today. The first is the perception of the head of an institution that formally prepares people with the essential tools to contribute to the creative development of new toys and games. The second is advice from an industry veteran who has "been there, done that, and got the T-shirt" vis-à-vis perseverance and commitment to new toy ideas. The third nails the reality that many inventors may be mature in stature but a bit juvenile in their creative endeavors.

The Origin of Inventors

Like all mortals, toy inventors are born. They pass through rebellious years of puberty before continuing with some higher education that leads them to the start of a career. Current members of the professional inventing community have diverse training—everything from the priesthood to a Ph.D. in psychology. Regardless of where they started, at some time in their lives, cosmic and celestial powers aligned to move them to use their creativity to originate ideas for new toys and games.

Many inventors worked at toy companies or in associated industries (retail, ad agencies, licensing, and so on). Then one day, driven by a strong sense of entrepreneurship, in response to a business condition like a merger or bankruptcy, or just because of an itch, they joined the ranks of the professional inventing community. Others started working for a professional inventor organization right out of design or engineering school. Then at some point, having developed corporate relationships and a savvy for the ebb and flow of the business, they broke out solo or joined others in a new start-up company. All these people share certain basic characteristics:

- ◆ **Capacity for reproduction:** Inspired by other inventors, they have the ability to motivate others to become toy and game inventors. This is done through various forms of mentoring. Professional inventors are a very sharing species.
- ◆ **Growth potential:** They mature in the business, honing their creative and entrepreneurial skills through constant exposure to a broad range of products, technologies, companies, executives, and experiences.
- ◆ **Unique metabolism:** The best and the brightest are high-energy, passionate people. Although biological energy is derived mainly from sunlight, inventors are energized by risk, opportunity, and challenge.
- ◆ **Movement:** Inventive people break the collective framework that imprisons noncreative types. Mentally and physically, no natural boundary corrals them.
- ◆ **Responsiveness:** Pros sense and respond to changes in their environment. The toy industry throws stimuli at them on an almost daily basis.
- ◆ **Adaptation:** Inventors learn to survive in a three-ring, Barnum and Bailey enterprise that, like its sister entertainment industries of film, television, theater, and music, thrives on trends, bally-hoos, egos, advertising, originality—and smoke and mirrors.

All in the Family

The other species of inventor swam in the right gene pool. These people grew up in the industry because of a parent who set the stage for them. The Fuhrer brothers maintain offices on the East and West coasts; Bob (Crocodile Dentist) is in New York, and David (Backwords) is in L.A. The Becker brothers, Jonathan and Roger, maintain the broker/agent business; Anjar (Othello) is at the Toy Center on Fifth Avenue, started by their father, Jim, 40 years ago. Adam, Andy, and Noah Kislovitz started their inventing business, The OBB (Diva Starz), after watching their parents create and build Colorforms. Martin Golfarb (Shark Attack) works with his father, the legendary A. Eddy Goldfarb (Stompers), in Northridge, California. When asked who got him into toy invention, Martin responds affectionately, "My pop!"

Another father/son team is the Ellmans (Mr. Potato Head), Julius (Julie) and Steve. Steve credits a home enriched by the inventions of Julie and his original partner, George Lerner, as well as an artistic mother, as the big factors in narrowing his career choice to creating and developing toy ideas.

Michael Kohner is another industry creative who grew up in a household deeply involved with the industry. His family ran Kohner Bros., the original maker of Busy Box, Busy Bath, Trouble, and other classics. Says Michael of his start, "I was raised in the business. It's in my blood." Though not mentioned by Michael, early exposure to the toy world at Kohner included experiences with the energy, drive, and product sense of Fred Kroll, whose industry tenure and over 65 Toy Fair appearances have touched us all.

Burt Meyer, credited with creating Lite Brite, Toss Across, Rock'em Sock'em Robots, and other classic toys and games, was a partner in the premier invention house for the toy industry, Marvin Glass Associates (MGA) in Chicago. Looking back at growing up in a rich toy environment, Burt's son, Steve, recalls many after-hours trips with his father to the MGA shop, where he saw new ideas in various stages of completion. "Often times I never knew which ideas really got produced until I saw them under a friend's Christmas tree a year or two later. I guess I learned pretty early by seeing my father's work that Santa had a lot of help making toys," smiles Steve. Today Steve heads Chicago-based Meyer Glass Design. Before managing a staff of 20 creatives that originates a range of concepts from preschool toys to electronic games, Steve was vice president of development at MicroProse, the computer gaming company.

Creativity Loves Company

Though not genetic residents of the inventing community, descendants of earlier key members of the industry-at-large also impact inventors. The most important is Alan G. Hassenfeld, chairman and CEO of Hasbro since 1989. Hasbro is the second largest toy company in the world and home to Hasbro Games, the world's largest game and puzzle marketer.

Hassenfeld worked his way up the corporate ladder in the business started by his grandfather in 1923. After graduating from the University of Pennsylvania, he took on a variety of challenges, including jobs in domestic and international marketing and sales. He was named vice president of international operations in 1972. He also held positions as vice president of marketing and sales, and executive vice president before being named president in 1984 and chairman in 1989.

In 1994, Hassenfeld was inducted into the Toy Industry Hall of Fame. His late father, Merrill, and late brother, Stephen, were inducted into the Toy Industry Hall of Fame in 1985 and 1991, respectively.

Another CEO born to the industry is at the helm of Pressman Toy Corporation, the third largest game manufacturer in the United States. The company was founded in 1922 by Jack Pressman; his son, Jim Pressman, was voted president in 1977.

Jim Pressman started very young. In 1959, he appeared on the cover of the company's catalog holding a toy doctor's kit. He started working for the family business in the late 1960s while on summer vacation from Boston University. Like Hassenfeld, Pressman worked his way up from manufacturing to the front office.

Though many years removed from the industry, arguably the single most important management contributor to the growth of a company during the 1940s through the mid-1980s was the Shea father/son team: James Sr. and James Jr. The long history of the game giant Milton Bradley is delightfully told by James J. Shea Sr. in a book titled *It's All in the Game*. Shea tells of assuming the presidency of Milton Bradley in December 1941, when the company was floundering so badly that a consulting firm recommended "liquidation."

After stopping the financial bleeding, Shea focused on "the kinds of games Americans want to play." In his search, he welcomed all inventors, and the takers were numerous. Shea was inducted into the Toy Industry Hall of Fame in 1988.

Early licensors/inventors included an engineer (Magic Mary), a recuperating patient (Candy Land), a newspaperman (Uncle Wiggily), retail store employees (Go to the Head of the Class), an accountant (Rack-O), and a teacher (Quizmo).

Never Too Young, Always Young at Heart

At one time the industry could claim members ranging in age from 8 to 80. The upper end of this range will remain anonymous. However, the underage inventrix was none other than Bettie Levy, in 1987 the elementary school–age daughter of co-author and co-creative principals in Richard C. Levy and Associates. She got through the door of Hasbro Games as a "junior associate" in the Levy organization. An obviously well coached Bettie then made a convincing demonstration of her fully playable board game concept, Here Comes the Bride, to the other co-author, who at the time was in a product acquisition position at Hasbro Games.

Bettie's creation did not make it at the world's largest game company because of "theme issues." Nonetheless, the game did make it into the Ungame Company line, where it remained on the market for several years. Time has passed, and Bettie has taken her degree training into another venue of the entertainment business. It is assured that if she has another toy or game concept in the future, it will be presented by her agents, Richard and Sheryl Levy.

Like Bettie, some youthful inventors may flirt with fame before they move to other careers in search of fortune. However, Hasbro Hall of Famer Greg Hyman started at age 13 and remains in the idea business today.

Before embarking on toy invention, Hyman started a business to outfit neighborhood homes with crude security systems. He says of the service, "I actually hot-wired several residences with sound alarms that an intruder would trip if there was a break at several entry points. Maybe I should have continued inventing security devices, but I doubt that it would have been as much fun as creating Alphie or Tickle Me Elmo," he concludes with a broad smile.

Several other pros recall an early start with their invention work.

Steve Ellman claims a beginning as a professional toy inventor at age seven. While blowing bubbles with his brother Fred, Steve accidentally dipped a large open-ended cardboard tube in solution to blow bubbles. The result was bubbles that were larger than normal. Steve recalls showing his find to his dad because he was so proud of the new size of bubbles. Julie Ellman eventually used the approach in the world's first musical bubble maker. "I should have asked Julie to put some of the royalties aside for my college fund," quips Steve.

Brendan Boyle, creator of Fib Finder (Pressman) and Aerobie Football (Superflight), remembers, "As a kid, I had a love for taking things apart, but I was often unable to put them back together." Gary Donner, inventor of Phase 10 Dice (Fundex) and Monster Stomp (Artistoplay), recalls, "I always loved to play games as a child and then as an adult. I began coming up with my own. There is great satisfaction in making a toy or game work."

As a highly precocious three-year-old, David Vogel remembers his parents taking him to the Thomas A. Edison laboratory in West Orange, New Jersey. While on the trip, Vogel told them he wanted to be an inventor when he grew up. Says David, "I've been tinkering ever since."

Richard Blank may claim the earliest intensive exposure to the toy industry, toddling into commercials at age 3 and making regular appearances in TV spots until age 15. "I've been coming to New York Toy Fair for 40 years," claims Blank. Richard reiterates his years of experience in which he has licensed over 100 products: "28 years of inventing, 18 years of character licensing, and 13 years as a lawyer mostly related to industry business." When asked who he credits with such a long but ongoing career, Richard simply says, "My father, David Blank."

Breaking in at an Early Age—and Without Know-Who

Young inventors like Bettie, Greg, Steve, Brendan, and Gary can jump-start their careers early through organized creative contests sponsored by companies such as Wild Planet (www.wildplanet.com) and University Games (www.ugames.com). These companies encourage children to use originality in designing their own toys and games. Inventors of all ages who want to know more about these programs should visit their websites.

Bob Moog, president of University Games started the National Young Game Inventors Contest (NYGIC) in 1995 to find kids (5–12) who had the creativity and imagination to invent and design board games. The model for the contest is similar to the Science Fair, in that it can be co-curricular or extracurricular.

Finalists are selected out of nearly 1,000 entries each year. Then a judge's panel selects the winning game. The game is manufactured in the following year. Winners include Take a Hike, Twisted Tales, Jungle Adventure Game, Rapunzel's Revenge, and Mouse Round Up (2002). The inspiration for the contest was Din-O-mite, the dinosaur adventure game, invented by nine-year-old Josh White in 1987.

The most successful game was Take-a-Hike, invented by five-year-old Derek Nelson. It sold more than 50,000 units and was translated into 4 languages and sold in more than a dozen countries."

As incentives, University Games offers the contest winner a trip to San Francisco, a home game and puzzle library, and a $10,000 savings bond for college.

Training for Today's Real World of Toy Invention

The skill sets most helpful in preparing a product for current company needs are changing as products become more sophisticated. In the future, career preparation will likely skew toward degrees in industrial design, computer programming, the arts (fine arts or graphic arts), engineering, and marketing or accounting. The ability to work in 2D and 3D CAD systems also is important.

The professional inventing business already has many members who were schooled as industrial designers. They were trained to think of ideas in three dimensions. Others formally trained to apply skills to the invention business are illustrators who can conceptualize in two-dimensional art/sketch renderings filled with graphics and detailed callouts of product functions.

The importance of good design to illustrate an idea cannot be overstated. Designers can often put a pretty face on an ugly idea. They can add the sizzle of an interesting form while defining the final function.

Outstanding programs for those preparing to enter the toy industry are available at the Fashion Institute of Technology in New York and the Otis College of Art and Design in Los Angeles.

F.I.T.: Learning to Be Elves

The Toy Design program at the Fashion Institute of Technology is the first degree-granting department of its kind. Enjoying a close relationship with the Toy Industry Association (TIA) and considered by many to be the best of its kind, F.I.T. has a unique curriculum that offers students the opportunity to participate in every aspect of toy design and manufacture. More than 120 F.I.T. Toy Design alumni work in almost all of the leading toy manufacturers and inventor groups, including ALEX, Binney & Smith, BMT, Disney, Hasbro, K'NEX, Leapfrog/Knowledge, LEGO, Lucas Arts, Madame Alexander, Mattel and Mattel Fisher-Price brands, Nickelodeon, Rose Art, and Wild Planet Toys. Each of these companies has toys on the market designed by F.I.T. alumni, many of whom have won industry awards.

The primary goal of the Toy Design Department is to train young designers to create products that have a lasting impact on children by stimulating creativity. The students at F.I.T. are educated to think beyond making passable toys. Explains program founder and chairperson Judy Ellis, "A really great toy invites discovery, enhances a child's play environment, and is fun, educational, and age appropriate." The faculty and students at F.I.T. believe that "really great" toys respect and honor children.

The program also strives to turn out inventors who are on the cutting edge of toy design. To do so, they must address both artistic and practical matters and learn to be mindful of financial, safety, and creative concerns. Inventor Steve Meyer says that one of the things that impresses him most is the way F.I.T.'s program simulates actual inventor and design groups. "The people coming out of the program have a very well-rounded understanding of the toy industry, which is what we look for in inventors," he says. The curriculum provides technical skills, production skills, marketing skills, and analytical and interpretive skills that allow students to translate their creative concepts into products that can be manufactured in a cost-effective way.

Competition to fill the 20 or so spots in F.I.T.'s Toy Design program is tough. As the applicant pool continues to grow in both numbers and diversity, F.I.T. looks for the most focused, responsible, and hard-working students. Foremost is the ability to draw and conceptualize: Students must be able to form original ideas and reproduce them on paper. In addition, successful candidates are driven, think like designers, and hold themselves to a high ethical standard. The department is designed so that people who succeed in the program will succeed in the industry.

Of the 21 or 22 new students who enter F.I.T.'s Toy Design each year, 50 to 60 percent come from other colleges or universities, or already have degrees and are re-entering school to study toy design. The rest come from F.I.T.

Toy Trivia

32. Which company introduced Trivial Pursuit in 1984?

a. Milton Bradley

b. Selchow and Righter

c. Parker Brothers

F.I.T.: A Look Inside the Toy Design Department

F.I.T.'s Toy Design Department is a rigorous two-year Bachelor's program that reflects the experience of an industry design team. Students must enroll full-time, and each student completes a summer internship and intense winterim experience. The classes are designed to build on each other; by the end of their schooling, students have created a number of prototypes and designed countless other concepts. They have a healthy portfolio filled with the kind of finished sketches, ideation sketches, and engineering drawings that toy companies look for. Students also have experience working with children in a variety of outreach programs under the Discover Together program, in which they interact with children of all ages and with different kinds of needs.

During the mandatory summer internship, students work at manufacturing and design firms on existing toy lines, brainstorming new product concepts, engineering prototypes, developing marketing strategies, and presenting their ideas to management— always bringing in work within budget and production guidelines.

411 To keep up on the fast-breaking news in the world of intellectual property, log on every day to www.ipo.org. Intellectual Property Owners' IPO Daily News is the best source for information across the complete range of IP issues.

F.I.T.: Life After

The Toy Design Department is proactive in placing its graduates, with 90 percent of students already placed in jobs before commencement. Every step of the process is overseen by director Judy Ellis, whose contacts and experience take the guesswork out of looking for a job. Ellis is the founder of the Toy Design Program, which she launched in 1989. An innovative educator and designer with an extensive background in curriculum and program development, Ellis shapes all aspects of the department. She provides an intensive and personal approach to education, counseling students through the program and in their professional careers.

A graduate of Parsons School of Design with a BFA in Communication Design, Ellis has enjoyed a career rich with educational and professional experience. As a professor of graphic design at Parsons for seven years, she launched the consulting company Graphics for the Environment, which counted among its clients the Amerada Hess Corporation, Clairol, and IBM. As a designer at Chermayeff and Geismar, Ellis designed an award-winning permanent bicentennial exhibition at the Smithsonian Institution and large-scale murals for IBM.

Neil Friedman, president of the Fisher-Price division of Mattel, counts many F.I.T. alumni among his employees. "The department has been an invaluable resource to the toy industry, and its graduates have been invaluable to the companies they work for," he says. "The F.I.T. Toy Design Department has given its students the ability to understand the workings of the toy industry, as well as unleashing the creativity that has enabled the companies they're associated with to grow to new heights and take products to new levels of success."

Pertinent information about applying to the program can be found on F.I.T.'s website (www.fitnyc.edu) or through the Toy Industry Association, which has a page dedicated to F.I.T.'s program (www.toy-tia.com/ATI/F.I.T.).

Toy Trivia

33. What is Barbie's complete name?

a. Barbie Jo Roberts

b. Barbara Jo Slate

c. Barbie Melissa Handler

Breaking In: Otis Toy Design

"Toy designers are the heart and soul of Mattel," says Matt Bousquette, president, Mattel Brands. "We have more than 600 designers, many of whom are Otis graduates. Mattel and Otis share a special relationship because of our mutual passion for designing innovative toys that capture the imagination of kids. There is a great deal of talent and creativity embodied in the Otis students, faculty, and graduates."

Otis College of Art and Design was founded in 1918. Located in Los Angeles, California, Otis recruits students from as many as 39 states and 26 countries with 77 percent of those students receiving some type of financial aid. Otis is the only four-year college that offers an accredited Bachelor of Arts degree in Toy Design. The program boasts a 95 percent job-placement rate of internships and graduates in such companies as Mattel, Disney, Hasbro, Pleasant Company, Equity Marketing, JAKKS Pacific, Strottman, Applause, Chicco, JMP Creative, Lanard Toys, and Neurosmith, among others. "The Toy Design program at Otis gave me a seamless transition from the classroom to the Toy Industry." says Gerry Cody, Senior Toy Designer for Sport-Fun Inc. "The faculty demanded critical thinking, and strategic problem solving."

At Otis, every member of the faculty is a toy industry professional. Martin Caveza is the founding chair of the Otis toy design department. "I created the Otis program based on the combination of abilities one needs to be a good toy designer," explains Caveza. "You've got to be a designer, an engineer, and a marketing person. Otis grads hit the ground running with their proficiency in these diverse areas." Before joining Otis, Caveza enjoyed a career at Mattel where he managed the Nickelodeon Brand Design group. During his 13-year tenure at Mattel, he managed and designed a vast array of products from concept through production within many different toy categories. An award-winning designer, Caveza currently divides his time between his chair responsibilities, consulting, and inventing toys for submission to the toy and pet industries. He graduated magna cum laude, with a Bachelor of Science degree in industrial design from Arizona State University.

Jennifer Lizzio is assistant chair of the toy design department. She received a Bachelor of Arts degree in advertising and English from Penn State University. She completed a mass communications program at the University of Manchester in England and received her MFA in creative writing from Emerson College in Boston. Before joining Otis, Lizzio enjoyed a 12-year toy industry career in the fields of marketing and advertising. She handled the Hasbro account at Grey Advertising, creating strategic campaigns for Parker Brothers. She also worked in marketing at Mattel on brands ranging from Games to Preschool to Dolls, and as Director of Marketing for Disney at Fisher-Price in New York.

Among the other toy industry professionals on the Otis faculty are Alan Cusolito, who works in the Games group at Mattel, developing hot products such as the Survivor board game, Harry Potter's Levitating Challenge, and UNO Attack. Eric Ostendorff is a design engineer who created the mechanism for products such as Fireball and OctoBlast. During Drew Plakos' 30-year career, he engineered products such as See

N'Say, Barbie accessories, and classic games like Perfection, Othello, and Electronic Battleship. Lili Davidson and Robin Smith have designed numerous dolls including Magic Nursery, Cabbage Patch, and Disney Princesses. Deborah Ryan designed such notable toys as Swan Lake Barbie, and licensed plush characters for *Sesame Street* and Warner Bros. These individuals represent only a sampling of Otis' award-winning faculty.

The goal of the toy design curriculum is to produce highly skilled designers who can translate ideas into merchandise that will be competitive within the marketplace. The curriculum focuses on prominent categories relevant to the industry. Sophomores design plush, infant, and preschool toys. Juniors concentrate on vehicles and action figures, while seniors focus on dolls, games, and corporate sponsored projects. In addition to stressing the technical and creative side of toy design, the program features a solid foundation of liberal arts courses such as child psychology, math for designers, business practices, history of toys, anatomy, and ergonomics, as well as communication and presentation skills. In conjunction with their academic studies, juniors and seniors have the opportunity to participate in summer internships at many of the toy companies affiliated with Otis. Additionally, interning students often move into full-time employment with these companies after graduation.

Otis has formed corporate sponsorship programs with Mattel and Disney, which not only underscore Otis' close alliance with the toy industry, but also prepare students for their careers. These unique partnerships enable students to work with seasoned professionals in a creative exchange that simulates a real working environment. For the Mattel Senior Studio Project, Mattel designers propose ideas and then critique students' work during an eight-week period. The final products not only have the potential of being marketed in the industry, but students also compete for cash prizes, scholarships, and jobs. In a similar scholarship program, Otis seniors design products based on existing Disney properties or newly developed internal initiatives. The students' work is then critiqued by a Disney creative team from concept through finished models.

To learn more about Otis Toy Design, contact Martin Caveza or Jennifer Lizzio at 310-665-6985 or go to the web at www.Otis.edu. For application information, contact the Office of Admissions toll free at 1-800-527-OTIS, e-mail otisinfo@otis.edu, or write to the Otis Toy Design Department C/O Otis College of Art and Design, 9045 Lincoln Boulevard, Los Angeles, CA 90045-3305.

Women in Toys

If you are a female inventor, a wonderful organization for networking and building friendships is Women in Toys. Founded in 1991 by industry veterans Susan Matsumoto and Anne Pitrone, Women in Toys (WIT) serves as a networking base for professional working women within the toy industry and related industries and to acknowledge and promote the achievements of its members. "There were so many wonderful women in the toy industry, but no real way for us all to meet each other," states Matsumoto on the primary reason she and Pitrone decided to start the organization.

Since 1991, WIT has sponsored a Toy Fair dinner every year, where hundreds of industry women have gathered to meet, renew friendships, network, and also honor an outstanding woman in the toy industry. One of the first honorees was Ruth Handler, founder (with her husband Elliot) of Mattel Toys.

WIT has also sponsored regional groups in the Los Angeles, New England, and San Francisco areas; seminars at Toy Fair on relevant topics in the toy industry; and a social hour and seminars at the Licensing Show. WIT offers many positive opportunities to its membership. Go to www.womenintoys.com for the latest membership information, applications, and fees.

Getting the Big Break

In business, breaking in is often the toughest step; creative work with toys is no different. The following three stories detail the paths taken by three major contributors to the creative product development side of the business today.

On Wisconsin Inventors

Peggy Brown offers a prospective on being more than a lone inventor. With partner Gina Hartliep, Brown started Milwaukee-based Alley Oop in 1991 and did everything from ideation to final product and package art, both as contract work and on speculation. After eight years at Alley Oop, she is now vice president of product development at Patch Products.

Toy Trivia

34. Who is the group publisher of *Playthings* magazine?

a. Maria N. Weiskott

b. Andrea Morris

c. Barbara J. Slate

Brown feels it would have been extremely difficult to start Alley Oop, a full-service design shop, had it not been for the experience and contacts gained working inside a large company like Western Publishing. First of all, there is knowledge of how an internal R&D process works, what services are needed, and how they are divided up and doled out to the outside vendors.

Brown says about showing a broad range of capabilities, "Having a portfolio of projects we worked on at Western was key to pitching other toy companies for work. And the contract design and development work we did for other major toy companies helped validate our own speculative invention work. Each completed product only added to our viability as a development source to prospective new clients. In addition, at a time when most toy companies were closing their doors to amateur submissions, our portfolio got us in with the professional inventors.

"Sometimes we were brought in to breathe fresh ideas into a struggling line. Sometimes we were brought in along with an army of independents to design and build products for Toy Fair, and frequently we were 'scapegoated' with hopeless products that nobody in-house had the nerve to kill themselves."

As an external vendor, Brown liked working with the middle-size companies best since big companies have deep development and art groups and don't really need much help. On the other hand, tiny companies often don't have the budgets to pay for outside development. Most of the middle-size companies have limited creative staff in-house, and need expertise to nip at the heels of the giants.

Brown says starting out as independent designers was exciting, but the realities of running a design business—or any business, for that matter—can be brutal. Instead of creating all the time like they did on the inside, the partners were faced with all the facets of small business: marketing themselves, writing proposals, pitching new business, and managing the details of insurance plans, leases, contract negotiations, lines of credit, personnel, payroll, lawyers, bankers, accountants, and on and on. They couldn't just spend eight hours a day making toys anymore.

Toy Fair was a huge event for Alley Oop because every one of its clients and every one of its prospects worldwide was within a three-block radius of each other for a solid week. "Although we made the rounds and toured all the major show rooms, it was really at the company parties where we did the best networking and got the most new business," Brown explains. "We did schlep the portfolio around to try for contract design work during Toy Fair, but generally toy company execs are in a selling mode during the show and don't have time or patience to be sold."

Over the eight years Alley Oop was open, they watched the industry change. Brown continues, "Initially we had some great success with inventions and made good income from option agreements on top of contract design income. As the years passed, however, it became harder and harder to land invention contracts, and even though the graphic design and illustration portion of our business grew steadily, the development portion slowed. Hasbro bought Western and closed its creative center. Many of our other clients throughout the industry were swallowed up, too, either by Hasbro or Mattel. By that time we had a tremendous toy and game portfolio and nobody to sell to."

In hindsight, she reflects, it was well worth the risk, but knowing how the business has changed, Brown would hesitate to do it again in today's climate without a pocketful of contacts. As a long-time toy person, she says it's good to be back in the trenches making product-development decisions and forming new toy lines rather than pounding the pavement or trying to collect accounts receivable.

"Everything I learned on the outside over the years bolsters the decisions I make every day on the inside," Brown says. "Many of my contacts are still around, going out on their own as consultants, and then later surfacing again with other toy companies." Concluding her thoughts about creative R&D and seeing ideas evolve into real products, whether inside a company or outside as a professional inventor, Brown says, "I guess once your heart is in the toy business, you're in it for good."

West Coast Innovators

Whereas Brown did the independent inventing scene before returning to corporate life, the K.I.D. Group of San Francisco has been an independent product source for 12 years. Dan Klitsner heads the group of eight designers who has met success and continue to meet the annual idea challenge. Among their most successful products are Bop-It, Bop-It Extreme (Hasbro Games), Crash Back R/C (Kenner), Mr. Piano (MegaBloks), Uno Blitzo (Mattel), and Keyboard Toppers (Hasbro Interactive).

Says Klitsner of his emergence, "I started out knowing I wanted to create things, but not sure what that profession was called. I was guided into engineering at U.C. Davis, where after two years I got a clear picture that being an engineer wasn't the answer. I wanted to come up with ideas and design the look and feel of product. Creating ideas sounded like more fun than specifying the draft angles and wall thickness of molded parts.

"Luckily, my father, an actor, knew I was unhappy and mentioned my dilemma to a graduate of the Art Center in Pasadena. Dad sent for a catalog. When I saw it, I knew I had found my calling and discovered that there was a field called industrial design. I fell in love with the vision of being able to earn a living thinking of ideas and using my hands to build models and design products."

After Art Center, Klitsner worked at a company where he conceptualized robots for home use and with engineers who were supposed to build them. This venture ended up as a bust, but he had fun. "I began designing consumer products for Discovery Toys while continuing to build some other nontoy clients to cover bills. I freelanced as an architectural illustrator as well as did work with corporate identity firms designing anything from airline interiors to cola bottles."

Klitsner developed over 15 products for Discovery Toys and then decided that it would be good to have more than one client in the toy industry. He started researching how the mass-market toy companies bought ideas from inventors and felt it was like a dream come true—that is, to pitch ideas to the companies whose toys he played with as a child.

Of special interest were game companies because he had always had the greatest time playing games with friends and family. He calculated that if 20 percent of K.I.D.'s time was speculating, he could absorb the overhead of a staff of three designer/model makers to work on toy ideas in the downtime between other nontoy projects. Eventually, to the plan was to transition to 80 percent inventing and 20 percent nontoy design work.

"It took five years to get there, but luckily that is the formula that seems to be working today. Over the course of a few months, I came up with a dozen ideas to take to Toy Fair 1990 to pitch to product acquisition representatives. My portfolio of successful products for Discovery Toys helped me get my appointments, but I knew that the ideas needed to be much more commercial than my preschool products."

Recalling his first day at his first Toy Fair, Klitsner says, "My first day in NYC, I had a meeting with Ron Weingartner at Milton Bradley. He seemed to like many of the concepts and encouraged me to continue coming up with ideas. Eventually, I licensed Go Go Worms to Milton Bradley, which was shown to Ron at that initial meeting as a sketch and video of a working prototype. I was ecstatic to have placed a game with such a well-known and high-quality company."

K.I.D. Group licensed or optioned several products in each of the next few years, and although many of them never hit the market, the advances funded more ideation time. Many of the concepts had features based on interactive electronics and were sold with the help of flashy computer simulations that showed motion, lights, and sounds.

"It seems today we need to build much more intricate prototypes, probably because the ideas are more sophisticated and the ergonomics are so tied into the interface," Klitsner concludes. "Occasionally, we can still license an idea based upon a faked video or simple mockup, but it all depends on the idea and its simplicity. My strong wish is for us to find more simple ones."

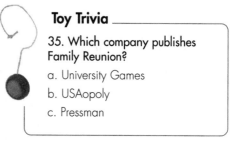

Toy Trivia

35. Which company publishes Family Reunion?

a. University Games

b. USAopoly

c. Pressman

The Game Diva of Connecticut

Cathy Rondeau had an interesting approach that ultimately helped her "break into" toy marketers. She did not ask them to license her item for *their* line; instead, she asked them to do contract manufacturing for *her* line. How's that for innovative?

She says of her contact with then industry giant Coleco, "I was hand-sculpting items and selling them at retail and wholesale. Lord & Taylor saw my stuff and placed a large order. There was no way to fill it on my own, so I looked into mold making and manufacturing in general. With three little kids, the time commitment for my own production was inconceivable. I wrote a letter to Coleco and detailed my situation and success. They took an option on the concept. I spent the next two years or so model making and pattern designing. After my sculpting projects, I kept the contacts by showing other ideas."

Of her early meetings to show concepts, Rondeau says, "My first meeting was with Jerry Wood. He was a professional and never made me feel like the neophyte I was. He helped me understand the process, and I feel he was fair with me. On the other hand, I had many other meetings at which the principals were less than professional or courteous. It can be a very rough business."

She continues, "In one meeting, a president of a company sat there and never spoke. He'd just dropped or raised his thumb after every submission. Today I wouldn't tolerate that treatment, but I was just a kid then. Today I make it a point not to work with people I don't trust or respect."

Preparation Goes a Long Way

As demonstrated by the experiences of Brown, Klitsner, and Rondeau, the pros know the importance of presentation and painstaking preparations for any face-to-face meeting with company representatives. The step-by-step details of how to make a pitch are covered in Chapter 7. However, the importance of the "big show" dictates extra emphasis on readiness, especially for inventors just breaking into the idea business.

You'll never break in if your powers of presentation aren't well honed. A carefully planned and rehearsed pitch is a must, since you're explaining and displaying concepts to viewers who are obviously unfamiliar with what they're about to see. You hope to get their full attention at such meetings, but often your presentation may be interrupted by "emergency" calls that break the continuity of any demonstration. You should be grateful if you're able to present without disruption. The importance of the presentation meeting demands the right amount of time, attention, and concentration by both presenter and viewer. However, if there are disruptions or distractions, you need to be flexible enough to deal with them.

411

Patent Search Room
Crystal Plaza 3, Room 1A01
2021 Crystal Drive
Arlington, VA 22202
Tel: 703-308-0595
Hours: Weekdays (except holidays)
8:00 A.M. to 8:00 P.M.

The inventor meeting is like a relay race in which a baton—the submitted idea—is passed on to the next runner. The inventor starts the race and must give a performance that inspires the next carrier to run as fast and hard as the inventor did on the first leg. If you are slow out of the box, juggle the baton, or run out of gas during the presentation, don't expect the carrier of your concept to be very motivated—if it moves ahead at all.

One of the strangest and most disruptive meetings took place between an inventor and co-author Ron Weingartner early in his career as a new product manager for an educational aids manufacturer in Chicago. He had an agreement to meet an award-winning educator from the upper Midwest. She had been in the running for Elementary Teacher of the Year in North Dakota and, coincidentally, was passing through Chicago on a summer vacation. Though Weingartner thought it was odd that she was traveling by bus, he agreed to meet her at the Greyhound terminal and have the presentation at a nearby hotel meeting room.

Little did he know that the July weather would be in the upper 90s and that the educator/inventor would have only 45 minutes between arrival and departure. With so little time, the meeting could hardly be moved to a more desirable location. Teacher-made models were taken out of two shopping bags, unwrapped, and shown in the noisy, crowded public bus terminal.

None of the models was kept for further review—not because of the temperature, the location, or the demonstration, but because they all lacked commercial potential.

Nonetheless, the lesson was learned: Never look at concepts when the meeting-place temperature exceeds 90°, and never, never look at items in a mass transit terminal—even to accommodate inventor schedules.

When asked how many items she can show effectively, Cathy Rondeau says it depends on the circumstances. "I rarely show more than three. It isn't likely that I have more than three things in inventory that are suitable for any given company. I've had people present products to me and it often seems when they have six or seven items [that] they are just throwing stuff against a wall to see what sticks. I am more likely to take projects further along in development than to sketch an idea on a napkin. I have, however, sold ideas by simply describing what I have in mind. The trick there is to trust the other person and to know that they have a capacity for vision. Unfortunately, most people are very concrete."

Asked how many no's it takes before she puts a concept back into her closet, Rondeau responds, "I don't put an idea away unless the reason given for rejection is something like a safety issue, or it has been done before, or it's simply cost-prohibitive. There are so many variables in the decision-making process, not the least of which is timing.

"I may put an item on the shelf for a bit, but if the idea keeps returning to me, then I usually feel there is some merit and the project is revisited. Sometimes it's simply a question of my having missed an angle or a new spin on the idea. As Rodin said, 'I invent nothing. I rediscover.' So much of what we do is about looking at something that already exists and putting our own little peculiar mark on it. And since I am a different individual every day, my concepts grow with me," concludes a daily rejuvenated Rondeau.

Toy Trivia

36. In which year did the teddy bear celebrate its one hundredth anniversary?

a. 2002

b. 2003

c. 2000

TIALIMAIDSANSSEA: Convergence of Creativity

If you can decode that string of 16 letters, you are well on your way to finding potential outlets for your future efforts.

As the industry turned the Y2K corner, it became less about doodling on a napkin, tinkering in the basement, or turning a lathe. Much of the invention business is now about information processing. Inventors as never before are in need of company pulses, consumer trends, marketing strategies, technologies, or glimpses of niche markets.

Those 16 letters represent organizations that can help you gather pieces of the market puzzle. This help should enhance new creations and presentations to marketers. An informed inventor's concepts stand better chances of survival. A rule to keep in mind is: If you know what's goin' on in the market, your latest offering will hit the hot button of marketers who must know what's goin' on.

Savvy professionals spend time at the industry functions sponsored by the TIA (toys and games), LIMA (licensing), IDSA (electronics), and NSSEA (education business). Whether surfing the websites of these organizations or walking the aisles of their shows, information will help to infuse relevance and currency into your ideas.

Trading Places

Trade shows are a very important element in the process of understanding the toy industry, keeping up with new product introductions, exposing yourself to innovative stimuli, and networking among corporate types, other inventors, vendors, and so forth.

Trade shows are not always the best place to sell ideas. Companies have paid tens of thousands of dollars or more—in some cases, millions—to participate in a trade show, and they're there to ring up sales. Companies attend trade shows to sell, not to buy. Having said that, frequently non–sales executives attend shows, too—people from R&D, marketing, and so on. For that reason, shows can be a great venue in which to meet because you're outside the formal office setting and everyone's more casual.

It was at a trade show that the inventors of the Spin Pop, four former postal workers, found Cap Toys. "It's one of those great American success stories," Deirdre Gonzales, Cap's vice president of marketing, told the Associated Press. The Spin Pop was introduced by Cap in 1993, and it took off. "It really sort of invigorated the field of interactive candy," Gonzales said. Since 1993, it has sold more than 90 million units.

The Cost of Admission

Trade shows do not typically charge professionals an entry fee. If you're in business and can show a business card and stationery, this is often enough. Some shows, though, like the American International Toy Fair, require three forms of identification that indicate affiliation with the toy industry. No one under 18, including child inventors, is allowed to attend the Javits Center exhibit halls.

Following below is a list of domestic trade events that are attended by professional toy and game inventors. This list is current as of spring 2003. Since a book has a long shelf life, and you may be reading this many years after initial publication, for the most current information, go to the Toy Industry Association or trade magazines, such as *Playthings.* Their respective websites are as follows:

1. www.toy-tia.org
2. www.playthings.com
3. www.expocentral.com

For the aforesaid reason, we do not list specific contact people—only numbers to the organizers. Shows are listed according to the month in which they historically take place, although certain domestic shows may rotate venues.

The most important domestic trade show is the American International Toy Fair. It operates yearly the second week of February in New York City. It's the place for serious players. If you can't visit the show or don't qualify for entry, you can purchase the Official Toy Fair Directory from the Toy Industry Association (TIA). It lists all exhibitors from A to Z, along with their product lines, addresses, phones, faxes, websites, and so on. You will find yourself referring to it throughout the year as an invaluable desktop resource.

Call the TIA at 212-675-1141 to see if copies are still available.

> **Toy Trivia**
>
> 37. Which company introduced Furby? The year was 1998.
> a. Mattel
> b. Tiger Electronics
> c. WowWee

January

International Consumer Electronics Show (CES)

Las Vegas Convention Center
Las Vegas, Nevada
Tel: 703-907-7600
Fax: 703-907-7602
Website: www.cesweb.org

The world's largest annual trade show for consumer technology, the CES showcases innovations from 2,000 manufacturers, developers, and suppliers of consumer technology hardware, content media, technology delivery systems, and related products. It attracts over 100,000 attendees from the United States and more than 100 other countries.

Dallas International Toy Import Show (DITIS)
Dallas Market Center
Dallas, Texas
Tel: 214-655-6100
Fax: 214-655-7646
Website: www.dallasmarketcenter.com

DITIS is designed to serve a targeted microretail audience. This is not a good show for inventors unless you have a previously arranged meeting.

HIA Annual Convention/Trade Show
Anaheim Convention Center
Anaheim, California
Tel: 201-794-1133
Fax: 201-797-0657
Website: www.hobby.org

February

American International Toy Fair
Jacob K. Javits Convention Center
New York, New York
Toy Industry Association, Inc.
Tel: 212-675-1141
Fax: 212-645-3246
Website: www.toy-tia.org/AITF

In 2003, the AITF celebrated its one-hundredth anniversary. This is the largest and most important U.S. toy industry trade show. If you are serious about your work, this show is a must

Note: In October 2002, the Toy Industry Association announced innovative changes to the toy industry trade show calendar to support future diverse buying trends. The most immediate change will take place in October 2003, when it will replace the New York Toy Preview with the introduction of the first "early mass-market toy show," scheduled from Tuesday, October 21, 2003, through Thursday, October 23, 2003.

The TIA says that with mass-market retailers more efficiently serviced during October, the February Toy Fair will be promoted as a show more specifically directed to the specialty market. As a result, the mass-market retailers will now have more time to spend at Javits or the ITC focusing on the smaller manufacturers.

New York International Gift Fair
Jacob K. Javits Convention Center
New York, New York
Tel: 914-421-3200
Fax: 914-948-6180
Website: www.nyigf.com

School Equipment Show
Phoenix Civic Plaza
Phoenix, Arizona
Tel: 1-800-395-5550 or 301-495-0240
Fax: 301-495-3330
Website: www.nssea.org

March

Western States Toy & Hobby Show
Fairplex
Pomona, California
Tel: 626-839-4911
Fax: 626-839-5091
Website: www.wthra.com

These respective shows have become the second oldest and second largest trade shows of their kind in the United States.

Dallas Toys Show
Dallas Market Center
Dallas, Texas
Tel: 914-421-3200
Fax: 914-948-6180
Website: www.glmshows.com

East Coast Hobby Show
Fort Washington Expo Center
Fort Washington, Pennsylvania
Tel: 1-800-252-4757 or 561-338-3177
Fax: 561-338-5066
Website: www.hobbyshow.com

The only full-line hobby show on the East Coast.

April

Toy & Hobby Fair
Pacific Northwest Toy & Hobby Association
Stadium Exhibition Center
Seattle, Washington
Tel: 206-714-7837
Fax: 206-244-7069

Ed Expo
National School Supply & Equipment Association
Tampa Convention Center
Tampa, Florida
Tel: 1-800-395-5550 or 301-495-0240
Fax: 301-495-3330
Website: www.nssea.org

May

International Juvenile Products Show (JPMA)
International Apparel Mart
Dallas, Texas
Tel: 856-638-0420
Fax: 856-439-0525
Website: www.jpma.com

Electronic Entertainment Expo (E3)
Los Angeles Convention Center
Los Angeles, California
Tel: 1-877-216-6263 or 508-875-3976
Fax: 508-875-7364
Website: www.e3expo.com

This event is a must if you create electronic amusements. Over 60,000 attendees from 70 countries view over 1,000 new interactive entertainment products at more than 400 booths.

Annual ASTRA Convention
Omni Interlocken Resort
Broomfield, Colorado
Tel: 847-375-4727
Fax: 1-888-840-2650
Website: www.astratoy.org

June

Kids Today—Building on Success
Hotel Roy Plaza
Lake Buena Vista, Florida
Tel: 336-605-1066
Website: www.cahners.com

Licensing Show
Jacob K. Javits Convention Center
New York, New York
Tel: 203-882-1300
Fax: 203-882-1800
Website: www.licensingshow.com

Licensing is a more than $177 billion business, and the June show in New York City has become a midyear meeting venue for toy companies and inventors.

July

Comic-Con International
San Diego Convention Center
San Diego, California
Tel: 1-800-266-4299
Fax: 619-414-1022
Website: www.comic-con.org

This is the world's largest comic book convention.

August

New York International Gift Fair
Jacob K. Javits Convention Center
New York, New York
Tel: 1-800-272-SHOW
Website: www.glmshows.com

GenCon Game Fair
MECCA Convention Center
Milwaukee, Wisconsin
Tel: 1-800-529-EXPO
Fax: 206-957-1862
Website: www.wizards.com

> Wizards of the Coast is the official co-sponsor of Gen Con.

International Miniature Collectibles Trade Show and Convention
Wyndham Inner Harbor
Baltimore, Maryland
Tel: 740-452-4541
Fax: 740-452-2552
Website: www.miaa.com

MAGIC/MAGIC KIDS
Las Vegas Convention Center
Las Vegas, Nevada
Tel: 1-877-554-4834 or 218-723-9792
Website: www.magiconline.com

> MAGIC, founded in 1933, is the largest marketplace for licensed apparel and accessories, with 1,800 exhibitors in 7,000 booths. It is of interest to designers and agents looking to license characters and designs.

> MAGIC KIDS is the largest marketplace for children's apparel, accessories, and footwear in the United States.

WWDMAGIC
Sands Expo & Convention Center
Las Vegas, Nevada
Tel: 1-877-554-4834 or 218-723-9792
Website: www.magiconline.com

> Concurrent with MAGIC and MAGICKIDS, *Women's Wear Daily* co-sponsors WWDMAGIC, which hosts over 1,000 exhibitors, 2,000 booths, and 5,100 product lines.

TAG (Toys and Games) Summit
Ritz-Carlton Huntington Hotel & Spa
Pasadena, California
Tel: 246-431-1025
Website: www.TAGsummit.com

This meeting addresses key industry issues, including marketing, toy safety, product development, and trends in the market.

September

International Model & Hobby Expo
Donald E. Stephens Convention Center
Rosemont, Illinois
Tel: 847-740-1111
Fax: 847-740-1112
Website: www.ihobbyexpo.com

Dallas Toy Show
Dallas Market Center
Dallas, Texas
Tel: 214-655-6100
Fax: 214-655-7646
Website: www.dallasmarketcenter.com

Toy Trivia

38. Who manufactures Beanie Babies?

a. Ty
b. Gund
c. Commonwealth

October

NSSEA Ed-U
Ernest N. Morial Convention Center
New Orleans, Louisiana
Tel: 1-800-395-5550 or 301-495-0240
Fax: 301-495-3330
Website: www.nssea.org

This association is comprised of 1,400 companies that market to schools.

Early Mass Market Toy Show
October 21–23, 2003
New York, New York
Toy Industry Association, Inc.
Tel: 212-675-1141
Fax: 212-645-3246
Website: www.toy-tia.org

Gift Shows

If there is a gift show within striking distance of where you live, it's a good idea to go, to get an overall feeling of what's in fashion. Maybe you'll be stimulated by something you see that you can translate into a product. It's hard to go wrong attending a trade show.

For current information on select gift shows, call 1-800-272-SHOW.

Others are listed here:

Dallas: 1-800-DAL-MKTS

Phoenix: 1-800-424-9519

Orlando: 678-285-EXPO

San Francisco: 1-800-346-1212

Minneapolis: 1-800-626-1298

Canadian (Toronto, Montreal, etc.): 1-888-823-SHOW

411
U.S. Copyright Office
The Library of Congress
Tel: 202-707-3000
Forms Hotline: 202-707-9100
Fax-on-Demand: 202-707-2600
TTY: 202-707-6737

(International trade shows are covered in Chapter 8.)

Says Ron Magers of M Design, inventor of Puppy Racers and Cybershot (Parker Bros.), "I've attended most shows over the years. I use them for the obvious updates, the personal contacts, and to see my licensed products on display for buyers. But most importantly, I look at what *not* to invent because it's been done before and is in a show booth already!"

A "No" Can Be a Beginning

New inventors burst onto the industry scene with an idea they believe has the highest commercial appeal. Many just fade away when they are rejected. Others take another road to success.

Three such memorable ideas were presented to co-author Weingartner as he gathered new opportunities for Hasbro Games. Two of the three ideas came from unknown sources. After preliminary introductions, each concept was shown in finished, playable form. The concepts were executed so well that they left few "what if/how to" questions. The inventors had what acquisition people always want: a great works-like, looks-like model.

In Case 1, David Beffa-Negrini, Bob Wilkins, and David Hall saw a market for an add-on board to traditional Monopoly. They were not full-time professional game inventors. The men had other business interests. Wilkins had the original vision and took it on and off the burner from 1974 to 1995, when there was a breakthrough in board design and they were ready finally to show it.

Weingartner saw as unique the combined two-surface Monopoly board with new cards, properties, and money. All elements tied in neatly, putting a new and provocative spin on classic Monopoly. Their game would have natural appeal to an installed base of millions and millions of "monopolimaniacs." On the downside, Monopoly was already a great game, and to expand it might be seen by purists as something of an intrusion.

But Hasbro Games elected not to develop the concept. Furthermore, Hasbro would not give the inventors the Monopoly brand license, which would have allowed them to take the concept to a third-party manufacturer or to market the concept themselves through alternate distribution. The inventors had a terrific idea and a great model, but they'd learned a hard lesson in creating for a company brand and then being rejected by internal management.

In Case 2, Mimi Kirk rode into the East Longmeadow, Massachusetts, offices of Hasbro Games from the great Southwest to pitch her creation: a game of swapping tales, sharing friendships, exploring self—a women's game.

The very appealing model unveiled Cowgirls Ride the Trail of Truth. The model was so nicely executed that conversation ensued about the components before actually getting into game play. There were denim cardholders, cast horse pawns, and attractive graphics on all elements. The board was a map of the Old West with catchy venues like Pregnant Pass, Career Move Hill, Emotion Ocean, and Menopause Mountain. Weingartner thought the look was terrific and the play was a hoot (if not a yahoo)! The play structure (a trivia-like Q&A game) might not have been unique, but everything about the design had a fresh look.

Hasbro Games passed. Its marketing mavens said the game would appeal only to half of the adult-social game market. Though cowboys could play, it was most effective when cowgirls shared deepest personal bunkhouse tales. Women might meet in book groups, card groups, and investment groups, but the conclusion was that they were not ready to saddle up in big numbers to share the truth of their innermost trails. Kirk went on to build the property into a line of Old West accessories for modern-day cowgirls. You can view her website at www.cowgirlsgame.com.

But corporate tastes change, and timing plays a part in decision making. Fast-forward five years to another niche game for women. Hasbro Games hitched its marketing wagon to a goddess rather than a cowgirl. It introduced Go Goddess at Toy Fair 2002, the product of a group of amateur inventors from south Florida.

In Case 3, Canadian Ken Evoy, M.D., and his wife, Janice, ran Isovoy, Inc., an invention business in suburban Montreal. Though they reviewed concepts primarily from Canadian inventors seeking to create the next Trivial Pursuit, the Evoys successfully licensed 23 concepts, of which 20 were their own. Irwin Toys of Toronto marketed their first game, Globetrotters. Mattel acquired U.S. rights for a $100,000 advance, though the game was never released stateside. Schmidt Spiele developed it for Germany and France. Parker Bros. sold it in Australia.

The Evoys' most successful item, however, was Pooch Patrol, marketed in Canada by Grand Toys, with U.S. rights licensed to Tonka. "My conclusion, at the time, was that bears and dogs sold the best of all plush animals," says Ken. "With an absence of a plush dog on the market, I prototyped, through a Chinese friend, a specially sewn changeable face on a dog. By moving the eyebrows and lips, one moment the pooch would look friendly (lovable) and the next look mean like a guard dog. This was not just another stoic piece of plush; Pooch Patrol dogs had emotion and protected children from their fears, particularly night fears."

Weingartner always enjoyed Ken's presentations; he usually had solid game ideas. In this case, Ken brought a fully working speech device called Sound Bytes that would record statements, chop and scramble them, and play them back in half-second increments. It played half the bits, then 10 bits, and finally the whole statement. In game play, the team leader would privately record a topic and then give verbal clues as players tried to guess the correct statement in the shortest time.

Hasbro passed on Sound Bytes because of another electronic item it was tracking. But Ken was determined to market what he felt was a great item. "I found venture capital, contracted a hardware engineer, and had the device produced offshore. After disappointing results from an ad campaign, I created a radio contest that chopped and scrambled statements for the listeners to guess. It built strong consumer awareness for Sound Bytes. Unfortunately, that awareness never translated to big numbers at Zeller's and other retail outlets." With Hasbro's promotion budget applied, Sound Bytes might have been a winner. But Canadian and American game players will never know how good the game was to play.

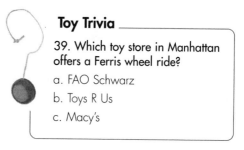

Toy Trivia

39. Which toy store in Manhattan offers a Ferris wheel ride?

a. FAO Schwarz

b. Toys R Us

c. Macy's

Common Thoughts from Uncommon Inventors

See if you recognize your feelings in those expressed by some of the professional inventors whose profiles appear in Appendix A on page 339. If you do, you may be further ahead than you thought. As diverse as the pros may be in age, size, sex, and training, there does appear to be a common bond among them in how they see business, how they started, what motivates them, their personal missions and goals, their expectations, and their emotions. One has the distinct sense that similar threads weave the community into a tight fabric.

Fun Facts

- Game trademark Gnip Gnop is ping pong spelled backwards.
- The first all-cloth Gerber baby doll was based upon a drawing by Ann Turner (Cook). It was sold from 1936-1939.
- The kaleidoscope was invented by Scottish physicist Sir David Brewster and was patented in 1817.
- The kite was invented around 2,500 to 3,000 years ago in China, Malaysia, or Indonesia. It is recorded that the earliest kites consisted of a large leaf attached to a long vine.
- There is only 1 correct answer and 43 quintillion wrong ones in the most popular puzzle in history, the colorful brainchild of Erno Rubik: Rubik's Cube.

Chapter 5

From Mind to Merchandise: Making an Idea Reality

"Most toy manufacturers function as other businesses in a rather structured and conforming manner. The independent inventor is our link to a special group of people who take the time to think out-of-the-box and with their entrepreneurial, non-conformist life styles bring the excitement of new creation that is a must for our companies. The independent inventor supplies the rich blood of life for new product development and future growth."

—Stephen R. Mickelberg, CEO,
S.R.M. Company, Inc.

How Toys and Games Are Developed

Ideas for new toys and games are not born whole. They emerge by degrees and transform over time. Like living organisms, there is tremendous variety among them. Their common denominator is that their origin is in curiosity and their growth is nurtured by a combination of intelligence, imagination, originality, motivation, persistence, and wonder.

Ideas won't keep. They go stale quickly, so something must be done with them. They are plans of action. Ideas are the stock and trade of a toy inventor, his or her prime assets. It is vital not only to know how to generate them, but also to know what to do with them at each step to the marketplace.

Independent toy inventors are prolific and entrepreneurial in spirit. It should come as no surprise that people in the U.S. economy have more individual freedom and more encouragement to innovate and be different than anywhere else on earth. The nation's marketplace is restless and ever-changing, with a constant demand for new products. We are, after all, a "throwaway/disposable" society.

Just as mere shape determines whether iron floats or sinks, so must ideas be well formed in order to survive. As the inventor's idea develops from its conceptual stage to a working prototype, it will go through many hands and many creative—and not so creative—minds. It has been said that an idea can turn to dust or magic, depending on the talent it rubs up against.

A new product idea is a fragile thing, and it doesn't take much to kill even the best one. It can be knocked out of consideration by a yawn. It can be butchered by a quip. It can be nitpicked to death by a scowl on the right executive's face. Rene Soriano, inventor of the preschool game Dot the Dog (Parker Bros.), says, "To make it all the way though the R&D and marketing process, the product has to sell itself all along the way. It needs the support and commitment of all the people inside who see, play, and plan it."

The longer a company holds a submission under active review, the greater the company's investment of time and personnel. "I make it a practice of following up every couple weeks, just to make sure my product is not sitting on a shelf in the inventor closet waiting for a slot in a meeting or forgotten," says Tim Moodie, inventor of the Rap Master Microphone.

In fact, there is a saying in the industry: "No comes fast; yes takes a long time."

Toy Trivia

71. Who founded Toys R Us?

a. Charles Lazarus

b. Sam Walton

c. Tyler Lawrence

In rare instances (rarer every day!), an inventor walks in with an item and out with a check, but these are the exceptions. Typically, a concept must pass a 30- to 45-day examination hurdle involving both R&D and Marketing. Then it can be another 120 to 150 days before the product is defined and specified to satisfaction. If it can be made for the right price, it is on its way to Toy Fair. An option fee may be paid after the first hurdle, with a full contract in place by Toy Fair. At smaller companies, all time frames may be compressed.

It is not uncommon for inventors to lose at least one key concept before each Toy Fair. The most prolific may lose even more. But there is a sense of loss by everyone. The sting is greatest with the loss of a well-developed concept late in the development process. The pros understand. If a licensed item falls out of favor, it is a major disappointment to every person who improved the design and began a marketing plan. Most disappointed of all is the inventor, who came *so* close and now has to try to sell the concept to another manufacturer. In such cases, many companies will give their model work to the inventor as a good faith gesture.

Of all factors brought to bear on a new idea, certainly the first for companies is their impression of the product, Andy Gatto said during his tenure as president of Match Box (USA). "The second is the consumer's impression of the product, and that order doesn't necessarily indicate the level of significance," Gatto said. "I think the consumer impression is to us the most important thing we deal with. If kids in testing ultimately like the product a lot, it makes it easier for us to invest the necessary human and financial resources to make the product go. If we have any reservations whatsoever about the consumer reaction to a product, then it's going to make the risk more intensive, and in today's economy you try to eliminate as much of the risk as possible."

Toy and game inventors share a single goal with their manufacturing/marketing partners. That goal is to have an idea become the next Hula Hoop or Trivial Pursuit, a megahit like Tickle Me Elmo or Furby. Creating for the sake of creating is not the task. Creating a toy that reaches retail and sells in quantity is the desired payoff.

In reality, however, of the 6,000 to 7,000 new products shown at Toy Fair each year, only 25 percent have the glide rate required to carry them into a second year. Even in Major League Baseball, a .250 average doesn't make an All-Star. In the toy business, that average is anemic as well, and the batting average lowers further when you go into the third year. Items with retail retention of four or five years are just about considered "classics."

There is no one way, no single procedure for firing the human imagination and sparking new ideas. It is always a challenge. The methods are as varied as the inventors.

Successful inventors have learned how to detect and follow what Emerson referred to as a "gleam of light that flashes across the mind from within."

"If there was a formula, an exact process to germinate ideas, it would have been plotted and charted long ago," the late Gordon Barlow once said. Barlow, a holder of nearly 400 patents, and considered a top creative thinker by toy marketers, created hits like Mouse Trap, Stay Alive, Pivot Pool, and Grape Escape.

"You never know exactly what will trigger an idea. It could be an object, a conversation, anything," says inventor Randice-Lisa Altschul. "But one thing is for sure: When the new idea hits my conscious level, it takes precedence over everything."

Greg Hyman, inventor of Alphie (Playskool), says he sparks ideas while lying on the nude beach on St. Martin.

And after the inspiration strikes and you have a serious commitment, what then? First comes the option money, then the advance on signing a contract. But, even after a contract, an item may fall. However, if it makes it to retail, the quarterly reports with checks finally start coming 30 days after close of each business quarter.

"It takes a lot of luck and connections. Tenth on a list is product originality," says Ron Milner, inventor of Hot Lixx (Tyco). "I think marketing forces are really the key to the whole thing. Ideas don't sell themselves. Ideas are sold often with some inventor's marketing concept to drive the idea."

Company Dreams

The pros may originate new concepts, but it is up to the marketer to transform the basic idea into a successful mass-market plaything. And that takes time. The play value and sales appeal of each idea put into the development cycle must be confirmed by a positive test result.

The carefully orchestrated steps taken by a manufacturer are intended to get the idea to market in an appealing form and at a price point. Today's mass-market producers need minimum sales of 200,000 to 300,000 units to justify an investment. The dream of any manufacturer is to produce a first-year million-seller and sustain product life as long as possible through new features, restyling, and extensions. It should be noted that companies selling to the specialty market are satisfied with far lower annual minimums and keep product alive much longer.

Every company is ecstatic when a new entry has solid sales for three or four years. The plan is for longevity, but too often an idea spawned in enthusiasm, launched with high expectations, and even supported by a multimillion-dollar media campaign disappears unceremoniously after a year or two (or less).

On the other hand, some strong sellers remain on Christmas lists year after year. Often parents buy playthings that they enjoyed as kids, such as Play-Doh, Mr. Potato Head, Boggle, Monopoly, Scrabble, Barbie, and Hot Wheels. These products are representative of items called *classics*, *staples*, or *evergreens*, which may undergo periodic cosmetic updates but are much the same as when they first appeared at Toy Fair. They can be counted on for virtually guaranteed annual sales. A classic seller is every inventor's dream—and every manufacturer's expectation.

The most successful companies are those with the most classics. E. David Wilson, president of Hasbro Games, says, "Our success is based on a solid, well-rounded line of staple merchandise that forms our sales and marketing base. Parker and MB had the classics, and that fact alone establishes Hasbro Games' leadership in the business." Hasbro acquired Milton Bradley and Parker Brothers in 1984 and 1991, respectively.

Every professional inventor may dream of a staple product that pays off regular royalties year after year. In reality, only a few top-echelon inventors receive hundreds of thousands or millions of dollars each year from a single solid hit. There just aren't that many sustained winners like Connect Four or Operation or Cabbage Patch or Pound Puppies.

Advances against royalties are nice for short-term cash flow. However, the true foundation of any inventor's business is the solid royalty base provided by a staple. But most toys are the casualty of fast-changing consumer interests. The pros know that annuities are rare.

> **Toy Trivia**
>
> 72. Which is National Inventor's Month?
>
> a. September
> b. December
> c. August

"There is no doubt that you start a product cycle each year looking for winners," says Mike Meyers, a former senior vice president of R&D at Milton Bradley. "You can see thousands of ideas in search of the best new ideas. Sometimes the potential hits are obvious. Most times you look for the germ of an idea that will transform during internal development into something everyone feels will be a sales success. Anywhere during that cycle, if the confidence level does not remain very high, all work is discontinued on an idea regardless of the investment in time, design efforts, and dollars."

The Pick of the Litter

Inventors' concepts picked by a manufacturer are moved into its structured design, engineering, fulfillment, and marketing cycles. Ideas must have a significant physical presence that takes them from the "what if/imagine this" stage into appealing, playable forms that get immediate favorable reaction by executives.

The most successful ideas have what many in the industry call a *wow* factor. This is some promotable feature that, combined with a market need, delivers obvious excitement. Cabbage Patch Kids come with adoption papers and one-of-a-kind looks, names, and birth certificates. Tiger Electronics' Furby had patented microelectronics that gave the impression of artificial intelligence through speech and sensors. Promotable dolls have reached the level of sophistication that they need nurturing and care of every conceivable bodily function. Games like Bop-It challenge players to mimic sequences of pulls, twists, and bops at an increasingly rapid pace. Whatever the hook, in today's toy-invention business, "Ya gotta have a gimmick." And you need the toy gods on your side.

The gimmick has to be working at the time of the initial presentation. The easiest ideas to sell are those that have a demonstrable form and function. If the idea has sounds and action, you need a "Wow!" reaction. If it's a cute and sweet concept, it should hit the "Aaahhh" chord with company viewers.

"When I meet with a manufacturer to present product possibilities, I make certain that every concept is workable, playable, and functional," says Jeffrey Breslow, president of BMT Associates of Chicago. "Each item has a limited time to make an impression, and I try to leave very little to chance, to the viewer's imagination. I don't want the manufacturer to guess at the new idea. I want the viewer to see the idea, feel the idea, hear the idea, and play with the idea."

The old saying, "Necessity is the mother of invention," came to life for Mike Satten, who created Sports Starters Baseball Glove (Playskool). Satten was teaching his son, Brett, to catch a baseball. The inventor realized that many baseball gloves have no flexibility and are inappropriate for younger children. To solve this, he created numerous prototype gloves in different sizes, pocket configurations, and bumpers before settling on a tricot model with a removable "catch guard" that prevents the ball from popping out.

Reflecting on his long career gathering external concepts to present to internal groups, Mike Meyers says more seriously than jokingly, "It seemed the idea needed to leap up and kiss everyone on the lips to ensure a positive group reaction."

United States Patent [19]

Lehmann et al.

[11] Patent Number: **4,817,209**

[45] Date of Patent: **Apr. 4, 1989**

[54] **CHILD'S BASEBALL GLOVE**

[76] Inventors: **Roger W. Lehmann**, 18 Flintlock Ct., Bernardsville, N.J. 07924; **Michael I. Setten**, 4 Farmers Rd., Kingspoint, N.Y. 11024

[21] Appl. No.: 223,291

[22] Filed: **Jul. 22, 1988**

[51] Int. Cl.⁴ A41D 13/10
[52] U.S. Cl. 2/19
[58] Field of Search .... 2/16, 19, 160, 161 A

[56] **References Cited**

U.S. PATENT DOCUMENTS

899,522	9/1908	Gamble	2/19
958,117	8/1908	Hartman	2/19
1,072,012	9/1913	King	2/19

Primary Examiner—Werner H. Schroeder
Assistant Examiner—Sara Current
Attorney, Agent, or Firm—Salter & Michaelson

[57] **ABSTRACT**

A child's baseball glove includes a hand member includ-ing a palm section, a finger section, a thumb section, and a webbing section connecting the thumb section to the finger section, and a padded pocket member which extends along the front side of the thumb section, across the base portion of the palm section, along the front side of the outer portion of the finger section and across the upper end portion of the front side of the finger section to substantially define the perimeter of a pocket in the glove. The glove preferably further includes an elon-gated padded retainer member which is detachably secured to opposite side portions of the pocket member and extends in outwardly spaced relation across the base portion of the palm section. The glove can be initially used by a young child with the retainer member in place in order to enable the child to more easily catch and retain a ball in the pocket of the glove, and after the child has developed an initial level of proficiency at utilizing the glove, the retaining member can be re-moved to enable the glove to be used in a manner simi-lar to a conventional baseball glove.

14 Claims, 4 Drawing Sheets

Child's Baseball Glove
Patented April 4, 1989
U.S. Patent 4,817,209

The Development Cycle: Milestones and Deadlines

Inventors need to understand product cycles, though every manufacturer may have slight variations of the development process. Hasbro provided general descriptions of three different product cycles, which may occur simultaneously when a line is put together. The specific cycle depends on the complexity of product or products to be developed and prepared for market. These timelines would be different for a smaller company.

1. Soft goods or plush toys may undergo a shortened development cycle of three to four months. During this time, designs are finalized, specifications are established, sewing patterns are created, materials are selected, and prototypes are safety-tested. A relatively short cycle is possible since most cute, cuddly, soft goods are simply a matter of style and design. Unless electronics or mechanics are added, there is no complex engineering, intricate molding, or special tweaking to maximize play value.

2. Board games and single-toy concepts are usually developed within a cycle of 8 to 10 months. Game rules are written so that all predictable situations and outcomes are covered for every play level. Once the idea is boxed and in the market, there should be no unanswered questions about how to assemble, play, and get maximum fun from it. In some cases, all that may remain of the original inventor idea is the basic play pattern or that special hook that captures important strategies of play. It is possible that the theme or much of the content will have been altered entirely. Finished color artwork will change the look of the inventor prototype. In some cases, early inventor graphics may be dropped in favor of popular licensed characters from the Cartoon Network, Sesame Street, Disney, PBS, or Warner.

3. A complete line with many related playthings requires 15 to 18 months of development and represents a major financial investment. Such line ideas may include both horizontal and vertical development. Horizontal development brings out variations on the same theme at similar price points, as in Hot Wheels vehicles of varied designs. Vertical development involves items at a varied scale of execution and price points.

In today's business, the premium is on speed to market. Dividing up development tasks and involving offshore sources have become the common method of expediting development and cutting costs. Omitting any critical stage or neglecting any detail merely increases the question of ultimate success.

High Marks Pass Testing

Companies are very different when it comes to how much they rely on market-research techniques, but most consider some research and testing valuable to check reaction to product ideas. New product concepts must hit the decision-making executives right in the stomach—or, more specifically, in the infamous "gut."

"I think the value of market research is overrated. Truly great toys still come from the gut," opines former Playskool president Steve Schwartz, who now is an active idea source as head of Schwartz and Associates. "I've tested products that have done very well and when they got to the marketplace, they were decimated by some product I never even knew was coming out. Research can never predict who your competition is going to be, and that's where you get blindsided all the time. I think if the toy is right and you feel it's right, you go with it."

Schwartz goes on to offer some limits of research: "You're testing against what's known. So when Hasbro tested the then-new concept that led to My Little Pony, we tested against Strawberry Shortcake, which was very powerful in the market. My Little Pony was an unknown with no advertising or anything, and we got destroyed in the research. The truth of the matter is that My Little Pony blew away Strawberry Shortcake once it got to the marketplace.

"We tested Cabbage Patch Kids and what the mothers said was, 'My daughter has no idea what adoption means and, boy, is this doll ugly!' So what did that tell us? And Mattel tested it also, and I believe Kenner tested it, too. I think Coleco probably didn't. That's why they took it and had a success."

Standard & Poor's toys analyst Paul Valentine says, "I think what is extraordinary is a company's rejection rate on what ultimately become highly successful toys. Cabbage Patch Kids were rejected by five major toy companies, including Mattel and Hasbro, before Coleco accepted them. Teddy Ruxpin was personally rejected by Hasbro's Stephen Hassenfeld, who was an industry legend in picking product. It was also rejected by Mattel. Coleco only made a nominal offer. Hasbro gave up the technology that became Lazer Tag. You look around the industry, and it's amazing to see the product rejected. You like to think there's some science and skill to it, but after a while you think all these guys might as well be using darts."

Fisher-Price CEO Neil Friedman, while a senior vice president at Hasbro, told the writers that "companies often rely heavily on market research, but a product will live or die of its own volition." Friedman used market research for support or to give preferences if a product was on a bubble or controversial. Friedman also used market research to help sway an issue one way or the other or to obtain a better definition. "You have to get products while they're hot and topical into the marketplace," Friedman said. His feeling was that too much market research could bog down a manufacturer.

Product Development Timeline of Key Steps

The following product development steps begin on the arbitrary month of November. It follows the typical steps taken by a large company. Not all steps apply to all companies. Some products, such as board games, for example, can be turned around in a few months.

November

◆ Product concept approval.

◆ Market research. The marketing, design, and engineering team links together to assess consumer reaction to new concepts by interviewing consumers about a product's attributes or observing children field-testing a product. Consumers' input is valuable in evaluating the potential of a new concept or in fine-tuning a product prior to its launch in the market.

◆ Preliminary costing.

◆ PTO model from shop.

December

◆ Preliminary takeover. The PTO conference is a critical stage in a product's transformation from concept to reality. At this phase, a product passes from the hands of designers to engineers, with close scrutiny given to such issues as design, cost, reliability, packaging, and manufacturing plans.

◆ Marketing line review.

◆ R&D model finished. The R&D model shop constructs product prototypes early in the development process. Later, model makers may fine-tune mechanisms and build models for use during the ongoing product review process. They also construct the hand samples required for Toy Fair, since full production of many new products begins later in the year.

January

◆ PTO package approval.

◆ Appropriation approval request.

◆ FTO (final takeover).

◆ Marketing line review.

February

 ◆ Final sculpture. Product sculptors work in consultation with design engineers and marketing managers to transform a product idea into reality.

March

 ◆ Preliminary drawing release.
 ◆ EDM review (engineering, design, and marketing).

April

 ◆ Final drawing release.
 ◆ Pattern release.
 ◆ Cost verification.

May

 ◆ Tooling start.

June

 ◆ Proving model review.
 ◆ Graphic model complete.
 ◆ Final engineering changes.

Toy Trivia

73. Hasbro's 1961 Sno-Cone machine offered how many delicious flavors?

a. 10
b. 15
c. 20

July

 ◆ MTO costing (manufacturing takeover).
 ◆ Final packaging specs.

August

 ◆ Final product specs.
 ◆ MTO.
 ◆ Marketing line review.

September

 ◆ Package and art release. Designing a product's packaging is an important part of the overall product-development and marketing process.
 ◆ Preliminary instructions.

October
- Art release.
- First shots (samples of molded parts).

November
- Marketing line review. All the functions involved in the creation of a product, including R&D and engineering, come together. Features such as design, packaging, and advertising are evaluated, and the overall design and production schedule is monitored.

- VSP (vendor sample pilot). Some products are manufactured by outside vendors. If so, before full production is begun, a sample product is produced by the vendor. Marketing, design, engineering, and R&D teams evaluate all aspects of the pilot product to determine whether it conforms to design and engineering specifications prior to authorizing the start of manufacturing.

December
- Final packaging.
- Final instructions release.
- Marketing line review.

January
- FEP (final engineering pilot).
- RTP (release to production).

February
- Toy Fair. Months of design, development, engineering, and marketing effort culminate in the unveiling of the year's new product line at Toy Fair each February. The sales force shows the line to representatives of the trade.

March
- Production start.

Companies see hundreds of toy concepts a month, and gut and historical perspective initially tell executives whether the product has some level of appeal. But no matter how innovative an item is, many companies believe in market research, especially quantitative research, which measures consumers' specific likes and dislikes. The larger companies do focus groups and, depending upon the product and risk, often also do quantitative research to establish whether the focus session results are accurate. Many variables can skew the results, including the number of groups, the socioeconomic backgrounds of the kids, the locations where they are conducted, the composition of the group, the quality of the moderator, and so forth.

Recalling his days at Western Publishing, George Propsom says, "We did extensive market research on girls' products when the phenomenon was Dungeons & Dragons role-playing for boys. We said there has to be something for girls, and conducted extensive testing. We met with psychologists. After a year and a half, we couldn't come up with anything. Then Cathy Rondeau came in with Girl Talk (submitted as Pillow Talk). We opened the game and said, 'This is what we've been looking for.'"

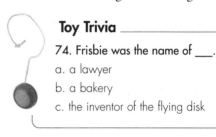

Toy Trivia

74. Frisbie was the name of ___.

a. a lawyer

b. a bakery

c. the inventor of the flying disk

It is extremely difficult to determine what people want. Given a blank slate, consumers—or parents of targeted consumers—are not likely to be able to articulate their basic play needs. They can't describe the perfect product from thin air, but if you put a product in their hands, they will react to what's good or bad about it. Therefore, the industry commonly gains insights into products through "negative testing," focusing on what is *not* liked about a concept or soliciting opinions about what nuances or features are missing from selected products on the market. In an effective product test environment, consumers can be brutally frank about their likes and dislikes, especially if there is an opportunity to see, feel, and play with something specific.

Usually the potential user and the potential purchaser are not the same. "We can never forget that we are dealing with two tiers of consumers," says Kate Stanuch, former associate director of market research at Hasbro and consultant to Radica Toys. "On one hand we have kids who will use the toy, and on the other is the parent who makes the purchase decision. When we talk toys and games with kids, it's all performance, fantasy, excitement, play patterns, and peer acceptance. With parents, toys and games are defined in relation to durability, repeat play, entertainment, and pricing issues."

One way to increase the likelihood of succeeding with your target audience is to pay attention to their interests. Elliot Rudell says that his designers take into account the broadest umbrella of interest for potential users. "Of course, we must know if there is anything like our idea already in the toy or game market; that is a given. But when we are doing our theme, our design, our *raison d'être* for the idea, we look at what else the target audience is into—where they are with TV, books, magazines, music, clothes, general interests. Our new toy or game concept has to appeal to the same senses that are diverted toward other things in the environment. When it becomes playtime, we are looking for the same energy and appeal that is coming at our users from everything else around them. In a sense, playtime has become entertainment time, and it now can be multimedia, not just a board game or a plastic toy."

Few inventors have access to large groups of players for extensive play-testing. Most do varying degrees of "kitchen research"—and more of them videotape these sessions, studying the players' reactions for ideas on changes and improvements. Play-testing is the only way to be certain of the appropriate age range for a product; it is the only way kinks and quirks can be identified and ironed out. Inventors have to put their idea into a playable form and play … and play … and play until they are sure everything is refined and ready to show to potential marketers.

At large companies, testing likely begins early and continues throughout development. It can be no other way. There are no Josh Baskins, as in the movie *Big*, at real toy companies. Adults decide on the selection, function, and structure of new toys and games, but for most products, children determine whether adult wisdom was accurate.

Advice from the Pros

"Good companies respond quickly to change; great companies create change."

—Robert Kriegel, David Brandt, co-authors, *Sacred Cows Make the Best Burgers*

Rather than rule in presumptuous isolation of kiddie consumers, management is inclined to test ideas with children at all stages of development. It is far better to get reactions early than to wait until they've got a warehouse full of miscalculations. Despite industry enthusiasm for a new toy or game, in the end, it is very possible that little Tyler, Bettie, Krista, or Stephanie—or their mothers—just won't like it. Early testing and accurate interpretation of consumer reactions helps to prevent costly and disappointing market rejection.

Steps to Product Selection

Step	Responsibility	Objective
1. General survey of opportunities	R&D and Marketing	Separate product wheat from chaff
2. Focus on manageable number of design projects	R&D and Marketing	Build a line with strongest candidates throughout
3. Define final product form and function, establish makers packaging	Designers, artists, engineers, model at target sell prices	Establish design and functional specifications
4. Review playability, consumer features, and point-of-sale appeal	R&D and Marketing	Build in all product features and make sure product and package convey benefits to consumer
5. Coordinate product, packaging, promotion, and advertising	R&D, Marketing, Advertising, and Sales	Position product to yield projected sales volume
6. Sign off of line introductions for Toy Fair	Senior divisional and corporate management	Approve investments in new product.

Product Development Magic

R&D takes an idea approved by executives and prepares it for manufacture as it continues to evolve through the development process. Mike Langieri says of the development drill he managed as vice president of creative development at Hasbro Games, "When new game concepts came to us, it was not just that they had be clever, cute, unique, appealing, innovative, and interesting to a target audience. We had to be confident that we could make the game and sell it at a price that allowed a reasonable profit. First we reviewed product with marketing. They had to give us the go-ahead to design toward a target sell price. Only then would we put all the development disciplines to work to determine if we could make a quality, highly playable game at that target price. Always considered was a desired profit level at the forecasted sales volume."

Toy Trivia

75. Who invented the Polygonzo novelty puzzler?

a. Howard Fleisher

b. Richard Blank

c. Paul Brown

Development disciplines are numerous. To get a sense of the true cost of an item, you must take into account much more than obvious factors like parts, labor, and packaging. There are expenses for artwork, design time, capital investment for tooling and equipment, and costs of advertising and promotion. It is impossible to do these projections for every new product concept.

The number of concepts under consideration is constantly being winnowed out. "Toy and game marketing is a very judgmental business," notes Langieri. "Often a great new concept is dropped and gets returned to the inventor not because the idea isn't good, but because there may be an alternative that ultimately will be more saleable, promotable, and profitable." Difficult as it is to accept, the return of an item doesn't always mean it's not good: It just isn't *as* good as the chosen one. And, unfortunately for the inventor who lost out, he or she will not see the winner until Toy Fair.

During the selection process, new products are played and played by internal designers. Their dimensions may be stretched and enlarged to convey greater price value and greater presence at retail, or they may be reduced in size to have a travel feature, possible collectability, or a lower price. Often internal staff is involved in product naming. Countless catchy names are considered and favorites are researched for prior use, with the final choice trademarked.

Products are safety-tested for puncture points, ingestion risk, toxicity, and durability under both intended use and misuse. Parts are sculpted and modeled into three-dimensional form. Every element is engineered and made functional. Parts may be added or taken away. Plastic is weighed and thicknesses are specified. Factory assembly is determined and costs are estimated by the manufacturer or are sent offshore for competitive cost quotations. Play instructions are written. Step-by-step diagrams are drawn, if customer assembly is required. Lively graphics with appealing colors may be specified. Appealing protective packaging is created. Every possible factor that has an impact on the bottom line gets examined. From an inventor's first prototype, a commercially viable product takes form through the input of numerous talents. What started as a hot inventor idea that gained commitment by senior management may later be viewed simply as just another plaything by kids.

Mike Satten, who has 32 years in the business, is so familiar with the long road to retail that he recites the process to a staccato beat. "Things have to pass through so many people. Imagine. You have to show it to a guy who has to like it. He has to take it back and show it to a group that has to like it. The engineering has to work. It has to cost out. It has to be tested with kids and then tested with parents. The trade has to see it. The trade has to like it. The agency has to see it. The agency has to like it. The agency has to do the commercials. The commercials have to be tested with kids and parents who have to like what they see. Then the trade has to see the product again with the commercial and like both. And after all that, it has to clear some manufacturer in China. It's mind-boggling."

Turning on the Spigot

When senior management decides that a product is a go, months of creation now dovetail into months of production. It is up to engineers, toolmakers, procurement people, and production staff to bring product through on schedule. Estimated costs become actuals; plans become reality.

"Once we know management is committed and we have the final specifications, we turn on all the capabilities, whether in our domestic manufacturing facility or at suppliers throughout Asia," says Dorothy Echlin, vice president of product engineering at Hasbro Games. "What we don't make or convert in our own plant, we procure from external suppliers, whether domestic or offshore. Our whole production team becomes dedicated to making the best possible product within the time frame and within a product's projected costs."

"The development process and manufacturing interface can be likened to a relay race," says Langieri. "Every part of the event takes an all-out effort to progress through some very clear objectives. You meet those objectives and keep moving farther along until you pass the challenge (baton) on to someone else. Although you move the product on to the next development stage, you remain involved so that a new product stands a better chance of finishing as a winner.

"In the toy business, we may not be passing a baton," he adds, "but rather the 'pass' may be an engineering blueprint, a CAD file, a batch of e-transmitted specifications, or a finely tuned mold. As the idea moves through progressive stages of development, it will cross the final schedule milestone through the involvement of many experienced and specialized people. If they all do their jobs well, the product—not the baton—will be passed along toward initial production."

Manufacturing then is called upon to make reruns as needed. The "new" becomes the "familiar" to factory fulfillment. Everyone involved hopes that production is called upon often to meet exceptional consumer demand. Product must be ready to meet the demands of retail accounts, where precise delivery to store shelves is the new order of the day. This "on demand" delivery is yet another challenge if a new item is to sustain life in the market place.

Shining a Marketing Light on the Line

While the daily details of product development and manufacturing move the new toy or game toward final form, periodic schedule updates and computerized tracking systems monitor the progress of a product on course toward market launch. As designers and engineers create the product, marketing focus is on package design and advertising.

"Our commercial for a new game is intended to capture strong points of difference between our product and everything else that is out there," says Dale Siswick, who has been both senior vice president of marketing and of R&D at Hasbro Games. "The TV spot has to be hard-hitting and memorable. If targeted at the child, we want the commercial to create reasons for the child to ask for the game. If targeted at parents, we want the commercial to be memorable so that the product is remembered when making a buying decision. If the commercial is our sales message on TV, our commercial at the store level is our package. We want that package to have as much energy, as much appeal as our most animated 30-second spot. In the stacks of boxes, in the aisles of choices, we want our package to stand out."

Line review is a time of assessment and a time to update R&D, marketing, sales, manufacturing, and senior-management issues. Each review, at any point along the development cycle, reports cumulative update information. If all does not fit into place, and if later information refutes previous conclusions, a new product candidate may fall from favor. The farther along a product is in the process, the more costly it is to abort its development. However, the financial gamble is never greater than when a product has gone to full term and thousands of units sit in inventory. With such risk in mind, a new plaything can be changed—or scrapped—right up to its Toy Fair debut.

"I've seen products fall at every step of the way during my years in the business," says inventor Jeffrey Breslow. "At first we want to know if the idea will be selected to go into the development cycle. But even after that happens and I have a contract as a firm commitment from a manufacturer, I know a product may be dropped unless it has strong buyer support pre–Toy Fair. At the Fair itself, without significant buyer intent to order, an item may be dropped. It is a tremendous disappointment to us all and a major financial setback as well. In this business, you learn that your item is never out until it is out—on retail shelves."

Advice from the Pros

"Embrace rejection. Sometimes it's the only thing you have going for you."

—Barbara Slate, creator of *Angel Love* and other comic books

Do Not Try This at Home

Often inventors become frustrated when ideas are not accepted and manufactured by established toy and game marketers. Their ideas never fall into the development flow as just outlined. At this point, many amateur inventors make what for many are financially disastrous decisions. Without a business plan and with little awareness of marketing pitfalls, they elect to self-publish or produce their ideas themselves. These entrepreneurs have little regard for true startup costs and generally do not know about production, how to establish and fill distribution pipelines, advertise and promote, and realistic profit projections after all expenses necessary to convert their beloved idea into reality.

Unfortunately, in the vast majority of such scenarios, the dream turns to disaster. If selling large numbers of toys and games is difficult for companies that should know what they're doing, it is virtually impossible for first-time inventors who *don't* know what they're doing to be successful. Not only is the danger that the inventor is left with inventories of unsold goods, but an ill-conceived product execution may forever damage the novel essence of a truly unique idea. It is virtually impossible for a new marketer to resurrect a tarnished product concept. A company would rather start with a fresh concept then rebuild an old one.

Pros know this pitfall. Ken Evoy, a Canadian inventor, counsels, "Don't mortgage the house. It is much safer to find venture capital. If you can't, maybe as a business proposition your idea was not meant to happen. The worst thing is to spend your money on 10,000 pieces, sell a few thousand, and [have] the rest end up in your garage."

Toy Trivia

76. What dolls are born at Babyland General Hospital?

a. Water Babies

b. Cabbage Patch Kids

c. Barbie and Ken

Richard Borg, inventor of Times to Remember (Milton Bradley), a 15-year pro doing contract game development and licensing to numerous European and U.S. game houses, agrees with Evoy. "Please don't mortgage the house and borrow money from relatives to self-publish your dream. There are a few examples of this path being the way to financial success, but there are hundreds of others who now have an attic, basement, or garage full of boxed dreams."

Toy Fair: Curtain Up, Light the Lights!

The payback on thousands of hours of creative effort and high-dollar investment begins at the industry rollout of a new item. Little about that rollout is left to chance. At the pre-Fair Toy Fair, products are displayed on pedestals for peak visual attraction. Enthusiastic, well-coached demonstrators extol product features and invite trade buyers to play. Nearby TV monitors, for mass-market product, flash supporting commercials. Those spots are one piece of a major-market media campaign for the new product.

The most common question asked at the American International Toy Fair? Without a doubt, "What's new?" Buyers know the past winners that continue to sell. Salespeople prefer not to talk about last year's overhyped launches that didn't meet expectations. The starting place for the coming year's business is with innovative new products, slick new packages, and hard-sell commercials.

The inventor, of course, takes pride in seeing his or her product on display and takes an interest in buyers' reactions. More than ever, he or she is now inextricably dependent on the manufacturer.

"When Toy Fair comes around, you either have items in the marketplace or you don't," observes Mike Satten. "If I don't, I feel I have wasted a year. The way I look at it, if you've beaten the odds, sold a few items, then you're a winner. If they happen to be well received, then you're a bigger winner."

"I come to Toy Fair to get a reading on what's new in general, but more specifically to see how our new placements are accepted by the trade," says George Delaney of Delaney Development. "I try to get to all the showrooms for a look at what we will be up against the coming year and to see where the holes may be in a line to get a running start on next year. But I particularly delight in visiting those showrooms where our items are being unveiled."

"Toy Fair is a highly charged and frenzied event. You go to keep up with the latest ideas and see inventing and marketing friends," says inventor Charlie Phillips. "There is a special twinge of pride when you see your products in a marketer's showroom." But as he explains, the end of the cycle is also the beginning of the next cycle: "Those displayed products are history to you now. Your main focus is on your latest creations, products that you hope to see displayed at a future Toy Fair. In the inventing business, you force yourself to think of the future and not pause too long in the glory of the present."

Toy Fair may be a time to bask in today's successes. It is also an opportunity to see colleagues, target future placement opportunities, build new relationships, and *kibitz* on such vital topics as where the industry is headed, what companies have been bought, and where executive friends have landed.

Noteworthy about New York Toy Fair 2003 was that both Mattel and Hasbro did not operate buyer showrooms and host inventors. Except for a small display for the media, and some senior executives walking around, they had no visible presence. This is likely to continue this way into the foreseeable future.

Company executives selecting 10 to 15 promotable items for the coming Toy Fair are thinking about the $20 million to $30 million gamble across an entire line of new playthings. They cannot help but be influenced by thoughts of the many industry departures, such as WOW, Coleco, Tonka, Galoob, Matchbox (USA), Western Publishing, Schaper, Ideal Toy, Tyco, and other marketers now gone to the industry's "Boot Hill."

Product development is a protracted and careful exercise. Just as in aviation, there are preflight checklists to be followed. Each manufacturer has some sort of centralized warning system that puts on the "Fasten Seat Belts" sign as soon as there is an indication of any lagging of an item under development or on shelves in the marketplace. Unlike aviation, however, there are no flight simulators in which executives can learn how to handle dramas and catastrophes. In the toy industry, every product launch is for real, so it is taken very, *very* seriously.

Toy Trivia

77. Twister was made popular when Eva Gabor played it on television with which host?

a. Jay Leno

b. Johnny Carson

c. Jack Parr

Fun Facts

- Bingo was originally called "Beano" in the United States. It was a game played at country fairs. A dealer would select numbered discs from a cigar box, and players would mark their cards with beans. If they had a winning card, they yelled "Beano!"

- A game that plays and looks like checkers was unearthed in the ruins of the ancient city of Ur in modern day Iraq. It dates to circa 3000 B.C. Checkers, as we know it today, has been around since 1400 B.C. In Egypt, a similar game was called Alquerque.

Chapter 6

Pat. Pend., ™, ®, ©: IP Firewalls

"For two centuries, the United States Patent Office has played a vital role in the scientific, technical, and economic development of our nation by granting inventors patents for their inventions. As Abraham Lincoln once stated, patents 'added the fuel of interest to the fire of genius.'"

—George W. Bush, President of the United States

IP Firewalls

Toy companies are built on two kinds of property. The offices and manufacturing sites are physically built on what is called real property. For example, Hasbro and Mattel, the global leaders of our industry, have substantial real property holdings around the world, from their headquarters in Pawtucket, Rhode Island, and El Segundo, California, to branch offices and factories around the world. But without their *intellectual* properties, they would be out of business. The IP is the lifeblood of all toy companies.

Intellectual property (IP) is defined as any product of the human intellect that is unique, novel, and unobvious, and that has some value when commercialized. IP encompasses ideas, inventions, patents, trademarks, copyrights, and trade secrets, to name a few of the elements covered under this umbrella.

411 The Office of Independent Inventor Programs was established at the U.S. Patent and Trademark Office in 1999. Reporting directly to the Director of the USPTO, the office gives independent inventors and entrepreneurs a direct channel to the highest levels of the USPTO. For information, call 703-306-5568, fax 703-306-5570, or e-mail independentinventor@uspto.gov.

Where would Mattel be today without intellectual properties such as Barbie and Hot Wheels? Where would Hasbro be today without such game brands as Monopoly, Clue, Risk, Connect Four, Battleship, Candy Land, Trivial Pursuit, The Game of Life, and Operation, to name a few? These brands have generated and continue to generate the money that allows the two companies to expand, develop in-house ideas, and acquire intellectual property, including innovations from the independent inventing community.

Watch for Falling Lawsuits

Few industries are as receptive to reviewing outside submissions as the toy industry. This is because it is a fashion industry, and no company can afford to be caught with its trends down. Product remains king in the toy industry—a lesson, by the way, that many stubborn, MBA-trained, financially focused executives still have to learn the hard way.

Unlike many industries, the toy industry doesn't normally require that a concept be protected before it is reviewed. There are many reasons for this, but perhaps the most important is that when the manufacturer licenses an idea, it may likely be on and off the market before a patent issues. A toy or game manufacturer, therefore, is more concerned that a product is original (has not been misappropriated) and does not infringe on existing intellectual property.

These concerns are very understandable. Toy companies are targets for unscrupulous, opportunistic inventors and lawyers who attempt to shake them down, claiming myriad types of IP infringement.

As the *Houston Chronicle* reported in its "Outlook" section, December 8, 1999, "With unpopular industries like tobacco and guns already under siege, an ambitious group of personal injury lawyers needed a fresh victim. They found one ripe for demonizing: those evil, manipulative, child-targeting, life-endangering manufacturers we all know and loathe, the toymakers."

This is not to say that there have never been cases in which toy manufacturers are in the wrong and get in trouble misappropriating an idea from an independent inventor or a competitor. They are far from unblemished, and each has had its share of problems. Such is the nature of this business. Intellectual property is a minefield across which even the most experienced and honorable companies can come into contact with an unseen hazard.

Sometimes the toymakers engage each other, as was the case when Hasbro went after Mattel in a battle over alleged patent infringement. Hasbro said that certain patents it has on an R/C vehicle, Ricochet, were infringed by Mattel's Rebound and Super Rebound R/C vehicles. Hasbro sued for damages. Ultimately, Mattel licensed the technology from Hasbro, according to a source close to this case.

Another example of companies going after each other was when OddzOn and Just Toys went to court over footballs. OddzOn sells the popular Vortex tossing ball, a foam football with a tail and fin structure. It said that a ball by Just Toys, called the Ultra Pass, infringed on its design patent (D346,001). OddzOn added claims of trade dress infringement and state-law unfair competition, asserting that the Ultra Pass line was likely to be confused with OddzOn's Vortex and that the Ultra Pass packaging was likely to be confused with the Vortex packaging. Just Toys denied infringement and asserted that the patent was invalid. On cross-motions for summary judgment, the district court held that the patent was not shown to be invalid and was not infringed. The court also held that Just Toys did not infringe OddzOn's on trade dress. OddzOn appealed the decision and lost.

Toy Trivia

40. Sea Monkeys are what form of life?

a. Primates that swim

b. Brine shrimp

c. A species of sea horse

So, both licensors and licensees must be very careful. It is not wise to play fast and loose with IP. Most of the inventors and manufacturers interviewed for this book have had a brush with IP problems, but few of the professional inventors ever go into a court of law against a toy company. Typically, problems are ironed out between the inventor and the head of a business unit, to preserve the relationship, and the lawyers are called off. Where elephants fight, grass does not grow.

In fact, one of the reasons companies work with a recognized cadre of professional product sources is that these inventors have a vested interest in not initiating litigation and, thereby, breach long-established business relationships. Inventors must continue licensing future ideas if they are to stay in business.

Speaking of Lawyers ...

Our publisher's lawyers want us to say that the information in this chapter is not intended to be legal advice. Thus, readers (that's you!) are cautioned that patent and trademark statutes (read: laws) and regulations should be carefully reviewed and understood before taking any action to apply for a patent, trademark, copyright, or trade secret.

The Pros Protect Their IP

Many independent inventors successfully obtain patents or register trademarks. Here is a sampling. Vic Reiling, a 32-year career creative source, claims to hold about 25 patents and 1 trademark. Squirt-gun maven Alan Amron reports 28 letters patents and 2 trademarks. Benjamin Kingberg, whose luminescent slate is sold worldwide, shows 26 patents and 6 trademarks. Greg Hyman, creator of the first preschool electronic toy, Alphie (Playskool), lists 17 patents and 2 trademarks. David Hampton, the electronic wizard behind Furby (Tiger/Hasbro), has 5 patents. Derek Gable, a former Mattel engineer and long-time indy creative, has been awarded 50 patents and 6 trademarks. Elliot Rudell, inventor of Gurlz (Irwin), lays claim to 60 patents and 25 trademarks. And Eddy Goldfarb, the dean of independent toy inventors, earned about 300 patents in his 55-year career, which is still going strong. Clearly, these pros want to protect their intellectual property.

The protection process is complicated and involves adherence to sophisticated legal requirements that are best handled by trained professionals. Therefore, you are strongly advised to employ an attorney or agent who is registered to practice at the USPTO to prepare, file, and prosecute your patent applications.

FirstGov.com Is Open for Business

There is a substantial body of literature on how to protect intellectual property. It is not the focus of this book to cover the subject in depth, but this chapter is designed to give you a primer on the subject and an overview of your options. If you have a computer hooked to the internet, we encourage you to visit Uncle Sam's new website www.firstgov.com, the official U.S. gateway to all government information.

FirstGov.com's powerful search engine, with its ever-growing collection of topical and customer-focused links, connects you to millions of web pages, from the federal government and local governments to foreign nations around the world.

On FirstGov.com, you can search more than 51 million web pages, including those of the U.S. Patent and Trademark Office (PTO) and the U.S. Copyright Office.

On the other hand, if you like to feel paper, turn pages, and use your yellow highlighter, a practical resource (warning: shameless self-promotion ahead!) is *The Complete Idiot's Guide to Cashing In on Your Inventions* (ISBN 0-02-864220-1), by this book's co-author, Richard C. Levy, and its publisher. There are 155 pages in the book dedicated to patents, trademarks, copyrights, and trade secrets, accompanied by author insights.

> **411**
> Learn how to search patents like a pro. The USPTO offers monthly training for its EAST, WEST and X-Search systems. Hands-on work stations are available. A prepaid $25 reserves you a seat at a class and includes one set of training materials. Off-schedule, three-hour personal training sessions are available for a fee of $120. Classes take place at the USPTO Public Training Facility in Arlington, Virginia. For up-to-date information, call 703-308-3030.

Patents

A patent is a grant of property right by the U.S. government to an inventor, acting through the Patent and Trademark Office (PTO). It gives you the right to exclude others from making, using, or selling an invention. But take note: What is granted is not the right to make, use, or sell, but the right to exclude others from doing so. The term of a U.S. patent is 20 years from the date of application, subject to the payment of maintenance fees. The right conferred by the patent grant extends throughout the United States and its territories and possessions.

Some interesting patent facts:

◆ About 325,000 utility patent applications are filed each year.

◆ A patent cannot be obtained for a mere idea or suggestion. A complete description of the actual device or other subject matter sought to be patented is required.

◆ A prototype is not required to secure a patent. The Patent and Trademark Office does not require you to submit working prototypes with your applications. In fact, nothing in the PTO rules and regs says an inventor ever has to make a proving model of his or her invention.

"The toy industry moves faster than the Patent Office, so the issue ought to be getting toys to market rather than patents to print," says Elliot Rudell, inventor of Playskool's Weebles. "Inventors spend their time best inventing. Licensees admire patents, by the way. And for that reason alone, they offer value to an inventor/licensor."

"I am of a mixed mind on patents," says Bruce Lund, inventor of Milton Bradley's Fireball Island. "[Patents] are costly and time-consuming to obtain. They are clearly of value in the case of items such as Furby and Super Soaker. However, most toys have a life span of six months, and a patent is of little commercial value. The problem is, we never know in advance which item we will later wish we had patented. There are several products that we wish we had patented years ago, and if we had, we would have been the beneficiaries of millions in royalties. Hindsight is 20/20. Nonetheless, today we patent all of the items we license."

Beyond its obvious value as a protection from competition, a patent can sometimes give an inventor leverage in negotiating royalties. The argument could be made that a patented item carries a higher value than a product without patent protection. After all, even if a patent is ultimately not allowed, during the years of its pendency, the manufacturer may legally mark the product and its package with the notice "Patent Pending." The average application pendency at the PTO is 27 to 28 months.

A patent is an impressive asset for any inventor to have at a presentation, even if it does not trigger a higher royalty. A patent certainly gives the item on the table an edge. But patents cost money. Kris Halvorson, a patent attorney with a Ph.D. in chemistry, based in Tempe, Arizona, estimates that the cost of a simple mechanical patent with lots of moving parts, one that needs two or three office actions, costs between $5,000 and $6,000. This cost includes PTO filing fees. Add to this PTO maintenance fees at the 3-, 7-, and 11-year marks, and the cost goes up another $3,000.

Howard R. Fine, senior vice president and general counsel to Tiger Electronics (a division of Hasbro, Inc.), says, "My approach to patent protection for toys is to be cautious. Patents are expensive to obtain and, because of the nature of the toy business, usually do not issue until long after a product's life cycle is over or nearing its end. Moreover, many toy patents are narrowed considerably during prosecution and provide a lot less protection than originally sought. Accordingly, in most instances, the expense of obtaining a patent is not worth the potential benefits."

Fine adds, "If a product utilizes a technology or incorporates a feature that may have applications outside the product at issue, or if the product is truly unique and likely to inspire knockoffs for years to come, a patent is good idea."

"In an industry where 'knockoff' products are very prevalent, patent protection is desirable, particularly in the case of significant product offerings," says Dale R. Siswick, senior vice president of R&D, Hasbro Games. "In the case of proprietary products, protecting one's investment is a necessary evil from those who prey on other's creativity and innovation."

George Propsom, director of product development at Team Concepts, a company that specializes in electronic items, says of patents, "I find in our area of the business that patents are relatively unimportant. Sure, it is nice to have a patent, but it needs to be applied to something truly unique. I saw someone a few years ago secure a patent on a folding game board. Come on, what was the patent office thinking? This patent holder then proceeded to go after everyone who produced games with game boards in them.

"The name of the game is to be the first to market with a unique idea. For the time and money it takes to receive a patent, someone else could beat you to the market with a similar product. The first one to market is the one who gets the credit and recognition for developing the product. Remember, a patent is only as good as the first lawsuit."

Agent David Kremer, a partner in 7 Towns, Ltd., the company that discovered Rubik's Cube in Hungary and brought it to Ideal, says about patents, "In the vast majority of cases, it is unwise to patent your ideas. The life cycle of products in the toy business is too short to make this a useful protection, and the cost of the average patent set against the average total royalties is too high a ratio."

An informal survey of both professional inventors and corporate executives reveals that everyone would rather have a patented product, if possible.

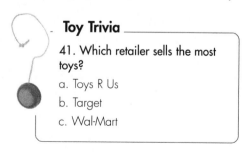

Toy Trivia

41. Which retailer sells the most toys?

a. Toys R Us

b. Target

c. Wal-Mart

Your Patent Options

You may apply for a *utility patent* if you have discovered or invented any new and useful process, machine, manufacture, or composition of matter, or any new and useful improvements thereof. Some toys and games that have been protected through utility patents include Norman and Arlene Farbricant's Dr. Drill 'n' Fill Play-Doh item (4,231,181), Lonnie Johnson's Super Soaker (4,591,071), and Eddy Goldfarb's Shark Attack game (5,163,863).

Jeff Conrad, vice president for outside development at Radica, says about utility patents, "If the invention/product has a mechanism, then it can qualify for a utility/ mechanical patent. This type of patent can be defended in court and is worthwhile as long as the inventor realizes the cost and time involved."

You may have heard about a *provisional patent* application (PPA). The term *provisional patent application* is misleading because it is not an application for patent protection at all. The purpose of a PPA is to formally establish a date of invention, should you need to ever prove it. Remember when you would mail something to yourself and not open the envelope, as a way to show the date of inception? This exercise is something like that.

In summary, the PPA provides you with a one-year period to further develop your invention, determine marketability, and seek a licensee. To obtain a patent, you must file a nonprovisional application within 12 months of the filing date of the provisional application.

You may apply for a *design patent* to protect any new, original, and ornamental design for an article of manufacture. The design patent protects only the appearance of an article, not its structure or utilitarian features. Some toys and games that have been awarded design patents are Gordon Barlow's SkeeBall (D269,358), Kenichi Sugino's handheld Nintendo game (D416,291), and Charlie Phillips and Ed Bick's Advance to Boardwalk game board (D293,121).

Radica's Conrad says about design patents compared to a utility patent, "A design patent can often be difficult to define and defend."

Patents Are Not Cheap—Who Pays?

If you want to have clear title to your patent as a licensor, you should pay the fees 100 percent, according to patent counsel. The moment a licensee pays even 1¢ of the expense, the licensee has a claim to ownership in your patent. If push ever comes to shove in a court of law, this investment, however minor, gives the licensee leverage. And if the licensee pays for everything, it becomes almost impossible for the inventor to effect a clean separation, even if a license is terminated, unless this issue is addressed up front. Good luck trying. Why would a manufacturer fund a patent and then give it back for free under any circumstances?

For the cash-strapped inventor, the arrangement may be made for patent expenses to be deducted from future royalties, or some verbiage may be added to the license agreement to the effect that the licensee will reassign the patent to its inventor for a designated dollar value when the product is no longer actively marketed.

Many inventors take care of the U.S. patent themselves and allow the licensee to pay for foreign patents, if it is felt advisable. Foreign patents are much more expensive to obtain than U.S. patents, and only the largest toymakers would even consider them. If they did, it would have to be for a major product introduction, usually involving a technology.

Yes, You Need a Patent Attorney

While the government says that you may prepare your own patent application (known as *pro se*), file it at the Patent and Trademark Office, and conduct the subsequent proceedings, if you are not familiar with such matters, you could get into considerable difficulty. And even if you are able to get a patent on your own, there is no guarantee that it will adequately protect your invention.

"The best thing for inventors to do is to write a first draft and then hand it to an attorney, since no one knows a product better than its inventor. Also, honest and early disclosure of prior art allows the applicant to diffuse often times off-kilter rejection points that could later have been brought up by the PTO," says Elliot Rudell.

Richard Besha, Esq., a veteran patent attorney at Nixon & Vanderhye, P.C., in Arlington, Virginia, agrees with Rudell. He says that books and computer software that imply that it is easy to do your own utility patents are not telling the whole story. "The danger is in the claim drafting," says Besha. "If you are not familiar with this art form, you could shoot yourself in the foot."

Even after many years of experience as a patent examiner, Besha says it was not until he had years of prosecution experience under his belt that he became proficient at claim drafting.

PTO Certified

The Patent and Trademark Office maintains a register of 21,160 active attorneys and 6,342 active agents who must comply with the regulations prescribed by the office. Those regulations require evidence not only that the person is of good moral character and of good repute, but also that he or she has the legal, scientific, and technical qualifications necessary to enable him or her to render patent applications.

To find a PTO-registered patent attorney in your area, go to the PTO website (www.uspto.gov) or call 703-306-4097.

Do Patents Matter?

Opinions are mixed about the value of patents. Most toy manufacturer licensing agreements require that the inventor attempt to secure a U.S. patent, at no expense to the corporation. On the other hand, the lack of patent protection is not a valid reason for 'a manufacturer to reject an item. The general attitude of a promotional toy company is that it will protect its market share through aggressive marketing, not patents.

"Patents can work when well written and well researched," continues California-based inventor Rudell. "The broader the claims, the bigger a target a patent presents itself for possible future disallowance, although disallowance actions are stringent in their requirements."

Patent Searching

"Locating prior art is one of the most important aspects of the patenting process," according to *The 21st Century Strategic Plan*, released by the PTO on July 5, 2002.

You can approach a search of prior art in three ways. Here are the headlines:

1. Hire a patent attorney, who will, in turn, hire a skilled patent searcher. The cost of the search is marked up and billed to you.
2. Hire a professional patent searcher yourself, and save a load of doh-re-me. There is no middleman.
3. Do it yourself at the PTO Public Search Room, at a Patent and Trademark Depository Library or online. Note: The problem with online searching is that it is extremely time-consuming and the keyword search capability is still very limited.

The risk of mining the collection of prior art yourself is that it takes experience to identify a field of search, select the right tools to perform the search, and determine an appropriate search strategy. Having said this, it is beneficial for every serious inventor to try a couple searches to get a feel for the process. Patent searcher George Harvill, of Greentree Information Services, specializes in toys and games. If you want to contact Greentree as part of comparative shopping, call 301-469-0902 or e-mail g.greentreeinform@verizon.net.

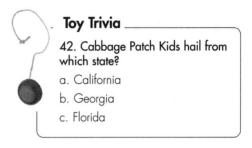

Toy Trivia

42. Cabbage Patch Kids hail from which state?

a. California

b. Georgia

c. Florida

Trademarks

Barbie. Clue. Connect Four. Etch-a-Sketch. Furby. G. I. Joe. Magnetic Poetry. Micro Machines. Monopoly. Nerf. Play-Doh. Taboo. Tickle Me Elmo. Scrabble. Uno. A trademark is any word, name, symbol, or device, or any combination thereof, adopted and used by an inventor, manufacturer, or merchant to identify goods and distinguish them from those manufactured or sold by others. Catchy trademarks are important tools in selling toys and games to manufacturers. Many IP and marketing professionals will tell you that trademarks are more important than patents.

Trademarks can be kept alive forever, whereas patents expire in 20 years. As long as the mark is being used in commerce and the proper maintenance fees are paid, it lives. For instance, the boar's head logo of Gordon's Gin is still alive and well (U.S. Trademark 21734); it was registered September 13, 1892, and claims a date of first use of 1769.

"There are more than six million words in the English language alone, and virtually all of them are registered," according to Julie Cottineau, a managing director at Interbrand, a brand consulting company.

A good trademark helps create immediate product identification. It helps tell the product's story. Just as trademarks are used by manufacturers to sell consumers, they can be helpful in giving the total product picture to the manufacturer.

Trademarks build goodwill between a product or service and the consumer. Nothing is more important. A strong, well-publicized mark frequently has value far beyond the physical assets of a company. It is a goodwill that spans generations. Consider the value of these game trademarks to Hasbro: Monopoly, Clue, Chutes and Ladders, The Game of Life, Twister, Scrabble, Operation, Connect Four, Candy Land, Cootie, Jenga, Ouija, Yahtzee, Hi! Ho! Cherry-O, Original Memory Games, Hungry Hungry Hippos, Ants in the Pants, Stratego, Battleship, Simon, and on and on. None of these games has any patent protection. It is all about trademarks and goodwill.

Companies aggressively protect their marks. The Mattel website, for example, displays this warning: "The likeness of the Barbie doll, character, silhouette and accessory icons, the color 'Barbie pink,' the stylized 'B' and other trademarks designated by ® and ™ are U.S. trademarks of Mattel, Inc."

Trademarks uniquely associate a product or a service with a particular source, even if that source is unknown to the consumer. Thus, trademarks help businesses build and retain demand for their products and services while enabling consumers to quickly identify and make a purchase decision based upon a recognized trademark. Because of their value, it is vital for every company—be it a multinational conglomerate or a one-product start-up—to make every effort to protect its trademarks.

Inventions can be named in many ways.

For the inventor:

Erno Rubik = Rubik's Cube

Beatrice Alexander Behrman = Madam Alexander Dolls

For its function:

Hula Hoop

Slip 'n Slide

Using initials or acronyms:

G. I. Joe

C.O.P.S

Using components or ingredients of the invention:

Silly Putty

Barrel of Monkeys

Using word combinations (such as repeated consonant sounds and rhyming words):

Gnip Gnop

Hula Hoop

A toy developer doesn't generally have to register a suggested product trademark before presenting it for review, but some do. "I registered an Intent-to-Use application on Family Reunion (USAopoly) within five minutes of thinking of it," said co-author Richard Levy, referring to his game. "I had that kind of confidence in my ability to create and license a board game under this mark. I am not always that aggressive."

Larry Mass, a professional inventor who created Rumblin' Thunder (Tonka) and Boglins (Mattel), among his 50 licensed products, says, "More often than not, we do not file an application for a trademark. In my experience, the manufacturer often prefers its own selection. However, if we love a name that we've created and feel it integrates perfectly with the toy/game, then we likely will file." Mass reports owning around 30 trademarks.

Dan Klitsner, head of K.I.D. Group of San Francisco, says of a name that fit his product from day one: "We felt Bop-It caught the key action in the game and showed the concept with that name. Players listen to audio commands that randomly instruct them to twist, pull, and 'bop' the game device," he explains. "The trademark Bop-It continued in use through the development process and remained as the name of the game on peg displays today."

Increasingly today, mostly because retailers are demanding products that have immediate consumer recognition, toy and game companies rely more on trademarks that they license or on their own classic house brands. Hasbro's Dale Siswick says, "An advantage of the license umbrella is that it authenticates individual products that fall under that brand. This is a real boost for the product, as long as the license sustains itself." He adds that branding is another way of providing some level of limited protection.

Searching and Filing Trademarks

Using the Trademark Electronic Search System (TESS), you can search online. Go to www.uspto.gov. TESS contains more than three million pending, registered, and expired federal trademarks. You don't need to hire anyone to conduct a federal search of trademarks. A word of caution: TESS does not search common law marks.

The USPTO also offers a wonderful system called the Trademark Electronic Application System (e-TEAS) that allows you to fill out a form and check it for completeness over the Internet. Using e-TEAS, you can then submit the form directly to the USPTO over the Internet, making an official filing online. Or, you can print the completed form for mailing to the USPTO. It's your choice.

For answers to questions about trademark filing requirements, call the PTO at 703-557-INFO.

Patent and Trademark Depository Libraries

Eighty-eight Patent and Trademark Depository Libraries (PTDLs) are located throughout the nation in prestigious academic, research, and public libraries. Their purpose, according to Carole A. Shores, director of PTDL Programs, is to "bring more information and help to all the people out there who need it and can't afford to pay big money to get it. We really listen to inventors, and when they bring requests in to us, we try very hard to give them what they want."

PTDLs receive current issues of U.S. patents and maintain collections of earlier issued patents. The scope of these collections may vary from library to library, ranging from patents of only recent years to some issued as far back as 1790. They have extensive trademark lists as well. Open to the general public, the PTDLs have all the official publications on patents and trademarks from the Patent and Trademark Office.

To be well rounded as an inventor, you should visit a PTDL if you're close to one and become familiar with its workings. There is no charge.

Many PTDLs offer interesting programs led by visiting experts. This makes them excellent venues for networking with other inventors.

Patent and Trademark Depository Libraries

To double-check phone numbers, addresses, etc., please call 1-800-786-9199, the PTO General Information Services number.

Alabama:

Auburn University Libraries, 205-844-1737

Birmingham Public Library, 205-226-3620

Alaska, Anchorage, Z. J. Loussac Public Library, 907-562-7323

Arizona, Tempe, Noble Library, Arizona State University, 602-965-7010

Arkansas, Little Rock, Arkansas State Library, 501-682-2053

California:

Los Angeles Public Library, 213-228-7220

Sacramento, California State Library, 916-654-0069

San Diego Public Library, 619-236-5813

San Francisco Public Library, 415-557-4488

Sunnyvale Patent Clearinghouse, 408-730-7290

Colorado, Denver Public Library, 303-640-8847

Connecticut:

New Haven, Free Public Library, 203-946-7452

Hartford, Hartford Public Library, 860-543-8628

Delaware, Newark, University of Delaware Library, 302-831-2965

District of Columbia, Howard University Libraries, 202-806-7252

Florida:

Fort Lauderdale, Broward County Main Library, 305-357-7444

Miami-Dade Public Library, 305-375-2665

Orlando, University of Central Florida Libraries, 407-823-2562

Tampa Campus Library, University of South Florida, 813-974-2726

Georgia, Atlanta, Price Gilbert Memorial Library, Georgia Institute of Technology, 404-894-4508

Hawaii, Honolulu, Hawaii State Public Library System, 808-586-3477

Idaho, Moscow, University of Idaho Library, 208-885-6235

Illinois:

Chicago Public Library, 312-747-4450

Springfield, Illinois State Library, 217-782-5659

Indiana:

Indianapolis, Marion County Public Library, 317-269-1741

West Lafayette, Siegesmund Engineering Library, Purdue University, 317-494-2872

Iowa, Des Moines, State Library of Iowa, 515-281-4118

Kansas, Wichita, Ablah Library, Wichita State Library, 316-689-3155

Kentucky, Louisville Free Public Library, 502-574-1611

Louisana, Baton Rouge, Troy H. Middleton Library, Louisana State University, 504-388-8875

Maine, Orono, Raymond H. Fogler Library, University of Maine, 207-581-1691

Maryland, College Park, Engineering and Physical Sciences Library, University of Maryland, 301-405-9157

Massachusetts:

Amherst, Physical Sciences Library, University of Massachusetts, 413-545-1370

Boston Public Library, 617-536-5400, Ext. 265

Michigan:

Ann Arbor, Media Union, University of Michigan, 734-647-5735

Big Rapids, Abigail S. Timme Library, Ferris State University, 616-592-3602

Detroit Public Library, 313-833-3379

Minnesota, Minneapolis Public Library and Information Center, 612-630-6120

Mississippi, Jackson, Mississippi Library Commission, 601-961-4111

Missouri:

Kansas City, Linda Hall Library, 816-363-4600

St. Louis Public Library, 314-241-2288, Ext. 390

Montana, Butte, Montana College of Mineral Science and Technology Library, 406-496-4281

Nebraska, Lincoln, Engineering Library, University of Nebraska-Lincoln, 402-472-3411

Nevada:

Las Vegas, Clark County Library, (Not Yet Operational)

Reno, University of Nevada-Reno Library, 702-784-6500

New Hampshire, Concord, New Hampshire State Library, 603-271-2239

New Jersey:

Newark Public Library, 973-733-7779

Piscataway, Library of Science and Medicine, Rutgers University, 908-445-2895

New Mexico, Albuquerque, University of New Mexico General Library, 505-277-4412

New York:

Albany, New York State Library, 518-474-5355

Buffalo and Erie Country Public Library, 716-858-7101

New York Public Library, (The Research Libraries), 212-592-7000

Rochester, Central Library of Rochester and Monroe County, 716-428-8110

Stony Brook, Melville Library, Room 1101, SUNY at Stony Brook, 516-632-7148

North Carolina, Raleigh, D.H. Hill Library, North Carolina State University, 919-515-2935

North Dakota, Grand Forks, Chester Fritz Library, University of North Dakota, 701-777-4888

Ohio:

Akron, Akron-Summit County Public Library, 330-643-9075

Cincinnati, Public Library of Hamilton County, 513-369-6971

Cleveland Public Library, 216-623-2870

Columbus, Ohio State University Libraries, 614-292-3022

Toledo/Lucas County Public Library, 419-259-5209

Oklahoma, Stillwater, Oklahoma State University Center for International Trade Development, 405-744-7086

Oregon, Portland, Lewis & Clark College, 503-768-6786

Pennsylvania:

Philadelphia, The Free Library of, 215-686-5331

Pittsburgh, The Carnegie Library of, 412-622-3138

University Park, Paterno Library, Penn State University, 814-865-6369

Puerto Rico:

Bayamon, General Library, University of PR, 787-786-5225

Mayaguez, General Library, University of PR, 787-832-4040 Ext 2022

Rhode Island, Providence Public Library, 401-455-8027

South Carolina, Clemson, R. M. Cooper Library, Clemson University, 803-656-3024

South Dakota, Rapid City, Devereaux Library, South Dakota School of Mines and Technology, 605-394-1275

Tennessee:

Memphis & Shelby County Public Library and Information Center, 901-725-8877

Nashville, Stevenson Science Library, Vanderbilt University, 615-322-2775

Texas:

Austin, McKinney Engineering Library, University of Texas at Austin, 512-495-4500

College Station, Sterling C. Evans Library, Texas A & M University, 409-845-5745

Dallas Public Library, 214-670-1468

Houston, Fondren Library, Rice University, 713-348-5483

San Antonio, San Antonio Public Library, (Not Yet Operational)

Utah, Salt Lake City, Marriott Library, University of Utah, 801-581-8394

Vermont, Burlington, Baily/Howe Library, U. of VT, 802-656-2542

Virginia, Richmond, James Branch Cabell Library, Virginia Commonwealth University, 804-828-1104

Washington, Seattle, Engineering Library, University of Washington, 206-543-0740

West Virginia, Morgantown, Evansdale Library, West Virginia University, 304-293-4695 Ext 5113

Wisconsin:

Madison, Kurt F. Wendt Library, University of Wisconsin-Madison, 608-262-6845

Milwaukee Public Library, 414-286-3051

Wyoming, Cheyenne, Wyoming State Library, (Not Yet Operational)

Copyrights

Copyright protection covers the form of expression rather than the subject matter. For example, the rules of the game could be copyrighted as a piece of writing, but this would prevent others only from copying the rules; it would not prevent them from writing another set of rules of their own or from making and using the game. Copyrights taken out today last until 50 years after the death of the author. Special rules apply to works created by employees as part of their jobs.

Toy Trivia

43. When G. I. Joe was launched in 1964, it was hyped as _____.

a. America's Movable Fighting Man
b. America's Combat Hero
c. The All American Soldier

The process of securing copyright protection is frequently misunderstood. In years past, it was necessary to fill out special forms and send them to the Library of Congress, together with a check and copies of the original work. Under the current law, no publication or registration or other Copyright Office action is required to secure copyright. Today copyright is secured "automatically" when the work is created, and the work is "created" when it is fixed in a copy or is phonorecorded for the first time.

Notice of Copyright

Before you publicly show or distribute your work, it is your responsibility to put a notice of copyright on it. The notice should contain the following elements:

1. The symbol ©, the word *Copyright*, or the abbreviation *Copr.*

2. The year of first publication of the work. In the case of compilations or derivative works incorporating previously published material, the year of first publication

of the compilation or derivative work is enough. The year may be omitted where a pictorial, graphic, or sculptural work with accompanying text, if any, is reproduced in or on dolls, toys, or any useful articles.

3. The name of the owner of copyright in the work, or an abbreviation by which the name can be recognized, or a generally known alternative of the owner. Example: © 2003 Richard C. Levy and Ronald O. Weingartner. Affix the notice prominently enough to provide "reasonable notice of the claim of copyright."

These points notwithstanding, it is still prudent to submit a formal application to the Library of Congress. This establishes a "public record" of your claim and entitles you to a certificate of registration (required if you have to go into court over infringement). The cost is $30 per application. Fees change from time to time, so log onto www.loc.gov or call 202-707-3000 to confirm the most current fee.

Fair Use

Many in the toy industry play fast and loose with copyright issues as they bend to pressures and demands by management and the market for their new products. There is frequently an attitude that they'll claim "fair use" and deal with it afterward if caught—for now, it's "Damn the torpedoes, full speed ahead!"

The so-called fair use doctrine has developed through a substantial number of court decisions over the years. This doctrine has been codified in Section 107 of the copyright law. You can read it in detail at www.copyright.gov/title17/92chap1.html#107.

Section 107 contains a list of the various purposes for which the reproduction of a particular work may be considered "fair," such as criticism, comment, news reporting, teaching, scholarship, and research. Section 107 also sets out four factors to be considered in determining whether a particular use is fair:

1. The purpose and character of the use, including whether such use is of commercial nature or is for nonprofit educational purposes

2. The nature of the copyrighted work

3. The amount and substantiality of the portion used in relation to the copyrighted work as a whole

4. The effect of the use upon the potential market for or value of the copyrighted work

The distinction between fair use and infringement may be unclear and not easily defined. No specific number of words, lines, or notes may safely be taken without permission. Acknowledging the source of the copyrighted material does not substitute for obtaining permission.

Board Games

Since there are so many inventors of board games, it is worth a special look at this category vis-à-vis copyrights. First and foremost, the idea for a game is not protected by copyright. The same is true of the name and title given to the game (except if it is a trademark) and of the method or methods for playing it.

Copyright protects only the particular manner of your expression in literary, artistic, or musical form. Copyright protection does not extend to any idea, system, method, device, or trademark material involved in the development, merchandising, or playing of a game. Once your game has been made public, nothing in the copyright law prevents others from developing another game based upon similar principles.

Some material prepared in connection with a game may be subject to copyright if it contains enough literary or pictorial expression. For example, the copy that describes the rules for Hasbro's Trivial Pursuit, or the pictorial matter that appears on the Endless Games' *Men Are from Mars, Women Are from Venus* game board or package may be registered.

For the most up-to-date information on obtaining copyrights, or for specific information on copyrights, contact a copyright information specialist at 202-479–0700 between the hours of 8:30 A.M. and 5:00 P.M. EST. Go to www.loc.gov. You can also send a written request to the Copyright Office, Library of Congress, 101 Independence Ave., S.E., Washington, D.C. 20559.

Trade Secrets

Arguably the most celebrated and legendary trade secret is the Coca-Cola formula. The ingredient called 7X is the mixture of fruit oils and spices that gives the syrup its signature flavor, and it's *very* important to the Coca-Cola Company to keep its formula secret.

A trade secret is a plan or process, tool, mechanism, or compound known only to its owner and those partners and employees to whom it is necessary to confide it. For example, the formulation for Educational Insights' Sea Monkeys is a trade secret. The trade secrets of a company are its crown jewels. Trade secrets are not patented because, through doing so, they would no longer be a secret and the owner would lose any competitive business advantage the secret afforded.

Trade secrets do not need to be registered with or granted by any government agencies. If you want to keep something as a trade secret, just take reasonable steps to keep your secret secret. Trade secrets are potentially unlimited in duration.

Independent inventors can have trade secrets, but simply classifying product-development information as a trade secret is not enough. Information that is known to the public or that can be easily gathered from reading trade publications, scientific journals, and so forth is not considered a trade secret.

If you haven't taken careful, deliberate steps to protect the trade secret, you may have compromised your secret. On the other hand, if the documentation you sign with the prospective licensee acknowledges your trade secret and promises (on behalf of the company and its employees) to hold your information confidential, then the use or release of this could be interpreted as willful and malicious misappropriation.

The Uniform Trade Secrets Act (UTSA) is legislation drafted by the National Conference of Commissioners on Uniform State Laws. Copies of the UTSA can be ordered from the National Conference of Commissioners on Uniforms State Laws, 676 North St. Clair St., Suite 1700, Chicago, IL 60611.

Forty states have enacted various statutes modeled after the UTSA, so do not rely on the UTSA without consulting with intellectual property counsel.

The best advice is not to reveal anything of a trade secret nature until and unless you have appropriate documentation agreed to and signed off on by an officer of the reviewing entity. Your nondisclosure document should be drafted by an attorney who specializes in trade secrets. Don't just assume that a patent counsel can handle it.

There you have them—patents, trademarks, copyrights, and trade secrets. Each provides a unique form of protection. But in the end, it is unique toy and game functions or a play feature, brilliant product execution, and an effective marketing campaign that will provide the most protection in the competitive industry marketplace.

Toy Trivia

44. Classic toy Snoopy Sniffer was introduced by which company?

a. Ideal

b. Fisher-Price

c. Playskool

Fun Facts

- Charles Pajeau, a stone mason, was inspired to invent Tinkertoys after observing his kids building structures comprised of pencils stuck into empty spools of thread. After some refinement of the components, the product was launched at a drugstore inside New York City's Grand Central Station.

- A school teacher in Cincinnati, Ohio, Joseph McVicer, created Play-Doh in 1955. It was derived from wallpaper paste and created for his sister's pre-school students. Rainbow Crafts, a Cincinnati, Ohio, company, sold a 1½-pound can of off-white Play-Doh to department stores in 1956. Since then, more than 700 million pounds of Play-Doh in all colors have been sold. The formulation remains a secret.

- Spirograph was created by Dennis Fischer, an Englishman. He took it to the 1965 Nuremberg International Toy Fair, where Kenner licensed the rights to make and market it in the United States. More than 30 million units have been sold to date.

- Master doll artist Bernard Lipfert designed about 80 percent of all American dolls during the decades of the '30s and '40s. A freelancer, he worked for just about every American doll maker. Lipfert was born on December 22, 1886, in Germany. He died January 6, 1974, age 87, at his home on Long Island, New York.

- Austrian Eduard Haas III created Pez candy in the late 1920s. Pez is an abbreviation of the German word for peppermint, "pfefferminz."

Chapter 7

Life's a Pitch: How to Sell Your Ideas

"Given two equally good concepts, the inventor with pizzazz, passion, showmanship, and a well-thought-out presentation will have the edge that could make the difference in a company taking or passing on an item."

—Mike Hirtle, vice president for concept acquisition and inventor relations, Hasbro Games

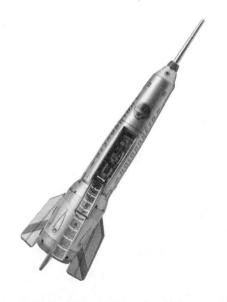

There's No Business Like …

"I lied," said San Francisco–based inventor Ralph Osterhout to a surprised Don Kingsborough, CEO of Yes! Entertainment, and Bill Radin, his vice president of engineering. The executives had made a special trip up from Pleasanton, an hour south of San Francisco, to see him on the promise that they would be viewing a "huge" new line of toys.

"I have only a single item to show you," the independent inventor fessed up.

Kingsborough, the man who also founded Worlds of Wonder and brought us Teddy Ruxpin in the mid-1980s, became infuriated and demanded to know what the item did.

"I invented this little wind-up car," Osterhout explained, pointing to what appeared to be a garden-variety vehicle. "It will cost you $40,000."

The CEO went ballistic. He was ready to storm out and drive the 60 miles back to his office. "This is a 35-year-old idea that nobody will buy!" he chided the inventor.

Smiling politely, Osterhout, a former U.S. Navy SEAL described by *Wired* magazine as a refugee from the covert world of high-tech weaponry, told the irate Kingsborough that he would demonstrate the car, but from the moment it started to move, Kingsborough would have only 10 seconds to license it. After 10 seconds, Osterhout would walk out and take the concept to a competitor, no matter how much he was offered.

Kingsborough became red-faced and started "swearing colorfully," recalled the inventor. "I calmly said that if he decided to buy the item in less than 10 seconds, he had to take me to dinner and purchase the most expensive bottle of wine on the menu."

Osterhout placed the tiny car on the conference table and pushed it back and forth rapidly to wind it up.

"Put your finger on top of the car," the inventor told the CEO. He asked Radin to time the car's performance with his wristwatch.

Kingsborough lifted his finger, and the vehicle rapidly accelerated about 4 feet down the table, snapped open lengthwise, and up popped a ramp with a tiny airplane on it. The plane's swept-back wings opened—and it self-launched off the ramp, flying out of the room and down the stairs.

"I'll take it!" screamed a jubilant CEO.

"Six seconds!" announced an amazed vice president.

"I'm hungry, and you're buying," quipped Osterhout.

The line was called Air Vectors. Ralph Osterhout shows that sometimes your style of selling is as important to closing the deal as what you are selling.

This dramatic presentation shows excitement, personal and conceptual; the importance of relationships; the quality of prototyping that's required; and the technical savvy inventors need to establish to get the commitment to a significant next step. Few new ideas are bought on the spot anymore. Few execs swing at the first pitch. And just because your item looks good does not mean it will get looked at. How many people do you know who are impeccably groomed but dull?

Once Upon a Time ...

In the decades of the 1950s through the 1980s and into the very early 1990s, it was often enough for an inventor to plant the seed of an idea with a company to qualify for a royalty. An inventor might present a basic breadboard, a marker rendering, or a partially developed idea (or, believe it or not, just whisper a concept in an executive's ear), and then sign a deal and qualify for a royalty.

In those years, it was not uncommon for an inventor to sell a concept and not see it again until it was unveiled at the next New York Toy Fair. Frequently, in such instances, an inventor did not even recognize his or her brainchild when it came out the other end of the development chute.

But for pro Charlie Phillips, whose inventing career has spanned 20-plus years, selling ideas has never been a walk in the park. He remembers coming to New York City in 1974 with four games to sell. "My wife's farewell assurance was, 'It's okay if you sell only three,'" he fondly recalls. "They are still on the shelf, unsold."

Phillips, who conceives about 200 ideas annually and owns New England R&D, continues, "I sold my first game to Hasbro. It was called I Vant to Bite Your Finger. It became a modest hit in 1978–79." After that meeting, Phillips told his wife, Ellie, that the game business could be easy. "I have never been more wrong in my life," says the highly successful inventor of a string of licensed games, including Clue, Jr. (Parker Bros.)

A former R&D director at a now defunct Twin Cities toymaker tells a story about when Marvin Glass, a legendary toy inventor, came in with a concept. Glass presented it with his signature showmanship and energy. Everyone loved it. Then someone from R&D piped up, "How do we make it?"

"That's your job," Glass said. The CEO agreed with Glass. They shook hands on the deal and went out for lunch, leaving the R&D team to figure out all the details.

A Clockwork Orange

Years ago, when the industry was filled with product-hungry companies, there was strong competition to see an inventor's latest first. It was also a time when some inventors could sell concepts sight unseen. Take Larry Jones, a 42-year industry veteran and the founder and president of Cal R&D.

Jones had scheduled a meeting with Kenner president Bernard Loomis in a hotel suite in Century City, Beverly Hills. Loomis, who has been inducted into the 1992 Toy Industry Hall of Fame, has credentials that include leading the charge to market for Strawberry Shortcake, Care Bears, and Star Wars toys among myriad other accomplishments.

"I was running late and my prototype was not ready. I could not reschedule," Jones says, recalling that all he had with him was a briefcase containing little more than his lunch in a brown paper bag.

The two old friends greeted each other and sat down, and Jones opened his case to get a pad of paper. "I tried to hide my lunch from view, as I was a little embarrassed," Jones recollects. "But he noticed it."

Loomis knew Jones was scheduled to see another toy company that afternoon, which was the reason for their morning meeting. To assuage the visiting executive, Jones told him the item was not ready but that he would send it ASAP.

Loomis got up and reached for the briefcase, accusing Jones of having a mock-up in it that he would not get to see but that the competition would. Jones quickly closed the case, waving Loomis off.

Jones says that after five minutes of back-and-forth ribbing, it got serious. "He turned red and was getting mad because I would not show him the item. So I finally told him that if he wanted to see what was in the bag, he would have to sign a disclosure document, which he did, and give me 5 percent and a cash advance of $10,000 sight unseen. He was so pissed. He agreed and signed a handwritten paper stating the terms. I was about to crack up, but felt I could play it a little further. I asked him what I was going to show at the afternoon meeting if he took what was in the bag."

Loomis went over and picked an orange out of a fruit basket. He tossed it to the inventor. "Show them this," he jested.

"I caught the orange, quickly got up, left the brown bag on the table, and exited the building. Of course, I took the signed paper with me," Jones said.

Later that same day, the friends spoke by phone. Loomis was cracking up over the incident. Jones, of course, tore up the paper.

Change Is Inevitable, Except from Vending Machines

Over the past dozen years, the industry has become much more difficult, even for the most talented inventors. A number of these independent creative sources, once fixtures in the industry, have disappeared from the hallowed, narrow halls and steep stairwells once trekked at the 200 Fifth Avenue Toy Center during Toy Fair.

It is not only inventors missing in action. The corporate scene has also undergone severe seismic activity. Executives and toy companies have slipped into deep faults, never to be seen again. Their names could make up a list as long as the product roster at the top of Chapter 1.

Benjamin Kinberg, an independent inventor for over 30 years, recalls when the toy industry was composed of literally thousands of small and medium-size companies and a handful of larger players. "Today the industry is almost completely dominated by two giants, Mattel and Hasbro," Kinberg says.

And although big-box, mass-market retailers like Wal-Mart and Target dictate a lot about new products, retailers are not immune to damage. Chain after chain has gone belly-up under the stress caused by mismanagement and ground-shaking consumerism. Unable to adapt, retailers have dropped like marbles in a game of Kerplunk. Ames, Bradlees, Caldor, Child World, Fingerhut, Hills, Kiddie City, LearningSmith, Lionel Leisure, Milton D. Meyer (a.k.a. Family Toy Warehouse), Montgomery Ward, Natural Wonders, Service Merchandise, Store of Knowledge, World of Science, Venture, E-toys, and Toysmart.com. And the huge chain K-Mart is on financial life support.

"It's a shorter list if I just tell you the ones that are around," says Frank Adler, executive vice president for sales and marketing at Uncle Milton Industries, responding to a writer about how many retailers have gone out of business.

Pat Duncan, the founder and president of Great American Puzzle Factory, comments on the biggest change she has seen in the past 22 years: "the explosive growth and then sudden demise of educational stores and up-market specialty retailers coupled with the increase in alternate channels of distribution such as mail order catalogs and e-retailing."

Companies that once provided opportunities for inventors have disappeared through acquisition by Hasbro and Mattel. Through bankruptcy or buyout, other corporate players have experienced industry fadeout: Aurora, Axlon, Azrak-Hamway, Buddy L, Child Guidance, Coleco, Colorforms, Fundimension, Gabriel, Galoob, Games Gang, Gilbert, Ideal, International Games, Irwin, Kenner, Knickerbocker, Knots, Kohner, Kransco, Leisure Dynamics, Marchon, Marx, Matchbox, Mego, Nasta, Nylint, Playtime,

Schaper, Selchow & Righter, Skilcraft, Superior Toy, 3M, Tiger, Tonka, Topper, Trendmaster, Tyco, Western Publishing, Worlds of Wonder .... There are others.

Mattel's vice president of game and puzzle marketing worldwide, Phil Jackson, sees the reduction of trade customers and the pressure on products to gain remaining shelf space as a huge change in recent years. He says, "Retailer consolidation and the need to perform or perish has reduced grass-roots and word-of-mouth opportunities to build a following for a game. There just isn't time. It has created a 'hit' mentality, much like TV programming or movie marketing's reliance on box office scores. There are just more great games than can fit on the shelves."

This dramatic paradigm shift has already left some toy and game inventors who could not understand and adapt behind like last year's Christmas toys. And the casualty list is likely to grow. Just as companies and retailers must reinvent themselves to survive, inventors must do likewise or risk perishing.

Hasbro's senior vice president for concept acquisition, the seasoned and savvy David Berko, agrees. Discussing the need for change within the professional inventing community and reflecting on the difficult current state of affairs, he jokes that it is possible that, "generations from now, people will not even know what a toy inventor is, except through the pages of this book."

The talents required for an inventor to succeed today involve more than creativity, "golden hands," and *shtikmeistering*. While inventiveness, technical expertise, and passion remain critical elements, the most successful inventors find themselves more involved with business, development, project management, and the marketing of their products.

411

Looking for prototype components? The Thomas Regional Director Company publishes industrial buying guides that provide listings and advertising to help you find companies, in 19 regions of the United States, that make just about anything you can imagine. To see if you qualify for a free subscription, call 1-888-REGIONAL or visit the website www.thomasregional.com.

Toy Trivia

45. Erno Rubik, inventor of Rubik's Cube, was a __ from Hungary.

a. mathematician

b. historian

c. surgeon

Challenges for Pros and Rookies

Like anyone who has ever been in sales knows, for those not doing it, it looks easy. But for salespeople actually making the cold calls, waiting for a key appointment, preparing the pitch, and, most important, coming away with the paper/order/deal, it's hard work. This reality gives inventors a doubly hard job. They have to come up with something new and fresh, and then find a licensee who will take the idea. Selling toy ideas indeed presents many challenges.

Challenge 1: Putting It Together

Inventors must work ever closer with their licensees, doing whatever is asked to bring a product to market. They must invest themselves in their concepts far beyond the idea or initial concept stage. This extended activity may include contracting specialized freelance engineering and design talent, sourcing components, conducting patent and trademark searches, doing initial market research, writing and editing rules/ directions for play, creating sell copy for packaging and promotional flyers, designing websites, contributing to key R&D and marketing meetings, and even doing PR.

Bottom line: If you want an idea to make the grade today, position yourself as *de facto* project manager. And you may not get paid for your personal time—just out-of-pocket expenses. This makes you the adhesive that holds things together and the lubricant that keeps everything flowing smoothly when problems arise or people lose focus, confidence, and commitment to a product that you think is a lock.

To be positioned as a multitasked inventor, you have to have "know-how" *and* "know-who." Perhaps no two people appreciate this more than Whit Alexander, 42, and Richard Tait, 39, the inventors of Cranium, the 2001 Game of the Year. The inventors had self-published their game before locking in an outlet. As they sat one day at a Seattle Starbucks discussing what to do about the problem, they realized that all around them were their target gamers, Starbucks consumers (25- to 35-year-olds).

As fate would have it, reports *Entrepreneur* magazine in its August 2002 edition, a friend of Tait's knew Howard Schultz, the CEO of Starbucks. Through this "know who," the partners got a meeting with Schultz and persuaded him to play Cranium. He liked it. Also fateful was that Starbucks had been contemplating selling a game. The guys soon signed a distribution deal to put games in 1,600 Starbucks by the winter of 1998. It's fair to say that without their personal Starbucks connection, Cranium would likely not have happened.

Company executives must reach a level of comfort with you and have total confidence in your capabilities. Obviously, this takes time. But it is easier to accomplish if you remember that you are always selling yourself first, and your innovation second. This way, if an idea is not accepted or the licensed idea goes south for reasons beyond your control, you will be invited back again and again. Remember, you cannot sell a person who isn't listening, and it's up to you to make someone hear what you have to offer as a development partner.

Your depth of involvement in each licensed product may mean fewer ideas generated and prototyped annually, but hopefully a higher percentage of placements and market launches because you'll be on the front line with the marketer. You need to provide such "value add" with every item. It comes under the heading of taking care of your customers. As the old saw goes, if you don't, someone else will.

The cross-pollination and synergism of corporate intrapreneurs and external entrepreneurs is what gets inventor products to market. It's a complex chain of people and events; if any individual link in the chain breaks, an entire project could flag. You need perseverance, dexterity, and leadership to organize and inspire multilevel teams of internal executives and external creative talents even as they navigate the turbulent and unforgiving seas of corporate bureaucracies. This is in addition to negotiating contracts, seeking market opportunities, and being willing to travel to far-away manufacturing facilities to see projects through to completion.

In summary, you will need a strong varsity team and a bench deep in talent. Today's inventors have to take much more responsibility for their products than in the past. An inventor who refuses to or cannot adapt to this environment never gets to be a "has-been"—he stays a "never-was".

California inventor David M. Hampton, the electronic wizard whose inspiration became Furby, spent two 40-plus–day stints in Hong Kong and at factories in China, away from his wife and sons, to ensure that the Chinese makers got the animatronic wonder toy manufactured to spec. While overseas, Hampton ran into fellow independent inventor Andy Filo, who was at Tiger's Hong Kong offices working on his licensed inventions. Tiger, now a division of Hasbro, was one of the first larger companies to encourage such inventor involvement. Tiger co-founders Randy Rissman and Roger Shiffman embraced outside inventors who could contribute to the development of what they licensed, and gave them the resources to get the job done.

Not all inventors can handle the intense involvement. On the other hand, some, like the partners in The Obb, excel under these conditions. Founded by Adam Kislevitz and his brothers Andy and Noah, they created Mattel's blockbusters Diva Starz, Mechanix Hot Wheels, and Air Rebound R/C. Their hot properties and deep involvement leave little time to commiserate and share some inventors' view of the down invention market. "While there are fewer outlets for new product concepts now than five years ago, companies expect more from inventors," says Adam. He goes on to explain that the manufacturer's needs have become much more specific, depending on where its strengths (real or imagined) lie. "Even in a market that has shrunk, each company is trying to establish its own identity." As a result, he says, many concepts need to be "custom made" for a given manufacturer.

Peggy Brown, vice president of R&D for Patch Products, a manufacturer of board games and puzzles, expands upon what Kislevitz describes. "Nowadays, on top of a great idea, it is not unreasonable for companies to ask inventors to provide all the game content, fully vetted and ready to be published, along with part drawings and even manufacturing cost estimates."

Toy Trivia

46. Chutes and Ladders is known by another name outside the United States. Which is it?
a. Snakes and Ladders
b. Oops & Downs
c. Chutes and Steps

Challenge 2: The Brandwashing of America

A good first step is to accept that entertainment licensing is here to stay, becoming a greater factor daily in the development and sale of toy ideas. Kislevitz observes, "Branding has homogenized the toy industry. Invention is now used in the context of a brand 'driver' item rather than as a standalone product."

If you want to sell more product, you must give more consideration to developing extensions to existing house lines or products based upon TV and film brands. This means a willingness to accept reduced royalties in some but not all cases. If Challenge 1 for inventors is to do more work, then sales Challenge 2 is to make sure the product happens even if layered by a character license.

Character licensing, discussed in detail in Chapter 11, is a $177 billion business worldwide. It shows no signs of weakening, in spite of frequent failures of licenses to perform. With exceptions like Furby and Cranium, both high-risk gambles by spirited, entrepreneurial toy and game marketers, the majority of new product introductions today are imprinted with well-known character licenses.

Years ago, if an inventor went to Fisher-Price showing a cuddly, soft little dog with expressive eyes and a playful function, the item, if accepted, would have been launched under a proprietary trademark. Today, the same concept would most likely be designed to resemble the blue canine star of the popular Nick Jr. television series *Blue's Clues*. In other words, even Fisher-Price, the maker and marketer of durable and distinctive playthings since 1931, and its retailers feel that this highly respected company needs licenses. A new TV name has more consumer drawing power than the name of a recognized manufacturer to reach mass-market sales goals.

A decade or so ago, an inventor might have shown a board game concept with an innovative feature, and the company would develop gameplay and some appealing graphics and offer it at an acceptable price point supported by an aggressive promotional plan. Today, that same new-game slot would likely be assigned to yet another version of Monopoly or UNO instead of taking a risk to build an unknown trademark.

The subhead of a story in *Time* magazine's October 25, 1999, issue read: "The big toymakers have a basic problem—they don't bother to come up with new toys anymore." *Time* reporter Karl Taro Greenfeld wrote that Mattel executives "can't remember the last hit toy the $4.8 billion company incubated without a movie licensing tie-in or an idea purchased from a smaller company." He said that the days when the firm was capable of organically growing a brand from the roots up seem long gone …. For the last decade, the company, along with rival Hasbro, has been relying on [company] acquisitions for sales growth."

William F. Dohrmann, who ran R&D between 1969 and 1998 at Parker Bros., Tiger Games, and Hasbro Games, and today owns Idea Development, an invention and idea representation business, says that entertainment licenses have a "choke hold" on the industry.

Just about every executive and inventor interviewed for this book expressed opinions about the pernicious effect of entertainment licensing on this industry, but no senior executive seemed willing to make the first move to change the situation. Almost everyone put the blame for the proliferation of licenses on the retailers, who, they claim, demand that a license be applied to a product. The use of a license crutch is particularly true when the trade sees a new low- or medium-promotion product. In fact, the largest retailers are acquiring rights and putting licenses on their own proprietary toy lines.

411

If you have been ripped off by an invention-marketing company or agent, the Federal Trade Commission (FTC) has a way for you to register your complaint online. Go to www.ftc.gov; you'll find it under Consumer Protection. Or, you call toll free 1-877-FTC-HELP.

A senior vice president at a major toy company said, on the basis of anonymity, that in the early days, movie studios promoted their films with huge ad campaigns, and this was a plus for the toy company. Today, he says, Hollywood does not do the same level of promotion. This forces the toy company to promote its products, which, in turn, helps the movie. And the studios have increased royalty demands.

"They should pay us," snapped the frustrated executive. "It has all turned around, and no one has the guts to draw a line in the stand. If no single company will do it, we should do it as an industry."

Toys R Us is licensing products directly from inventors as a way to increase its margins and get exclusive products, and to broaden its Pavilion line. Can Wal-Mart and Target be far behind?

Challenge No. 3: The MBA Syndrome

When the industry was filled with seasoned and aggressive toy and game marketers, independent inventors created concepts for people with a nose for product, passionate risk takers genuinely excited by the scent of innovation. Company owners and presidents even went out themselves to visit inventors and hear pitches. This still happens at smaller companies, but at the larger marketers, where inventors have their greatest chance of making meaningful royalties, the most senior executives are more interested in shareholder value than product value. Final product selection and line building has been delegated to MBAs and financial types, many with no roots in or feel for the mass-market toy industry.

But the old-timers knew what it took, and it went beyond business models and Excel spreadsheets. It was a combination of business and whimsy. Bernard Loomis, a former president of Kenner Products, was one of the first and most outspoken critics of MBAs and their case-study method of management back in the 1980s, when MBAs began to influence the toy industry.

Loomis told a writer in a 1990 interview, "Management must work to overcome the MBAs. The toy industry has had a sickness that American industry has, and it's managing earnings and working for Wall Street. At the root of it is this inability to run a company where the company wants to go in a natural way. The assumption that if the stack of paper is high enough an answer will come out of it is one of the most negative things that has ever happened. We've taken the best minds and we've talked them into going to business schools. They are coming out as automatons believing research is the answer. There is a place for research, but it is not the guiding tool. You're not going to do research and identify what's new and different. You're going to get a good look at yesterday."

Many MBAs are spectators, not athletes. Their process can infect companies with inaction. By the time they get done studying an opportunity, the opportunity is gone. They are so busy listening to statistics that they forget they can create them. They are so busy measuring public opinion that they forget they can mold it.

B-school logic, traditional forecasting, and overanalysis immobilizes and sterilizes ideas and idea people. Driven by a desire to please Wall Street and increase the value of their personal stock holdings, many of these men and women come to the industry from outside, rarely lasting very long at a company. They spend more time with the investment community than the inventor community. Many have never visited their own companies' R&D departments. Under their watch it is a pump-and-dump, day trader mentality.

The bottom line is, no guts, no glory. "Many things go into making a decision. But after a product has met all the tests, it is still the knowing 'gut' that separates the wheat from the chaff. It's unfortunate that there are so few active 'guts' left in the business," says Mike Meyers, who used that intuitive sense when viewing the many thousands of concepts he saw as head of R&D at Child Guidance, Aurora Toys, Marx Toys, and Milton Bradley.

Fred Kroll, inventor of Trouble (Kohner/Hasbro), who in 2003 marked his sixty-fifth year in the industry, observes, "No expertise in finance can help a company bring out saleable merchandise. It takes somebody who understands what sells and why. Too many toy companies—many floundering with their stock prices at three-year lows—have the wrong people at the top. Instead of product and marketing people, they rely on 'bean counters' who have no idea which items will sell and which should be skipped.

"If one looks at the closeout section of Toys R Us, you will see how many of the products of so-called 'majors' are marked down from 30 to 75 percent and still sitting on the shelves," Kroll points out.

Instead of the highest management taking responsibility for product line selection, there are elaborate layers of product reviews comprised of personnel who by themselves may be talented contributors. However, once they're in committees, their ability to make the important "gut" decisions based on industry experience, product sensitivity, and consumer awareness is diluted, and "groupthink" takes over. "Doers" become "reviewers." Many inventor concepts fall into this committee wringer and are returned to sender as yet another "pass."

Challenge 4: The N.I.H. Syndrome

When toy people use the initials N.I.H., they are not referring to the National Institutes of Health. In toy talk, N.I.H. stands for Not Invented Here, and is a syndrome from which some companies suffer. In effect, N.I.H. sends the message to the external inventing community that all new ideas worthy of entering that company's product line will originate with internal R&D. There may as well be a "No Help Wanted" sign posted on the door, or it may be demonstrated more subtly by a quick return of an inventor's concept with a terse note: "Pass."

It is not sound business for a company to be branded N.I.H. No one and no company has the corner on fresh ideas, even if the company has gone through a string of successful years. When the internal well runs dry—and they all do—you can bet they'll call on external inventors to prime the creative product pump. And a bad policy will change. N.I.H. usually is abandoned with different administrations.

It's Fun, but It's Serious Business

Unless you're out there knocking around the toy and game industry every day, you will never get the proper feel for the soul of the business—its character, its nuances, its subtleties, its golden rules, and its personalities. Its cast of characters is as colorful as the toys they create.

If you are a wannabe or a first-time inventor, you will never get what you want unless you can help the company insiders get what they want. And you won't know what they want unless you are on the alert, networking daily by phone, e-mail, and personal visits. This swirl of essential activity is why toy invention for the pros is a full-time job, and it's what makes them successful year after year.

"You must approach it as a business," advises veteran inventor Jay Smith. "You must have the skills that a business has in marketing and sales, finance, and operations. I think to be well rounded is the key to success, in addition, of course, to being very clever and creative. If you have one great idea and sell it, that's luck, but if you're going to do it over a long period of time, it has to be a business."

How tough is it? Says Smith, "If you have 1,000 ideas, you put 100 into sketch form, maybe 10 into prototype, and 1 may get sold. You have to recognize those odds."

Bruce Lund, inventor of the Geo-Safari Talking Microscope (Educational Insights), says the new kids on the block can expect two years without any income. He adds, "You have to be crazy to think you can make a living in this business. Don't expect wealth overnight. Be prepared to struggle."

Toy Trivia

47. Who invented Etch-a-Sketch?
a. Amanda Shiffman
b. Arthur Granjean
c. Michael Ross

Even when a product is licensed, it does not mean financial freedom for the inventor. In the first place, many companies, especially the larger ones, eat like elephants and s--t like sparrows. Much more goes in than comes out. And even if a product does make it to retail, don't pop open the bubbly—and don't quit your day job—until it proves itself and you start cashing royalty checks.

Attacks of the Killer Lawyers

When asked why they might be reluctant to see wannabe/first-time inventors, company executives consistently give answers centered on wariness: of how an inventor might react to rejection, and of legal action should there be a dispute or misunderstanding.

The threat of legal action is a significant reason the doors of some companies are firmly closed to amateur inventors. Busy toy executives don't need to spend time in depositions or in costly law suits. Casual inventors are often stung by the rejection of their once-in-a-lifetime creation, and all too often they retaliate with litigation at the remotest hint of an infringement or overlap with a marketer's subsequent introduction.

When amateurs insist that they haven't seen anything like their idea on the market, it usually means they haven't done more than a cursory search of toy company catalogs or their local toy stores. More important, they judge that its absence from the market can only mean that a manufacturer never had a similar idea. Never do they consider that the company might have judged the idea to be not strong enough to survive market conditions. It is often impossible and inconceivable for casual inventors to accept two key points:

1. Just because an item is not in a marketer's current line doesn't mean that the company doesn't have it in development, or didn't think of it in the past and shelved it.
2. Similar concepts can originate from two sources. This frequent occurrence is known as *parallel development*.

With the flurry of concepts swirling around the industry, there is always a strong likelihood of overlap or duplication. Much "invention" borders on reinvention or the use of a slight nuance of a previous play format. How much can an inventor do with a game board, spinner/dice, and pawns other than change themes, rules, or artwork? How many parts of a toy dog can wag, flap, roll, or strut? How many special gears or microprocessors can add animation or sound?

Pros don't like rejection any more than the amateurs, but they understand and live with the reality that only so much product can be done in any single year. They rarely get into legal entanglements with the companies. They may not like it that their concept was only a smidge different from an item ultimately selected for market, but they usually regard that as better execution or spin of a similar idea rather than a rip-off. And they may not like it that a manufacturer is now getting around to marketing a concept similar to one of their past ideas, but they know that the toy market is often a matter of timing.

Pros know that their business relationships with manufacturers are based on, among other things, trust and ethics. They are in the business of living off their ideas, not living off legal settlements. As Phil Orbanes, a former vice president of R&D at Parker Brothers and now president of Winning Moves Games, says, "There is a greater legal risk [to marketers] in having an unknown inventor come in cold."

"Unfortunately, we live in a litigious society," Mike Meyers says. "We have to be very, very careful not only to protect what we're doing inside, but also to protect the professionals we're working with, because as soon as someone opens a box or a letter, you begin to be in a compromised situation.

"Usually big companies are targets for legal action because when you have size, it's assumed you have deep pockets. There have been suits. There are always threats of suits. There is no satisfaction in a successful defense; even when the company wins, there can be a tremendous financial loss. Nothing is gained by a moral victory that isn't greatly eroded by lost time and expense."

But even with policies in place to limit legal exposure from unknown claimants, lawsuits are an ongoing problem. Some firms spend hundreds of thousands of dollars each year defending themselves against a wide variety of complaints. Some are valid; others are not. For example, many so-called paper-patent inventors get patents on concepts they never even prototype or attempt to sell. Such an inventor merely hopes to one day find an infringement to take action against.

Every inventor who has been in the industry for a few years seems to have a story about an idea that was misappropriated or was at least a close call. "You go to an executive's birthday party on a Sunday, and on Monday your good friend says, 'So sue me,'" laments one prominent

411 Join an inventor organization. Membership will connect you to a network of like-minded colleagues, encourage an exchange of ideas and solutions, and provide access to what is going on within your inventing community, locally, and, by extension, nationwide. For a state-by-state listing, go to www.patentcafe.com/ inventor_orgs/clubs.html.

developer who asked not to be named. We co-authors, with long careers in the industry, feel that toy company executives are on the whole honorable professionals who value their relationships with independent developers and do everything possible to maintain the balance in the flow of ideas between in-house and outside development sources. They also know that if they intentionally cheat inventors, the pipeline would soon be empty.

"We play hardball with our developers. And we'll take advantage of whatever situation we can, just as I would expect them to do. After all, business is business, and we're all experienced professionals," admits the senior vice president for R&D at a major manufacturing company. "But the last thing we want to do is rip off an inventor. Word would spread like wildfire, and all of our sources would dry up instantly. There is nothing to be gained and everything to be lost."

Perhaps companies see amateurs as loose cannons for two reasons. Historically, amateur inventors have been divided into two types: paranoid and more paranoid. They trust no one and hesitate to reveal their ideas, even to their own patent attorneys. There is constant fear of being cheated. Such an attitude is more destructive to an inventor than the actual hazards inherent in licensing intellectual property. Certainly, there are high-profile accounts of people who got ripped off. It's a risk that goes with the territory. But too much caution can kill an idea by depriving it of life-giving exposure for the purpose of improvement. Few ideas can grow locked in the mind or computer of an isolated, overprotective inventor.

For that matter, companies believe they can afford to let a few thousand ideas pass them by. When asked if he thinks the majors should be afraid of missing a blockbuster by not seeing all first-time inventors, Meyers, who saw thousands of ideas just from the pros each year during his long career at Milton Bradley and Hasbro Games says, "There's no proof that a company will. Major marketers could see 10,000 products a year, but how would you process 10,000 products? How do you keep the sanctity of those products? How do you separate them? It's not practical. It can't be done and still do the other progressive R&D functions."

To illustrate his point, Meyers says that one agent to whom Milton Bradley recommended amateurs needing representation told him that in 20 years of seeing Milton Bradley's referrals, he has never found a single worthwhile product among them that would fit the MB line.

Toy Trivia

48. Which company today manufacturers Matchbox?

a. Mattel

b. Galoob

c. Hasbro

Preparing to Play the Big Room

Remember the saying that if a man builds a better mousetrap, even though his house may be deep in the woods, the world will beat a path to his door? Maybe this was the case back in 1889 when Ralph Waldo Emerson penned it, but it's not true in the world of toy inventing. For the most part, it's just the opposite. Toy and game developers of new and better products must be prepared to beat a path to a manufacturer's door. And often, after a long, hard journey, the door might be locked.

The consensus among the pros is that successful toy development and licensing works out to about 10 percent creativity and 90 percent tenacity and marketing skills. Creativity is a natural gift; either you have it or you don't. Marketing talents, on the other hand, while intuitive to a great extent, are learned through experience. Amateur toy and game inventors become pros the same way amateur athletes do: through training and competition.

Before you take a product to a marketer, it is a good idea to build a presentation around basic elements that will show the reviewer that you are prepared. In addition to using them as talking points for the product during the meeting, you can leave many of these elements behind if the company keeps the item for further consideration. Bring enough copies for everyone. Do not ask the company to make copies.

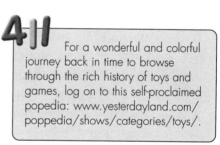

For a wonderful and colorful journey back in time to browse through the rich history of toys and games, log on to this self-proclaimed popedia: www.yesterdayland.com/poppedia/shows/categories/toys/.

1. **Instructions:** Write a step-by-step instruction sheet. Take nothing for granted. The worst thing that can happen is to have someone at the company forget how to operate or play your item. If you can, make a demo video. A few pictures of a new concept are worth thousands of words when trying to sell it.

2. **Marketing:** Highlight your item's advantages over an existing product. Explain what makes it unique, and suggest where it might fit into the market relative to pricing, competition, newness, and "hook." Don't tell manufacturers how many millions of dollars it will make, however; you have no factual basis for such projections.

3. **Advertising:** It's always a nice touch if you can provide some clever tag lines, slogans, and advertising hooks. They probably won't be used, but this shows you're thinking about the bigger picture—life after production.

4. **Play value:** Present the results of any independent testing or "kitchen research" you may have conducted. Again, include photographs or videotapes. Use casual acquaintances in play sessions, but never support an idea with the testimony of someone who loves you: You may never hear the truth.

5. **Engineering:** Include technical back-up that will give the licensee's engineers or designers a head start. If you're not an engineer, offer to bring in such skills if the product is accepted for extended review. The offer may be declined, but it shows confidence that there will be later stage development.

6. **Manufacturing:** Take a stab at estimating the hard cost. This may be difficult without complete specifications and a works-like model. If you have offshore associates and are comfortable releasing the concept for examination, confirmed costs will be even more impressive to the marketer.

7. **Trademarks:** If you have done a trademark search at the PTO, include the results. Never present a concept using a trademark you know is not available. If the marketer falls in love with the mark and subsequently finds out it is not available, the product could go south in a fit of disappointment. It's always better to use no working trademark than a bad working trademark.

8. **Patents:** Share with the manufacturer the status of any patent actions you may have taken: searches, applications, or issued patents.

9. **Packaging:** If appropriate, design a package to show the product's visual strengths on retail display. Again, this can be difficult without a works-like model in the anticipated size dimensions. It may be adequate to show existing product forms as examples of possible merchandising styles. A package can be extremely powerful especially if the trademark is killer.

10. **The future:** Through marker drawings and explanatory text, illustrate accessories, line extensions, and potential directions for your item. It doesn't hurt to show the marketer you are thinking beyond the core idea and know there can be a big picture for your IP. Extra representations are also good records of the originator of extensions, should that become an issue in the future.

Don't go into a key presentation without back-up tools. Bring along a first-aid kit for your prototype. In transit to the presentation, no matter how well your prototype is protected, something could come loose or, worse, break off. The emergency kit should include at least the following items:

- Mini screwdriver set
- Fresh batteries suited to your model needs
- Super Glue
- Markers
- Hardened steel file
- Double-sided tape
- Blue tak, a reusable, removable adhesive
- X-acto knife (pack in suitcase if flying)
- Chewing gum (for model)
- Altoids (for you)

Toy Trivia

49. Who is known as Dr. Toy?
a. Stevanne Auerbach
b. Fred Kroll
c. Roger Shiffman

If you are traveling with an electronic toy or game model, you'll also want to have a soldering gun and select supplies to make repairs to blown components, broken traces, or other mishaps.

Ready for Prime Time

Michael Langieri has spent nearly 40 years in the creative/selling and creative/buying arena, on both sides of the conference table. His experience includes years inside as a key R&D person at Child Guidance, Aurora Toys, and Marx Toys; he also has headed the game development department at Milton Bradley. In addition, Langieri has lived by his design talents outside at his own firms, Design America and currently Toy Genius. He originated, reviewed, or presented thousands of concepts and offers a perspective on the all-important meeting between inventor and manufacturer.

Here are tips that have worked for Langieri as he has scheduled and worked new concept presentations:

1. Arrange for a personal review of your idea. Never send in a model or a prototype, unless it's absolutely impossible for you to be there. A special relationship might circumvent the need for personal presence, but products are best demonstrated and questions are answered most quickly and accurately by the inventor.

2. Deal with the highest-ranking product reviewer you can, one on one, if at all possible. That way, attention is focused on the product, not lost in the distraction and varied attention spans of a large group.

3. If a reviewer doesn't know you well or doesn't know about your significant accomplishments, quickly refresh that person's memory before showing your new idea. Nothing breaks the ice better than a quick rundown of your industry track record or a chatty exchange of recent industry rumors or facts.

4. While every inventor loves his or her own idea, try to have some objective information about intended user(s). Relate the play experiences of potential consumers exposed to the idea during development and your thoughts on how this might project into the marketplace.

5. Make the presentation professional by showing your knowledge of how the idea fits into a company's product categories. Do your homework. Study corporate product lines. Companies have expertise in certain categories, and bringing them something far removed from their discipline is usually a wasted effort. Equally key is your personal appearance and attitude. If you expect to sell an idea in today's market, you have to be in step with today's market in every way and with every action.

6. If the product idea you're suggesting doesn't fit the manufacturer's needs, probe the possibility of some "customizing" to make it more viable. The best thing you can do is to try to keep the project moving forward.

7. Suggest the possibility of working a concept further. Sometimes, if the representative/manufacturer has a special way to clarify and improve the idea, suggest a "work for hire" agreement. Then the marketer has a vested interest, which might increase the likelihood of it being viewed more favorably at a later a date.

Advice from the Pros

"Be informed. Don't live in a self-created vacuum."

—Mike Meyers, former senior vice president of R&D, Hasbro Games

8. Always close the meeting with a clear action plan detailing what will happen next and by what dates. There may be an "on-the-spot" sale, but more often there is merely a "hold" of an idea to move it into the manufacturer's product selection process. Inventors must not lose sight of the fact that they have something unique, something magical. The goal is to gain at least a positive, proactive response from the manufacturer.

The R.I.T.E. Stuff

Dan Klitsner, head of Klitsner Industrial Design (K.I.D. Group) of San Francisco, has a fun formula for determining whether a new idea is ready to show a potential licensee.

"I have an acronym that I use to measure salability of an idea. It has to be R.I.T.E. All four of these lettered rules need to be present for an idea to have a reasonable chance of getting licensed. Kind of like four legs of a table."

- ◆ **R = Relationships.** You need a relationship with product acquisition contacts and resources. No idea is worth investing in without knowing the person well who you are relying on to sell it internally.

- ◆ **I = Idea.** It had better be a good one that is fresh and worth pursuing. Your knowledge of what has come before is critical.

- ◆ **T = Timing.** This is mostly blind luck, but you can increase the odds. Being two days late is harder to accept than being two years late— and it happens all the time! Being right is sometimes harder than being wrong in that case. You can help yourself zero in on timing through good communication with your No. 1 contact at a company.

Toy Trivia

50. Silly Putty was discovered in the New Haven labs of which company?

a. Union Carbide

b. General Electric

c. Elmer's

- ◆ **E= Execution.** You might have the right seed idea, but the wrong design, personality, style, scale, age group, and many other little details. A knowledgeable and talented designer can increase odds here and make or break a concept. Inventors always whine, "I thought of that," and "I showed that exact same idea," but usually some critical detail made all the difference in the perception of the toy company.

If any one of the four elements is removed or diminished, it is probably not ready to show yet, counsels Klitsner.

Make sure your presentation is strong enough to sell on its own without you explaining it. Enjoy the process as much as the goal. You have to be better at accepting rejection than accepting success, since it will happen 90 percent of the time—less if you are very, very lucky. Enjoy making your idea better or continuing to show it until the timing aligns with a company's needs.

Companies Don't Buy Ideas

The pros know that the farther along the form and definition of an idea, the better chance the concept has to catch the attention of the product screener. A looks-like, works-like prototype will help convey to corporate executives the excitement you hope to achieve with your product.

Jamie Filipeli, who has seen thousands of inventor presentations in her years as manager of external resources at Mattel, advises, "The biggest mistake is to come into a product meeting with a three-ring binder with volumes of sketches. Select your best four to six concepts—the optimum are works-like or looks-like models. If you are not in a position to take a concept to model, at least have a nice drawing or rendering that conveys your concept clearly."

411 Every serious inventor's library needs the annual "Official Toy Fair Directory and Year-Round Resource Guide," published by the TIA . To order a copy, go to www.toy-tia.org or call 212-675-1141.

To have any chance at all of a sale, there must be a bonding process between the item and those considering it. Consumers often purchase products by emotion, not by logic; this holds true for toy executives, too. After all, if you scratch these execs deep enough, when they're not making hard decisions about new products for their companies, they're *consumers.*

Prototypes should be as sophisticated as necessary to make the item understandable. Some companies, for example, want to see a prototype that is play-testable: It can be given to a group of people who have never seen it before, and they can experience it without detailed explanation. At the very best, the prototype should look like it just came out of the retail package so that users in a consumer test environment can jump into its use quickly.

Any concept with a mechanism should be proven out with a functioning sample. Product screeners know all too well the importance of trying to demonstrate inventor models in subsequent internal meetings. They lament that they don't see why they must spend time coaxing a mechanism into working, especially if the malfunction occurs in a key product review. "If it is a design concept or a fashion concept, marker renderings may be fine enough. But if it is supposed to work someday, it should work on the day of its first exposure," says David Maurer of Hasbro.

Through the Eyes of the Beholder

David Berko has been at thousands of inventor demonstrations over the years, looking for new products on behalf of a variety of toy companies. Currently he meets with external product sources as the senior vice president for concept acquisition at Hasbro. Berko offers this list of do's and don'ts—useful advice to new inventors and a refresher for some of the most experienced inventors.

204

◆ *Do* make sure your presentation is at a point that it can sell itself. Once you have presented a product, it has to survive on its own in the corporate organization.

◆ *Do* your homework. There is nothing worse than seeing an item that has been in the company's line for 10 years.

◆ *Do* bring back good ideas that have been rejected if you think something has changed in the marketplace. But give it time—and not just a week or two.

◆ *Do* follow up, but don't call every day. Give it a few weeks.

◆ *Do* listen to feedback and try to respond. The company gives this information to help you as well as itself.

◆ *Don't* work on products based on a trend or fad that is at its peak. You can be sure companies have been aware of these products for some time. Companies notice that there are products based on this trend on every street corner.

◆ *Don't* work on items from another company and expect a company to be interested. Hasbro would not be interested in Barbie accessories, and Mattel would not be interested in a new idea for Mr. Potato Head.

◆ *Don't* assume that the executive you are presenting to can read your mind. Explain concisely what your idea is without omitting anything important.

◆ *Don't* try to sell something that has already been rejected. Once a company says no, don't try to talk them into changing their minds; they'll only send it back again, which is a waste of your time as well as theirs.

◆ *Don't* lie. Berko once rejected a product based on safety reasons. The inventor didn't know that a particular component in the product was potentially unsafe. Once Berko informed him, the inventor said that he would put the item on the shelf and not try to sell it. Sometime later, when Berko moved to another company, he saw the same item in the inventor closet, from the same inventor who was still trying to sell it.

◆ *Don't* oversell. The company has only seconds to get the idea across to the consumer. If you need a 30-minute intro to get your point across, the company probably won't be able to sell it, either.

Toy Trivia

51. Where is GI Joe's scar?
a. Right cheek
b. Forehead
c. Chin

You Have Options

You can take three paths to the sale of your idea:

1. You can solo, equipped with the best representation of your new concept, and try to open doors to an marketer and give it your best pitch.

2. Associate with a recognized inventor, if you can make a convincing pitch so that the established pro is convinced that it will be in his or her interest to postpone proprietary work and take on your proposal.

3. Contract the services of an agent, who then becomes the rep for your idea. Some have design capability that will enhance your idea. Use only agents who have a proven track record in the toy and game industry, and with whom you have met personally.

If you take either of the latter two paths, be prepared to have these pros contribute to your product in creative ways, as well as share in any remuneration.

Finding a Home for Your Brainchild

Much of what has been outlined so far in this chapter explains how the industry views the first-time inventor and what you'll need to get into a company to make a personal pitch. Here are a few more thoughts about finding the right door and being prepared if it opens.

The first move is yours. And it is not an easy one. Long before you worry about how to get through the door and sell your concept, you must have a door in mind. It will be hard enough at the right door.

When an idea is finally licensed, every inventor needs to ask this question: "Can the company deliver?"

The designation "Inc." after a company's name can signify "incomplete" if you've picked the wrong one. A line of products at Toys R Us does not always mean a successful company.

Public Companies

Information is power. Here is how to get some information about the important issues, numbers, and personalities before signing on with an unknown marketer. If the company is public, a great place to get background facts is the Securities and Exchange

Commission (SEC). This federal agency provides the fullest public disclosure to the investing public. It has all kinds of revealing documents on file. You can learn …

- ◆ What the company produces, the percentage of sales for any one item or line, whether it's seasonal or nonseasonal, and so on.
- ◆ How much money the company spends on R&D.
- ◆ How much the company pays out in royalties.
- ◆ How much the company spends on advertising.
- ◆ Details on manufacturing and significant background on production capabilities.
- ◆ Whether the company is involved in any legal proceedings.
- ◆ The security ownership of certain beneficial owners and management. This is vital to understanding the pecking order and internal power structure. Here you will see who makes what salary and owns how much stock (including family members), and what percentage of the company equity such insider holdings represent.

The easiest way to access the SEC data bank is via the Internet, at www.sec.gov.

Private Companies

Private companies are not easy to scope out. The best way to reach a comfort level is to get the names of some inventors from whom the company has licensed products. Call the inventors, e-mail them, or use any other means to uncover distress signals about a potential licensor. Most inventors are willing to share, in confidence, specific known pitfalls if asked. But remember, it is always to your discretion on how you process any free advice and handle your conclusion on the potential of a privately held company.

Advice from the Pros

"Present ideas in person, not by mail."

—Mel Taft, former senior vice president of R&D, Milton Bradley; and current member of the board of directors, Radica USA

Never Say Die

When you are out there trying to find a home for your idea, often it will tax the limits of your patience, enthusiasm, and hope. When you're just about to put your idea on the shelf, the best advice is to just keep trying.

If you're lucky enough to get a corporate executive on the telephone, it is vital to establish your credibility as a reputable inventing source and introduce the product concept in 90 seconds. This requires very precise, attention-getting statements. Do not dwell on your personal resume or provide a coy, veiled description of a product that includes unrealistic promises of sales and marketing potential.

Advice from the Pros

"Don't try to own 100 percent of nothing."

—Richard M. Blank, Esq., agent

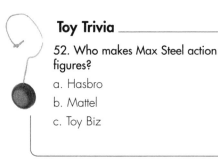

Toy Trivia

52. Who makes Max Steel action figures?

a. Hasbro

b. Mattel

c. Toy Biz

One corporate inventor-relations executive says, "It is amazing how many callers insist their hot invention is similar to or better than some product we know has sales on the decline. All that shows me is that the invention is too late and the inventor does not know the market. To get an executive's attention, emphasis should be on new and unique features, not on similarities to a dying product."

Inventor Don Ullman of Ullco Toys recalls the many phone calls he placed to company product representatives that most often went unanswered. "I knew that since I was just starting out, my name wasn't in many Rolodex or e-mail files," says Ullman. "Once my Rainbow Riders Game (Ravensburger) and Shrinky Dink Oven (Spin Master Toys) made the market, calls for product appointments were returned more quickly. Prior to that, my style was just to be a nuisance with frequent calls until I got the attention of the right company representative."

Round Pegs in Round Holes

If you want to do the selling yourself, a reoccurring question is: Where will a product have its best chance of fit and success? A rule of thumb is to have submissions follow a company's category direction and marketing goals. No two companies have the same needs.

The easiest way to get a feel for the product a company normally sells is to visit the nearest Toys R Us or check the shelves of Wal-Mart, Target, Kay Bee Toys, or a similar toy store. You will find many company product lines represented.

It will be less profitable for you to work with a manufacturer whose toys and games are not carried by a major chain. However, a visit to specialty toy stores may offer clues if you have a niche/edgy new idea that might sell in lesser quantities without promotion often at a higher price than in the mass market.

Jeff Conrad, a vice president at Radica, advises, "If I were an amateur inventor, I would get on an airplane, go around the country, and visit major retail stores and just look at what's there." He complains that because the amateur does not do any homework and operates in a vacuum, 80 percent of what he gets from them has been done before. In fact, their submissions are often a bellwether for tracking trends. When amateur inventors begin sending him a groundswell of products in a particular category, that usually marks the last year of a particular phase or craze. "This is because they are hearing about it way down the line," Conrad concludes.

Mel Taft agrees with Conrad that there is a lot to learn from regular store checks. In fact, when Taft headed R&D at Milton Bradley, he encouraged his staff to get into stores, particularly during holiday time. Taft said, "I would often tell designers to moonlight in the stores during the Christmas season to get real up-close with consumers and to see firsthand shelf movement of the company and competitive product. That's still a good way to learn the reality of the marketplace, especially for a new inventor if he or she has time."

But keep in mind that following established product lines with a new related submission can be a double-edged sword. It may be suited to what the marketer does best—however, companies may feel like they've seen the idea before.

Taft adds, "Inventors should at times take a gamble and force the company to think with them out-of-the-box or push the envelope into new areas. However, such ideas should be supported with as much research and current statistical information that will get the company excited about the totally new direction."

Advice from the Pros

"If you don't love the business for all its faults, fuggetabboutitt!"

—William F. Dohrmann, former senior vice president of R&D, Hasbro Games and Parker Brothers

Final Thoughts on the Presentation

A new idea is a delicate thing. It can be killed with a sneer or a yawn; it can be stabbed to death by a quip and worried to death by a frown on the right man's brow. Therefore, how it is presented is critical. Don't give the viewer a chance to be negative. Whatever is said at you, return with an upbeat and enthusiastic response.

Advice from the Pros

"Learn as much as you can about your market. Then step back and really ask yourself what is missing."

—Loren Taylor, president, Taylored Concepts

You must get an executive's attention to make a sale, and that action, by its very own high visibility, becomes a vital component in your presentation. Remember, you are a stranger. You are untested. Therefore, you will stand out. Do it properly, and you will always be welcome. Mess it up, and it will haunt you. Your credibility is the most critical factor, much more than the toy or game under your arm. It is impossible to put a value on the ability to make an encore performance.

The toy industry operates on development and review cycles. But it is critical to keep in mind the time of year when you show ideas. If you are showing at Toy Fair in February, in all likelihood the viewer is thinking license and release for the subsequent Toy Fair, 12 months away. If it is midyear, most likely you have missed the coming Toy Fair and are "early" for consideration for the next Toy Fair 18 months away.

Always have a clear picture of the corporate calendar. If it is unacceptable with your placement calendar, it's best to try a marketer whose timing is more in synch with your interests. Usually the bigger the marketer is, the more competitive and crowded the "opportunity well" is. Other products are already in work, and what you are showing will have to nudge out an earlier choice or be put on track behind it. If your idea is held for further review, know when you will hear about status and the general timeframe for which your idea is being considered.

On Finding a Pro Partner

Finding a pro to review your idea may be as difficult as getting through the door of a company. The reasons are similar: concern for potential legal hassles, the time to teach an external new creative about the industry, internal priorities with full royalty that cannot be altered for partial royalty endeavors, and maybe a touch of N.I.H. As is true with most companies, it will take a lot of convincing to get through the door of a professional inventor's studio, office, or think tank. It may even be more difficult.

The advice and preparation outlined on the proceeding pages also applies if you attempt to win over a professional inventor and become a coveted "associate." In your favor is the sense most have that they cannot create everything.

The pros know that someone, somewhere outside their walls will catch the next fad or technology breakthrough that will make a lot of money when commercialized in a new toy or game. The wannabe/amateur/first-timer has to convince the pro that what he or she has can be the next blockbuster. The incentive is the payoff of big bucks for all involved.

Toy Trivia

53. Who made He-Man action figures?
a. Playmates
b. Toy Biz
c. Mattel

Finding an Agent

In the serious game of Let's Place the Idea!, make frequent checks to see if you are close to winning. Has the timer run down with no decision to go solo, or has there been no forward progression from early moves? Has the Chance card not led to an association with a professional inventor? It may be that the dice should be rolled with a known industry broker/agent and run to the finish.

In fact, many of the pros responding to us for this book felt that getting a known agent partner may be the most beneficial avenue for a start-up inventor.

(Note: The fact that an agent has been interviewed for or mentioned in this book does not signify our endorsement of his or her services. We recommend that you conduct an interview with prospective agents—and, by all means, call three or more inventor references before you sign on with anyone. Any agent worth your consideration has at least three or more satisfied customers.)

Professionals interviewed for this book generally feel that agents can provide an important service to inventors who do not have experience licensing toy and game IP, or connections to potential licensors. At the same time, clearly it is a minefield, and you must be extra careful when considering an agent.

Twenty-eight-year veteran inventor Elliot Rudell says, "Some of them are honest and great and I am thankful for their role in the industry." Inventor David Vogel, Vogel Applied Technologies, offers, "The real ones are great and extremely valuable. The fakes are hideous parasites who should be euthanized." New York City-based inventor, Joseph J. Wetherall, concurs. "If they are legitimate, brokers and agents can be invaluable to an independent inventor."

The field of invention representation is, alas, loaded with so many frauds that more than 15 states have already passed legislation to protect inventors from these carrion birds. According to *Time* magazine, May 23, 2001, as many as 25,000 would-be inventors are ripped off annually. Richard Apley, former director of the USPTO's Independent Inventor Program Office, says that the scams ring up about $200 million a year. The average loss per inventor is $20,000 for useless services.

What to Watch for When Interviewing/Signing an Agent/Broker

1. **Services:** See what the agent offers and make sure it is what you need. It's horses for courses. If the agent does not have a successful track record in your field of invention, you may want to go elsewhere.

2. **Exclusivity:** Is the agreement for one concept, or many? Be careful not to sign anything that's too broad in scope, especially before you have experience with the agent.

3. **Timeframe:** Be comfortable with the length of time the agent wants to tie your product up.

4. **Rights:** Know exactly what you are handing over to the agent in terms of the scope of representation.

5. **Escape policy:** Perhaps more important than anything is your ability to get out of the agreement should the agent not give you his or her best efforts.

6. **Fees:** Just about everyone interviewed for this book said that if an agent asks for up-front money, go to the next candidate on your list. Further, be very careful of agents that charge for market evaluations. The best agents take their percentage of advances and royalties, and do not charge on a fee basis. Inventor percentages average 50 percent of any deal.

7. **References:** Make sure you talk to at least three satisfied clients of an agent before signing up. If an agent is unwilling to share such names, again, move along. Legitimate agents will have no problem sharing the names of satisfied clients.

8. **Party to contract:** You want to be a party to any licensing agreement. The companies are usually willing to cut two or more cheques and multiple copies of quarterly reports. Do not allow the agent to receive your money.

Toy Trivia

54. Who made the Tick action figures?

a. Bandai

b. Tomy

c. Hasbro

9. **Authority:** Make sure you're not turning over contract-signing authority to your agent. Make sure that you know exactly what you're getting into.
10. **Confidentiality:** Be sure you understand how the agent is handling the confidentiality of your ideas, what the agent warranties, indemnification, and so forth.

USA Submissions

Here is a listing of some agents. You may wish to expand this directory by asking toy companies and inventors for their favorites.

- Jonathan S. Becker
  Anjar Company
  200 Fifth Ave., Suite 1305
  New York, NY 10010
  Tel: 212-255-4720
  Fax: 212-633-1183
  Website: www.anjar.com

- Pete Carr
  Cactus Marketing Services
  1553 S. Military Hwy., Suite 101
  Chesapeake, VA 23320
  Tel: 1-888-215-7040
  E-mail: npcactus@erols.com
  Website: www.cactusmarketing.com

- George Delaney
  Delaney Product Development
  6956 Hawthorne Lane
  Hanover Park, IL 60103
  Tel: 630-837-2952
  E-mail: DeLaney116@worldnet.att.net

- Michael Kohner
  12 Rhoda Terrace
  Parsippany, NJ 07054
  Tel: 973-335-1015
  Fax: 973-335-5396
  E-mail: mkcnorth@worldnet.att.net

- Andrew Berton/Adam Wolff
  Excel Development Group, Inc.
  1123 Mount Curve Ave.
  Minneapolis, MN 55403-11128
  Tel: 612-374-3233
  Fax: 612-377-0865
  E-mail: info@exceld.com
  Website: www.exceld.com

- Frederick Fierst
  Fierst and Pucci, LLP
  64 Gothic St.
  Northampton, MA 01060
  Tel: 413-584-8067
  E-mail: fred@ent-atty.com

- Jeff Hibert
Hibert Interactive
625 13th St.
Manhattan Beach, CA 90266
Tel: 310-796-0207
E-mail: jeff.hmm@ix.netcom.com

- Paul A. Lapidus, IDSA
The Together Group/NewFuntiers
9882 Cow Creek Dr.
Palo Cedro, CA 96073
Tel: 1-800-846-0701 or 530-547-4412
Website: www.newfuntiers.com

- Frank Young & Liz Farley
Franklin Associates
6381 Maple Road
Mound, MN 55364
Tel: 952-495-1016
E-mail: toydoc@uslink.net

- Mike Trunfio
Invention Incubator
69 Graymore Road
Waltham, MA 02451
Tel: 781-373-1776

- Gary Carlin
Inventor's Greenhouse
198 Tremont St. #505
Boston, MA 02116
Tel: 617-422-0922
E-mail: garycarlin@aol.com

- Robert B. Fuhrer
Nextoy
200 5th Ave., Suite 1011
New York, NY 10010
Tel: 212-243-1050
Fax: 212-645-1365
Website: www.nextoy.com

- Shelly Goldberg
Lot O Fun Marketing, Inc.
17257 Quesan Place
Encino, CA 91316-3935
Tel: 818-788-9087
E-mail: lotofunsg@aol.com

- Michael & Lynn Marra
Marra Design Associates, Inc.
7007 Dakota Ave.
Chanhassen, MN 55317
Tel: 952-937-8141
Fax: 952-937-8141
E-mail: MDA1Mike@aol.com
Website: www.marradesign.com

- Howard Jay Fleisher
RoyaltyPros
16 West 23rd Street, 4th Fl.
New York, NY 10010
Tel: 212-366-6876
Fax: 212-366-6862
E-mail: howard@royaltypros.com
Website: www.royaltypros.com

- Carol Rehtmeyer
Rehtmeyer Design & Licensing
1952 McDowell Road, Suite 207
Naperville, IL 60563
Tel: 630-717-9304
Fax: 630-717-9384
Website: www.toyngames.com

- Dan Lauer
Haystack Toys, Inc.
8631 Delmar Blvd., Suite 300
St. Louis, MO 63124
Tel: 314-983-9220
Website: www.haystacktoys.com

U.K. Submissions

- Jessie Fotherby
  Cactus Marketing
  Studio One, The Cork
  Undercliff Road West
  Felixstowe 1P11 8AQ, UK
  Tel: 44 139 427 5275
  Fax: 44 139 327 5275
  E-mail: games@cactus-uk.freeserve.co.uk
- Mark Cochrane
  The Games Agency
  Ground Floor, 21 Elmdale Road
  Clifton, Bristol
  BS8 1SH, United Kingdom
  Tel: 44 117 974 4711
  E-mail: mark@thegamesagency.com
- Iain Kidney/Philip Harland
  Games Talk
  Little Coster, Blunsdon Hill
  Blunsdon, Swindon
  Wiltshire, SN2 4BZ UK
  Tel: 44 179 370 5291
  E-mail: lain@gamestalk.demon.co.uk

- Jacqui Lyons
  Marjacq Micro
  34, Devonshire Place
  London W1N 1PE
  Tel: 44 171 935 9499
  E-mail: jacqui@marjacq.com
- David Kremer/Christine Trussell
  Seven Towns Ltd.
  7 Lambton Place
  London W11 2SH England
  Tel: 44 171 727 5666
  E-mail: DeanneD@seventowns.com

Judy Flathers, senior coordinator of inventor relations at Hasbro Games, has spent 27 years in R&D and has been involved with external inventors. She often takes calls from first-time inventors who phone the East Longmeadow, Massachusetts, maker of many of the world's most popular games. Apparently, when you are the biggest producer of such classic games, inventors call with what they believe are ideas equal to or better than the company's bestsellers.

Toy Trivia

55. Which movie was produced by former toy inventor Avi Arad?

a. *Superman*

b. *Spider-man*

c. *Dick Tracy*

Advice from the Pros

"Concentrate on ideas that require TV promotion, as that's where the money is."

—Michael Kohner, agent

Says Flathers about the endless phone calls, "I try to be as helpful and understanding as I can, but I must deliver the message that our policy does not allow acceptance of unsolicited idea submissions from first-time sources. I've had some pretty persistent and convincing callers through the years, but the company policy stands at the end of each phone call."

"We do not recommend any specific name on our list," says Mike Hirtle, the vice president in charge of inventor relations at Hasbro Games. "It is up to the inventor to check out the agents and select one that offers the most comfort from a business point of view. That decision to go with a broker/agent has to be based on whatever is best for the inventor and his or her plans for the idea. The names on our broker list are product sources that I regularly see on my travel swings in search of new opportunities for Hasbro Games."

Hirtle says that he has heard many inventors exclaim through the years that he will miss an idea greater than Monopoly if the caller must go through a broker. Hirtle says, "Inventors are generally reluctant to align with another form of product representation. However, I try to assure them that if the idea is so great, I will see it because brokers are just as eager to make a sale of perhaps an improved concept and will call the No. 1 game company first if it is truly a quality opportunity."

Agents are, indeed, the surest way for amateur inventors to have their products reviewed by R&D or marketing departments at the major companies. Agents understand their important role in bridging the gap between the less-established part-time inventors and the industry manufacturers. Agents also recognize that some individuals in the nonprofessional inventing community may often be no less creative than people in the larger design groups. They merely lack time, experience, or the resources to learn the business and fully develop and sell ideas themselves.

It is best to deal with an agent who comes highly recommended by a well-known manufacturer or a satisfied client. Agents are as varied as the people and products they represent. The toy companies know who the best ones are, and many will often share a list of favorites, if asked.

"An agent is an extension of an inventor's dream," says Loren Taylor, of Taylored Concepts, an inventor-agent who has also held senior management positions at toy companies. "He or she must be able to guide and nurture that dream in every way possible." Taylor adds that a good agent helps make a concept better and doesn't just pull dozens of them out of a hat. "A good agent is a bridge to a manufacturer and must be every bit as effective in communicating with the manufacturer in the absence of the inventor. To be a good one, you have to have vision and be totally trustworthy."

David Kremer is the owner of Seven Towns, Ltd., one of the most successful brokerages in the business. His father, Tom, found the Rubik's Cube in Hungary and licensed it to the Ideal Toy Company. It has sold 125 million "official" units to date.

It's no surprise that Kremer sees agents as a valuable resource who more than pay for their commissions with solid deal terms and contractual knowledge. However, he warns first-timers, "Never pay any cash; only give away a future percentage." He does not believe in paying for evaluations or protection, or to have someone take on a concept.

"If you're new to the business, an experienced agent with a demonstrable track record is a great plus," says Hank Atkins, who created the hit puzzler Roadside Rescue (Binary Arts). "Sharing royalties with this person will be worth it. However, stay away from any agent that requires money up front."

Alien Autopsy (DaMert) inventor Belinda Recio says of her experience with agents that they can be of great help. "But ultimately, it's still the inventor's responsibility. So, if you hire an agent, don't simply sit back waiting for things to happen. Stay involved and keep thinking."

Inventor Ralph Baer, who in 1980 became the first person to draw interactive symbols on a television screen, says some agents may not even know what they are presenting, but they play golf with all the right people and bring in unbelievable advances. "But then there are the rest of them," he says.

"Some are good, some are not," says pro inventor Mary D. Ellroy, who goes by the nickname GameBird. "The best advice I can give is for an inventor to call a toy company and see which agents the company likes to deal with. If you don't like selling or you're new to the industry, get an agent."

Randi Altschul, inventor and president of Dieceland, of Cliffside Park, New Jersey, has no confidence in agents, either. "I think that most I have met are snakes who try to take advantage of inventors and take much more than they deserve." Her advice: "If you can do it yourself, go for it."

Toy Trivia

56. Which company marketed Wrist Racers?

a. Knickerbocker

b. Ertl

c. Galoob

Overall, the professional inventors and executives we interviewed for this book gave agents high marks, but everybody agreed that you have to do your homework before signing up with one, and you must choose one that shows passion for your idea and treats your business interests fairly.

Agents Describe Their Work

Pete Carr, director of marketing for Cactus Services, Inc., the firm responsible for the placement of Scattergories at Hasbro Games, says, "We do not restrict ourselves to toys and games, although more than 50 percent of the submissions we see fall into this business." Ninety-five percent of the products submitted to him do not pass a phase-one review. Ten to 20 percent do not even make it through the initial telephone or mail screening. But those products that do make it are brought in-house for three to four months of a three-phase evaluation that he says can cost his company a minimum of between $10,000 and $12,000.

The very first product to pass the evaluation in 1988 was Scattergories. The inventor, Gunther Degen, paid Cactus several thousand dollars as a retainer, what Carr describes as a "get-serious fee," plus something in the range of 30 percent of any advances and royalties.

Marra Design Associates in Chanhassen, Minnesota, is owned and operated by Michael and Lynn Marra. Mike, an engineer, started his career in 1971 at Hasbro. MDA is a toy-and-game screening facility. It filters out those ideas that have little chance of making it in the marketplace, and it gives the inventor an objective recommendation on possible alternative actions. The Marras then represent the strongest candidates to major manufacturers.

"Our clients are crucial to the toy and game industry," says Mike. "I see the function of an agent as an extension of the marketer as well as the inventor. We evaluate inventor concepts, preparing the best for presentation to appropriate marketers whose lines we know by attending the Toy Fair and by maintaining close communication with corporate inventor relations and R&D/marketing personnel. We can do R&D and engineering assists as well as negotiate license agreements."

The Marras count among their biggest successes 1313 Dead End Drive (Hasbro), Simpson's Trivia (Cardinal), and the 30-Second Cotton Candy Machine (General Creations).

Paul Lapidus, who heads NewFuntiers in Palo Cedro, California, has been in the toy industry for 25 years and claims placement of 25–30 products during that time.

Trained as an industrial designer, Lapidus has experience that includes years as design manager at Playskool before becoming an independent product source. He later expanded to represent other inventors' ideas as well. Lapidus shares the disappointment of seeing an aborted project, whether one of his own concepts or an idea he represents for a client. "It is horrible news to find out a product has been dropped due to cost, lack of buyer support, or any other reason that dooms a great idea. This happens about 25 to 30 percent of the time in our experience. Licensing a product is tough business."

Michael Kohner has had a 37-year career, with 27 of those years spent as an agent in New York City and Parsippany, New Jersey. Kohner, who is well represented globally with licensed products such as The Tooth Fairy Game (Drumond Park) and Froggy (Ravensburger), uses a stable of reliable developers to meet identified product's needs. He also looks at first-time inventor concepts. Kohner sees inventors as "the lifeblood of a marketplace where consumers are always looking for new leisure products."

As an agent, Kohner provides a unique service to small-market companies, where he sells a finished product for specific noncompete territories and then gangs production runs in his offshore production sources. On one hand, he can broker just the idea (supported by a fully engineered model), to attract large U.S. marketers. Or, he can broker the fully developed idea all the way through to finished inventory, as he does successfully in European markets.

Whereas many professional inventors spend 20 percent of their time selling their own ideas, hardworking agents may spend 50 to 60 percent of their time in aggressive efforts to place the works of a stable of creative first-time sources. Often the relationship between the inventor and the agent becomes a true partnership. Both parties have strong vested interests in the property. The inventor has the ability to create the idea; the agent has the wherewithal to sell it to a toy company.

There is no standard royalty split between agent and inventor. Most agents work on a 50/50 split; with others, the split could be 60/40, with the higher percentage going to the sales function. The task of making the idea a reality with some major marketers is often harder than conceiving the idea itself. Jeff Conrad, a vice president at Radica Games, believes that the amateur must be willing to take a little less money in return for the agent's talent in getting products placed with the major manufacturers. The premise is that a shared percentage is infinitely better than 100 percent of nothing. Amateurs who balk at the business arrangements between themselves and agents may be missing a key point. Just because an agent agrees to represent a product is no guarantee of placing it. The agents may do months or years of work before succeeding with a product—if they succeed at all.

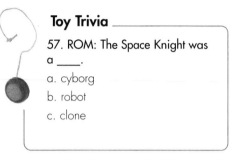

First-time inventors should search the agent ranks for the one that appears most able to represent the idea, offers the best business terms in the inventor's judgment, and presents a satisfactory plan showing which companies will see the idea. Some timeframe should be specified for the agent to represent the property, and the elements that will be returned to the inventor should be clarified. This is particularly important if design work has been added during the agent/inventor relationship.

Invention Marketers: The Con Game

Do not confuse agents and brokers recommended by toy companies with another, quite different breed of middlemen: invention-marketing firms. Numerous horror stories abound about unsuspecting amateur inventors in general—and toy and game creators among them—being fleeced by these invention companies who take hungry novices for a very costly joyride.

These slick invention marketers sign up lots of products and place nothing—except of their hands—in the pockets of trusting inventors. Like carrion birds, invention marketers kill for food, seeking to trap inexperienced, frustrated, casual inventors through hard-sell ads on late-night radio and television shows, midday commercials for the out-of-work, and direct mail. Attorneys general in dozens of states are trying to make these predators an extinct species. The U.S. Federal Trade Commission has retired several of them for good.

As positive as executives were about dealing with professional agents, not a single one had anything good to say about invention-marketing services. Most of their contact appears to be through unsolicited mailings that are nothing more than form letters containing very general information. There are no efforts by firms to make personal contact with the toy company hierarchy. Acquisitions executives don't seem to have any use for these sources, and often the envelopes remain unopened. Invention-marketing services thrive on doing cookie-cutter marketing studies and patent work all for "phase fees," with no understanding of product requirements in today's toy and game market.

If you have a complaint to register against an invention marketer at the federal level, or to learn whether there has been an action against a particular person or company, call toll-free 1-877-FTC-HELP, or use the online complaint form at www.ftc.gov.

States including California, Connecticut, Illinois, Iowa, Kansas, Massachusetts, Minnesota, Nebraska, North Carolina, Ohio, Oklahoma, South Dakota, Tennessee, Texas, Utah, Virginia, Washington, and Wisconsin have protective legislation for inventors.

If you're dealing with a professional toy agent or fall into the clutches of an invention marketer, you are entitled to ask questions about past success in the industry. This success should be measured by the number of products placed and the money earned from royalties for inventor clients. Most reputable agents will encourage you to speak to other clients they represent as references.

More Golden Rules for the Inventive Psyche

As you are out there selling ideas, some days uplifting and successful, and others disappointing and flat, everything in this book will in some form cross your path. While we believe there has been much to absorb and internalize, this is the last batch of "golden rules" to live by in the world of idea selling. May the force of this book be with you, and may your ideas earn royalties.

Never take yourself too seriously. Keep your ego out of projects; it can be a major cause of failure. Regardless of who has the original idea, every product becomes a team effort at some point. In this way, development is no different from the collaborative efforts to produce feature films, recordings, ad campaigns, and theatrical productions. Successful toys and games are the product of numerous creative and business forces that cross-pollinate and energize each other.

Never take your product too seriously. It is sobering to realize, but the world will survive without your product. The manufacturer will probably survive without your product. You might need it to survive, but no one else will! The main objective of the outside developer is to get the product to the most influential executives under the most favorable conditions. All kinds of minor problems along the way could, if permitted, get you off-course.

You are always selling two things—yourself and your concept. Personal credibility is critical. If you cannot sell yourself, you will never command enough respect from corporate executives to champion your product. Do it right the first time, and you will be welcome anytime, whatever the concept. You cannot put a value on the ability to make an encore. Ninety-nine percent of what is sold happens in Act II. Leave a poor impression, and you may never return. Therefore, how you come through the door and what you bring deserves considerable thought. In those important product meetings, who you show, how you show, and what you show are keys to building the relationship with a company's personnel that set the tone for the future when you have yet another brilliant idea. As is so true in life—and definitely in the world of invention selling—first impressions are lasting impressions.

Toy Trivia

58. Adver*teasing* was published in 1988 by _____.

a. Milton Bradley

b. Cadaco

c. Pressman

One of the best inventors cum salesman, Elliot Rudell, sums it up. As for the future of independent toy and game development, most pros agree with him: "It'll always be hard. It'll always be frustrating. It'll always be a crapshoot. It'll always be exhilarating. There will always be idea knockoffs and ethically questionable companies to work around. But there will always be a need for great product."

It is that need for great product that weaves the creative fiber of the independent toy inventor inextricably into the toy industry. Inventors are a remarkable, renewable natural resource that satisfies the industry's insatiable appetite for novel and innovative product. Without the continuous and nutritious supply of new concepts provided by external inventing sources, the toy business as we know it today would not exist. Invention, after all, is the fount of all sales and the economic future of the industry.

Fun Facts

◆ Magna Doodle was created in Japan in 1974 by Japanese engineers working for the Pilot Pen Corporation. They were trying to develop a dustless chalkboard when they invented what has become one of the world's most popular drawing toys. More than 40 million units have been sold to date.

◆ According to a Yale University study, the scent of Crayola is among the 20 most recognizable to American adults.

◆ Californian Ed Headrick, inventor of the modern "Frisbee," died at age 78. Headrick's son said his father's ashes will be molded into a limited number of "memorial flying disks," which will be distributed to family and friends and sold to help fund a museum. Source: *The Washington Post*

◆ Mickey Mouse's image is reportedly the most reproduced in the world. Over 7,500 products bear his likeness.

Chapter 8

Foreign Licensing:
Going for Euros and Yen

"For years we tried to get by with only product conceived internally. It didn't work. Our outlook was too insular. We now get ideas from the outside inventor community. We insist they stay involved with implementation. The concepts are better. The end product is better. It has an edge that we would not get from the inside. These guys—the outside guys— think differently than normal people. We are looking straight ahead. They are looking forward but sideways, at the same time."

—Barry Tunick, president
and CEO, Estes-Cox, Inc.

Selling Across the Ponds

Most U.S. toy manufacturers sell their products overseas through subsidiaries and distributors, and direct to retailers, to the tune of an estimated $6 billion in sales annually, according to the TIA *2001–2002 Toy Industry Fact Book.*

The product of many U.S. toy inventors reaches foreign markets by sublicense, through U.S. licensees. An example of this is an inventor who gives worldwide rights to a U.S. company that, in turn, exploits them overseas through its relationships with foreign companies. Giants like Mattel and Hasbro have their own offices around the world and do very little sublicensing.

It is noteworthy that many American companies sublicense products from overseas corporate and inventor sources, in hopes of making them happen here. Examples range from a Japanese craze like Pokemon, which Hasbro picked up for the U.S. market, to Pressman's Who Said That?, an Australian game.

Toy Trivia

59. Marvin Glass was a well-known toy inventor from ____.

a. Chicago

b. Boston

c. Los Angeles

Passport? Visas? Up, Up, and Away

Some inventing pros attend foreign toy fairs, meet regional marketers, and strike their own offshore deals.

Michael and Lynn Marra, of Marra Design Associates in Chanhassen, Minnesota, invented and licensed the hugely successful Cotton Candy Machine to General Creations. They license directly to European companies and have found that …

1. European markets are smaller. If a European manufacturer wants to sell in other European countries, the language barrier increases the cost of instructions, graphics, and shooting television commercials for each country.

2. Europeans have a more cerebral mind-set. They are willing to play with products that integrate strategy at all levels and educational features, whereas the U.S. market looks for items that have sizzle and that deliver instant gratification.

3. Much smaller unit volume means keeping tooling cost minimal or trying to find a product that does not require tooling. That is why most U.S. products that need heavy tooling find their way to European markets under license. Often a sublicensee can buy production from a second set of tools that belongs to the U.S. marketer. Few products originate in Europe and make it to the American market; they are typically found in specialty stores.

4. Overall, disposable income is lower in Europe, which affects the amount of money spent per child for toys and games. In countries that spend more per child (such as France), toy and game revenues are limited by population.

"We always pitch product to our worldwide manufacturing friends with the expectation that securing a license will add incremental income," the Marras conclude. "Using this approach has proven worthwhile."

Chicago inventor Bruce Lund says, "We have done a great deal of foreign licensing, with little success in Hong Kong and Japan, but a lot of success in the U.K. and Europe."

Lund continues, "I have a great fondness and respect for many wonderful European toy companies. Each country has, or had, its own unique toy companies with a distinct flavor of products appropriate to national tastes. In general, the people are a joy to work with and [are] incredibly dedicated. They are a great source of innovation to the toy industry."

Lund's enjoyment of working with Europeans and placement success notwithstanding, he has not seen great financial success overseas. Therefore, he laments, "We have decided to de-emphasize our international licensing efforts."

Cultural Quirks

Nextoys' Bob Fuhrer has broad experience in marketing ideas worldwide through his working relationship with Casio Creative Products and sublicensing through major licensees. Fuhrer has this to say about doing business in Europe and the Asian rim: "The U.S. is the largest market in the world; therefore, U.S. companies are most likely to make the investment in an idea since the return on investment should have a fast payback. Items that can cross over cultures through a combination of play value, design, language, and style are rare. Many products can be successful in some territories but failures elsewhere. Our own examples are Gator Golf, Dragonfly R/C, Fishin' Around—all great successes in the U.S., but [with] erratic results elsewhere."

Fuhrer is also aware of how nationalism and cultural differences can affect selection. "There is a territorial style to different cultures. Japanese products tend to be mechanized with engineering beauty, whether in simplicity or complexity. Products that seemingly could or would never be designed by typical American toy designers come from Japan, such as The Dancing Flower, Transformers, and Pokemon. Europe tends to develop and create "brain" games, such as Guess Who?, Mastermind, and Who Wants to Be a Millionaire. Japan is great at skill and action games like our

Crocodile Dentist, Gator Golf, Fishin' Around, as well as Hungry Hungry Hippos, Mr. Mouth, and others. Such product has come from the minds of Japanese creators and is then matched with U.S. marketing."

Fuhrer concludes, "There are ideas created and marketed throughout the world, but the worldwide inventory of all concepts is competing for very limited retail space and financial investment."

Keepin' the Nations United

Multilingual Howard Jay Fleischer, who has worked as an inventor and international licensing agent for over 15 years, says, "I have learned that a really great toy or game has no borders or language barriers. Fun always means fun!

"However, the business of toy and game licensing requires patience and understanding of subtle cultural differences among diverse peoples of the world," he adds.

Fleischer's main point is that as inventors look upon opportunities abroad, they must take the time to evaluate the business practices of each country as well as to understand the retail consumer. "Since the legal systems abroad are very far away and very expensive, doing business with the wrong partner can strip you of a successful future with your Million Dollar Idea," he warns.

"After many pitfalls and costly experiences, it is not worthwhile for me to do business abroad," Fleischer concludes.

Toy Trivia

60. In which country was Trivial Pursuit invented?

a. England
b. Australia
c. Canada

The Trade Show Circuit

If you want to learn about opportunities abroad, the best way is to attend foreign trade shows. Some of the major international trade shows are listed here:

January

The Toy Fair
(Previously British International Toy & Hobby Fair)
ExCeL
London, England
Tel: 44 020 7701 7127
Fax: 44 020 7252 5925
Website: www.britishtoyfair.co.uk

2003 marks the fiftieth anniversary of this most important British toy fair. The show typically offers 400 exhibitors from 40 countries. Attendees number around 16,500 from 60 countries.

Canadian Toy and Hobby Show
Metro Toronto Convention Centre
Toronto, Canada
Tel: 905-660-5690
Fax: 905-660-6103
Website: www.cdntoyassn.com

Univers D'Enfants Salon International Du Jouet
Paris Le Bourget Exhibition Park
Paris, France
Tel: 33 140 1600 15
Fax: 33 140 1603 58
Website: www.univers-enfants.com

Spielwarenmesse International Toy Fair
Nuremberg Exhibition Center
Nuremberg, Germany
Tel: 203-882-1300
Website: www.toyfair.de

This is the world's leading trade show for toys, with more than 3,000 exhibitors from 54 nations and more than 74,600 trade visitors from 120 nations each year. If you want to pick one foreign toy fair to attend, this would be the one.

Hong Kong Toys and Games Fair
Hong Kong Convention & Exhibition Centre
Hong Kong
Tel: 852-2584-4333
Fax: 852-2584-0249
Website: www.hktoyfair.com

In 2002, more than 28,300 people from 114 countries and regions attended Asia's largest toy fair.

Salon Internazionale del Giocattolo
Fiera de Milano (Milan Fairgrounds)
Via Petitti 16, 20149
Milan, Italy
Tel: 39 0232 5621
Fax: 39 0233 1415
Website: http://chibicart.fmi.it/default_e.asp

Feria Internacional del Juguete y El Juego
Valencia, Spain
Tel: 34 96 386 1100; 212-922-9000 in USA
Fax: 34 96 363 6111; 212-922-9012 in USA
Website: www.feriavalencia.com/feju/index_uk.htm

London Toy Fair
Harrogate International Centre
Vening House, South Road
Weybridge, Surrey, KT13 9DZ
Tel: 44 01 932 828877
Fax: 44 01 932 828811
Website: www.harrogatefair.com

This trade show is for the north of England.

March

Australian Toy, Hobby, and Nursery Fair
Melbourne Exhibition Center
Melbourne, Australia
Tel: 61 39 320 2600
Fax: 61 39 320 2622
Website: www.austoy.com.au

Children's World
International Exhibition of Toys and Educational Games
Ekaterinburg, Russia
Tel: 7 3432/493012, 493017, 493027
Fax: 7 3432/493019
Website: www.uralexpo.mplik.ru/chi/chi_next_eng.htm

April

Stockholm Toy Fair
Nacka Strand
Stockholm, Sweden
Tel: 46 8 506 472 51
Fax: 46 8 506 472 59

Bangkok International Gift & Toy Show
BITEC Center
Bangkok, Thailand
Tel: 662-366-0258
Fax: 662-366-0261

May

ABRINQ
Brazilian International Toy Fair
Expo Center Norte
Sao Paulo, Brazil
Tel: 4191 8188
Fax: 4191 0200
Website: www.abrinq.com.br

This is Latin America's most important toy trade fair.

June

Japan International Toy Fair
Metropolitan Industrial Hall
Tokyo, Japan
Tel: 81 3 3829 2513
Fax: 81 3 3829 2549
Website: www.toynes.or.jp

September

Licensing Europe
MOC Congress & Exhibition Centre
Munich, Germany
Tel: 49 6172 307 972
Fax: 49 6172 307 940
Website: www.licensingeurope.net

Toy Trivia

61. Playskool's Dr. Drill 'n' Fill was invented by which dream team?

a. Norman and Arlene Fabricant

b. Larry and Terry Mass

c. Elliot and Robyn Rudell

October

Shanghai International Toy, Baby & Gift Fair
Shanghai, PRC
Tel: 86 10 6603 3782
Fax: 86 10 6603 3964
Website: www.goalmark.com

Sponsored by German Spielwarenmesse eG, the organization that organizes and manages Nuremberg, the exhibition covers an area of 7,500 square meters, of which over 20 percent is occupied by overseas exhibitors. The overseas enterprises include those from Germany, Britain, Spain, Israel, Mexico, Columbia, Korea, Thailand, Hong Kong, and Taiwan. With China's WTO accession, China's toy makers face international competition because overseas enterprises have set their eyes on the Chinese market.

Seoul International Toy Fair
Convention & Exhibition Center (COEX)
Seoul, Korea
Tel: 82 2 795 9505
Fax: 82 2 795 0401

Hong Kong International Toys & Gift Show
Hong Kong Convention & Exhibition Center
Hong Kong
Tel: 852 2311 8216
Fax: 852 2311 6629
Website: www.kenfair.com

And if you want to keep abreast of what's going on offshore on a continual basis, here are the most active foreign trade associations:

Australian Toy Association, Ltd.
North Melbourne
Tel: 613-9320-2600
Fax: 613-9320-2622
Website: www.austoy.com.au

Brazilian Association of Toy Manufacturers
Sao Paulo
Tel: 55 11 816 3644
Fax: 55 11 211 0226

British Toy & Hobby Association
London
Tel: 44 207 701 7271
Fax: 44 207 708 2437
Website: www.btha.co.uk

Canadian Toy Association
Ontario
Tel: 905-893-1689
Fax: 905-893-2392
Website: www.cdntoyassn.com

China Toy Association
Beijing
Tel: 8610 6603 3782
Fax: 8610 6603 3964

Chinese Taipei Toy Manufacturers Association
Taipei
Tel: 886 2257 11264
Fax: 886 2254 11061
Website: www.taiwan-toys.com

Danish Toy Trade Association
Randers
Tel: 45 79 50 5029
Fax: 45 75 33 8819

French Federation of Toys & Juvenile Products Manufacturers
Paris
Tel: 33 1 4016 2570
Fax: 33 1 4016 2571

Hong Kong Toys Council
Hong Kong
Tel: 852 2732 3188
Fax: 852 2721 3494
Website: www.toyshk.org

Advice from the Pros

"Beyond creativity, inventors need an ability to feed off people's wants and needs."
—Phil Orbanes, president, Winning Moves

Toy Trivia

62. Which company markets Mr. Potato Head?

a. Pressman

b. Hasbro

c. Mattel

Hungarian Toy Association
Budapest
Tel: 36 1 209 8939
Fax: 36 1 209 0387

Italian Association of Toy Manufacturers
Milan
Tel: 39 02 806041
Fax: 39 02 80604392

The Japan Toy Association
Tokyo
Tel: 81 3 3829 2513
Fax: 81 3 3829 2549
Website: www.toynes.or.jp

Korea Toy Industry Co-operative
Seoul
Tel: 82 2 795 9505
Fax: 82 2 795 0401
Website: www.kotoy.or.kr

Mexican Association of Toy Manufacturers
Mexico, D.F.
Tel: 525-604-2442
Fax: 525-604-2442

Spanish Association of Toy Manufacturers
Madrid
Tel: 34 91 541 1305
Fax: 34 91 541 3543
Website: www.aefj.es

Association of Swedish Suppliers of Toy & Hobby Articles
Stockholm
Tel: 46 8 678 80 01
Fax: 46 8 679 96 65

Thai Toy Industry Association
Pravet
Tel: 662 366 0258/9
Fax: 662 366 0261
Website: www.ttia.or.th

Dealing in the international arena takes resilience and the spirit of adventure. Travel can be hectic and expensive. The world political climate makes travel to many locations where toy events are held trips of anxiety and delay.

But the world is a global village, and the more of it that you cover, the more familiar you will be with the requirements to license ideas. Those ideas exposed to non–U.S. marketers can be launched in offshore settings just as they might be in the United States. Payback will be smaller, but you get a sense of satisfaction and you get to see the world. Many factors for selection and inventor responsibilities are the same in Bangkok, and Budapest as they are in Boston. The object remains to get a fair and equitable license agreement for your idea.

If you are not up to carrying a passport and an electronic Franklin translator, you might try the route of an agent with an international track record. The list of agents can be found in Chapter 7. *Note:* The fact that an agent has been listed in or interviewed for this book does not constitute the authors' endorsements of his or her services to represent ideas in the international market place. Do your own diligent research to determine the best means to get your product represented offshore.

If you decide to embark on a foreign adventure, here is how to say "I am an inventor and I have something for you" in some important languages.

Chinese: *Wo Fa-Ming Wan-Ju. Ni Yow Shing Chu Ma?*

Italian: *Io sono inventore, e ho qualchecosa per voi.*

Portuguese: *Eu sou um inventor, e eu tenho algo para voce.*

German: *Ich bin Erfinder, und ich habe Etwas fur Ihnen.*

French: *Je suis en inventeur, et j'ai quelque chose pour vous.*

Japanese: *Watashi wa hatsumeisya de ate, anatani misete agetai mono ga arimas nga, … ikagadeshouka!*

Spanish: *Soy inventor, y tengo algo para Usted.*

Fun Facts

- Illustrator Rosie O'Neill created the Kewpie Doll in 1909 for Ladies Home Journal.
- Mattel designer Ira Gilford created the first in-house Hot Wheels design.
- The Brio Corp. took its name from its founders, the Brothers Ivarson, who hailed from Osby, Sweden.
- Fisher-Price's classic red-and-blue scalloped packaging was introduced in 1958.
- Fisher-Price introduced Puffalumps in 1986 and went on to sell 10 million units in the next nine 9 years.
- In the late 1830's, the first organized toy factory in America is reported to have been the Tower Toy Company of South Hingham, Massachusetts.
- In 1964, Mattel's Changeable Charmin' Chatty Cathy could say 120 things through interchangeable records that the child inserted into the doll's left side.
- Wisconsin entrepreneur Pleasant Rowland was the first to recognize that girls 7 to 12 were an underserved market. Wanting to give them an alternative to Barbie and Cabbage Patch, she combined books with soft dolls designed to represent and teach about eras of American history. She sold her company to Mattel in 1998 for $700 million.
- Toy mogul Louis Marx was featured on the cover of Time magazine, December 12, 1955.
- Hasbro's Playskool brand has its roots in the Playskool Institute, founded by Lucille King, a former school teacher. She started making wooden toys for preschoolers.

Chapter 9

Molding the Deal:
The Gets and Gives

"An important consideration when negotiating a license agreement is to remain focused on the big picture. A lawyer does a tremendous disservice to his client by utilizing negotiation tactics that others perceive as unfair or needlessly heavy-handed. It is, in fact, possible for a lawyer to vigorously represent the company while still maintaining a sense of fairness, respect, and goodwill for all parties involved. In this manner, the lawyer can protect the company's legal interests while simultaneously serving its business purposes by fostering positive, productive relationships with its partners.

—Howard R. Fine, senior vice president and general counsel, Tiger Electronics (a division of Hasbro, Inc.)

It's midday. The game inventor has just come back from gathering eggs in the hay mow on his rural Pennsylvania farm and is about to prepare a luncheon omelet when the phone rings.

ITG: "Hello, this is Barbara at In The Game."

Inventor: "Hi!" (holding breath)

ITG: "I have good news. We want to move ahead with your submission, Humpty Dumpty chess. We have to move fast, though, to get it into previews and the New York Toy Fair."

Inventor: "That's great to hear." [an understatement, after months of waiting!] "They really like it?"

ITG: "Very much so. There are modifications planned to the board and game play, but the concept tested well."

Inventor: "Do they need anything else from me?"

ITG: "Just your signature on a license agreement. Here are the key deal terms the company proposes."

Toy Trivia

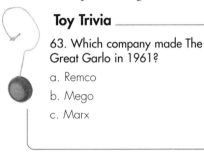

63. Which company made The Great Garlo in 1961?

a. Remco
b. Mego
c. Marx

Advice from the Pros

"Success isn't in the concept. It's in the execution."

—Pleasant Rowland, founder, The Pleasant Company

Barbara and the inventor discuss the terms before the deal sheet is sent to Legal, where a license agreement will be worked on by a lawyer who would not know Humpty Dumpty chess from Mickey Mouse mah jongg. The inventor settles on a 2 percent royalty, since Barbara argues that he really didn't invent chess and rumor has it that Humpty Dumpty belongs to Warner Bros., so ITG will have to pay a third-party character license. The inventor further acquiesces to the low-ball royalty because Barbara assures him that the game will be heavily supported by TV advertising and trade promotions.

Hard negotiating aside, the inventor feels relieved since there was no time left before Toy Fair to show the concept to another company, and he wants to finish making the omelet. Despite reduced financial terms, he is thrilled that his game will likely be at Toy Fair and at least some royalty income will trickle in from his spin on an all-time classic strategy game.

Time to Play "Let's Make a Deal."

Negotiating contracts is a skill that can be learned. People tend to make it complex. It is not. Here are some general guidelines.

- Assume that everything is negotiable. If something is not, you have nothing to lose by asking.
- Never fear to negotiate. Never negotiate out of fear.
- Know going in how you will respond to counteroffers. Have alternatives. Know your bottom line. In short, have a strategy for compromise.
- Negotiation is mostly about listening. You must understand where the other side is coming from. Once you do, keep listening.
- Negotiation is about give and take. Figure out what is the most important thing to the company. Then figure out a way to give that to them, all the time watching out for what is vital to you. This is not always possible to accomplish, but it should be the goal of both sides.
- Be human. Don't be afraid to share your troubles and issues. You should not be trying to outsmart the company. An amicable agreement benefits both parties.
- Don't be afraid to shop around for the best deal. Your focus should be on quality, commitment, and the marketing plan, not just the key deal numbers.
- If time is of the essence to you, this will put you at a distinct disadvantage. If time is of the essence to the company, conversely, they will be at a disadvantage.

> **Toy Trivia**
>
> 64. Which of the following products is marketed by S.R.M?
> a. Air Trigger
> b. Speed Force
> c. Call of the Jungle

This chapter is not a primer on license agreements. It is an overview of the environment you will face while negotiating and licensing a product. We are not lawyers. Do not consider anything we write or report to be legal advice.

Lawyers: Not Always Deal Breakers

Nicholas Caroll, the author of *Dancing with Lawyers*, says that people see they can do a lot of legal work themselves. "The law is not so mysterious; once you get past the jargon, it's mostly bureaucracy as usual." However, sooner or later, you will have to deal with lawyers if you become successful. They are partners in the ritual of contract negotiation, something you will have to participate in if your licensed product is going to get to market.

Reflecting on his early days in the business, Howard Wexler says, "I never felt that I needed a lawyer. Now it's gotten uglier. Hard times have set in, and very often hard times bring out the ugliness in people. I find myself having to be more a businessperson than I ever wanted to be."

Melody Maxim, wife of inventor John Maxim, inventor of Bumble Ball (Ertl), who lovingly calls her his "Mouthpeace," handles their contract negotiations. She feels that two parties working toward a common goal—a successful product—should be allies, not adversaries. However, she observes, "That doesn't seem to be the case once the licensing agreement negotiations are initiated. It would be ideal if one attorney would draw up an agreement that is as fair as possible to both parties, but that's unlikely to happen. Toy companies usually have 'in-house' attorneys, and it is the attorney's job to negotiate what's *best* for his or her client—not necessarily what's 'fair.' This makes it necessary for the inventor to either understand all the fine print or have his own attorney. Unfortunately, my experience is that for every attorney involved, you can add three or four weeks, plus one of your kids' college funds, to the cost of the deal!"

Toy Trivia

65. Who designed Pigs in Clover, a puzzle?

a. Charles M. Crandall

b. Phil Orbanes

c. Milton Bradley

"'Please sign our standard contract,' translates to, 'Get ready for battle,'" warns Greg Hyman, inventor of Talking Barney (Hasbro). "Unless you are quite experienced in guerrilla warfare and are a fan of pain and suffering, I suggest using your own attorney."

Hyman continues, "Do you possess the necessary expertise? You may think that you have all your ducks lined up, but the other side is usually a skilled marksman (or markswoman) aiming to shoot down those ducks."

Inventor/agent Mike Marra of Marra Design Associates says, "If each side has a dream team of lawyers who generate a dream contract, the deal is only as good as the parties feel about working together. Should one team sign with ill will, the dream team lawyers will make all the money."

Here's a view from the other side: Hasbro attorney David Dubosky, vice president of games and licensing, says, "When I look at the world of misery that so many of my lawyer colleagues must work in, I find it more than satisfying to know that my job is basically aimed at making a product that makes people happy. There are far worse ways to make a living, especially if you're a lawyer. And even on my worst days, when negotiations become trying, I always try to get a little perspective by reminding myself that, hey, this is about Mr. Potato Head, for crying out loud!"

Attorney-Client Relationships

Early on in your career, it is advisable to develop an attorney-client relationship. Many lawyers are savvy in the ways of the industry, nobody more than former corporate counsels for major toy companies. If you can hire a former senior corporate intellectual property lawyer, especially a veteran of Hasbro or Mattel, consider it seriously. This person may even know the players who want to license your product. He or she will surely know what pitfalls you should avoid. But whomever you hire, make an informed decision based upon references and a face-to-face meeting. And don't sign anything (except autographs) until your lawyer has seen it.

The attorney for the toy manufacturer has a client, too. For in-house counsel, the client is senior management. But business decisions will be made by you and a member of corporate management, respectively, not the lawyers on either side.

Some smaller companies use outside counsel. Many years ago, inventors negotiated directly with these hired guns, but that's rarely the case anymore. Companies want to keep their legal bills down, and having an inventor talk to a billing machine on retainer is not the way to do it. So someone at the company acts as a buffer, calling the lawyer only when necessary, and the deal gets done.

If you hire an attorney, do not think that he or she will do it all. You must make critical decisions. No one has more to gain or lose than you. The reality is that a lawyer may not be able to negotiate a better deal when it comes to key terms. In the end, you, not the lawyer, are the one with a vested interest in sustaining the future relationship with the marketer.

Executives set parameters like advances, royalties, and guarantees. These are not legal issues. They are calculated according to formulas using sales and earnings projections against sales and marketing expenses. For example, advances are not numbers pulled from thin air, but a percentage of what a company estimates it will generate the first year for you in royalties. A rule of thumb is that the advance be one third or one quarter of the amount of money the company expects to pay in royalties that first year.

Even though your attorney may not be able to better the numbers or change other terms and conditions to favor you, he or she will at least be able to explain the agreement so that you understand what you are signing. Nonetheless, you want to be on the front line. You must understand what plans the company has for your item. You cannot make decisions relative to the contract in a vacuum. You need to understand the company's business issues.

At larger toy companies, deal memos are transmitted back and forth through inventor relation departments. These folks have the responsibility of directing and monitoring the memo traffic as it goes in and out of legal and marketing departments for everyone's chop. At the opposite end of the spectrum, the president of a small company often works directly with an inventor on contracts. Many smaller manufacturers may not run their agreements by counsel. They rarely have in-house counsel, and they're as afraid of getting hosed by an outside lawyer as the inventor.

In-house lawyers do not mind negotiating with inventors because, in many ways, it is easier than dealing with opposing counsel. Corporate types know that many inventors suffer from "sellitus" and will sign anything. Companies use this to their advantage. "Sellitus" is a disease that overtakes inventors, amateurs, and professionals who have not sold a product for awhile and need the victory (or an advance).

Let your lawyer do the finer legal points after you have worked out the key business issues with your executive contact. This modus operandi is good for a couple reasons:

1. Inventors create product, and thrusting and parrying in a game of verbal swordsmanship with an attorney is not their definition of fun. It is like having one's oxygen shut off for most inventors to work with an attorney. Lawyers are trained for this type of battle and love it.

2. You can focus on building a personal relationship with those running the business, help develop your product, and start new ones.

Flying CAP (Combat Air Patrol)

Lawyers see themselves as protectors, providing air coverage for management. They see their mission as saving executives from themselves. But lawyers are not responsible for the product or for making profits. If your concept can boost company revenues, the executive shines. The lawyer may see things only in black and white (though the better ones do not), but good executives live in a world of black, white, and gray, knowing that calculated risks bring results.

When the inventor licensed Adver*teasing* to Cadaco, a major issue was indemnification. The game required players to recall advertising trivia. But who would indemnify Cadaco against possible legal actions from the thousands of companies whose advertising slogans, trademarks, and copyrighted jingles would appear in the game without permission?

Cadaco's outside counsel insisted that the inventor take on this responsibility. The inventor refused, telling the company not to do the game if it was unwilling to take the risk. In fact, seeing the concern that Cadaco's lawyer expressed, the inventor insisted that the company indemnify him. News of the stalemate reached the president. He and the inventor spoke at length about the situation, and the president decided to indemnify the inventor and go full speed ahead.

Adver*teasing* became a megahit, selling over one million units. There was never a peep about the IP used in the cardware. The only call they got was from the then chairman of Procter & Gamble: He wanted to know where to buy quantities of the game.

Cadaco's lawyer was correct to question the risk. In the end, according to a chief counsel for a major toy company, who spoke on the basis of anonymity, "The most important part of any agreement is liability because it is the greatest potential for loss." But the president took the calculated risk. Assessing the cost of a mistake vs. the benefits of a hit, he went with his gut. He figured that if anyone complained, he could order a running change and pull the card.

Most successful products are typically the most risky, and this risk may involve a deal point. When negotiating, always go back to the executive if you feel a lawyer is being overly protective to the point of blowing the deal.

Toy Trivia

66. Who invented Scrabble in 1931 while he was out of work?

a. Charles Darrow

b. Afred M. Butts

c. Alex Randolph

Do It Your Way

Societies thrive not on triumphs in domestic debates, but on reconciliations. Nothing will ever get done if every technical disagreement is turned into a civil war. Alas, not all opponents believe this. Some people need to pound the other guy into the ground to feel good.

In the 1980s and early 1990s, there was a popular type of management called "management by objectives." It caused many companies to make stupid decisions on routine common-sense matters. The basic concept is to …

1. Set goals for employees.
2. Measure their progress in achieving their goals.
3. Compensate them based upon their achievements.

Robert Jones, a partner in the accounting firm of Harriton, Mancuso, and Jones, P.C., in North Bethesda, Maryland, pointed out flaws in the system. "The problem is that the most important goals especially in the case of toy companies—customer satisfaction and relationships with creative resources—are the most difficult to measure. So management sets goals that can be quantified. These goals usually focus on short-term profit rather than long-term success. Employees focus their efforts in the wrong place, and frequently, such effort is counterproductive."

The most basic rule is to conduct *your* business in *your* style. You should set the pace. Do not allow yourself to become caught up in a lawyer's timetable and priorities. Things tend to get worse under such pressure. And don't roll over just because a corporate lawyer insists upon something. Remember, the company *wants* to license your concept, or you wouldn't be talking to its lawyer!

Lawyers tend to intimidate nonlawyers. If you allow it, they'll confound you with facts, blind you with Latin, and plague you with precedents. Insist on clarity over form. Do not be afraid to ask the company lawyer to interpret something. If you do not understand something, ask. If you still do not understand, ask again. Asking dumb questions is easier than correcting dumb mistakes. The best lawyers will take the time to explain the ramifications of what they are asking you to sign. If a lawyer suggests that you get your own lawyer to interpret it for you, you'll know to be even more careful. This is not a good omen. Have everything spelled out to your satisfaction so that the intent of what you are signing is clear to you, the other side, and any third party who might be asked to read and interpret the agreement at a future time.

As you embark on a negotiation, remember these observations:

1. Exceptions always outnumber rules.
2. There are always exceptions to established exceptions.
3. By the time one learns the exceptions, no one remembers the rules to which they apply.

The Deal

Getting what you want doesn't have to be at someone else's expense. There really are win/win situations. It comes down to whether you and the manufacturer are looking for a relationship or a transaction. If you want a relationship, both sides must be willing to make concessions. Everyone knows what a good deal is.

Here is a model example of the difference between a relationship and a transaction. (The names are not used because we were told this story on the basis of anonymity.)

A senior marketing executive happened to comment on how well one of the inventor's items was performing. "Then why am I not making any money?" responded the puzzled inventor.

"I don't know. What was your deal?"

"Six percent."

"Hmm. Then the eagle should be screaming," quipped the senior vice president.

Both men ran to get copies of the license agreement. It took no time to find the problem. What was supposed to have been a 6 percent royalty was shown as 3 percent. "I must have been asleep!" groaned the inventor.

"You clearly were," said the executive, reminding the inventor that he wasn't there when the deal was consummated.

The inventor asked what could be done. Without giving it a second thought, the VP said, "Let's fix it."

The two agreed that from that day forward, the company would pay 6 percent. A settlement agreement gave the inventor, in a separate payment, half of what he would have made over the 3 percent up to that point in time. They also set an appointment for the executive to visit the inventor to see new products.

Good relationships are the foundation of any business, and these two guys went on to do many more products together.

In the end, contracts are only as good as the people who sign them. Jason Smolen, an attorney who has negotiated thousands of agreements, says, "If a contract is good, it gathers dust on the shelf. If you need to keep looking at it, you're in trouble."

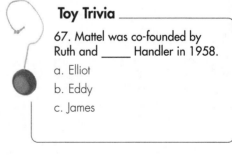

Toy Trivia

67. Mattel was co-founded by Ruth and _____ Handler in 1958.

a. Elliot

b. Eddy

c. James

The Negotiation

Some people see negotiation as a battle. Others see it as a dance. But it all begins with paperwork. As they say in the theater, if it ain't on the page, it ain't on the stage.

The savvy inventor asks the licensee for its contract. It is important to take a look at it before you propose that your agreement be used as the basis for the deal. You'll be surprised how often a company gives you something you forgot, that you were too timid to request, or that your attorney overlooked. It happens. So sit quietly and listen. Try to get the company to commit first.

One inventor we interviewed on the basis of anonymity said he once wanted a $20,000 advance but would have settled for $10,000. When asked how much he wanted, he responded, "What is it worth?" The senior vice president of R&D replied, "I thought we would offer you $30,000."

The inventor knew that this meant that he could probably bump the number up by at least $5,000, but he decided not to get greedy. By taking the opening offer, the executive could go back to management and report a victory. The inventor was $20,000 ahead of what he would have accepted, so he had a win already.

Another story we heard went like this. A senior vice president of marketing called an inventor to make him an offer on a line of plush toys with a mechanical action. The inventor asked for $50,000 and got it. There was no hemming and hawing. The inventor got off the phone and kicked himself for not going for a higher number. After a few hours, he just could not take it. He called the exec back.

"What would you say if I asked for an extra $25,000, and we made the advance $75,000?," he queried.

Advice from the Pros

"The larger companies can afford—and, in fact, do carry out—serious research prior to launching new concepts. However, if this research were reliable, then the larger companies would 'get it right' more often than the smaller companies."

—David Kremer, inventor/agent, Seven Towns, Ltd.

"But we agreed to $50,000," responded the perplexed executive.

"I know, but, honestly, it was too easy. I could tell by your fast response that I could have asked for more and received it."

"Okay. Let's make it $75,000, and don't call back unless it's with another great product," he told the stunned inventor. (P.S. The product never made it to early trade reviews. There were technical issues.)

Many corporate inventor licenses have been slowly forged and burnished over the years by professional inventors and their experienced legal advisors.

While not giving anything away to the inventor, such agreements may cover esoteric points that even all the pros do not know.

In today's highly volatile business atmosphere, with public companies under extreme pressure to enhance shareholder value, the bean counters have unleashed their lawyers to go over agreements and even attempt to take a few pounds of flesh out of an inventor's standard deal. What were once pretty simple agreements are now frequently overlawyered documents.

While interviewing people for this chapter, we heard an astonishing story of a major company actually going back to inventors and asking them to reduce their royalties on certain evergreen items. Some-one in the hierarchy decided that the inventors had received royalties long enough. Not a single inventor we spoke to agreed. "It left the taste of lukewarm parsnip juice in my mouth," said one inventor. He added that when the company was printing money with his product, no one called to *increase* his royalty.

Toy Trivia

68. What did Denis Fisher, a British electronics engineer, invent?

a. Etch-a-Sketch

b. Spirograph

c. Lie Detector

The Timetable

Whatever you do, remember that the length of a business contract is typically inversely proportional to the amount of business the product will generate. A typical negotiation scenario goes like this: A company representative calls with the exciting news that they want to license your concept. This is the kind of call every executive likes to make and every inventor likes to receive.

The inventor, of course, wants to get an agreement signed and sealed quickly—and deposit that advance. The lawyer wants to hold on to the company's money for as long as possible and still make sure the product doesn't fall out of the line. (This could happen for too many reasons to list.) For a while, this arrangement clearly benefits the manufacturer, but as things move along and the manufacturer invests more and more money and assets in the inventor's product, it is risky for the company not to have clear title to the product.

Companies have gone into Toy Fair without inventor products under license. When it happens at a large company like Hasbro and Mattel, it is usually because the legal department is overloaded and the lawyers were working on other priorities.

The biggest risk is not that the inventor will welsh on the deal, though it could happen. The real risk is that the inventor becomes incapacitated or worse, and suddenly the company finds itself dealing with total strangers who have greatly different motivations than the inventor.

Option Agreement

The following is a sample agreement that often precedes the licensing document. In effect it is the marketer's first formal commitment to the inventor's idea. With a monetary payment, the marketer is buying time to review the idea further and take the idea off the market while a final decision is made. Agreements may vary by company but the important issues are: what is the amount of the holding fee, how much time is being bought, and what does the inventor get back if the marketer decides not to enter into a full license agreement.

OPTION

THIS AGREEMENT made as of this __ day of ___, 200__, between _____, located at _____ (hereinafter "LICENSOR"), and _____, located at _____ (hereinafter "LICENSEE").

WHEREAS, LICENSOR has invented a _____ (hereinafter "Item"), and

WHEREAS, LICENSOR has presented the Item to LICENSEE for evaluation and possible licensing; and

WHEREAS, LICENSEE wishes to review and evaluate the Item;

It is therefore agreed between the parties as follows:

LICENSOR agrees that LICENSEE may examine and evaluate the Item for a period commencing on the date of this Agreement and ending on (insert date) ("Review Period"). LICENSOR represents that, to the best of its knowledge, it has such rights in and title to the Item as to enable it to grant LICENSEE an exclusive license for its manufacture and sale. LICENSOR agrees that it will not license or disclose the Item or similar items during the Review Period to any other person, firm, corporation, or other entity in that would compete with LICENSEE.

LICENSOR agrees that should LICENSEE wish to license the Item, LICENSOR will enter into a mutually satisfactory licensing agreement for the exclusive use in the (define territory, e.g., US, Europe, worldwide, etc.) of the Item with LICENSEE or a subsidiary or affiliate designated by LICENSEE.

In consideration of the foregoing, LICENSEE agrees to pay to LICENSOR the sum of $_____, along with other good and valuable consideration, the receipt of which is hereby acknowledged. If LICENSEE decides to license the Item, it will so notify LICENSOR, by a written confirmation sent to LICENSOR at the address specified above, mailed no later than the last day of the Review Period, and both parties agree to negotiate a licensing agreement within thirty (30) days thereafter. In that event, LICENSEE may apply the above-referenced paid consideration against any royalties payable under the executed license agreement. In the event that LICENSEE does not elect to use the Item, it is agreed that LICENSOR shall be entitled to retain the entire sum payable hereunder.

IN WITNESS WHEREOF, the parties have executed this Agreement as of the date first written above.

LICENSOR: _____ LICENSEE: _____

Title: _____ Title: _____

The Agreement

If the toy gods are smiling, your next step will be a license. Here is a template for a typical license agreement that contains many key issues of importance to inventors (licensors) and companies (licensees). *It in no way is meant as legal advice.* We include it as a reference document only. Its terms and conditions have been taken in bits and pieces from myriad licensing agreements. What applies to your specific situation will be unique to your deal. We hope that you and your counsel are able to adapt parts of this agreement to your specific needs, put some personal English on it, and come away with a fair deal.

Toy Trivia

69. Who was nicknamed the "Henry Ford of the Toy Industry"?

a. Louis Marx

b. Marvin Glass

c. A. C. Gilbert

This template is a vehicle to get your idea to market. Just like a motor vehicle you drive to Toys R Us, the basic conveyance can be souped up and modified. It is up to you and/or your lawyer—not us—to make certain that, through careful negotiation, your vehicle gives you and your product a comfortable ride to the marketplace. There is likely nothing in this document that a company has not encountered when negotiating with an inventor.

Throughout the agreement, the authors and inventor/agents Michael Marra, Paul A. Lapidus, and Robert Fuhrer, make observations or comments. Marra has been in the industry 31 years, 18 years inside companies and 14 years as an inventor/agent. Lapidus has been in the game 27 years, 25 years as an independent inventor/agent. And Fuhrer has been working with the elves for 25 years, 21 years as an independent inventor/agent. You'll find their comments and some notes from the authors in bold, italic type throughout.

AGREEMENT

AGREEMENT made this ___ day of _____, 20__, by and between _____ (hereinafter referred to as LICENSOR) and _____, LICENSEE, a _____cor-poration with offices at _____, (hereinafter referred to as LICENSEE).

WITNESSETH

WHEREAS, LICENSOR represents and warrants that it is the creator, inventor, designer, and owner of (name product), hereinafter referred to as the ITEM;

WHEREAS, LICENSOR hereby warrants that it is the sole and exclusive owner of all rights in the ITEM, and that it, to the best of its knowledge, has the sole and exclusive right to grant the license herein; and

Note: *It is important that you qualify anything you really do not know for sure with the words "to the best of my knowledge." Do not permit anyone to tell you this phrase cannot be included or that it is meaningless.*

WHEREAS, LICENSEE is in business of manufacturing and selling toys and games;

WHEREAS, LICENSEE is desirous of obtaining the sole and exclusive rights to manufacture and sell the ITEM in (USA, worldwide, etc.);

Note: *Define the territory. Allow the licensee rights only in areas where the licensee has demonstrated the ability to successfully commercialize product.*

Fuhrer: *Because the culture and taste of each nation can be so diverse, territorial restrictions should apply. Some products, such as word games, may be suitable only by language restrictions. Some thematic uses, such as animals or popular culture icons, may be very restrictive for international sales. This can get sticky because most of the major global manufacturers want "rights throughout the universe" but will usually be reasonable that sales must commence by a certain date in respective territories.*

Dividing territories can be complicated, especially with the European union. USA rights usually become "North America" and include Canada, military bases, and sometimes Mexico. It's possible to specify separate nations in a territories such

as Latin America (for example, Brazil), Asia (for example, Japan), and Europe (for example, the U.K.).

Further impediments ensue when a product is attached to a license—such as Sesame Street—that has a strong USA presence but may be weak elsewhere. This means the product might have to be substantially redesigned for a suitable character or in generic form in another country, R&D, and/or tooling expenses and resources that have to be expended in addition.

Also, each nation has its own safety, tax, and customs laws, making the whole process tricky. The main reason to divide territories is to try to ensure proper distribution with a distributor that genuinely wants the product and doesn't just "inherit" it from a parent company.

For purposes of this Agreement, a contract year shall be from January 1 to December 31, except for the first contract year, which shall be from the date of execution of the Agreement until December 31, 20__ (year agreement is written\executed).

Note: *Having the contract year is helpful since most companies' fiscal year is the calendar year. Plus, some contract terms may depend on payments.*

NOW, THEREFORE, for and in consideration of the sum of One Dollar ($1.00) and other good and valuable consideration, receipt of which is hereby acknowledged, and for the performance of the mutual covenants hereinafter to be performed, it is agreed as follows:

DEFINITIONS

Item: As used in this Agreement, the term Item refers to the ITEM described herein above, and any Improvements, Accessories, or Extensions thereto, whether developed by or for LICENSEE.

Improvements: As used in this Agreement, the term Improvements means any design or technical refinements or advances made by or for LICENSEE and reflected in the ITEM as marketed.

Accessories: As used in this Agreement, the term Accessories means any products making use of the ITEM, as well as equipment developed by or for LICENSEE designated for use with the ITEM.

Extensions: As used in this Agreement, the term Extensions means any products that are sold independently by LICENSEE under the ITEM trademark—i.e., products that trade on the name of the ITEM, but are not necessarily marketed as accessories to the ITEM.

Collateral Merchandise: As used in this Agreement, the term Collateral Merchandise means products that are sold under the ITEM trademark or trade on its good will.

Note: *You may not want to grant these rights. If not, omit this reference. Or, you may want to allow for certain collateral merchandise and not others. If so, spell it out here. Collateral merchandise could range from T-shirts to tennis rackets. Whatever you decide, always put a performance clause in with milestone dates. If a licensee does not do something by a date certain, those specific rights return to you.*

1. LICENSOR hereby grants, assigns, and transfers to LICENSEE the sole and exclusive right, privilege, and license to make, reproduce, modify, use, and sell, and to have made, reproduced, modified, used, and sold, the ITEM and the subject matter of the patent application which is to be filed on the ITEM pursuant to Paragraph 4 hereof.

2. All rights and licenses not specifically granted to LICENSEE herein are reserved by LICENSOR and, as between the parties, are the sole and exclusive property of LICENSOR and may be used or exercised solely by LICENSOR.

Note: *This is a critical clause. It makes clear that it was never your intention to give the licensee any rights that are not called out specifically in the agreement.*

Fuhrer: *How categories are defined is very important, particularly for technologies. It is essential to separate categories of use as much as possible. Is the license for vehicles, video games, dolls, board games, or sporting goods? If prospects exist to broaden product categories, efforts should be made to retain those rights. Does the licensee have the capability to exploit all markets and potential?*

3. This Agreement shall be for an initial period of _____ years, beginning the date hereof. If LICENSEE meets all its obligations hereunder, and LICENSOR earns a minimum of $_____ per year in royalties, or $ _____ in total per year, LICENSEE will have the option to extend the initial term for an additional _____ years, under the same terms and conditions as the initial period. After the first _____ years, the license will automatically renew for additional _____ year periods, unless either party gives notice, by certified mail, of its desire and intent to let the license expire at least _____ days prior to the end of the term in effect.

   If LICENSEE doesn't meet aforementioned minimum payments, and it wishes to extend the license, LICENSEE may do so by making up the short fall to the LICENSOR.

4. (a)   LICENSOR agrees to bear expenses of obtaining patent protection in the USA, and any and all such patents will be in the name of and remain the property of LICENSOR during and following any termination or cancellation hereof.

Marra: *I insist that my licensees do diligence on all intellectual properties involved in a license. To that end, I include the following clause 4(b):*

(b)   LICENSEE will conduct its own patent, copyright, and trademark searches and satisfy itself that the ITEM does not infringe anything in any of these fields, and once satisfied, LICENSEE agrees to indemnify, defend, and save harmless LICENSOR from and against all damages, costs, and attorney fees resulting from all claims, demands, actions, suits, or prosecutions for patent, copyright, or trademark based upon use of the ITEM or its components and all forms of the ITEM as produced and sold by LICENSEE, its subsidiaries, affiliates, and Sublicensees. LICENSEE shall be given prompt notice of any claim against LICENSOR and shall have the right to defend such claim with counsel selected by LICENSEE. LICENSOR agrees to cooperate with LICENSEE in connection with the defense of any such claim.

(c)   LICENSEE acknowledges that LICENSOR makes no representations or warranties as to the patentability of the ITEM or the ability to copyright, trademark, obtain a trade name for, or otherwise protect the ITEM. LICENSEE acknowledges that notwithstanding any lack of protection afforded by patent, copyright, trade name, or trademark law, LICENSEE shall be bound by all the terms and conditions hereof.

Marra: *Foreign patents are very expensive because each country has its own fee structure. They cumulatively can run in the tens to hundreds of thousands of dollars, depending on how many countries are engaged. Since the inventor does not have control over the manufacturer's distribution network, I recommend adding the following clause to limit cost and realize some royalty income. This works for the USA, too.*

LICENSEE shall obtain registration or application for additional patents, trademarks, trade names, and copyrights, as deemed necessary and appropriate by LICENSEE, in its sole discretion to protect the ITEM consistent with the rights granted to LICENSEE hereunder. LICENSOR agrees to cooperate with LICENSEE to obtain or apply for said registrations and applications. Any such registrations and applications (other than any registration or application for patents, trademarks, trade names, and copyrights already applied for or obtained by LICENSOR) will be at LICENSEE's expense, except that solely in the case of application(s) for a United States patent(s), LICENSEE may apply for and procure said application(s) in the name of LICENSOR, and deduct half of the expenses for the United States application(s) from United States royalties otherwise to be paid LICENSOR on the ITEM, to a maximum of $___ thousand dollars. LICENSEE may apply for and prosecute such patent applications outside the United States as LICENSEE may determine necessary. LICENSEE shall bear all costs and expenses associated with any foreign patent filings and applications, provided that, in the event royalties thereafter accrue from sales in a foreign country, then there shall be deducted from any royalties otherwise due to LICENSOR from sales in such foreign country, fifty percent (50%) of the cost of the patent filings and applications in such country, up to an aggregate of $___ thousand dollars for each foreign country. LICENSOR may, at its sole option, apply for such further or additional patent protection on the ITEM in the United States or any foreign country at LICENSOR'S expense. LICENSOR shall advise LICENSEE of any such application.

(c)   To the best of LICENSOR's knowledge, the ITEM does not infringe any patent rights.

(d)   LICENSEE shall clearly mark ITEM and its packaging, containers, advertising, and display cards with *Patent Pending*, until and unless LICENSOR advises LICENSEE that a US patent has issued, in which case LICENSEE will cause *Patented* to appear on the ITEM and its packaging.

(e)   LICENSEE agrees to clearly mark the ITEM, its packages, containers, display cards, and advertising messages with the following legal notice:

_____ is a TM of _____.

Used With Permission. All Rights Reserved.

Note: *If you have a trademark on the product to be licensed, there should be a clause to this effect.*

wherever LICENSOR marks the ITEM with its legal notices, and in the same typeface and point that it uses for its legal notices. LICENSOR reserves the right to have LICENSEE change said notice, but no requested change shall apply to goods at retail, goods in transit, goods in warehouses, goods in progress, or any component for the goods until exhausted.

(f)   LICENSEE acknowledges and agrees that LICENSOR is the owner of all right, title, and interest in and to the trademark and in the good will associated with the trademark. LICENSEE shall not in any manner represent that it has any ownership in the trademark.

(g)   All trademark notices and all other written material placed on the ITEM or its packaging or ads associated therewith shall be sent to LICENSOR, the trademark holder, for approval at least _____ days prior to distribution of the ITEM. Failure of LICENSOR to notify LICENSEE of disapproval within ___ days after receipt of the notice or other written material shall be deemed approval of the notice or other written material.

5. (a)   LICENSEE shall pay LICENSOR a _____ percent royalty on all Net Sales of the ITEM, if sold on a domestic basis.

(b)   LICENSEE shall pay LICENSOR a ___ percent royalty on all Net Sales of the ITEM, if sold "Letter of Credit" from any foreign country.

(c)   In the event LICENSEE sells the ITEM as a premium, the royalty rate shall be ____ percent of the revenue derived by LICENSEE from the sale of ITEM as a premium. For the purposes of this Agreement, the term "premium" shall be defined as including, but not limited to, combination sales, free or self-liquidating items offered to the public in conjunction with the sales or promotion of a product or service other than the ITEM, including traffic building or continuity visits by the consumer, customer, or any similar scheme or device, whose primary purpose in regard to each of the sales described above is not directed at the sale of the ITEM itself and the prime intent of which is to use the ITEM in such a way as to promote, publicize, and/or sell the products, services, or business image of the user of such ITEM rather than the ITEM itself.

(d)   LICENSEE shall pay LICENSOR ___ percentage of any gross revenues (including all advances, guarantees, minimum payments, and royalties) received by LICENSEE from third parties for collateral merchandise (including *physical adaptations* such as uses of the ITEM and its improvements and accessories thereto in toys of all kinds without limitation); and *nonphysical adaptations*, which include uses of the characters embodied in the ITEM and its improvements and accessories thereto in comic strips and comic books; clothing; paper goods; breakfast cereals; video and computer games; posters; home video versions of TV programs and motion pictures; TV; print; film; animation (cartoons) and characterizations and performances; newspaper, magazine, and book fictionalizations; and other media of entertainment or enlightenment without limitation, whether existing today or not yet invented. Should LICENSEE itself use such a right for collateral sublicense rather than licensing it to a third party, then royalty payable to LICENSOR shall be the same as on the ITEM. LICENSEE shall promptly provide to LICENSOR a copy of each collateral sublicense.

Fuhrer: *I ask these questions, among others, when considering allowing a company to sublicense. (See 5[e].) Does the company holding the master license have its own distribution in another territory, or will it sublicense? If it is a sublicense, royalties can be substantially reduced because most companies put in a royalty-sharing clause for sublicenses. Plus, the royalty rate may be based on unfavorable pricing.*

(e)   It is further agreed that any sublicense for the manufacture and sale of said ITEM in any foreign country (outside USA, Canada, and Mexico—NAFTA) shall require payment to LICENSOR of _____ percentage of any and all monies received, including but not limited to royalties, advances, guarantees, and consultation fees it may receive under such sublicenses after deduction for payments made to outside parties for effecting the sublicense, not to exceed _____ percent of the monies received, with royalties payable to LICENSOR being no less than _____ percent of the sales of said ITEM. LICENSEE shall promptly inform LICENSOR of any foreign sublicense it grants with respect to said ITEM, and LICENSEE shall send LICENSOR a copy of its licensing agreement with all respective Sublicensees.

Marra: *Paragraph 5(f) is the language I recommend to cover closeout sales.*

(f)   The royalty provisions of this Agreement shall not apply to "closeout sales" by LICENSEE or its affiliated Sublicensees. The royalty provisions of this Agreement shall apply to "closeout sales" by any unaffiliated Sublicensees where LICENSEE receives any payment from such Sublicensees arising from or related to such sales. "Closeout sale" is defined as any sale that occurs after twenty-four (24) months from the date of this Agreement at a gross sales price of less than seventy-five percent (75%) of LICENSEE's usual price, when made in contemplation of ceasing sales of the Item. In the event that closeout sales continue for a period in excess of six (6) months, then all sales that were previously classified as closeout sales shall be reclassified as royalty-bearing sales hereunder, and LICENSEE shall immediately pay to LICENSOR all royalties on such sales based on the definition of net sales appearing in Section 5(a) hereof. From and after the date of such payment, a "closeout sale" for purposes of this Agreement shall be defined as any sale at a gross sales price less than seventy-five percent (75%) of LICENSEE's gross selling price during what had been previously classified as a closeout sale, when made in contemplation of ceasing sales of the Item. LICENSEE shall continue to provide LICENSOR with royalty statements during the period of any closeout sale.

(g)   The term "Net Sales" is defined as sales computed on prices charged by LICENSEE to its customers for the ITEM, less a deduction not to exceed ____ percent to provide for freight allowances, sales allowances actually credited, customary trade discounts (but not cash discounts), volume discounts (not to exceed usual industry practices), to the extent taken, directly applicable to the sale of the ITEM, and less returns (but not for exchange) that are accepted and credited by LICENSEE. No deduction shall be made for uncollectable accounts. No costs incurred in the production, sales, distribution, or exploitation or promotion of said ITEM shall be deducted from any royalties payable by LICENSEE to LICENSOR, nor shall any deductions from royalties be made for taxes or bank-handling fees of any nature. LICENSEE cannot barter or trade or do so-called "chargebacks" on the ITEM without computation of full royalties.

(h)   All royalties payable by LICENSEE to LICENSOR shall accrue on the date an ITEM is invoiced, billed, shipped, or paid for, whichever occurs first.

(i)   All payments required by this Agreement shall be made to LICENSOR in U.S. dollars and, if requested by LICENSOR, via bank wire transfer.

6. Upon execution of this Agreement, LICENSEE shall concurrently pay LICENSOR the sum of $_____, as a nonrefundable, guaranteed advance against royalties. In no event shall such advance payment be repaid to LICENSEE other than in the form of deductions from payments due under Paragraphs 5 and 6 hereof.

Marra: *I like to get a reasonable yearly advance whenever possible for myself and my clients. It's not unusual. Keep in mind that the operative word is* **reasonable**, *especially if it is structured with the company's product cycle and unit volume in mind. I designed the following clause to cover this:*

LICENSEE also agrees to pay LICENSOR the sum of $_____ thousand dollars, on or before January 6 of each successive year of the term of this Agreement, commencing January 6, 20__, except as provided in subparagraph below. Such amounts shall be treated as guaranteed nonrefundable advance royalty payments that can be recouped by LICENSEE only against royalty payments due under Paragraph __.

LICENSEE shall be excused from making the advance royalty payment stated in subparagraph above with respect to any year by giving notice to LICENSOR no later than the August 31st preceding the January 6th *(the dates need to be suitable to the manufacturers product cycle)* on which the advance royalty would be payable of its intention not to continue with the marketing and sale of the ITEM. Such notice shall have the effect of terminating this Agreement, except for any provisions hereof that are continuing in nature, such as the payment of royalties arising out of continuing sales and shipments of the ITEM.

7. LICENSEE hereby agrees to divide all advances and royalty payments due between to LICENSOR according to the following percentages and mail each inventor's payment, together with duplicate quarterly account reports, to their addresses as noted in the preamble of this Agreement.

Inventor #1: ___%

Inventor #2: ___%

And so forth.

Note: *Paragraph 7 can be modified for a single inventor.*

8. (a)　LICENSEE agrees to introduce ITEM no later than NY Toy Fair 20__, and within ____ months thereof begin shipment in commercial quantities of the ITEM; subject, however, to provisions of Paragraph 15 hereof relating to occurrences beyond LICENSEE's control. LICENSEE further agrees to use its best efforts to manufacture, promote, and sell the ITEM to satisfy demand.

(b)　If LICENSEE fails to meet either of the aforementioned deadlines, or ceases manufacture for ____ days, this Agreement may be terminated, at the option of LICENSOR, and all rights, title, and interest in the ITEM granted by LICENSOR to LICENSEE will revert to LICENSOR. LICENSEE will, in such case, return to LICENSOR all samples provided by LICENSOR.

9. LICENSEE has the right to change the form of the ITEM as submitted by LICENSOR and to produce and sell it under new form(s); provided, however, that all the provisions of this Agreement shall apply to said new form(s) of the ITEM.

10. (a)　LICENSEE shall annually furnish to LICENSOR, free of charge, _____ *(insert number)* samples each of each ITEM in its packaging prior to its availability at retail. In the case of foreign product, LICENSEE shall provide to LICENSOR, free of charge, _____ *(insert number)* samples each of each ITEM in foreign-language packaging.

(b)　LICENSEE may give a reasonable number of product samples to trade accounts for their review, free from any royalty obligation, as long as they are given away for free.

(c)   LICENSEE shall send LICENSOR copies of its 20__ catalog, sell sheets, and price lists and subsequent copies of both for each year the ITEM is offered for sale.

Marra: *Add the following clause, if appropriate.*

LICENSOR will receive from LICENSEE *(insert number)* copies of any television commercials and/or *(insert number)* copies of audio cassettes of any radio commercials for the ITEM.

11. (a)   LICENSOR represents that it has no knowledge that production and/or sale of the ITEM, in the form originally submitted to LICENSEE, infringes the rights of others. If a formal lawsuit is brought against LICENSEE, in a court of competent jurisdiction, concerning title or ownership to the ITEM, during the term of this license, LICENSOR agrees to fully cooperate with LICENSEE in the defense thereof. LICENSEE will pay all legal fees and will pay any LICENSOR travel and board expenses incurred by LICENSOR for any appearance connected with such lawsuit, farther than ___ miles from LICENSOR's offices.

Lapidus: *We do not believe that indemnifying 100 percent of all royalties paid by a manufacturer on the sale of products utilizing a licensed property is fair or reasonable. Our bottom line is simple. If a company makes money utilizing one of our licensed properties, we should continue to be paid all or a negotiated portion of royalties, as long as it is not found that we knowingly entered into an agreement under false pretenses.*

(b)   LICENSOR agrees to indemnify, defend, and save harmless LICENSEE against actions brought against LICENSEE with respect to any claim or suit that LICENSOR is not the originator of the Item.

(c)   LICENSOR agrees to indemnify LICENSEE against losses, claims, and expenses with respect to losses, claims, or expenses that arise only from an act or omission by LICENSOR that is done in bad faith.

(d)   LICENSOR shall not indemnify LICENSEE on claims whereby LICENSEE has been said to have been previously shown an ITEM similar to the ITEM by the claimant. LICENSEE warrants that it has never seen an item similar to the subject ITEM.

(e)   LICENSOR agrees to indemnify and hold harmless LICENSEE from and against any claim of infringement of trade secrets arising out of LICENSEE's sale of the ITEM.

Marra: *Most companies have very stringent indemnity clauses, and the following is only one simple way to keep some of your royalties. Trying to find middle ground can be a challenge because my experience has found the indemnity section of any contract the most difficult to negotiate.*

    (f)   With respect to any claims against LICENSOR falling within the scope of such indemnifications, all Losses shall be recovered by LICENSEE from and only to the extent of payment paid or due LICENSOR hereunder. *(Limit repayments to either paid royalties or royalties due.)*

    (g)   In the event an infringement is determined against LICENSEE by a court of competent jurisdiction, LICENSOR's liability for such infringement will not exceed ___ percent of the amount of royalties that begin to be earned on the ITEM, starting on the date LICENSOR are first notified, in writing, and sent by certified mail, of the filing of such lawsuit, and only if the original design submitted by LICENSOR is cause for said infringement. This __ percent is limited to the country in which the alleged infringement occurs. One hundred (100%) percent of royalties will continue to be paid to LICENSOR in countries in which no alleged infringement has occurred. Any funds withheld by LICENSEE from LICENSOR shall be held in an interest-bearing escrow account until such lawsuit is resolved. Said account shall be periodically reviewed by LICENSEE and LICENSOR, and a portion of held funds released if said claim is stalled. At the time of resolution, all escrowed funds and interest earned on said funds will be returned to LICENSOR, less agreeable deductions for legal or settlement costs paid by LICENSEE.

    (h)   LICENSEE agrees to indemnify, defend, and save harmless LICENSOR from and against all damages, costs, and attorney fees resulting from all claims, demands, actions, suits, or prosecutions for copyright, trademark, and personal injury based upon use of the ITEM or its components and all forms of the ITEM produced and sold by LICENSEE, subsidiaries, and affiliates.

Lapidus: *We live in a society in which individuals have a propensity to litigate whether or not they have just cause. They may take action because they know companies may settle cases to avoid publicity or the high cost of prosecuting an unjust litigation. Since anybody can make claims and bring suit against a manufacturer, we do not believe we should be responsible for attorney's fees, expenses, and any other loses incurred in such a controversy, if in the end it is found that there was no breach in any of our warranties.*

In the unlikely event a breach is found in any of my warranties, licensees expect to retain all rights to the licensed property that are not found to be part of any material breach of their warranties.

Lastly, if a company decides to compromise or settle a controversy by making a payment of monies to an individual, company, or organization in an effort to avoid publicity or continued costs, and the company does this without reasonable evidence of a breach in my warranties, then no deductions should be made from the royalties due to me.

(i)   LICENSEE agrees to cover LICENSOR under its product liability insurance providing protection for itself and LICENSOR against any such claims or suits relating to product manufacture or materials failure, but in no event in amounts less than $__ million dollars and within ____ days before manufacture of the ITEM coming hereunder, LICENSEE will submit to LICENSOR a certificate of insurance naming LICENSOR as insured parties, requiring that the insurer shall not terminate or materially modify such without written notice to LICENSOR at least ____ days in advance thereof.

Note: *Indemnifications are very important—perhaps the most important clauses in a license agreement. Do not sign an agreement that does not provide strong indemnification, especially as it relates to product liability. As the* **Houston Chronicle** *reported in its "Outlook" section on December 8, 1999, "With unpopular industries like tobacco and guns already under siege, an ambitious group of personal injury lawyers needed a fresh victim. They found one ripe for demonizing: those evil, manipulative, child-targeting, life-endangering, manufacturers we all know and loathe: the toymakers."*

12. LICENSEE shall, within ____ days following the end of each calendar quarter, starting with the month following the quarter in which sales of the ITEM commence, submit to LICENSOR a report covering the sales of the ITEM during the preceding quarter, said report setting forth the number of ITEMs sold, the gross sales, the net sales, and the royalties due for the stated period, as reflected by LICENSEE's books of accounts. Royalties paid later than __ days after the due date shall be subject to interest at a rate equal to the current prime rate at Chase Bank of New York, times the number of days until payment is made in full to LICENSOR. Such quarterly statements shall be submitted whether or not they reflect any sales.

13. (a)   LICENSEE agrees to keep, at its headquarters, full and accurate books of account, records, data, and memoranda respecting the manufacture and sales of the ITEM in sufficient detail to enable the payments hereunder to LICENSOR to be determined, and LICENSEE further gives LICENSOR the right, upon reasonable written notice, at its own expense, to examine, or to have its representatives examine, said books and records, only insofar as they concern the ITEM and not more often than once in any calendar year, and upon reasonable notice to LICENSEE, for the purpose of verifying the reports provided for in this Agreement. In the event LICENSOR shall examine the records, documents, and materials in the possession or under the control of LICENSEE with respect to the subject matter, such examination shall be conducted in such a manner as to not unduly interfere with the business of LICENSEE. LICENSOR and its representatives shall not disclose to any other person, firm, or corporation any information acquired as a result of any such examination; provided, however, that nothing herein contained shall be construed to prevent LICENSOR and/or its duly authorized representative from testifying, in any court of competent jurisdiction, with respect to the information obtained as a result of such examination in any action instituted to enforce the rights of LICENSEE under the terms of this Agreement. This right of audit shall extend to two years after the termination of this Agreement.
Note: *If you are considering an audit, no one has more experience than Elliot Greller, CPA. Tel: 1-800-724-4063.*

(b)   In the event that any audit of LICENSEE's books and records indicates that royalties have been underpaid by ___ percent or more of sales subject to royalty, LICENSEE will reimburse LICENSOR for reasonable costs and expenses of the audit. Payments found to be due LICENSOR as a result of an examination shall be paid immediately with interest at the highest rate permitted by law, plus ___ percent, from the date the payments should have been made to LICENSOR.

14. (a)   If LICENSEE shall at any time default by failing to make any payment hereunder, or by failing to make any report required under this Agreement, or by making a false report, and LICENSEE shall fail to remedy such default within ___ days for money, and ____ days for reports, after notice thereof by LICENSOR, then LICENSOR may, at its option, terminate this Agreement and the license granted herein by notice to that effect, but such act by LICENSOR shall not relieve LICENSEE of its liabilities accruing up to the time of termination. In the case of a subsequent default, the time period within which to remedy the defaults shall be reduced to ___ days for money, and ___ days for reports.

In the event LICENSEE commits ___ or more defaults and corrections thereof of any nature during the term of this agreement, and any extension, as to which LICENSOR has given notice, LICENSOR may terminate this agreement at the time that LICENSOR learn of such third or more defaults by giving LICENSEE written notice thereof.

(b)   If this Agreement is terminated, LICENSEE shall not sell or otherwise deal in the ITEM, nor shall LICENSEE sell or transfer the tooling to any person, company, or corporation, unless said person, company, or corporation signs a license agreement with LICENSOR.

(c)   The rights to commercialize the ITEM in foreign countries (outside the USA, Canada, and Mexico—NAFTA) are conditioned upon introduction of the ITEM in the USA, as required herein, and the signing of a sublicense or sales deal with a foreign country within *(insert time limit)* after the U.S. introduction of the ITEM. If any foreign rights revert back to LICENSOR, LICENSEE shall have the right of first refusal as OEM vendor for any LICENSOR Sublicensees.

Marra: *Add the following clause so that the inventor can recover the intellectual properties and goodwill.*

(d)   Immediately upon expiration or termination of this Agreement, for any reason whatsoever, all the rights granted to LICENSEE hereunder shall cease and revert to LICENSOR, who shall be free to license others to use any or all of the rights granted herein effective on and after such date of expiration or termination, and to this end, LICENSEE will be deemed to have automatically assigned to LICENSOR upon such expiration or termination, all copyrights, trademarks and service mark rights, equities, goodwill, titles, designs and concepts, and other rights in or to the ITEM.

LICENSEE will, upon the expiration or termination of this license, execute any instruments requested by LICENSOR to accomplish or confirm the foregoing. Any assignments shall be without consideration other than mutual covenants and considerations of this Agreement. In addition, for whatever reasons, LICENSEE will forthwith refrain from any further use of the trademarks or copyrights of any further reference to any of them, direct or indirect.

15. It is understood and agreed that if LICENSEE does not introduce the ITEM at the NY Toy Fair in February 20__, LICENSOR may give notice to LICENSEE of its desire to terminate this Agreement for that reason and, if LICENSEE does not within ___ days resume the manufacture and sale of the ITEM, this

Agreement and the license granted herein shall terminate as of the end of that ___ day period.

16. It is understood and agreed that in the event an act of government, or war conditions, or fire, flood, or labor trouble in the factory of LICENSEE, or in the factory of those manufacturing parts necessary for the manufacture of the ITEM, prevents the performance by LICENSEE of the provisions of this Agreement, then such nonperformance by LICENSEE shall not be considered a breach of this Agreement and such nonperformance shall be excused, but for no longer than a period of __ months on any single occurrence.

17. LICENSEE agrees that if this Agreement is terminated under any of its provisions LICENSEE will not itself, or through others, thereafter manufacture and sell the ITEM and all rights to the ITEM, including the merchandising rights, and to any trademark or patents filed hereunder shall automatically revert to LICENSOR.

18. (a) LICENSOR agree that LICENSEE may assign this Agreement to an affiliate corporation, provided, however, that such assignee shall thereafter be bound by the provisions of this Agreement.

    (b) LICENSEE shall have the right to assign this Agreement, provided that it sells its entire business in said ITEM as a going concern, with LICENSOR's approval, not to be unreasonably withheld, so long as LICENSEE management remains in place or if such management does not remain in place, it is to an entity known to LICENSOR and that has a trusted relationship with LICENSOR.

19. (a) In case of the Receivership or Bankruptcy of LICENSEE, by reason of which LICENSEE is prevented from carrying out the spirit of this Agreement, this Agreement shall terminate and the rights hereunder shall revert to LICENSOR. In the event of such termination, LICENSEE agrees to pay all royalties accrued at the date of termination.

    (b) If LICENSEE, at any time after the execution of this Agreement and prior to and during the preparation of said ITEM for production, display, and offering for sale, shall elect not to produce, display, offer, or manufacture said ITEM, which election shall be in writing sent by Registered or Certified or Express Mail to LICENSOR, then LICENSOR's sole and exclusive remedy shall be to retain the advance against royalties, as provided for in Paragraph 6 hereof for breach of this Agreement, and such Agreement shall thereafter be of no further force and effect, and the license shall be deemed cancelled and neither party shall have any claim against the other.

(c)   At expiration of this Agreement, unless it is terminated due to a default by LICENSEE, LICENSEE may dispose of product on hand or in the process of being manufactured at the time of termination for a period not to exceed _____ days after termination, provided that payments and statements are rendered when due.

20. All notices wherever required in this Agreement shall be in writing and sent by Certified, Registered, or Express Mail to the parties care of the addresses set forth in the preamble to this Agreement.

21. If any provisions of this Agreement are for any reason declared to be invalid, the validity of the remaining provisions shall not be affected thereby.

22. This Agreement shall be binding upon and inure to the benefit of the parties hereto and their successors and assigns as herein provided, and said successors and assigns shall be liable hereunder. LICENSOR may assign its rights to receive royalties under this Agreement.

23. This Agreement shall be deemed to supercede agreements heretofore entered into by and between LICENSOR and LICENSEE on this ITEM.

24. It is expressly agreed that LICENSOR is not the legal representative of LICENSEE and has no authority, expressed or implied, on behalf of LICENSEE to bind LICENSEE or to pledge its credit.

25. LICENSOR and LICENSEE hereby agree to hold the terms of this Agreement confidential.

Marra: *For those inventors who do not have a lot of money to drag out a court case with a large company for many years, try arbitration; it's quicker and cheaper. However, the judgment is final because there are no appeals. Remember, you are rarely (if ever) really judged by a jury of your peers. I recommend including the following clause:*

The parties agree that any material dispute arising under the terms of this Agreement shall be submitted to binding arbitration pursuant to the rules of the American Arbitration Association applicable to commercial disputes. The Federal Rules of Civil Procedure shall apply to discovery of documents relating to the dispute.

The party seeking arbitration shall give written notice of arbitration to the other party of the specific dispute for which it seeks arbitration. Within ten days from receipt of the notice, each party shall submit to the other the name of an arbitrator. The two arbitrators so selected shall choose a sole arbitrator who shall preside.

The arbitrator's qualifications shall be knowledge of the toy industry and commercial law and availability in the time frame required by this arbitration provision. The arbitrator shall make written findings as part of any award. Such findings shall be based on the substantive law if the State of __. The arbitrator's award shall be rendered within forty-five (45) days of the date of the arbitration. Each party shall bear its own costs of the arbitration and shall equally share the arbitrator's fee and expenses.

The arbitration shall be conducted in (city, state) and shall be conducted within thirty (30) days after the sole arbitrator has been selected. The award of the arbitrator shall be final and shall be entered as a final judgment in any court having jurisdiction over the party against whom enforcement is sought.

26. This Agreement shall be construed in accordance with laws of the State _____.

IN WITNESS WHEREOF, the parties have executed this Agreement in duplicate originals the day and year first hereinabove written.

LICENSOR _____   By: _____

LICENSEE _____   By: _____

Words to the Wise

Having published the preceding agreement template, we hasten to remind you that, like snowflakes, no two agreements are exactly the same, no matter how many you draft. Different products require different terms. Different companies have different requirements and flexibilities. And once you add the personalities, well, it gets even more interesting. To quote Heraclitus, an early Greek philosopher who wrote about opposing forces and their delicate balance or state of tension, "It is impossible to step into the same river twice, for fresh waters are ever flowing in upon you." Following his metaphor, the important thing is to jump in and get wet!

Toy Trivia

70. Who was the first president of the Toy Manufacturers of America?

a. Benjamin F. Michtom
b. A. C. Gilbert
c. Edward P. Parker

Finally, keep these 20 points in mind as you negotiate.

1. Select your words carefully. Lord Chesterfield reminds us, "Words are the dress of thought."
2. Trust yourself. Most of this is common sense.
3. Prioritize your negotiation. Time is money.
4. Be sure of your facts. Double-check everything.
5. Do not be deterred because your mind has calculated that the opposition is too great.
6. Do not capitulate to names and institutions.
7. Do not be overly impressed with the opposition's intellectual achievements. Even bacilli are cultured.
8. Avoid the temptation to overwhelm. You must not be perceived as either an egomaniac or a victim.
9. Thou shalt not committee. A simple problem can be made insoluble if enough people discuss it.
10. Make only deals that you are comfortable and confident making.
11. Don't bring up the artillery until you bring up the ammunition.
12. Empty barrels make the most noise.
13. Pillage before you burn.
14. If you bite the bullet, you'd better be able to stand the taste of gunpowder.
15. Not until a contract has been in force for six months will a contract's most harmful stuff be discovered.
16. Yea, though you may walk through the alley of the shadow of debt, show no hunger.
17. Some victories are not worth winning.
18. Don't turn a technical disagreement into a civil war.
19. Never murder a person who is committing suicide.
20. If you find yourself in a hole, stop digging.

Fun Facts

- Bubble solution is one of the best selling toys of all time. Evidence of bubble play can be seen in the work of seventeenth century Flemish painters who depicted children blowing bubbles with clay pipes.

- The term "doll" comes from the Greek word, "eidolon," meaning idol.

- Frenchman Johann Maelzel made the first speaking dolls in the 1820's. He also invented the metronome for the piano.

- Ma Jong has as many names as stories of origin. It is also known as: Mah Jong, Mah Jongg, Ma Diao, Ma Cheuk, Mah Cheuck, Baak Ling, and Pung Chow. The most common belief is that the game was developed by Confucius, the Chinese philosopher, about 500 B.C. Ma Jong is Chinese for hemp bird.

- Independent inventor Reuben Klamer, according to the book, *A Toy Is Born*, created weapons and gadgets used in *The Man From U.N.C.L.E.*, a television series.

- Marbles made of baked clay have been found in prehistoric caves. It is believed that ancient Romans played marbles 2,000 years ago.

- The largest jigsaw puzzle measured 51,484 feet and consisted of 43,924 pieces. It was assembled in Marseilles, France, on July 8, 1992, according to Guinness.

- Historians feel that the tinplate toy industry may have started in Nuremberg, Germany.

- Barbie's first pet was Dancer, a horse (1971).

Chapter 10

Batteries Not Included: How Product Is Powered

"Radica is one of the few manufacturers of toys and games that was founded by an industrial designer and game inventor, Bob Davids. As a result, we have a very healthy respect for the importance of creativity and innovation inbred in our culture. We also have about 15 trained industrial designers on staff—quite a lot for a company our size. However, we also understand that it would be extremely limiting to be dependent upon a small group of creatives when there is such a large community of outstanding talent in the inventing community."

—Pat Feely, CEO, Radica USA

How a Product Is Powered

A look at how toy marketers describe their products in slick printed catalogs, impactful CDs, hype-filled PR releases, video news releases (VNR's), whiz-bang websites, and other ballyhoo leaves little doubt about how much show business there is in the toy business. Furthermore, the industry has become forever intertwined with and dependent on character licensing and original programming as ways of gaining faster consumer recognition for their toy and game lines.

Many years ago, when Hasbro licensed a line of action figures for younger boys called COPS from Marvin Glass & Associates, it was launched with a multimillion-dollar advertising campaign and its own syndicated animated television series produced by Sunbow Productions. "This line of urban law enforcement figures were 'Fightin' Crime in a Future Time!'" recalled Kirk Bozigian, the vice president of Boys Toys Marketing at the time of the line's introduction. "All the good guys and their vehicles had unique cap-firing weaponry that gave a big-bang effect for what was called 'crossfire fun.'"

Advice from the Pros

"Don't be afraid—and, in fact, try to learn to enjoy this—to tear your entire product apart. There may come a time when finessing and noodling just is not enough—and you will know this by the reactions you get and don't get. Tear it apart and see what it might really want and need to be."

—Susan Adamo Baumbach, vice president of R&D, Pressman Toys

Hasbro and Sunbow wrote an action-packed back-story against which to sell the assortment of characters. The story, set in the twenty-first century, gave organized crime the upper hand in its struggle against the law. Under the evil influence of CROOKS, crime had spread across the country like wildfire. The fear was that a total collapse of law and order could happen at any time.

Would COPS be the next G. I. Joe for Hasbro? The birth of the new line had all the trappings of a NASA rocket launch with sky-high expectations. Unfortunately, COPS never gained altitude with consumers, and it fell silently off the sales charts just like several earlier lines.

COPS had been preceded by Air Raiders, with air-activated missile launchers, and Visionaries, an Abrams Gentile Entertainment creation, with great holographic effects in the play pieces. "But at the time, Hasbro was very aggressive about promoting new toy lines that had magical features, and we felt consumers would respond to supporting media programming to drive store purchases," Bozigian recalls. "Today, the odds are against those types of full-line launches without megastudio/network programming. Bozigian today is the vice president of R&D at DML Associates and is heading development work on a special line of action figures based upon NYPD and FDNY licenses.

Dino Riders was another effort to hook kids on dinosaurs long before *Jurassic Park*. In fact, it originated not in Hollywood, but in the creative mind of Jim Alley, then the senior vice president of R&D at Tyco. Against a mandate from Dick Gray, president of Tyco, not to explore the boys' action-figure category, Alley did behind-the-scenes development and spent time and money on the concept. Set in an imaginary land *circa* 50,000 B.C.E., the world was locked in endless winter. Cavemen struggled for survival against giant prehistoric mammals. Collectible plastic Dino Riders found powerful allies to join them in their battle against the highly sculpted and equally plastic Rulons.

Mike Hirtle, then vice president R&D at Tyco and now with Hasbro Games as vice president for concept acquisition and inventor relations, said, "We held our collective breath when the line, clearly targeting the boys' action-figure category, was first shown to Gray. It was a major internal development, and we nervously waited for his reaction. Fortunately, it was favorable, and the line was given support of a multimillion-dollar advertising budget."

In addition, here was a toy company creating fully animated Dino Rider Ice Age adventures that were offered to kids on bargain-priced videocassettes in toy stores to drive purchases of the large toy line. Tyco got more than two strong sales years out of the line. Just as important, Dino Riders vaulted the company into the then-hot boys' action-figure category.

Mattel went to even greater lengths during its run with its Masters of the Universe action-figure line. The California toymaker backed a feature-length motion picture starring its macho characters. The brainchild of now independent pro Derek Gable, while he was working for Mattel, Masters of the Universe took children to the fantasy world of Eternia, a place beyond all time. Characters such as He-Man, "the most powerful man in the universe," and Skeletor, "Lord of Destruction," played out the story line around Castle Grayskull, the centerpiece of the toy collection.

Toy Trivia _____

78. Who authored *The Monopoly Companion?*

a. Phil Orbanes

b. Bill Dohrmann

c. Mike Gray

Media and Product Blitz

Such earlier efforts were intended to hook consumer interest through multimedia build. Today the industry looks to Hollywood to do the cinematic creation and then licenses rights to launch movie characters into the toy world. Toy companies leave the creation of important backstories to the talents of Spielberg and Lucas. New toy and game products are orchestrated to hit toy shelves just as movie-goers line up at the box office. In the ideal world of licensing, the carryover impact of the movie should result in toy sales at TRU, Wal-Mart, Target, and other mass merchants.

"The reality is that movie licenses offer no guarantees whatsoever, and they usually require huge financial commitments," says one major company executive, on the basis of anonymity. "If a film gets bad prelaunch buzz, toys can be DOA when their containers are opened on the West Coast docks. If the film gets panned or the word of mouth is not good, the toys will stiff, no matter how innovative they are. And in the case of a blockbuster movie, the toys and games may only sell for a few weeks anyway. It's a real crap shoot."

The same coordinated release of toys and media characters holds true for television programming. For example, huge numbers of Power Rangers and Pokemon SKUs were waiting on retail shelves as the shows lit up tubes across America. Indeed, show business is part of the toy world, and, increasingly, proprietary inventor items get sucked into the vortex as co-mingled outpourings of internal and external ideas are needed to support the latest hot entertainment property.

In the final analysis, however, consumer demand, not designs and backstories, makes one product more successful than another. "Toys are not sold. Toys are bought," points out David Leibowitz, now an industry analyst with American Securities Corporation. "As each child on the block gets a new product, he invites other friends to play with it. If the peer group enjoys it, they're going to tell whomever the toy-buying member of their family is to get it for them. You replicate that experience in enough parts of the country, and you have a winner. You can fool a parent, you can fool a retailer, and Lord knows you can fool an analyst, but you can't fool a child."

Successful toys and games must always appeal as products. But the transition of a good idea into a mass-marketable plaything is only the beginning. Here are the five most important elements for cutting through the clutter of consumer choices: packaging, pricing, personality, promotion, and public relations.

It's not enough for the inventor's neighborhood kids to like the new plaything, or even that it tests well within a company's formal focus groups. "We see hundreds of good-playing games each year as we put a new line together," says Dale Siswick of Hasbro Games. "A game's playability is only one part of the success formula. We have to answer questions about other elements in the success formula before we can feel good about a product's chances in the market." Siswick enumerates key questions like the following:

- Can the product price overcome any consumer resistance and avoid a buying choice with similarly priced competitive items?
- Can the product be tied to some hot fantasy or strong character personality?
- Does the package merchandise well and exude high product expectations while displayed on retail shelves?
- Is there a memorable point of difference about the product that will pop in the TV spot?
- Does some element of the product make it newsworthy and support a strong public relations campaign?

"The more elements the product has working for it, the more energy it will have at retail," says Siswick. "The stronger the integration of product with package and promotion, the more likely there will be a consumer purchase, after-purchase satisfaction, and word-of-mouth support."

The sheer mass of product offerings is an indicator of the volatility of the toy and game industry. According to the Toy Industry Association, 150,000 playthings are available from various companies. Each year producers "churn" their lines, dropping mediocre sellers and adding new products in hopes of catching greater sales. In such a product-intensive environment, the independent toy inventor exists to answer the manufacturer's call for something better, something cheaper, or something not done before.

Toy Trivia

79. Which year were in-line skates patented?

a. 1985

b. 1759

c. 1878

Product

Inventors know there is a huge annual demand for new products. Paul Lapidus, founder of NewFuntiers, agrees. "Toy and game inventing can be more lucrative than most other areas of product design. Manufacturers in this business actively seek out new ideas from the inventing community-at-large. Unfortunately, many other industries seem uncomfortable working with outside inventors and do not regularly invest the dollars on new products to the levels you find in the toy business."

If the toy business has an insatiable appetite for new ideas, it also provides the professional inventor huge targets for creativity. The 2003 *Playthings Buyers Guide* differentiates some 650 categories of toys and games that manufacturers bring to the market place. The doll category alone has 27 different types, from baby to fashion to walking dolls. And there are another 25 separate categories of doll accessories, ranging from clothing to furniture. This type of product array offers inventors a very large target for their creativity.

Is your specialty game development? The industry recognizes 52 different categories of games from *A* to *W*: action games to word games.

The many product categories give inventive people much room to roam. The inventor has not only choices of categories and types playthings, but also a focus on age and sex and play environments. For example, will the end user be preschool or adult, boy or girl, artistic or athletic? Will play take place outdoors or indoors? And is use seasonal, depending on water in summer or snow in winter?

Although the industry thrives on product ideas, the demand is not always for totally innovative approaches in new designs. There is something to be said for new products that bear a similarity to items from the past. Truly innovative products offer no experiential reference. They are unknown and unproven. Both the toy trade and the consumer are sometimes less than willing to try unfamiliar products. Push the envelope too far, and it may go undetected.

Use of ideas born in the past and rehashed in the present may reflect not necessarily innovation, but reinvention. In fact, the industry often touts resurgence of the known as "back to basics." As long as there is no IP infringement, a new spin on an old play format or product form is a time-honored tradition among inventors and manufacturers. It is quite common to hear such comments as, "It plays a lot like a yo-yo, but it has a new twist," or "It doesn't look like a Frisbee, but it's a flying disc revisited."

Though he created many unique concepts in his long career, inventor Ted Wolf saw part of his role as "adapting previously known devices to previously unknown products." Inventors do not speak only of "original," "innovative," "never before," and "unique" in describing their creations. "Recombining" is an acknowledged skill of the toy pro.

The history of toy inventing is filled with stories of successful products that came about through a new interpretation of long-established playthings. Invent a new toy truck? There was nothing exceptional about the specs: the basic two axles and a chassis. But what Eddy Goldfarb and his then-partner Del Everitt brought to an eager market of young boys was the off-road craze in toy scale. Goldfarb recalls, "Here in southern California we started noticing a lot of four-wheel-drive, off-road vehicles and thought they would make a nice toy item. But what we wanted to do more than anything was to make it very, very small; very powerful, but not so small that you wouldn't be able to tell how you could insert the battery. We used known truck brands but changed them to make them more macho."

Goldfarb first took his 4 × 4 concept to then-toymaker Kenner. The manufacturer bought it immediately and made plans to introduce 8 to 10 items. After Kenner worked for three months, Goldfarb was surprised to learn that the company's design department had changed his original concept and showed Kenner president Bernie Loomis a big vehicle—not at all what Goldfarb had submitted. Ironically, Loomis reportedly complained, "I didn't want big ones; I wanted small ones." After three or four more months of redefining, Loomis told his people to give the concept back to Goldfarb.

Goldfarb then took the concept to Schaper Toys and sold it on the spot. Schaper made the vehicles according to the inventor's original concept and named them Stompers. There were well over 200 models, and many millions of units sold worldwide. Stompers remain on the market today from a company called Tilcon.

Invent a new wealth-accumulation real-estate game? It's certainly been done before, by the all-time favorite, Monopoly, and a host of clones over the years. But Jeffrey Breslow of BMT Associates wove the charisma of billionaire developer Donald Trump into a wheeling/dealing investment game and sold it to Milton Bradley as Trump, the Game.

It took Breslow three or four months to put the deal together after reading Trump's best-selling book three times to get a feel for the man. "We told him that if he gave us the rights, we would spend our money to develop a game. If he liked what we created, then we would sell it to the right company. Trump flipped over what we showed him," says Breslow. "It was a great-playing game. We had many toymakers who wanted to market the game even without the Trump name. We were very satisfied with the product, and the tie-in with Trump just made it even better."

Toy Trivia

80. Name the restaurant chain founded by inventor Nolan Bushnell after he sold Atari Corp. to Time Warner in 1976.

a. Chuck E. Cheese

b. Roy Rogers

c. Fudruckers

The magic of the Trump name attracted Toy Fair buyers to the new game with an old and tried theme. They bought hundreds of thousands with hopes that consumers would want to play the role of a real free-wheeling real-estate developer. Game players never made the crossover from Boardwalk to Breslow's effort to win them over with a new real-estate game, and Trump faded quietly from the toy world, hardly making a dent in Monopoly sales during its short life.

Pricing

Inventors are expected to create magic for pennies. On the matter of pricing, the late Gordon Barlow said, "In my 30-plus years of designing, I've had too many ideas turned down by manufacturers for costing reasons not to take production issues into mind as I design a new toy. At the outset, I just let the concept flow. When I know I'm really on to something, I try to step back and formulate some engineering and production parameters in my design as suggestions to the manufacturer."

Barlow knew that in the end, his thoughts as an inventor didn't matter. An inventor might view a concept to be a retail bargain at $14.99, but a manufacturer that has to sell it targets a $9.99 price. When there is such a wide differential, the decision on a product will be not to accept it into a new line. In establishing a product cost, a point is reached at which nothing more can be taken from a toy or game to reduce costs to increase the profit side.

How important was the shaking feature in Tickle Me Elmo? Would the toy have been a megahit without it? Ron Dubren, the toy's co-creator, comments, "They almost decided not to include the shaking because of cost considerations."

Everyone involved with the development and marketing of new toys and games must ask the question, "At what price is it a 'go' product?" To the inventor, the latest hot concept is extremely valuable. The more pieces that are sold, the higher the rewards are. At the same time, the inventor wants to hold on to the integrity of the original vision. Naturally, every inventor feels that all kids will want the creation—maybe even two or possibly a whole collection. It is not surprising that the inventor is deeply emotional about the creation. If the originator doesn't have emotion, how can a manufacturer or consumer be expected to show interest?

In the end, it is often a tug of war between creativity and market reality, which is to make money. It is the marketer's tough job to place a "price-value" on an idea. Both marketing and manufacturing analyses are done to determine a sufficient profit margin, an exercise that determines whether a product lives or dies. What's the bottom line? The profit dollars generated from sales, not the gross dollars, measure true success for the company.

Staff designers and engineers establish the product's dimensions and component specifications. The amount of decoration, the number of parts, how things work, how things get made, and the choice of materials all influence the cost, as do labor rates on product assembly and packaging.

Those manufacturers best able to plan all product details will have the best pre-production estimates and more accurate post-production costs. Every new product carries a burden of startup costs for molds, fixtures, and other tooling; costs for product and package artwork; and costs for advertising and promotion until sufficient numbers of units are sold to pay back the investment. Startup costs are a major reason why it is hard for many new products to capture market share from well-established products, even though the new products may be more innovative. The old standbys have already paid back their investment dollars and, therefore, can be sold for much less than the new entries.

The toy company establishes a sell price to the retail trade that includes a fair profit above all product, promotion, and administrative costs. Retailers add their markup from the price they pay to the manufacturer, and that becomes the consumer's price. Some stores keystone the price (double manufacturer's sell price); others choose a full 40 percent markup; some take a short markup and offer discounted pricing.

It is up to the sharp-eyed consumer to find the best price. Price variations splashed in the Sunday circulars reflect retailer differences in pricing strategies. Retailers do what they think is best to move merchandise. Those with the best selection and the sharpest prices usually attract the largest consumer traffic and sell the most product. Toys R Us, which specializes in toys and games, offers the best full-range selection. On the other hand, Wal-Mart and Target have other consumer product lines from which to pick up profit, so they can use a strategy of a short markup on toy lines.

Pricing must be acceptable to two buyers. The first is the retail store or trade buyer, and the second is the consumer buyer/shopper. If either buyer feels that the product does not merit the price, the new toy or game will be a failure for the manufacturer.

Initially, the trade buyer must accept the new product in its package with supporting promotion plans as viable to occupy retail shelf space. If that hurdle is passed, then the buyer's mark up is applied to the marketer's price to get the "everyday price."

At this point, the buyer makes the judgment that that price will be perceived as a value to the shoppers.

And it is this second tier of buyers that will determine whether what gets on the shelf will be successful. If those buyers are willing to pay the sticker price and take the toy to the checkout in big numbers, the retailer and the manufacturer will have a winner.

Industry veteran Randy Karp, president of the Chicago-based Executive Sales Group, says, "There is a strong symbiotic relationship between perceived value and pricing. Even a pop star diva has a limit on what she may charge her loyal followers for a ticket. The difference is, she's a star and has loyal followers.

"If we're talking about a nonbranded, nonpromotional item, there's no loyal following and no immediate recognition. Its value is purely based on the amount of product or features offered relative to price. And that price has to compel not only the consumer, but also the buyer for the retail chain. Even if the concept is innovative, if it's nonbranded and not promoted, the manufacturer had better not get greedy. If the toy is not priced right out of the starting gate, competition will knock the pricing legs right out from under them, with a disparity in cost that will cost that manufacturer credibility with their customer.

Pricing is about the consumer wanting a deal they can't refuse. It doesn't have to be a ridiculous deal, but a reasonable one relative to the value they place on that product," Karp concludes.

"A problem with retailing today," continues Karp, "is the Monty Hall Syndrome. This is when stores keep marking down prices such that it says to loyal customers, 'You weren't smart enough to wait. You were dumb enough to buy some of our product at the wrong time. Sorry, but we have another deal for you today.'"

"Basically, it's a broken promise," says Karp. "And when people aren't consistently honest with people, they loose credibility. That's what's happened to the Monty guys, while the Wal-Marts of the world keep forging ahead. Consumers have taken their shopping elsewhere. The fickle pricers will perish and Sam Walton shall inherit the earth."

Toy Trivia

81. Toy inventor A.C. Gilbert won an Olympic medal in what type of sport?

a. Track and field

b. Skiing

c. Swimming

Considering the high stakes involved in launching a new product, manufacturers obviously must rely on more than just gut-level intuition when choosing new product. The more controlled and better managed the whole rollout process is, the more likely a new introduction will be on target to meet sales expectations. When applying the hard realities of product cost and investment to a new toy or game, it becomes clear why only 1 idea in 100 makes it to market.

Personality

Kids like to play with friends. So when making products for kids, manufacturers like to have help from a friend whom kids have given high TV or movie ratings. The desire to bring instant recognition to a toy or game leads manufacturers to the world of licensing. Licensing is the business of leasing the right to use a legally protected name, graphic, logo, saying, or likeness in conjunction with a product, promotion, or service, according to the Licensing Industry Merchandisers' Association. The 2003 *Playthings Buyers Guide* lists more than 750 licensed properties in its 2003 issue, and inventors and manufacturers make wide use of these properties in each year's new toy lineup.

In 1980, sales of licensed products worldwide were $10 billion. In 1990, sales of all types of licensed products worldwide hit $66.5 billion. And in 2002, sales from such enhanced products topped $177 billion worldwide, according to the fall/winter issue of LIMA's, *BottomLine*. Goods emblazoned with a licensed identity are on everything, on everybody, and everywhere.

"Modern licensing was started by the Walt Disney Company," explains Stan Weston, a founding father of entertainment licensing. "The Howdy Doody property in the early 1950s started what I consider modern TV licensing. Then you go into a much more expanded list of properties, ranging from a classic like Snoopy to all the current superheroes and super-villians."

Such longstanding industry favorites as Sesame Street, Barney, Clifford, and the Warner and Disney characters, to name a few examples, continue to move millions of products each year. The average royalty paid by a toy company for a license is in the range of 10 to 12 percent of net wholesale dollars. In the escalating demands of hot properties, mid- to upper-teen percents are being paid by toy companies, with Hasbro topping out at 20 percent for the rights to Star Wars, according to the November 2, 1999, *Motley Fool, Daily Trouble Report*. People who spoke on the basis of anonymity placed the royalty at a staggering 25 percent.

Licensing is a sophisticated way of marketing and merchandising products that crosses many industries with a ubiquitous presence. Toy manufacturers and retailers are always seeking new methods of attracting and holding customers, and licensing represents a coordinated attempt to reach that consumer.

Knowledgeable toy and game inventors have been aware for many years that having the right license on their products can potentially mean lots of extra income, even if they have to take reduced royalty for the tie-in. Some professional inventors, therefore, clothe their designs with an existing license to show a contemporary spin on their own idea.

"Adding a licensed character to a toy or game has the obvious benefit of bringing an identity to the product," says Cathy Meredith, vice president of licensing at Hasbro Games. "It should have a positive impact on sales. However, just putting a personality onto the artwork or into the molded pieces will not make a bad product good. Though many people are comfortable seeing familiar faces on toys and games, it can be a tricky business for the manufacturers. If the personality weakens in the marketplace, ratings drop, or some unforeseen public event casts badly on that personality, that kind of news can take the product down with it. A superhero is a help in this business; on the other hand, nobody wants to play with a fallen hero."

"Certainly Sesame Street, Warner, and Disney have shown that licensing is tremendously important, but they're not panaceas either. You put them on a bad product, and you get a bad result," warns Steve Schwartz, former president of Playskool. "I think in terms of some of the hot licenses, it's all timing."

Much of the appeal of a licensed property comes from the design and graphics that can be built in by the unique personality. A strong, recognizable figure catches the consumer's eye and rivets interest on the product at point of sale and throughout repeat play. The popularity of personalities, celebrities, and events flavor the tone and form of playthings stacked on the toy shelves. This is evident on any walk through a toy store.

Even a megaproperty like Stars Wars may not bring anticipated success if expectations are too high. The success measure of Star Wars in retail wars is ongoing since all episodes have not reached the critical eyes of consumers. Hasbro can only hope that later consumer acceptance pays off the price to play with the fantasies of Lucas's figures. Toy Land's Product Boot Hill is jammed with former favorites that never lived up to advanced billing.

Vic Reiling, an independent inventor for nearly 30 years, has learned to live with licensed properties. Notes Reiling, "When I come up with a new concept, I don't necessarily plan it for any specific celebrity or personality. I make my concept relevant to what is going on with kids and wherever possible weave a contemporary feeling into my design. The more 'now,' the better. When it comes to a specific personality being applied to one of my concepts, what they add is entirely the call of the manufacturer.

Usually I'm asked to take a reduced royalty when some cartoon character or super-hero is added to the product plan. If a mouse or bird can double the sales of one of my concepts, I am very interested in such a partnership. I want to see my ideas sell."

Stan Weston once said that to a toy company, licensing means "presold." A good product that's properly priced and manufactured can be given an added presold advantage over a competitive item when identified in a logical way with a well-known license or property.

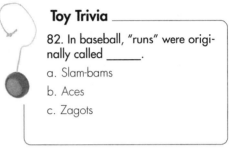

Toy Trivia

82. In baseball, "runs" were originally called _____.

a. Slam-bams

b. Aces

c. Zagots

Package

Could any industry other than toys deliver an empty box and get people to pay for it in droves? In what other industry would an executive approve selling empty boxes?

"It certainly worked," beamed Bernie Loomis, as he reflected with pride on his decision to ship empty boxes to toy stores in 1978 upon realizing that Kenner would not have its Star Wars product ready for Christmas.

"I said to myself, hey, the kid is going to get a lot of things Christmas Day. I am going to give him the prettiest picture of Star Wars, and I am going to make a deal with his parents, not with the child: Pay me for the figures, and we will deliver them before the end of May. And I limited the sale to 500,000 units. The parents read it and understood it."

Loomis's scheme worked. The empty boxes flew off the shelves, and one of the most gutsy marketing gambles of any industry went into the history books. "If there is any genius involved, it is the genius of being able to function alone and make a decision," suggests Loomis.

"Product packaging, especially for nonpromoted products, is absolutely critical," says David Shapiro, vice president of marketing at Pressman Toys. "It has to set itself apart from the sea of packaging a consumer looks at while standing in the game department without a clue of exactly what it is they want to purchase. It has to be visually appealing, communicate fun and entertainment, while at the same time giving the consumer enough information to motivate them to pick it up and read more about it. No wonder an art director's office is littered with drafts of package ideas that don't quite get it all right!"

Salesmeister Karp agrees. "Like a silent salesman seated on a store shelf, a package must convey the manufacturer's intended message to the consumer in mere seconds. In a cluttered environment of noise, and distractions inherent in a typical shopping experience, it must stand out from all the other 'Please buy me' wannabes and *grab* that consumer at the point of sale. If successful, our silent salesman has even less time to *close* the deal. To do so the message must be clear, package attractive but uncluttered, price and value right for that particular consumer's age and lifestyle, with the kinds of features that distance them from the also-rans.

"Creating a great toy package is an even greater challenge. Picture one Santa trying to outdistance another. Now our silent salesman is sharing shelf space with the best of the best, selling fantasy and dreams to an audience that has seen and heard it all: the children.

"Dazzled by an array of sights and sounds from a world of technology the likes of which have never been seen before, the threshold for wowing kids is at an all-time high. From the Internet to game systems with more power than the average computer had only years ago, and with an appetite for special effects that sent George Lucas back to the drawing board, the average kid is a *darn* tough sell.

"So the package says to itself, 'How can I get Johnny drooling over me?' The competition is not just shelf-mates. It's every other item in every other department loaded with silent sales-hype all vying for the same attention. Many are celebrities. That's right, they're TV toys that have made several sales calls to Johnny long in advance of this visit. Toys are in the most challenged packages in the entire merchandising world.

"A nonpromotional, basic toy. Talk about climbing a mountain. The investment in a charismatic package that knows how to grab and close is one of the most important investments a company can make. All the R&D and marketing research means little if the packaging is milk toast."

Manufacturers know that packages must be dropped, kicked, crushed, punctured, and baked during tests to measure how well they protect valuable contents. Underpacking a product can have disastrous effects at retail. Consumers see a damaged package on a shelf to mean concealed product damage, and instead they will select a crisp, unscuffed container. Crushed and abraded packages will be left on shelves as poor reflections on the product, the manufacturer, and the retailer.

Toy industry packages are expected to go beyond merely carrying the product to the consumer. Though kids seldom put toys and games away, reusable boxes can keep pieces orderly and safely together.

Perhaps as important as protection for products in transit and storage after purchase, packages must merchandise products in the store. Whether hung from hooks, stacked on shelves, aligned in point-of-sale displays, or loaded into dump displays, packages should draw attention to the product inside. In the high-traffic aisle of mass-market retail stores, packages must be an appealing, attention-grabbing billboard that stops the consumer and invites handling and examination. Packages can be the final influence on a decision to buy on the spot ... or not.

Says Dale Siswick, Hasbro Games' senior vice president for R&D, "Packaging is terribly important in the competitive retail environment. Consumers are making buying choices in a matter of minutes, possibly even seconds. You want your package to convey a price-value relationship that makes consumers feel the purchase was a good value for the price. A large package in good structural condition, showing and promoting an attractive product, goes a long way toward helping the product move off the shelf. Packaging must close the sale at shelf level."

Many toys are displayed in open-faced "try-me" packages. The charm and aesthetics of the plaything come through the polystyrene film or thermal-formed blister. Consumers see exactly what they are getting. A "try-me" package allows a consumer to activate an in-store product demonstration. Packages often use high-energy photography or illustration to capture the product in use and convey the promise of endless hours of after-purchase entertainment.

On so-called set-up boxes, every square inch of the six panels is used for sales messages. Even the box bottom carries a story of features and benefits. The two side panels and two end panels usually shout a product's name and show a miniature reproduction of it. The box face is the most important panel, and no package is successful without a powerful mix of type and graphics. Product vitality and personality must come through on this facing. Consumers should be given a promise of fun through a dynamic product representation with age-appropriate happily playing kids. Features and benefits are either shown or listed. The product name is carried prominently on all panels.

Toy Trivia

83. Whose invention is the "Iris Dome"?

a. Chuck Hoberman

b. Buckminster Fuller

c. Ron Milner

Promotion Begins at Home

Ad agencies are extremely important to toy companies. They create the image that the child sees. They do the commercials, and that's what sells mass-market toys and games. It's an advertising-driven business. To hit the big sales numbers, items need memorable TV spots.

In 2001, *AdAge* reports that Mattel spent $448.6 million on advertising, placing it 66th of the nation's leading advertisers. Hasbro, at $194.1 million, ranked 127th. Interestingly, a truer number for promotion expenditures would be to combine royalties paid for character licensing to other ad forms, since the intention of both is to build rapid consumer awareness.

In current marketing plans, however, television is a major line factor, and inventors delight in having a TV-promoted toy or game. "One of the major changes I've seen in the industry through the years is the extensive use of television commercials to promote toys and games," says toy inventor Eddy Goldfarb. "I recall bringing product concepts to top executives, and if they had a favorable gut reaction, we had a deal. Now the decision-making process has been strung out, much of the reason being the tremendous expense associated with promotional campaigns.

"I feel I am making a major investment of time and effort to come up with a new concept. I prefer to get that concept placed with a manufacturer who is also making a major investment," adds Goldfarb. "Although I have no control over the decision, that means making my item a promoted new entry. With TV support, the product will have a running start on the thousands of other new products introduced each year at Toy Fair."

The most important reasons for the inventor wanting television promotion are:

1. It guarantees trade buyer support, which translates into bigger initial orders.
2. It creates consumer demand at retail, which triggers reorders.

Even if TV fails to move the product, an inventor can make more money from a TV-promoted loser than a nonpromoted winner at a small company. This is because inventor royalties are paid on quarterly shipments, not sell-through.

Says Paul Lapidus, former design manager at Playskool and now head of new product source NewFuntiers, "Let's face it: With all of the options parents have when shopping for toys and games, a memorable commercial is a real boost for a product in this business. No toy or game is a certain, guaranteed success until both the trade and the consumers make it happen, often motivated by a TV spot."

"We only do TV items," says Larry Jones, head of Cal R&D. "I guess a lot of other guys will do non-TV toys. I'll tell you from this standpoint, and I've been in the business since 1969, the only way you have staying power in this industry is to generate royalty income, and a solid TV-promoted item will help you survive."

Marketers, of course, know that they cannot silently introduce a significant new toy or game into the market and expect a hit. Consumers do not look at playthings as necessities. Most parents enter a toy store in search of what they or their kids have seen in a TV spot that has sent them shopping.

Whereas some TV commercials target parents, others target children. Messages for parents tend to create an impression that children will benefit from and enjoy the promoted plaything. This is certainly the approach of preschool commercials. Messages for children aim to create excitement and a lasting impression so that they will ask their parents for the toy by name. Parents will make the decision to buy, but they are strongly influenced by the demands of their children.

Marketers know that if there is no presell by a hard-hitting TV spot, the product will be lost among the thousands of toys and games stocked at mass-market retailers. Promotion must get the consumer through the doors of the local toy store looking for a specific product. Once in the store, product design, interesting packaging, appealing personality, and the right price may close the sale. But the whole motivation for the consumer to buy many playthings starts with the television commercial.

Major marketers seldom flinch to create million-dollar media campaigns if the forecast supports those expense levels. Between the commercial's production costs and the media buy, a seven-figure campaign may be minimal to get the attention of the trade buyer and ultimate consumer. In many cases, the promotion budget exceeds all the other costs of developing and bringing a product to market.

This expense causes a marketing and financial dilemma for the promoters. To afford TV, marketers know there must be high sales forecasts, since few products can stand a per-unit TV cost load of a dollar or more to pay back those creative and media expenses. Without a top-selling performer, a campaign may end up in the red and erode the anticipated profits presented in the product plan. When early product sales are not responding to TV, it is not uncommon to cut the media budget to stop the financial bleeding.

According to the TIA, studies have shown that toys with heavy advertising budgets generally result in lower consumer prices than those backed by smaller ad budgets. As a result, the average retail profit margin for television-advertised toys is now 15 to

25 percent, while the average for nonadvertised items may be between 35 and 40 percent. Several factors contribute to this phenomenon.

At the store level, retailers use TV-promoted toys in their local advertising to create competitive prices against other retailers. In addition, at reduced prices, these toys are used as "loss leaders" to build general store traffic and create rapid inventory turnover. On the supply side, the high demand created by TV and other advertising allows for economy of scale and the procurement of raw materials in volume, thus further lowering the toy's costs and ultimate retail price.

Retailers expect the marketers to support their toys and games with TV commercials. Ten to 15 years ago, it was common to find 4 or 5 items in a given line with TV support. Now marketers have plans for all new major introductions to be supported on television. Retailers value their shelf space too much to commit to a product without a TV budget to help pull it from their stores. And increasingly, if there is no TV support, they expect a known character license to be on the product to get pull-through.

Tyco Toys made a daring move and exhibited marketing finesse when introducing a new multimillion-dollar line of toys called Dino Riders the day after Christmas. That's right: *after* Santa had gone home. According to Neil Werde, marketing director for the product, in 1987 Tyco felt that it was worth the risk because after Christmas there would be less advertising clutter to cut through on the tube, and the cost of media would be a fraction of what it would have been the week before Christmas.

Toy Trivia

84. Boric acid was responsible for what accidental invention?

a. Play Doh

b. Super Ball

c. Silly Putty

Tyco Toys was able to do a 2-minute animated TV spot and air it for the price of a 60-second commercial. In addition, kids have lots of buying choices the day after Christmas. There are gifts to be returned and exchanged, and they have gifts of money to go out and spend. Werde says the innovative scheme moved $3 million worth of product in the first quarter of 1988. The first full year, the company did $48 million in Dino Riders.

"At one time I was concerned about the play value of every item I bought for my stores," says one major mass-market buyer who asked not to be identified. "But today, I am more interested in how much money the marketer is planning to spend on promotion to create inventory turn than in what's in the box."

Is it possible to have a successful toy today without television promotion? Jeff Jones, director of new products and technology at Racing Champions/Ertl, says, "Absolutely yes. The key is a solid promotional plan, basic grass roots marketing, and good PR."

In fact, in some ways, TV may be the lazy way to market a toy. The cost of TV to the levels required to break through the clutter is prohibitive to all except the largest toy companies. If you analyze the most successful toys, such as Furby, Cabbage Patch, Tickle Me Elmo, and others, most did not come by their popularity through TV advertising.

Advice from the Pros

"Marketing is a battle of perceptions, not products."

—Al Ries and Jack Trout, co-authors, *The 22 Immutable Laws of Marketing*

Public Relations

Marc Rosenberg, senior vice president of marketing and advertising at Hasbro Toys, and one of the industry's most creative and astute showmen, says, "A successful PR campaign can *make* a toy. The third-party endorsement that comes from media stories lends a credibility that can't be bought with TV advertising or through any other means. A few well-placed stories, and you can be off and running toward the next Cabbage Patch, Teenage Mutant Ninja Turtles, or Furby."

Public relations people know that bringing attention and interest to a toy or game before a large audience can only help sales. Consumers have a natural tendency to "join in the fun" or "share the experience" when they become aware of a hot, topical product. Tournaments, play-offs, challenges, and high-visibility celebrity endorsements get the media coverage that builds demand for products in the marketplace. Such events are also economical and effective. Not only do they build sales, but they also focus favorable public attention on brand names that leaves a lasting positive impression.

Picture, if you will, a toy disk being hurled almost a quarter-mile through the southern California skies. The 1,126-foot toss becomes a world record for an Aerobie, a disk-shaped toy invented by Alan Adler. The challenge is set for all ages to match. The news brings sales of this performance flying disk not only from those who want to play, but from those who seek the competitive test of breaking a world record.

The high school gymnasium is filled with tables containing setups for the popular word game Scrabble. In this arena of intense, concentrated play, word-game buffs are battling for supremacy in a regional contest sponsored by the game's manufacturer. The winner will move on to the national championships. The National School Scrabble Championship is scheduled for April 2003 in Boston. Only a game, yes, but the activity for over 1 million kids in 20,000 schools has passed beyond play and is now an ongoing competition with 13 state or regional championships in 13 locations.

Beyond school competitions, there is a biannual World Scrabble Championship, which in 2001 had representatives from 40 countries compete in English, up from 20 countries represented 10 years ago. Twenty-five thousand avid word game players belong to the National Scrabble Association, according to executive director John Williams. When asked what has made Scrabble so successful, Williams explains, "It appeals to a 7-year-old playing the word *cat* for 10 points and the champion playing *quixotic* for 100 points. No two games are even close to being alike."

Mark Morris, director of public relations at Hasbro Games and an experienced advertising and PR professional, says, "Event publicity can create a great deal of excitement and capture the attention of the media, if done correctly. Of course, the 'newness' of some games gives you an advantage, and we select a handful of new games every year and create special publicity programs for them. The media like anything new, or, at least, they'll take the time to review it."

Morris gives as another example the 37-year-old game Twister. Well known for its vinyl mat with different-colored printed circles, the game's director spins a spinner. Players must place their hands and feet on those colored circles without losing their balance. They twist, turn, and contort until the one left standing wins.

"Twister was given a tremendous boost when Johnny Carson got into the game on his show with then-popular Eva Gabor. Everything was so spontaneous and frolicsome that for weeks after the show, people called and wrote to find out where they could buy the game," says Morris. Mel Taft, who at the time was vice president of R&D and licensed the game from Reyn Guyer, recalls, "Some in the company were reluctant to do the game because they felt we would be criticized for putting sex in a toy box!"

Whatever came out of the box, picture many hundreds of the 54×69–inch vinyl mats strewn around the football field of the University of Massachusetts. It was May 2, 1987, and thousands of people were simultaneously playing Twister. This was the largest organized group of contortionists ever brought to the game at one time. News of the mass play session motivated a lot of others to try the game. In fact, through the years, Twister has been a fad among college students. This is interesting consumer support for a game originally targeted at kids ages six and up.

"Whenever we see that a game has real PR possibilities, we exploit all channels of exposure," says Hasbro's Morris. "Some games that may be perfectly good-playing games may not have PR opportunities. PR can often complement TV advertising to get maximum public exposure for new products."

LEGO is in a very unique position from a PR point of view. How many companies have theme parks devoted to their products? LEGOlands in the United States (California), Canada, Germany, and Denmark host millions of visitors annually. It is hard to visit a park and not come away with a desire to get into building with LEGO bricks. That park experience is worth a lot of hard-sell TV commercials that are usually fleeting "Buy me" messages. Public relations efforts such as the park and other programs at LEGO build the popularity of LEGO products through real-life experiences.

> **Toy Trivia**
>
> 85. What do the initials PVC mean?
>
> a. Polyvinyl chloride
> b. Polyamide viable cachou
> c. Plastic vehicle—car

Long Live the King

Toy and game companies know the vital elements needed to support their commitment to a strong idea. What starts with excitement for a new idea takes heavy investment in packaging, promotion, licensing support, energetic PR, and efficient pricing to launch the new idea into the toy trade. Mission control for such a launch is in the sales and marketing offices of major manufacturers. Additional power for launching toys and games into the marketplace comes from time, people, and dollars—all of which must be heavily committed to get the product into sales orbit.

Professional inventors, the very sources of the magic and excitement of new toys and games, have little or no input into the marketing and merchandising needed to make an industry hit. An inventor delivers basic ideas and then relies on the licensee to execute new products effectively using all the available skills and resources of the company. The product may be intended for play; the business side is intended to make or exceed sales and profit goals.

The key decisions affecting final product form, function, market presence, and salability are beyond the control of a product's creator. Phenomena like Trivial Pursuit, Furby, Nintendo, PlayStation 2, and other hot sellers could be delivered to consumers in plain brown boxes. But few such phenomena in the business and playthings need attractive packages. Classic or fad toys and games may sell on nostalgia and word of mouth, but new items need strong TV support in major markets if they are to reach high-volume sales levels. Without strong ad campaigns, the trade is noncommittal and consumers are left to search out potentially popular playthings in spotty distribution.

In an industry in which product has long been recognized as king, the inventing sources of these new product ideas are certainly part of the royal court. In today's mass market, filled with competitive consumer choices, new kings are made through excitement, hype, and major company investment and commitment. Kings are not born quietly into brand pedigree. What is needed is the right combination of product, pricing, personality, package, promotion, and PR to attain the elusive winner's crown.

Fun Facts

- Sixteen-year-old Minh Thai, a Vietnamese refugee, won the World Rubik's Cube Championship in Budapest, Hungary, in 1982. He solved the puzzler in a record-breaking 22.95 seconds.

- A $2 million Monopoly set was created by San Francisco jeweler Sidney Mobett in 1988. The board was made from 23-carat gold, and rubies and sapphires were in the chimneys of solid–gold buildings. The dice sported 42 full-cut diamonds for pips.

- The world's most popular video game system is the Nintendo Game Boy. It sold more than 100 million units between 1989 and 2000. This was an average of more than 1,000 units per hour.

- The name POG is derived from Passion Orange Guava, a juice produced by a dairy on the island of Maui, Hawaii. POG collecting started in Hawaii, but some milk cap experts think it's a modern version of a 600-year-old Japanese game called menkos. Menkos means "small mask" in Japanese.

- Springfield, Massachusetts, lithographer Milton Bradley personally went on the road circa 1860 selling his Checkered Game of Life board game. The first year he moved 45,000 copies.

Chapter 11

Brandwashing: Entertainment Licensing

---

*"Inventors should embrace the myriad opportunities
entertainment licenses provide. It is no longer
acceptable for a company to simply slap a label on
an existing product and expect the consumer to pay
a premium. Companies need innovation, and it is
worth an inventor reducing a royalty for the potential to participate in the megadollars generated by
many successful licenses. Rather than being locked
out by inactivity, I encourage inventors to see licenses
as a major opportunity and create innovative
product for these brands."*

—Roger A. Shiffman, co-founder, Tiger Electronics

Legend has it that, while bear hunting in Mississippi in 1902, President Theodore Roosevelt decided to spare the life of a cub that a member of his hunting party had roped and dragged around for him to bag. Political cartoonist Clifford Berryman of the *Washington Post* memorialized this event the next day, showing the 43-year-old Roosevelt refusing to shoot the scared black bear, saying that he took only prey that had a sporting chance to defend itself.

The following day, in Brooklyn, New York, toy and novelty store owners Morris and Rose Michtom, Russian Jewish immigrants, saw the cartoon panel and, like many people in the nation, were struck by Roosevelt's compassion. Rose was inspired to create a stuffed toy bear, which Morris, a marketing maven, called Teddy's Bear and put in the store window. It became an instant hit with customers. After more than a dozen people asked to buy a Teddy's Bear, Morris sent one to the president for his children and asked for permission to call it the Teddy Bear. Soon a letter arrived from 1600 Pennsylvania Ave. in which the president said they were welcome to use his name, though he doubted it would help sell the bears.

The association with President Roosevelt helped sell so many stuffed bears that the couple, realizing there was more money in manufacturing and marketing soft bears than in owning a store, started a toy company. It became the Ideal Toy Company, which remained in family hands until the 1970s, when it was acquired by CBS.

May I See Your License, Please?

The Mickey Mouse watch. Sesame Street preschool toys. Barbie key chains. Kawasaki musical instruments. Warner Brothers Trivial Pursuit. Elvis UNO. Buffy The Vampire Slayer board game. Star Wars toys and games. Harry Potter products. Direct-to-retail lines such as Target's National Geographic franchise, and Clifford at Toys R Us. Rather than developing a brand from scratch, companies increasingly prefer to license the rights to a recognized brand, with all its goodwill, and transplant it onto products.

Licensing is imprinting a character, image, logo, signature, design, personality, or highly recognizable entertainment property on any product for the purpose of heightening its awareness and sales. It is a way of marketing and merchandising products that crosses many industries. Like the Michtoms, today's manufacturers and retailers are always looking for new means to attract a customer base to their stores, and licensing represents a cooperative effort to reach that consumer. Licensed product raked in a staggering $177 billion in 2002 worldwide retail sales, according to LIMA's, *BottomLine*.

Twenty to thirty years ago, when the majority of the inventors and executives interviewed for this book got into the industry, major toymakers created their own proprietary lines of action figures and launched them with the synergism of multi-million-dollar advertising campaigns and syndicated animated series.

Toy companies opted to move away from original invention, be it in-house or inventor-generated proprietary product, and deeper into entertainment-licensed product. This is part of what Jeffrey Chester, executive director of the Center for Digital Democracy, calls the "brandwashing of America."

Early in his career, Jerry Houle, a former Licensing Industry Merchandisers' Association (LIMA) Licensing Agent of the Year, was involved at Fisher-Price with research that showed that kids as young as two and a half can identify character images that they see often and will select related products. Houle says, "Consumers with an identity or loyalty to a licensed property want to buy goods related to that character because they want to broadcast their 'membership' in that property. Broadcasting that membership becomes part of their persona."

Charles Riotto, president of LIMA, told attendees to the December 2001 Licensing to Kids conference that licensing is recognized as an integral piece of the process in building communication strategies: "Its ability to deliver cost-effective results in strengthening brand awareness, extending product ranges, and generally increasing market share can no longer be ignored. Today more than ever, owners of children's properties are increasingly looking to licensing to help them secure higher levels of visibility, stretch their ad/promo dollars, aid in retail penetration, and generate new sources of revenue."

According to the October 21, 2002, issue of the *Toy Licensing Letter*, kids ages five to eight account for 41 percent of licensed merchandise sales from entertainment/character properties—the largest share of any age group in that sector.

Advice from the Pros

"Trust your process."

—Barbara Slate, cartoonist/writer for many Marvel and DC comics

411 Copyright does not protect names, titles, slogans, or short phrases. In some cases, these may be protected as trademarks. Copyright protection may be available for logo artwork that contains sufficient authorship. If you are unsure, contact the U.S. Patent and Trademark Office at 1-800-786-9199 for expert advice.

What Marketers Say

Despite prerelease hype, demographic support, and related glitz surrounding a new or reintroduced license, it remains a crapshoot whether a licensed entertainment property will connect with consumers. Best-seller book lists, Q ratings, and box office receipts may gauge success of a property in its original form, but shelf movement at Wal-Mart, TRU, and Target is the only success gauge of interest to a toy marketer. When the prelims are over and the lucrative deal is in place, only the *cha-ching* at checkout registers measures whether the licensee's expectations have been met by the license.

When the planets align for a particular property, licensing can be a very powerful tool. But, as you might expect, when so much money is at stake, industry leaders' opinions vary on the efficacy of licensing and which properties to wager on.

Toy Trivia

86. Who invented the Super-Soaker?

a. Lonnie Johnson

b. Eddy Goldfarb

c. T. J. Waterman

Mike Meyers, a consultant to Hasbro since he retired as senior vice president of R&D at the company's game division in 1992, says that licensing has become an excuse not to be creative. "Everyone is looking for a guarantee, and some companies think that entertainment licensing gives it to them. In many cases, it actually has increased the financial risk-reward. I hesitate to name some examples, but I think we all know which ones they are."

Every industry executive we interviewed blamed the lack of innovative toys and games on mass-market retailers who require licensed properties. Yea, though the marketers walk through the valley of the shadow of debt, they fear no license. "Our president has never seen a license he did not want," moans one senior vice president.

The retailers interviewed blamed no one. They clearly want items emblazoned with entertainment licenses or well-known brands. "Sometimes you get the gold mine. Sometimes you get the shaft," says one buyer, who asked not to be named. "But I'd prefer to go with the known over the unknown."

To give you a sense of the present environment, here is a sampling of observations from industry marketers. It is followed by comments from a major retail buyer on what she expects from licensed and nonlicensed toys.

Alan Dorfman, founder and president of Basic Fun, says that brands represent a safe harbor, especially in today's very cautious retail environment. Dorfman is a Philadelphia-based marketing maestro who made his impressive imprint on the toy industry through the innovative idea to attach to key chains miniature, fully working replicas of popular toys and games. His first product, the Super Soaker key chain, sold over five million units. He licensed rights from Larami.

Dorfman explains that the retail buyer needs to ensure success on the space he or she is responsible for, and brands minimize risk. "They offer familiarity to the consumer, as well as value, experience, and function. A consumer is willing to spend more for a familiar brand, especially if it gives the security in the purchase (which is often more valuable than a small savings). When needing to choose how to commit their shelf space, buyers will choose a branded item over an unbranded item most of the time."

In conclusion, he points out, "We—not only our company, but our competition—frequently get caught up in the fear of missing out on a license opportunity."

A senior vice president for a major toy marketer, who spoke on the basis of anonymity, expands on Dorfman's observation. "In our desire not to miss a great opportunity, we frequently throw caution to the wind. There is perhaps no better example than how much Hasbro paid Lucas for the rights to *Star Wars*. The industry needs to approach licensing with more discretion and carefully assess pros and cons of a property before making a commitment."

"Entertainment licensing is a squirrel-cage existence," says another anonymous senior industry insider. "You get trapped, and it's hard to get people to make a major introduction without the leverage of a new film, television series, or popular performer."

Danny Grossman, founder and president of Wild Planet Toys in San Francisco, says that entertainment licensing has had a profound impact, both positive and negative, on the toy industry. "The advent of licensing has clearly helped maintain the freshness and dynamism of the toy industry by linking to the ever-changing content of the entertainment industry. Furthermore, there are many cases where the benefit of play has been enhanced by the use of a license.

"Harry Potter LEGOS are an example of a toy that becomes greater than the sum of the parts when you add the magic of characters and story. Unfortunately, in most cases, the increase in the use of licenses has meant a diminution of resources available to create great innovative product. Given that the manufacturer has to pay for the use of the license, that payment almost always comes at the expense of the features of the product."

Grossman is also concerned that, in too many cases, association with a license is more likely to make the product a closed-ended experience for the child rather than a platform for his or her imagination. "This will often occur because the child believes that the toy can or should be used only in the manner they have seen on the entertainment property," Grossman opines.

Nancy Zwiers, president of Funosophy and the former Mattel senior vice president for worldwide Barbie collectibles, licensing, and new business ventures, explains the classic risk/reward trade-off as it applies to licensed brand equity like this: "We all know owning a home requires a bigger risk in the form of bigger investment and bigger commitment. But once you buy, you *own* your home—you make the design and remodeling decisions and cash in on the home's appreciation over time. Conversely, leasing an apartment or home requires much less up-front investment and commitment. However, you are beholden to the landlord and you have no residual value when the lease expires. Now apply that same own-or-lease decision to brand equity. Building your own brand equity requires more investment and commitment, but you are in control *and* you benefit financially from the brand equity appreciation over time."

Advice from the Pros

"The upside is never with one of your brands. Brands pay the rent. They are the bulk of a company's profitability. They are steady and reliable, but we see spikes from new hit products like a Furby, FurReal Friends, Hit Clips, and other new ideas."

—David Berko, senior vice president of concept acquisition, Hasbro

Zwiers says, "Licensing is a growing phenomenon in the toy industry because the industry players—manufacturers and retailers alike—are looking for ways to lower risk, often at the expense of big wins."

Thirty-five–year veteran Jack Dromgold, senior vice president of sales and marketing at Singing Machine, says that while he always liked a hot Lion King or Star Wars license, often by the time you get licensed product to market, children's interests have moved on to another area or the license is over. "You are then stuck with inventory at both places—the retailer and the manufacturer—and neither is happy. That's how closeouts happen, and nobody wants that."

In the optimum situation, licensing lessens the danger for the manufacturer and the retailer, and makes clearance potentials seem less intimidating. Every child from the days of Flash Gordon to Luke Skywalker, from Gene Autrey to Batman, from Rin Tin Tin to Barney yearns to be a hero made bigger than life on the big or little screens. Character-licensed products let that happen.

What Does the Retailer Want?

Asked what she looks for in licensed and nonlicensed products, the senior toy buyer for a leading big-box retailer offered this list, on the condition of anonymity:

- Hot licenses need to have something behind them—a TV show, a movie, success in other countries, or elements of previously successful licenses.
- How much is the manufacturer putting into the license? Its own creative, TV money, or resources?
- What is the license worth to the manufacturer in dollars?
- What would my market share be on that type of license?
- Is pricing in line with other licenses?
- What other licenses are competing for this same consumer at the same time?
- Will the license become evergreen or flash out after the season?
- Is the product going into a proven format or something totally new?
- What is the manufacturer going to do to drive the awareness of the license or item?

Here is what the buyer looks for in a basic product:

- Value for the money
- A higher margin than license goods
- Whether it's a proven format or new
- What the manufacturer is doing to drive sales
- Sales estimates for the season
- Whether the product fits the guest
- Whether the product (store name withheld) brand has look, feel, and value

Where does this leave the inventor? Phil Jackson of Mattel also sees the need for inventors to be proactive with new licenses. He says, "We will consider signing on licenses that are brought to us by inventors, but we seldom go to the inventor community for help in developing license based games. We do work with inventors to create games based on core Mattel brands, but they must show innovative fresh thinking with a point of difference. We want to be on-trend and culturally relevant."

The current quantity of licensed products clearly reduces placement opportunities for independent inventors, but opportunities exist nonetheless for those who can modify their business model. "Licensing is the god now," says inventor Jim McCafferty, president of JMP Creative. "We have to figure out how to make the god happy."

To survive in this environment, inventors need to think more about line extensions to existing brands and must be willing to take a smaller piece of a larger pie.

Randy Altschul created the Miami Vice game, based upon the TV show license for Pepperlane Industries. David Fuhrer created Bounce Around Tigger, marketed by Mattel under a Disney license. David Hampton engineered interactive Yoda, done by Tiger, under license from Lucas. Parker Brothers' Disneyland game came from Brian Hersch, licensed through Disney. TV Guide: The Game, by David Hoyt, was published by Hasbro under license from the TV Guide Magazine Group. Bob Jeffway created Kick 'n Splash Cabbage Patch for Mattel, under license from Original Appalachian Artworks. In each of these instances and many more, inventors found a home for their innovation.

A good living can be made creating for licensed properties, but it takes a whole different inventor approach—and there is a new business to learn and a new set of relationships to establish. Inventor Marc Segan, whose hits include Fisher-Price's Triple Arcade, says that licensors often don't want to confuse their message with some unusual, inventive product—even though many say they would like more imaginative products representing their properties. Segan explains that licensors mean that they'd like more investment in their properties: expensive design and tooling to give more value to the consumer. "They're only sometimes interested in invention. Invention, on the other hand, costs money and increases risk, whether we inventors like it or not. Still, we dream on and succeed."

Toy Trivia

87. Where is Hasbro located?

a. New Haven, Connecticut

b. Providence, Rhode Island

c. El Segundo, California

Going to the Source

One way for inventors to tie in to entertainment license opportunities is to reach the IP agent or owner before the toy marketer becomes involved.

Tiger co-founder Roger Shiffman, one of the industry's most successful marketers and greatest showmen, tells a story of an inventor who wanted to create for Harry Potter. But instead of going first to a toy company, he called up the licensor, Warner Brothers, and showed them what he had in mind. Warner sent him to a toy licensee with its endorsement, and a deal was struck.

In the case of the Men Are from Mars, Women Are from Venus board games, published by Mattel in 1998 and Endless Games in 2003, co-author and inventor

Richard C. Levy saw the sleeping giant of an opportunity before any game publisher. Levy took his vision directly to author John Gray and convinced the relationship guru to allow him to create a game and approach potential licensees. Had a game publisher approached Gray and made a deal, it would not have had any room in it for an inventor royalty. But because Levy was prepackaged in the deal, the numbers worked for his licensees.

Levy has put together similar win/win/win deals using licensed properties to create the Duncan Yo-Yo key chains, Uncle Milton's Ant Farm Game, Martin Luther King Jr. Game, and Magnetic Poetry: The Game, to name a few.

Prolific Chicago inventor Jeffrey Breslow, a founding partner of BMT Associates, understands this modus operandi very well. Seeing an opportunity for Milton Bradley to have a real-estate trading game that would compete with Parker's Monopoly, Brez approached building magnate Donald Trump and secured his co-operation. Trump, The Game, was born. Among other Breslow third-party licensed properties were a series of Dummies games for Pressman and MB's Planet Hollywood game.

Another Windy City inventor, David Hoyt, a former trader on the floor of the Chicago Board Options Exchange, approached Tribune Media Services with an idea to extend its syndicated word puzzle JUMBLE. JUMBLE appears regularly in over 600 newspapers, with a combined readership or more than 70 million. Hoyt first sold TMS on JUMBLE Crosswords. Then he extended his relationship through the creation of JUMBLE-branded puzzlers Crosswords for Kids, TV JUMBLE, JUMBLE Brainbusters, and JUMBLE for the Classroom. Hoyt has become an integral and well-respected part of the TMS/JUMBLE creative family.

These examples illustrate how proactive inventors can thrive in today's license-driven environment. Rather than trying to place only original concepts, these inventors and many others have joined the hunt for licenses, securing IP rights and building products around them before approaching a marketer. They have gone beyond pure invention to become marketing-driven product packagers.

If you want to pursue such third-party opportunities, Richard Blank, a former vice president and secretary of LIMA, recommends these first steps:

- ◆ Pay attention to brand licenses and follow the character license industry. Educate yourself.
- ◆ Build relationships with licensing agents and companies that are active with licensing.
- ◆ Try to come up with ideas that enhance characters, and go to the licensor as well. If the licensor likes an idea, it may influence the licensee.

Toy inventors should utilize licenses, not fear them. Independent inventors who want a slice (or even a slab) of the licensing pie need to get out of their studios and workshops, put on marketing hats (or associate with a marketing-driven inventor), and creatively marry their product-development skills and original concepts to third-party licenses. We've said it before, and we'll say it again: Licensing is here to stay.

When asked where independent inventors fit in the world of licensing, John Gildea, former Hasbro corporate vice president of licensing and promotions, says, "Licensing is a key part of the toy business, and inventors should embrace it with their best ideas. Most licensors would love to have creatives scope out their license to give a read on how it can be interpreted into toys and games before it goes to a licensee. Once a product is assigned to a licensee, that licensee most likely needs fresh thinking and A-plus ideas in order to meet guarantees and maintain the brand."

Elliot Lederman, vice president of licensing and merchandising for the Universal Studios Consumer Products Group, sees the independent inventor as a potential key component in getting the *wow* factor into licensed products. He says, "Everyone wins if a licensed property can be combined with the best and most innovative products. All parties benefit, including the inventor, licensor, licensee, retailer, and consumer. If the idea captures the essence of the licensed property in a unique way, it can become a best-seller at retail. The additional volume produced by combining an inventor's concept with a licensed property should make up for the potential reduction of the inventor's royalty percentage."

Lederman believes that there can be an alliance between an inventor and a licensor. "If the inventor establishes a relationship with the licensor, the inventor has no risk to present his or her concepts. They are in the business of developing unique product; our core business is developing and licensing entertainment content. And our having seen a unique proprietary idea should be added value during the pitch to a potential licensee—especially if they may also be an existing licensee for the licensed property. Conversely, if the license is still available and an inventor makes a passionate pitch of his idea with the license, that may get the licensee to connect with the license. The sale of the idea with the license makes a nice, complete package."

Lederman, who personally reaches out to independent inventors, feels it is critical for inventors to have a dialogue with licensors. The Universal executive is extremely proactive in this regard and enjoys noodling opportunities with the pros.

The Inventor's Edge

The inventor has an advantage in some instances because he or she thinks about the product, not just brand equity. Most licensing agents pitch the strength of a brand—the sizzle—and depend upon licensees to come up with product—the steak.

Bob Fuhrer of Nextoy sees marketer deals for licenses sometimes eroding what inventors can provide. "The huge advances and guarantees lead to what I call 'label slaps.' Companies put new labels on generic product. Often licensed products coming to market are just generic rehash. If I have a fresh concept for a licensee and want to make a solid sales pitch, I have to determine if I want to invest in dedicated art. If there is no sale, I lose, and there is no way I can show the prototype to another company.

"Licensing definitely affects my economics of doing business. If a license is involved, it is generally expected that I take a third-party royalty of 3 percent. If there is no other royalty-bearing license, I can expect a more normal deal. But with character licenses involved, I have to hope that at half the normal royalty rate there will be twice the sales."

Inventor Paul Lapidus of NewFuntiers agrees. "In my view, the toy industry moves forward on breakthrough product fueled by innovation. Licenses only move sales, and at different paces, depending on the strength of the license. Often marketers can't afford innovation when paying a high license fee. Even if they license an idea from an inventor, economics may prevent marketers from using an idea to its fullest extent. They end up selling the character and not the potential of the idea.

"It is costly to prepare a toy or game concept for a specific license. You are essentially spending and preparing for a one-company show. If the idea doesn't move the licensee, all that costly art and model work to dress the idea for a license is wasted. Even if you hit, you know you are going to get 3 percent for a *wow*, while the character licensor is more likely at the 15 percent level."

> ### Advice from the Pros
>
> "Saying there's no competition for a product destroys an inventor's credibility—in many cases, if there's no competition, there's no market. Understanding the concept of competitive advantage is invaluable."
>
> —Dr. Debra Malewicki, director, Wisconsin Innovation Service Center, University of Wisconsin–Whitewater

When asked about the flood of new licenses, Fuhrer replies, "I get a surprising number of inquiries from independent inventors with great designs for figures, complete with backstories. I merely tell them how tough that category is because of the many entertainment companies that create characters and have the resources to package it all together with a cartoon series, publishing deals, and support through their own channels. A visit to the New York Licensing Show would give a quick reality check of going against all of those properties already being shopped."

Advice from the Pros

"Always make sure you have a clear and concise answer to the question, 'Why would a kid play with this?'"

—Duncan J. Billing, general manager, Hasbro Toy Group

Universal Studios' Lederman sees another value to the Licensing Show for inventors: "It is critical for inventors to have dialogue with licensors. That information may inspire inventors to think about new licenses in the entertainment pipeline, which should lead to unique new opportunities everyone wants to see in the toy industry. The New York Licensing Show is a great place to start that dialogue."

Staying Power Gives Product Power

Mel Taft was one of the first industry executives to see the potential of licensing. Says Taft of his early efforts as head of R&D at Milton Bradley, "I felt we had to do something to get the trade to buy more of our line. After Candy Land, Uncle Wiggily, and Game of States, they really didn't need us for commodities like chess and checkers. The answer seemed to be with early TV tie-ins. We produced Howdy Doody first, followed by Hopalong Cassidy. The trade got the connection and licensing spiked our sales. It was such a big thing that we bought full page ads in *Life* magazine in 1957. From then on, I kept one eye on new licenses and the other on our chief competitor at the time, Ideal Toy Company. I was particularly pleased when we were able to license Concentration as a boxed game show. It became our first million-seller."

A snapshot of the line 20 years later showed how Milton Bradley continued to tie in licenses to its game assortments. The 1974 Six Style Game Assortment included the Addams Family, Casper the Ghost, Yogi Bear, Scooby Doo, Hound Cats, and Speed Buggy. It sold to the trade for 60¢ each, with an intended retail of $1.

Advice from the Pros

"Treat your ideas like they are your business, not a single shot to make millions."

—Brian Mehler, director of product development, Maui Toys

A higher-priced Four-Style Game Assortment featured Columbo, Wildlife, Fastest Gun, and Planet of the Apes, all with a trade price of $2.40 and intended retail of $4. Though some of these licenses applied to early board games survive today, they have emerged as megamedia properties and would never be released on modestly priced SKUs like these assortments. Licensor guarantees and royalties and licensee expectations would never permit such placement.

Endless Games has picked up on the consumer interest in TV game shows started years ago by Milton Bradley and offers a long line of favorites like Password, Concentration, Family Feud, Newlywed Game, What's My Line?, $25,000 Pyramid, Beat the Clock, and The Price Is Right. Says Kevin McNulty of his product strategy, "I knew these were game staples and fun to play. I tied up rights through Mark Goodson Productions and Sony, and churn these wonderful games every couple of years so there are always at least four at retail. They may go back many years, but there is still plenty of attraction to them."

When asked about licensing today, McNulty responded, "Licensing has gotten out of hand. There is too much at retail. For me, I'll take a game that can make a license rather than a license that makes a game." This is why Endless Games balances its line with original product such as Route 66: The Great American Road Trip Game, Encore, and Two Out of Three.

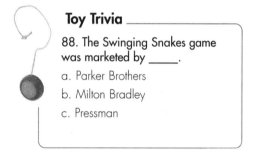

Toy Trivia

88. The Swinging Snakes game was marketed by _____.
a. Parker Brothers
b. Milton Bradley
c. Pressman

That Was Then, This Is Now

Some 30 years ago, Playskool took the licensing plunge on two play sets. At the time, miniature environments of real-world settings were a strong category in the preschool market. "What better segment of business for licenses?" thought the late Art Taylor, vice president of marketing for Playskool, and Mel Taft, senior vice president of corporate research and development at parent Milton Bradley.

Taft recalls the excitement in capturing the McDonald's and Holiday Inn licenses. "We were able to design great play value into the play sets of a well-known restaurant and hotel chain. Buyers were supportive when they saw what we had created in sturdy molded plastic with a collection of appropriate play elements. The product looked great, the packaging was great, and everyone at Playskool was enthused about these licensed play sets."

What we didn't count on was a bit of a consumer backlash from parents. Apparently, there was a resistance to letting kids play with settings where real-world intentions are to eat and sleep. Looking back, fast food was only in the early stages of acceptability, and a hotel setting didn't relate strongly enough to kids, whereas themes like a zoo, playground, or airport were okay. The licenses hit some sort of nerve, and the parents didn't buy at levels we projected. We sold a couple hundred thousand of each, and in two years they were gone."

Co-author Ron Weingartner was head of Playskool R&D in the mid-1970s. "Our mission was to catch the then No. 1 preschool marketer, Fisher-Price. Character licensing was one strategy to make our products more appealing. We had great licenses: Disney, Sesame Street, and Snoopy on puzzles, and Charlie Brown was the key figure on a line of little sports products. We had excellent success with *Gilligan's Island*, the world's first floating bath toy."

But Playskool's experiences applying licenses to preschool items was something of a mixed bag. For example, Playskool offered a Good Humor ride-on, when the category was dominated by the nonlicensed, macho Big Wheel. The sweet Good Humor vehicle slowly melted away in the heat of competition with the big, bad wheelie.

"During my years with Playskool, licensing was always there, but it didn't automatically mean management would pursue a new business direction merely on a license's potential strength with consumers" says Weingartner. "I felt Playskool should extend beyond single-item marketing and offer products that would set the total environment for the toddler/preschooler. One concept was Sesame Street furniture for the nursery. I had one of our designers create actual size foam-core models of a Big Bird Bookcase, Oscar Toy Box, and Bert and Ernie Night Stands. A well-known Chicago-based furniture-design engineer studied the structural specs for manufacturing direction.

"I stopped short of getting the acceptance of Sharon Lerner and Chris Cerf, who at the time did licensing approvals for CTW. When the concept was readied for management review, I was excited and there was high anticipation by R&D personnel. After pitching the Sesame Street license and the new business opportunity, I was stunned by the flat-out rejection. I was told, 'This is not product for the toy buyer. It's for the furniture buyer!' Daaaaa! Personally, I didn't understand why a salesman couldn't walk down the hall with a great license on great product and find the right buyer."

The situation is no different today. Companies tend to do only the products its sales force or reps handle. They rarely strike out to build new relationships. Marketers can only hope that they make a commitment to what Jerry Houle calls a real or potential "franchise" property. "If you can find a property that translates through various media, it can only increase consumer exposure and a demand for new forms of its images," says Houle. "The popularity grows, and if it all leads to a major event like a megamovie, sales of products using the license can go through the roof. The Muppets did this in '79, Ninja Turtle did this, and most recently Spiderman did this."

Industry licensing pros like Houle and Cathy Meredith have seen just about every license that has emerged in their 37 years in the business. Their choices of successful, evergreen franchise licenses include (in alphabetical order): Barbie, Blue's Clues, Bob the Builder, Cabbage Patch, Care Bears, Harry Potter, Muppets, Nascar, Pokemon, Power Puff Girls, Scooby Doo, Sesame Street, Star Wars, Strawberry Shortcake, TMNT, and Winnie the Pooh. But many other licenses are ready and able to push products in today's market.

You Pick 'Em

The *2003 Playthings Buyers Guide* lists almost 800 licenses available to toy and game marketers—or any merchant of consumer products, for that matter. And you can be assured that new licensed characters are being created in Hollywood studios and TV production shops right now. Some, like Spider-Man and Batman, can scale buildings; others, like Superman, can fly over them. Others, like James Dean, Elvis, and The Three Stooges, tug at past memories. On the comic strip side are Dick Tracy and Annie, to name a couple. Cartoon characters, movie celebrities, and toy-industry action figures are all ready to make a fresh impression on whole new product categories and for a whole new wave of consumers.

Attorney Andy Levison, who began outlicensing TSR's D&D figures and has closed hundreds of licensing deals, says licenses have a generational life. "Properties burst into the industry and live in product lines for two or three years. The good ones may be put on the shelf to resurface for new consumers, for collectors. Licensors of such properties come back with marketing support, good management, and workable approval systems. When evergreens come back, they bring millions of impressions in consumers' minds—look at Raggedy Ann and Andy, look at Betty Boop."

Levison points to some past licenses that might be inactive in toys and games but that exist on the Cartoon Network, classic movies, or cable placement, just waiting to recycle back into the industry. He explains that these kinds of properties can give a real jump-start over a brand that is expected to build from scratch with or without promotion. People remember Strawberry Shortcake, Teenage Mutant Ninja Turtles, Cabbage Patch Kids, and Pound Puppies. When these are applied to new products, they make immediate noise.

Hasbro Games' Cathy Meredith knows there is no shortage of new license opportunities at the world's largest game marketer. From her position of gathering the latest from the license world, she says, "I see many properties. It can be as high as 40 a year, of which 20 are serious candidates in their development and potential. In addition, we have our own rich in-house licenses, which offer great brand-building possibilities. We take our best shots for new games from a big licensing mix each year."

John Gildea, who had a corporate view of licensing opportunities says, "Each year we would look at between 50 and 75 new opportunities for master licenses, reviewing pilots, scripts, and support plans, most from TV and movies. In most cases, TV had the advantage if it was a syndicated show airing five times a week. We looked for properties with the highest viewer impressions. Licensing is all about character recognition; it's all about eyeballs."

As the world's largest jigsaw puzzle maker, too, Hasbro has an additional need to license artwork and artists. Says Meredith about this segment, "Computer-generated graphics have exploded on the art scene. I must see 300 to 400 opportunities for puzzle art annually, which compete with game licenses for the few slots in our puzzle line."

A Magenta Dinosaur, a Yellow Bird

Licensors take their properties very seriously. Since images of licensed characters have equity with consumers, their owners diligently protect them. Licensors establish design and style guides with tight specifications that licensees must follow to the letter (or feather). Approvals are required all along the way as license-bearing products evolve. Production schedules can grind to a halt without periodic licensor approvals. Package and product graphics, parts' sheets, directions, and preproduction pieces must all be approved. No inventories can be built or product shipped to stores without the magical licensor "okay."

Contractual agreements with huge financial stakes are signed off on by upper management, but it's when the property enters a marketer's development pipeline that the license has real impact. The goal is to generate sufficient product to pay back advances, guarantees, and commitments. From the first pencil sketch to color illustration, to sculpted figures, licensees must submit their work for licensor approvals. Anatomic detail must be accurate in 2D and 3D form; correct character attitudes, markings, and vitality must be captured in all reproductions. The goal is to have the character's appearance identical on games, embodied in toys, printed in books, and so on. The integrity of its design is sacred.

Donna Christian, who headed the department responsible for all copy on game boards, packages, and directions at Hasbro Games, remembers the demands of licensors. "All elements had to pass through the licensor. With some licenses, that meant four or five pairs of eyes had to give signatory approval, and often they couldn't agree among themselves. Working with our internal licensing people, our own treatment guide was put into place to avoid misunderstandings." When Hasbro was doing 3D Disney games, Donna put out 15 pages for Disney people on how she and her team would treat punctuation, grammar, logos, legal lines, and any other editorial detail.

The following is a summation of the types of requirements licensors place on toy and game companies:

- No TV ads can be run without written approval.
- No limitation is put on the licensor to grant to others licenses for other uses.
- No use of licenses as premiums is allowed by the licensee and its customers.
- No part of the guarantee paid to the licensor is repayable.
- Sales activity must be reported within 30 days of initial shipments.
- Upon demand, the licensee must provide an audit by an independent CPA.
- Licensees slow in paying pay penalty fees after the due date.
- The licensee must keep the books open for two years, in case the licensor elects to audit them.
- The licensor will be held harmless in suits brought against the licensee on specific issues.
- The licensee should obtain liability insurance.
- Only artwork approved by the licensor in writing can be used.
- All art forms created by the licensee are owned by the licensor.
- The licensee must create original artwork and holds the licenser harmless from claims that it isn't original.
- The licensee must prominently display proper trademarks and copyrights.
- The licensee must strictly comply and maintain compliance with quality standards.
- The licensee cannot manufacture, sell, distribute, or promote licensed products without written approval.
- Modifications to products must be approved in advance.
- Characters may not be mixed for promotion purposes without approval.

◆ The licensee cannot sublicense any rights.

◆ The licensee may not sell through certain outlets.

◆ The licensee must conduct all business related to the licensor's product in an ethical manner and must comply with government laws.

◆ The licensor may terminate the license for any 14 ways in which there may be a breach of or noncompliance with the agreement.

Licensing Can Bring in the Winners

The following lists from TRSTS show the No. 1–selling toys and games over the last decade of the 1900s. Some conclusions: No. 1 represents huge numbers. The biggest sellers are known brands, whether character licenses or brands that marketers built themselves. Exceptions are Furby and Giga Pets, by entrepreneurial Tiger Electronics. Wouldn't you like to be the inventor with the original idea for any of these blockbusters? Bottom line item is 1991, top line item is 2001 on each list

No. 1–Selling Toys 1992–2002

Item	Maker	$/Millions	U/Millions
Leap Pad Book Assort	Leapfrog Ent.	$79,650	5,650
Hot Wheels Basic Cars	Mattel	$83,100	109,200
Hot Wheels Basic Cars	Mattel	$74,400	86,700
Furby Assortment	Tiger/Hasbro	$191,400	6,800
Plush Teletubbies Assort	Hasbro	$89,500	3,600
Giga Pets Assortment	Tiger/Hasbro	$18,200	1,800
96 Happy Holiday Barbie	Mattel	$40,800	1,200
Baby Sister Kelly	Mattel	$22,500	2,300
Power Rangers Figures	Bandai America	$56,100	10,100
Plush Talking Barney	Hasbro Toy Group	$39,900	1,200
Super Soaker 50	Larami Corp	$16,200	1,600

No. 1-Selling Games 1992–2002

Item	Maker	$/Millions	U/Millions
Trivial Pursuit 20th	Hasbro Games	$25,595	870
Pokemon Booster Blister	Wizards of the Coast (Hasbro)	$15,400	5,800
Pokemon Series 2	Wizards of the Coast (Hasbro)	$36,400	11,500
Pokemon Base Set Booster	Wizards of the Coast (Hasbro)	$55,200	17,300
Bop It	Hasbro	$21,400	1,200
Bass Fishing	Radica	$23,200	1,300
Wheel of Fortune Handheld	Tiger/Hasbro	$15,600	800
Monopoly	Hasbro	$17,600	1,800
Jenga	Hasbro	$18,000	1,200
Jenga	Hasbro	$5,400	400
Jenga	Hasbro	$4,500	300

The Pitfalls of Licensing: Pow! Zap!

Some say that toy marketers use licensing to guarantee sales success. This is not always true, and it's not a path without its own pitfalls. There is always the danger that kids will not like the toy applications of the license, or that moms and dads who gave high ratings for a TV or movie encounter will pass the property in the aisles of TRU or Target. There are other risks, too, whether it is a celebrity falling from grace or a rich financial deal with questionable return on investment.

One of the first celebrities to impact a hot license was Evel Knievel in the late 1970s. His daredevil exploits and red, white, and blue image made him a living action figure. The fact that his stunts reportedly caused him to break

411

If you are interested in the impressive and inspiring 140-year history of FAO Schwarz, read *FAO Schwarz: The Original Toy Story*, a commemorative publication created by Maria Weiskott, editor-in-chief of *Playthings Magazine* and her team. The 70-page, 8½ x 10½ magazine was released in the fall of 2002 and may still be available from FAO or *Playthings*.

every bone in his body at one time or another only contributed to his notoriety. Ideal Toy seized on this macho icon and in 1974 produced an ever-expanding line from action figures to motorcycles, to rocket cars, to play sets. Other toy novelties and nontoy products were in the licensing mix as he jumped his vehicle over shark tanks, buses, and assorted landmarks. Knievel was a marketer's dream.

Then—pow! Knievel was so infuriated by what he felt was a distorted and inaccurate book on his life that he physically assaulted the author, his former PR agent, with a baseball bat. While Knievel did hard time, sales plunged as the public took a dimmer view of his behavior than would likely be inflicted on Hollywood and sports figures today. Though there is some interest in a small line of his vehicles today, there is no question that the broad line appeal ended with Knievel's one bad off-track stunt.

When George Lucas decided he would create and produce a *Star Wars* trilogy, the buzz over who would get the master toy license could have drowned out the roar of an attacking X-wing. Who would not want the rights to a property that generated $4.5 billion and had moved 250 million action figures at retail since 1977?

The universe of potential takers was wide open, owing to a major financial miscalculation. In 1977, Lucas granted Kenner Products exclusive rights in perpetuity to Star Wars for a $100,000 annual fee. Kenner made millions of dollars selling Star Wars figures. Hasbro acquired Kenner in 1991 with that fee in place. But sales of Star Wars toys were lost on the dark side of the planet. What accountant worth his abacus wouldn't conclude that The Force hardly justified the toll? According to *Forbes* magazine, "A Hasbro accountant figured he could save the company $100,000 by not sending George Lucas a check." The rights were terminated, and the license was up for grabs.

Galoob, the licensee of independent inventor Clem Hedeen's Micro Machines and a major marketer of boys' toys, saw Star Wars as an opportunity made in a distant galaxy. The company progressively built a Star Wars line that was doing $120 million by the end of 1997. Apparently, this growth convinced Lucas that there was great interest in other life forms, and he announced that his trilogy would be subject to new licensing rights.

The 1997 battle for rights to market Star Wars toys began among industry giants Hasbro, Mattel, and then-independent minimajor Lewis Galoob Toys. After ratcheting the financials into hyperbolic orbit, Mattel was the odd Ewok out. In October, Hasbro was awarded the master toy license and Galoob won the rights to small-scale figures, vehicles, and play sets that would go under its Micro Machines brand.

Hasbro and Galoob reportedly paid Lucas hundreds of millions of dollars in cash advances spread over the release of the three episodes. In addition, the financial package included equity positions for Lucas in both toy companies. Royalties are reported on the upside of 20 percent of toy shipments; some insiders say it's closer to 25 percent.

Zap! For the love of space, Hasbro, on September 28, 1998, bought Galoob for $220 million in cash, announcing that "the deal combines the two firms' separate licenses for toys based on the Star Wars franchise."

Mattel, the world's largest toy company and Hasbro's arch rival, was awarded by Warner Brothers the right to produce toys and games based on its Batman; Superman; Looney Tunes, including Bugs Bunny; and Justice League characters, for the next five years. The deal is estimated to be worth between $200 million and $500 million. Mattel reportedly won the licensing rights in part because Warner Brothers was delighted with the toys and games it produced for *Harry Potter and the Sorcerer's Stone*. This agreement gives Mattel the lucrative Batman rights, which were held until the end of 2002 by Hasbro.

Advice from the Pros

"Even if you can do the initial presentation in person, make a video to leave behind if the concept is retained for further internal review. The video can be simple and informal, but you need to demonstrate the 'unique feature' in the first 20–30 seconds to get your audience hooked. An extended attention span is not guaranteed on the receiving end. Then follow with technical details, additional features, and so on. The video is a good backup to keep you alive if the prototype malfunctions or is difficult to demonstrate."

—Richard J. Maddocks, lead designer of advanced development services, Hasbro

Entertainment-licensed product should continue to drive the toy industry. The 2002 holiday season saw these new films: *Treasure Planet* (Disney), *Fat Albert* (Fox), *Pokemon* and *Pinocchio* (Miramax), *Lord of the Rings: The Two Towers* (New Line Cinema), and *Harry Potter and the Chamber of Secrets* (Warner Bros.). Set for 2003 are *Winnie the Pooh* (Disney), *Cat in the Hat* and *Sinbad* (Dreamworks), *Bulletproof Monk* (MGM), *Lord of the Rings: The Return of the King* (New Line Cinema), *Charlie's Angels 2* (Sony), and *The Hulk* (Universal Studios).

Hasbro and Mattel are not alone in their reliance on entertainment licenses. Examples abound. Here are just a few. Fun 4 All, a toy and novelty company, signed up as the master toy licensee for the Osbournes. From Ozzy Talking Heads to Sharon Coin Banks, Kelly Bendables toys to Jack Slammers talking plush—and even Osbournes Snow Globes—Fun 4 All's irreverent new offerings captured the undeniable appeal of TV's coolest and highest-rated happy family.

Bandai America, a subsidiary of the third-largest toy company in the world, Japan's Bandai Co. Ltd., opened a U.S.–based front in the American toy market in the mid-1970s as one of Nintendo's first licensees. Bandai America has grown from its Nintendo beginnings to become the master toy licensee of some of the most popular properties in children's toys and entertainment, including the Mighty Morphin Power Rangers, Digimon, and Gundam product lines.

Bandai America has built an action-figure empire by strategically leveraging its brands with complementary children's television programs such as the 10-year-strong *Power Rangers* and *Digimon: Digital Monsters* series, both featured on the Fox Kids Network. In 1999, Bandai America introduced Gundam to the U.S. market through a partnership with the Cartoon Network in celebration of Gundam's 20-year history in Japan.

Even LEGO is not immune from entertainment license fever. The LEGO Group, makers of the world's best-selling construction toys, entered into an exclusive agreement with Lucas Licensing, Ltd., to market Star Wars construction toys worldwide.

Toy Trivia

90. A horseshoe-pitching version of tic-tac-toe is called ___.

a. Toss Across

b. Ringers

c. Bean Bag Toss

Take 'Em in a Package, Take 'Em Early

Some of the major entertainment companies are developing and packaging franchise licenses. Dan Romanelli, president of Warner Bros. Worldwide Consumer Products, told *Licensing!* in September 2002, "We are in the business of creating franchises unlike we ever did before. These properties are global, with significant revenue, and we are investing heavily in them. This move should signal to the retail community our even greater commitment to brand continuity."

That commitment by Warner was immediately bought up by Mattel. It took the master toy license agreement for Looney Tunes, Baby Looney Tunes, Batman, Superman, and Justice League characters through 2007. This packaging of properties to a single licensee ended the Batman toy rights with Hasbro and brought the Warner collection into the Mattel lineup, which already includes Harry Potter, SpongeBob SquarePants, Masters of the Universe, and Yu-GI-Oh.

Direct to Retail

Whereas the Warner–Mattel affiliation may signal the packaging of licenses for marketers, other entertainment sources are going directly to retailers for marketing deals. An example is the DIC Entertainment involvement with Toys R Us. Though only a recent arrival on the kid-vid screens, Liberty's Kids debuted on PBS in the fall of 2002. Toys, school supplies, and other products become available exclusively at TRU starting 2003.

The addition of Liberty's Kids expands the growing exclusive licenses at TRU that include Discovery Animal Planet, Cabbage Patch, Home Depot, and E.T. TRU also maintains an expansive line of proprietary games marketed under its Pavilion brand.

Time will tell what these aggressive moves mean to the independent inventor. On one hand, Mattel takes the doubt out of who will market a large stable of properties. This gives inventors a broad target with ideas suited to the newly acquired licenses. On the other, TRU will determine immediately what ideas fit its exclusive licenses and can guarantee those selected ideas shelf space if there is approval of the concepts.

Dressing the Products for Success

So how has the shadow of licensing engulfed the toy industry of today? Jerry Houle, self-proclaimed licensing pioneer, offers this merger of factors: "There has always been licensing, but in the past five years, there has been an explosion in media, TV, internet, and video games, all offering extendable opportunities. At the same time, there is much potential product to sell; traditional licensees are faced with a consolidation of retailers. As controllers of shelf space, retailers are in a "driver" role of what brands to merchandise. Sensing the strength of retailers, some licensors are cutting out licensees and doing direct deals with retailers. We are seeing retailers like Toys R Us and Saks Fifth Avenue seeking to develop a quarter of shelf goods being unique to that chain through internal development, private label, or exclusive licenses."

Houle adds, "Some licensors continue to misunderstand the key ingredients of licensing and focus solely on the deal rather than building from the power of the product. The goal of the licensee and the retailers is sell-through to a satisfied consumer. Licensors should see these three elements as stakeholders in their property and partner with them to manage a license for success."

Cathy Meredith sees not only escalation of licenses, but also the escalation of the financials expected by licensors. "Some licensors have great expectations in royalties, guarantees, merchandising programs, and even TV support, all the while that they slice the license thinner."

Building Q president Woody Browne has been in licensing for over 20 years. He also sees royalties as an issue. A former three-term president of LIMA, he says, "If you start at 8 percent, and go to 10 percent, and, if it is a home run, go to 12 percent because all the tooling costs are amortized, which puts the gross margin up, then the company is healthy. When the percentages start at 14 or 15 percent and they're tiered to 25 percent, it is crazy."

John Gildea sees consolidation of media partners as one of the biggest changes in licensing in recent years. "Disney, AOL-Warner, and Viacom control the content and distribution of programming and, through that, the heat for their licenses. Independent TV stations are gone. Other producers and licensors are forced to take other routes, like PBS. That worked for Barney and Teletubbies, but that venue is getting crowded."

Commenting on the issues with some franchise licenses, licensing attorney Andy Levison says, "To meet the guarantees, there is often a flood of product that most often just denigrates the license. Licensees try to sell as much product while paying the high royalties to meet the financials. Sometimes a licensor would do better to carve out marketers who can best execute and distribute to segments rather than assign one master licensee. All would profit by doing the products they do best."

Levison's view of the importance of product first has the confirmation of "game guys" with over 100 years of cumulative experiences in the industry. Phil Orbanes, who has 33 years of experience at Parker Bros and Winning Moves, says, "Entertainment licensing on this industry's products tends to stifle innovation and leads to short, jarring life cycles of toys."

Bill Dohrmann, who for 30 years has headed marketing and development efforts at Parker, Tiger, and Hasbro Games, offers a nostalgic view. "Obviously the impact of licensing has been profound, and all of us traditionalists would love to see many more new entries out there just because they are fun and original … with no connection to this or that license."

And Mel Taft, chairman of the Gamesters by virtue of his 54 years in the business, chides marketers paying off-the-chart royalties and giving tremendous dollar guarantees for licenses: "It only causes quality to suffer and at the same time escalates prices to consumers. Somehow the marketer has to make back those huge investments."

And It All Depends on the Kids

What better summary statement about licensing than what has been attributed to unidentified industry experts? "Properties are cyclical entities, dependent on fickle kids and strong marketing campaigns." The operative factor is "fickle kids." Even with strong marketing campaigns by licensors, a flop is always possible unless there is consistent consumer passion for the product that carries the character image. As the hype builds for the next supposed megaproperty, may the licensee, the inventor, and the consumer beware!

Creating Toys for Nontoy Brands

Alternative markets are open to toy and game inventors, one of the most fertile and potentially lucrative being premiums. These are products used to motivate consumers favorably toward a goal, which is usually the increased consumer purchase of a particular product.

According to *PROMO* magazine, in 2001 the premium incentives industry generated an estimated $26.3 billion (a 2.4 percent decrease from 2000). Business incentive programs, which include travel incentives, accounted for $21.9 billion of this figure (a 3 percent decrease from 2000). Consumer-targeted programs accounted for $4.3 billion of this figure (a 1 percent increase from 2000).

The promotional products industry was estimated at $16.0 billion (a 10.4 percent decrease from 2000).

Any product with a perceived value can motivate a target audience, and there are many companies whose business it is to motivate children toward a purchase. Two great examples are breakfast cereals that offer in-pack premiums and fast-food chains such as Burger King and McDonald's that give away toy premiums with purchases. All kinds of packaged goods aimed at kids use premiums.

To find out which ones use such novelties, just run up and down the aisles of supermarkets and look at packages, scan the free-standing inserts (read: discount coupons) in weekend newspapers, and look at the windows in fast-food eateries. The targets of opportunity are clearly marked.

If you decide to go after the premium market, understand this basic fact: The company is not in the business of selling or giving away premiums. It is in the business of marketing its brands and premiums help to increase its shipment and share.

Premium offerings operate under the principle of "slippage." People tend to collect so many needed proofs of purchase and then lose focus before reaching the required number. This is what the manufacturer counts on. If every coupon were to be redeemed, the brand would be in big trouble. So don't be surprised if you hear the consumer goods brand manager not hoping for 100 percent redemption.

Corporations have standards when selecting a premium. To help you organize your thoughts, here are a few key ones:

- Suitability (perceived value) to target audience. It is vital that an idea match the brand's key consumer.

- Pricing. Always shoot for the lowest possible price point. Corporations have strict guidelines. For example, cereal in-pack premiums usually cannot be more than 5¢ each.

- Potential for breakage and defects in manufacture. Premiums are generally sent nationwide via UPS, unless they are in-packs. Items with a low possibility for breakage are favored. Premiums also have QC standards.

- Mailability. Companies take everything into consideration, including the cost of envelopes and cartons.

- Reliability of supply. You may be asked to line up a second manufacturing source to ensure that it can supply the program.

These are key terms you'll want to know. Others are found in the book's glossary, "Talk the Talk."

- **Advance premium**   Given to a new customer on the condition that the company will earn it back through later purchases.

- **Bounce back**   Additional offer mailed with a self-liquidator. Frequently associated with the first premium.

- **Combination sales**   Tie-in of a premium with the purchase of an advertiser's product at a combination price.

- **Direct premium**   Dealer incentive that is part of a point-of-purchase display.

- **Free**   The magic word often has strings attached. In the trade, an item given with purchase, at no extra cost over the selling price, may be described as free.

- **Free-standing insert (FSI)**   Newspaper supplement in which companies offer coupons and premiums. Usually drops on Sunday.

- **Fulfillment house**   A distribution center for premiums; usually an independent concern from the offering company.

- ◆ **In-pack**   A direct premium enclosed inside a product package.
- ◆ **Keeper**   A premium offered in direct sales marketing for the acceptance of free trial sales merchandise.
- ◆ **Loader**   A dealer incentive given with a specified product purchase. This is for the dealer, not end consumers.
- ◆ **Near-pack**   A direct premium, typically in the grocery business, that is stacked on the shelf not far from the promoted product.
- ◆ **On-pack**   A direct premium that is shrink-wrapped to or otherwise held in place to the outside of a product package.
- ◆ **Self-liquidator**   Consumer premium offered for proof of purchase and cash to cover merchandise cost, postage, and handling.
- ◆ **Sprint**   Brief campaign within a longer premium program.

Reaching the Decision Maker

The path to the decision maker is not as obvious as it is in the toy industry. Companies all seem to work slightly differently in this regard. At Fortune 500 companies like Procter & Gamble, General Foods, and General Mills, for example, departments are charged with the purchase of premiums. Other companies rely on their ad agencies to bring them such opportunities. And in other instances, brand managers and even people in the executive suite may influence the purchase of premiums.

Cleaning Up on a Toothpaste Premium

"While brushing my teeth one morning, I was focused on the tube of Crest toothpaste in my hand when a Eureka moment hit," recalls co-author and inventor Richard C. Levy. "I envisioned a Big Wheel–style trike having a large Crest tube as its mainframe. I called it the Crest Fluorider.

"I immediately shared the idea with my associate, Gary Piaget, and he did a marker rendering. My next step was to call ride-on manufacturers—Empire, and Coleco—to see if someone thought I was on to something. The idea was turned down, albeit politely, by everyone who did outdoor wheeled goods.

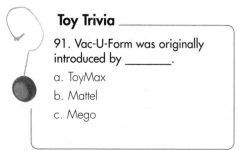

Toy Trivia

91. Vac-U-Form was originally introduced by _____.

a. ToyMax
b. Mattel
c. Mego

"Then I took a shot in the dark. I talked my way through the front-line defenses and into the Crest brand group at Procter & Gamble's headquarters in Cincinnati, Ohio. It was early in the morning, and the most senior brand manager picked up the line."

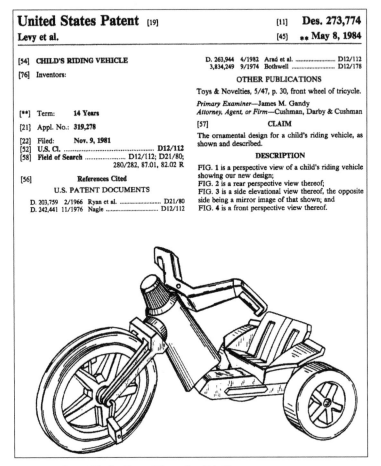

United States Patent [19]

Levy et al.

[11] **Des. 273,774**

[45] ** **May 8, 1984**

[54] **CHILD'S RIDING VEHICLE**

[76] Inventors:

[**] Term: **14 Years**

[21] Appl. No.: **319,278**

[22] Filed: **Nov. 9, 1981**
[52] U.S. Cl. D12/112
[58] Field of Search .... D12/112; D21/80; 280/282, 87.01, 82.02 R

[56] **References Cited**

U.S. PATENT DOCUMENTS

D. 203,759   2/1966   Ryan et al. D21/80
D. 242,441 11/1976   Nagle D12/112
D. 263,944   4/1982   Arad et al. D12/112
3,834,249   9/1974   Bothwell D12/178

OTHER PUBLICATIONS

Toys & Novelties, 5/47, p. 30, front wheel of tricycle.

Primary Examiner—James M. Gandy
Attorney, Agent, or Firm—Cushman, Darby & Cushman

[57] **CLAIM**

The ornamental design for a child's riding vehicle, as shown and described.

DESCRIPTION

FIG. 1 is a perspective view of a child's riding vehicle showing our new design;
FIG. 2 is a rear perspective view thereof;
FIG. 3 is a side elevational view thereof, the opposite side being a mirror image of that shown; and
FIG. 4 is a front perspective view thereof.

Child's Riding Vehicle (Crest Fluorider, P&G)
Patented May 8, 1984
U.S. Patent 273,774

Levy's "Have I got an idea for you ..." resulted in an exchange of faxes and a request to see a rendering. From there it quickly moved to a request for a looks-like physical model, made to scale. Piaget, a talented industrial designer with "golden hands" and toy industry prototyping and manufacturing experience, contracted to have one made with someone he knew in upstate New York. P&G paid for it. Simultaneously, the inventing team took out trademark and patent protection on the intellectual properties.

A few months later, Levy and Piaget were asked to supply 800 sample trikes for a test. P&G cut another purchase order. A deal was made with a manufacturer in New Jersey, who subcontracted part of the job to a factory in Pittsburgh. Suddenly, the toy inventors were manufacturers.

The concept tested so well that P&G gave the inventors a purchase order for the first 30,000 units.

Advice from the Pros

"Select your best five or six concepts for presentation. Do not come into a presentation with dozens of sketches that are not fully thought out."

—Jamie Filipeli, director of inventor relations, Mattel

"We make toothpaste, not toys," the brand manager told Levy when the inventor asked for a royalty deal. "If you want to see kids riding Fluoriders all over the country, you'll have to produce it for us."

The P&G executive outlined how much they could afford to pay for the product to be delivered to a Minnesota fulfillment warehouse; he could have cared less how much of that price went to the inventors. It was a bottom-line deal.

In 1982–83, the guys found themselves supplying Crest Fluoriders for what became a $12 million premium program. Their Crest Fluorider was sold nationwide through displays in more than 30,000 supermarkets and was promoted through a television spot. In addition, P&G distributed 100,000 Crest Fluorider coloring books to dentists. For this right, the inventors were paid a flat fee.

The nation's No. 1 brand of toothpaste used its Fluorider to increase shipment and share of its product through a box-top redemption program. The inventors had their first taste of the lucrative premium market and saw how they could apply toy-inventing skills to it.

Levy and Piaget did another ride-on program, the Jell-O Popcycle for General Foods. In this case, the trike, with its Puddin' Pop mainframe, was a so-called "dealer loader." After the program was over, the supermarket (the dealer) was allowed to keep the product, a $30 retail value. It was not sold to consumers. This was a less expensive way for General Foods to get a bang out of the product.

In 1984, Levy/Piaget created a patented inflatable that caught flying discs for Post Pebbles breakfast cereal, featuring Fred Flintstone. This was promoted to consumers through an FSI in Sunday newspapers. As in the aforementioned cases, the inventors handled the manufacture through a subcontractor.

Levy and his associate, Emily Kelly, did two in-pack programs for Ralston-Purina's Cookie-Crisp cereal, which required the inventors to arrange for production of two million fortune cookies each time, a small number, by cereal standards, but profitable for everyone. Levy's next premium was a gift-with-purchase plush dog for The Fashion Bug stores. It was also a win for all parties. This initiative required Levy and his associates to travel to Korea and supervise the line startup at a factory outside Seoul.

Fast Foods, Fast Money

Inventor Jim McCafferty, who created Manley's animatronic hit canine, Tekno, and X-Men Action Heads for Takara, has also been hugely successful creating premiums for the likes of Pepsi, Frito Lay, Taco Bell, 7-11, Pizza Hut, Arco, Subway, KFC, Dairy Queen, and dozens of other companies.

"The category is very challenging for the independent inventor because it is very marketing- and promotion-driven," says McCafferty. "Since we work in these promotional arenas, we are aware of a company's strategic positioning of its products, and invent to and are able to give them focused presentations for their needs.

McCafferty says there are lots of opportunities because so many companies want to attract attention to their brands without having to discount. Through premiums, a company can create a higher perceived value and do not have to compete on price. "Premiums are the best defense against having to rely solely on price," McCafferty says.

Some of McCafferty's most successful premiums have been interactive products, such as the Magic Straw and Morphing Cups he created for Pepsi to give the consumer a more novel experience with their products. Tens of millions of the two products have been sold.

While Levy had to manufacture the premiums he did in the 1980s and early 1990s, McCafferty says that today premiums are typically sold to the brand, which then has them manufactured. The manufacturer pays the royalty.

Advice from the Pros

"Practice is just as valuable as a sale. The sale will make you a living; the skill will make you a fortune."

—Jim Rohn, business philosopher

When not inventing toys, inventors Laureen and Maureen Trotto put their considerable creative and business talents to work creating premium programs for the likes of Pepsi Cola, Frito Lay, Pizza Hut, and KFC (as in, Lil Drum Stix: Munchin' to the beat of a different drum).

Paul Lapidus of NewFuntiers has had considerable success creating premiums. To license in this category, Lapidus says that low-cost manufacturing and high level of play value are crucial when designing premiums. Lapidus has been able to accomplish this in premiums for fast-food restaurants like Taco Bell, Hardee's, Carl's Jr., White Castle, Dairy Queen, Blimpie, Long John Silver, Church's Chicken, Sonic Restaurants, Ruby's, and Little Caesar's."

He continues, "If you can create a flexible design and then do variations, so much the better. I did this with Spinner Darts. It is a flexible plastic disk with five, six, or eight suction cups evenly spaced around its periphery. When thrown with a simple flick-of-the-wrist motion, the Spinner Darts will stick to any smooth surface. I have been able to use these safe darts in promotions with Denny's Restaurants, Post's Honeycomb Cereal, Coca Cola, Colgate, and the Discovery Zone. I have also been able to use this unique dart in toy products with Placo Products and Talicor, Inc. The darts have taken many forms over the years, and every promotion has been successful."

Toy Trivia

92. Which game was advertised as the first board game that glowed in the dark?

a. Green Ghost

b. 1313 Dead End Drive

c. Séance

Meal Time Is Play Time

Toys in fast-food restaurants today are as expected as order windows, double cheeses, and super-sizes. Countless times each day, youngsters tie food stops with other functions.

Toy licenses attract kiddy consumers to fast-food outlets just after indoor facilities, but ahead of the food fare. Toys have been inextricably tied to the sales of billions of burgers.

Happy Meals contain tasty morsels and the latest hot toy properties in miniature. When a program is in place usually for one month, happy burger eaters gobble up a bonus of 35 million to 50 million toys. Bigger promotions like Beanie Babies and Furby may reach 65 million levels and higher. Why go to TRU or Wal-Mart if you can get these playful *chotchkes* free with your fries?

The toy industry is in a state of flux. Inventors no longer rely 100 percent on toy companies as the sole outlets for their creativity. It is necessary to pursue new avenues for revenue streams, such as premiums. Toy companies no longer depend on the major retailers; they, too, need new outlets, such as drug store chains, supermarkets, theme parks, and booksellers. Starbucks is even selling games now. And the retailers no longer depend as much on toymakers. TRU is manufacturing much of its own products. Wal-Mart just opened a huge base of operations in Shenzhen, north of Hong Kong, through which it is dealing directly with the factories for open-market and custom goods. In other words, it's not just the inventors who have to change their business models. Everyone is reacting to the chain reaction started by the gatekeepers, the toll collectors between products and consumers, the mass-market retailers.

The reliance on entertainment licensing notwithstanding, the enterprise of independent toy and game development remains a target-rich environment for the most creative and entrepreneurial inventors. But as in any highly competitive arena, the elephants must keep up with the bandwagon.

If at first you do not succeed, redefine success. In some ways, there have never been greater opportunities for those to whom the elves whisper.

Advice from the Pros

"After you have some protection on your invention, tell *everyone* you know about it. I mean *everyone*—former and current neighbors, business associates, friends. Tell all your relatives. Don't forget your high school and college friends. Odds are that one of these people holds one of keys to success that you're looking for."

—Joanne Hayes-Rines, publisher, *Inventor's Digest*

Fun Facts

- Uneeda started making dolls during World War I, but it was not until the 1960's that it had a product take off big time; troll dolls.
- The French card game "Mille Bornes" translates to A Thousand Milestones.
- The earliest known playing cards can be traced to China, A.D. 969.
- Mancala is known as the national game of Africa.
- Backgammon is known in France as Trictrac.
- In every modern language, except English, checkers is known by some variant of dama (woman). It was once known as "chess for women."
- Cribbage was invented by Sir John Suckling (1609-1642). It was once spelled Cribbidge.

Chapter 12

Interactive Invention: Opportunities in Video Games

"Interactive entertainment provides a large challenge to independent inventors. Interactive entertainment is all about storytelling and puzzle solving. In this segment of technology games, it's the execution of the story that is more important than in traditional game inventing. In today's interactive market, companies invest $2–4 million just to develop a game and then another $3–5 million to advertise it.

"There are many ways to invent interactive toys and games using the PC as a multimedia tool. As technologies converge and ITV emerges, I see a major new growth market in interactive toys for ITV. Both of these markets are growth opportunities short and long term. Companies that are receptive to technology innovation are Leap Frog, Intel Toys, Mattel, V-Tech, and others."

—Tom Dusenberry, founder and former
CEO of Hasbro Interactive

You Want to Invent Video Games?

The creation and design of video games and other kinds of high-tech, interactive entertainment take skills and equipment far beyond what even the most prolific and successful toy and game inventors possess. When asked to describe the scene for independent inventors in the video game market, high-tech toy inventor Ralph Osterhout described it as "brutally difficult."

It's a Different World

The cryptic domain of video game design is inhabited by geeks who understand words like MUD connectors, Half Life, Quake level, milestone CD burns, and porting. Most write code. And they spend endless hours roaming worlds of simulated cities, villages, and fabled islands, running and gunning, battling fire-breathing dragons, morphing monsters, facing and delivering death and dismemberment, and pointing and clicking their way to a quest.

The purpose of this chapter is to give you some rudimentary background in video gaming and offer a feel for the business. Few inventors have successfully crossed over from the world of molded plastics to that of multimedia flash—and when it happened, it was typically enabled by a toy industry relationship.

If you control a license, perhaps based upon one of your own toys or games, there may well be interest in it as the basis for a video game. In this case, you would do the license deal and become a producer of the video game, not unlike writers who are fortunate enough to have their books translated into feature film or television fare. If you happen upon a whiz-bang technology that has video game application(s) and you know how to wheel and deal, as many pro toy and game inventors do, this is another avenue into this lucrative enterprise.

The surest route to a career as a game designer, in-house or independent, is to be young enough—in age, not just mind—and to enroll in a video game design course. Today you can earn an accredited Bachelor of Science degree in video game art and design at certain institutions. At the same time, you can intern at video game development houses. And, above all, you should play every game you can, starting with oldies like Galaxian, Centipede, Zaxxon, and Space Invaders, if possible.

Today the war for consumer dollars is between platforms like GameCube, Game Boy Advance, Xbox, and PlayStation 2. And bigger battles are on the horizon. Experts predict that the market for interactive entertainment will reach $49 billion worldwide. In 2002, video games were $10.3 billion vs. $9.4 billion in 2001, according to the TIA.

It Started with Baer Essentials

Ralph Baer knew he wanted to do more than become the Maytag repairman of malfunctioning TVs after using his electronics genius to fix fragile post World War II sets. After seeing all those dysfunctional television sets, Baer was ready to develop a higher-quality product or do something to expand the 40 million sets that had flooded American households at that time.

Born in Germany in 1922, Baer, who is Jewish, was ousted from school in 1936 after Hitler turned the country into a war machine in 1933. Two years later, at 16, Baer fled with his parents to the United States, where he eventually enrolled in a National Radio Institute correspondence course for radio and television repair. His first formal education did not come until after service in the U.S. Army in World War II, when he attended the American Television Institute of Technology in Chicago and earned a Bachelor's degree in Television Engineering.

In 1951, while designing and building a TV set at Loral in New York, Baer was the first to suggest incorporating a game into a TV set and as a gifted engineer, he had the skills to do more than suggest it. Baer went on to deliver on that "Eureka" moment in September 1966 with a 4-page proposal to make every one of 40 million U.S. home TV screens into a game display.

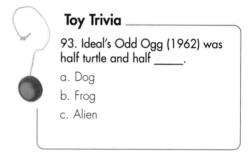

Toy Trivia

93. Ideal's Odd Ogg (1962) was half turtle and half _____.

a. Dog

b. Frog

c. Alien

Games? Yep. Baer's efforts led to the invention of the home video game in 1966. His first patent, filed in 1967, became the pioneer patent of the industry. Baer modestly describes his "real" job as an engineering manager at Sanders Associates, a defense contractor based in New Hampshire where he worked for more than 30 years starting in 1955, as "designing and developing hundreds of millions of dollars worth of military electronics, including radar test equipment and display systems for NASA." But it was his inventive genius that led to 100 patents worldwide and his induction into the American Computer Museum in 2002 as the "Father of Video Games."

From that 1966 event of playing video games on an ordinary TV set, other Baer designs ultimately turned into many of the entertainment features popular in video games today. Baer was the first to invent and design a TV target shooting game using a light gun in 1967. He was the first to create a two-player sports video game in 1967. In 1968, he demonstrated that a ballistic ball and paddle could be addictive. In 1969,

Baer had the first programmable home video game console which played multiple video games. In the early 1970s, Baer was the first to use video game cartridges, the first to couple video display with an audiotape player, first to demonstrate "Instant Replay" and the first to demonstrate interactivity between a TV and entertainment software. Though much of Baer's early work was done as a consultant to Coleco, Milton Bradley benefited most from his inventive genius.

In 1977, Baer began a prolific association with Marvin Glass and Associates, the Chicago-based toy design firm that made the correct read on the dawn of electronics in mass-market game play. Working closely with MGA partner Howard Morrison, Baer invented and Glass licensed electronic Simon to Milton Bradley. The popular tabletop game is still marketed by Hasbro 25 years later. Baer went on to thrive in the toy industry. From 1979 to 1981, he created a series of microprocessor-controlled, handheld games like Maniac (Ideal), Computer Perfection (Lakeside), and Amazatron (Coleco). In 1985, he did an electrooptical toy, Laser Command (Kenner). Then he went back to his TV roots in 1987 and created Smarty Bear Video (Galoob). This plush bear interacted with and talked to its friends on the TV screen while playing a VHS cassette containing a cartoon and nested data and voice.

Baer straddled sophisticated defense projects at Sanders/Lockheed and mass-market consumer electronics with toy and game companies. He was one of the first to see the Nintendo game system demonstrated before it was formally unveiled in the United States in 1985. "I knew Nintendo had something special. Something that could burst from the ashes of other early game systems and personal computers into the reborn gaming arena at the time," Baer recalls.

Advice from the Pros

"When you consider marketing a new product, it is a good idea to do a patent search, even if you do not intend to patent the concept. This lets you know if you are infringing an extant patent. Better to know before the expense of design and production than to find out later you have a partner."

—George Harvill, president, Greentree Information Services

Toy Trivia

94. King Zor (1962) was a fighting _____.
a. Gorilla
b. Cyborg
c. Dinosaur

Revolution

The most prophetic genius could not have looked into a crystal ball to foretell the feverish competition between Nintendo, Sony, Sega, and Microsoft. Most certainly, few could see that blips on a monochromatic television screen would lead to system software that delivers such high-resolution 3D graphics that it increasingly mirrors reality.

Today's video games are edgy, feverish, in-your face, finger-twitching, pulse-raising fun. They are big business. Grand Theft Auto 3 for PlayStation 2, from Rockstar Games, reportedly sold seven million copies in its first year. Add five million more units sold for original PlayStation.

Todd Zuniga, associate editor of the *Official U.S. PlayStation Magazine*, says, "GTA3 changed what games are, how we play them, and how we talk about them. It blurred the lines between games and cinema, and defined interactive entertainment's code of immortality."

Terry Donovan, COO/vice president of marketing for Rockstar Games, told the *Official U.S. PlayStation Magazine* about Vice City, "Try the word *epic*. Given the Rockstar philosophy, it's slightly more than a film now. A linear 120-minute film experience no longer, I feel, competes with a video game. I like going to the cinema, but it's not the same as a 100-hour video game." Clearly, producers now see the interactive software experience as comparable, if not superior, to a movie.

And so must the fans. In 2002, sales of video games and hardware outgrossed the $8.4 billion box office receipts for theatrical films. Video software sales alone are on pace to exceed box office sales, and the battle will be won by which medium produces the most blockbusters.

Sean McGowan, a long-time toy industry analyst at Gerard Klauer Mattison & Co., feels that video games keep improving because producers can do things that were before impossible. He says, "There is an attitude that you have to design and develop games that push the limits, or your competition will. And games do not seem to be price sensitive— at least, those titles in the top 30."

Indeed, the top 30 games enjoy incredibly rarified sales, considering the number being sold. Exciting print ads and websites fuel explosive sales. Video game zines are ready to

Advice from the Pros

"Do your homework and research on prospective companies for fertile ground before spending time and money developing concepts. Be aware of similar or comparable products in the category when you make your presentation. This will help if you have to explain your positioning of the concept and why it is important for the company to pursue."

—Richard J. Maddocks, lead designer of advanced development services, Hasbro

help consumers preview and rate hundreds of titles. To wit, an April 2002 magazine broadcast 900 games rated. By July, the number had risen to 1,000; by October, the list had expanded to 1,148 titles. By the time the November issue began circulation, 23 more games had been added. Apparently, there has not yet been a product glut.

Toy Trivia _____

95. Shaker Maker cast items out of _____.

a. Plaster of Paris

b. Alginate

c. Goop

Tom Dusenberry, the former founder and CEO of Hasbro Interactive, foresees a distribution problem looming. "The industry has too many game platforms to support. A retailer has to find shelf space for PC Games, PlayStation Games, PSII Games, Nintendo Game Boy Advance and GameCube, and Microsoft's Xbox. All this, plus the need for space for all the games, adds up to a log jam. We need to find a way to successfully use the retail store and Internet commerce cooperatively."

Video Games on Review and Preview

Marketers insert free demo disks into video game magazines, and publishers offer tips and secrets to ensure that mere mortal players can rise to the challenge, the mission, and the combat.

It is possible to browse the Internet for sample displays of many popular games. A visit to the websites of key producers gives a downloadable sampling of current or soon-to-be-released titles. Some include these:

www.capcom.com	www.acclaim.com
www.thq.com	www.eagames.com
www.activision.com	www.rockstargames.com
www.segasports.com	www.playstation.com

The industry even accommodates players who want to have a special advantage in their game-playing experience. Cheat prompts are posted on a number of sites, including these:

www.cheatcc.com

www.happypuppy.com

www.gouranga.com

The latest buzz and ratings of hot video games and industry news can be seen at this sampling of websites:

www.ign.com

www.avault.com

www.gamespot.com

www.gamedaily.com

Toy Inventors on Video Games

Inventor Sean Mullaney, of Bang Zoom, takes a dim view of video games, saying, "Video games suck the life out of people!" He has a simple remedy for the condition: "Buy one of our remote control vehicles and get outside."

Game inventor Charlie Phillips sees video games as a threat that traditional toy and game companies must deal with. Says the 30-year industry veteran, "Sales show that video games represent an explosive category, while traditional toy company growth has been comparatively modest in recent years." Phillips goes on to say, "Video game play is the cool thing to do when you are over 10 years of age. It has great appeal to kids in that it compresses time, presents a different place, and lets them play God. These games are a hot topic with kids."

Mullaney may be just promoting his R/C inventions with his observation. Or he may have seen the psychomotor effects on a solitary player mesmerized by images on a TV screen. Often the only moving parts on the player are hand digits depressing controller keys. Mulaney, licensor of more than 50 concepts, may also be subscribing to the long-held view that healthy play is a social activity among peers that, if done beyond the comforts of a sofa, offers the added benefits of physical exercise and fresh air.

Phil Orbanes, the head of Winning Moves, lived through Parker's early entry into electronics and cartridge-based games. He takes a more philosophical view of the current co-existence of traditional and video games. Orbanes feels that video games provide a good outlet for solitary play and teenage hormone release.

Advice from the Pros

"If your concept has a clever new twist on a mechanism ... a works-like model is always helpful in demonstrating the feature."

—Jamie Filipeli, director of inventor relations, Mattel

Traditional toys sales may be surviving, but at a more modest rate than the video game segment. An October 2, 2002, *Brand Week* report on toys quoted NPD's Funworld toy-tracking unit statistics that 2001 annual sales rose 1.7 percent, compared to a rise of 10 percent for video games (both hardware and software sales).

Toy Trivia

96. Small plastic molding sticks are melted and forced into molds to make figures that snap together in this activity toy.

a. Super Injector

b. Vac-U-Form

c. Shaker Maker

Doug Lowenstein, the president of the Interactive Digital Software Association (IDSA), spoke of the huge potential of this category in his opening remarks at the annual 2002 E3 trade show: "There's no doubt that video games are deeply imbedded in our society. It's clear that the industry's surging growth is no passing fancy and that the millions of Americans who played video games yesterday play them today, and will still be playing them tomorrow."

Someone Else's Dog Is in This Fight

Walk the aisles of Best Buy, Circuit City, or Electronics Boutique, and you will see many familiar toy brand facings. Monopoly. Risk. Tonka. Barbie. Matchbox. Hot Wheels. Upon closer inspection, however, it is not Mattel and Hasbro supplying their respective famous names. They out-license their brands to experienced software producers and bank a royalty on the conversion of their brands to game consoles and PCs.

Dusenberry had the foresight to convince Hasbro that its brands could be more than plastic parts and ink on board games. As the prime mover behind the launch and growth of Hasbro Interactive, he had this to say about the strategy of the fledgling software operation: "There was a three-pronged strategy to enter what I knew would burgeon into a white-hot market. First, we would take the well-known Hasbro brands from both toys (Tonka) and games (Parker and Bradley), and move quickly into interactive form. Second, we would seek out well-known former electronic game brands from Atari or the arcade business, such as Frogger. Third, we would create original content that we knew would be costly and time-consuming."

After four years, Hasbro sold this business segment to software producer Infogrames. Much of Dusenberry's product efforts remain alive under Infogrames' logo. His ventures into adding character and entertainment licenses to software also impacted many new titles at Infogrames. Dusenberry observes about the software business, "There has to be a commitment over the long haul as well as whether the short-term goal is growth or profits. There are a lot of producers today who will have to learn these lessons and make those choices."

Mattel took a somewhat similar approach to get into the market with an interactive line, by mining megabrands Barbie and Hot Wheels. The world's No. 1 toymaker took a giant step when it acquired The Learning Company as a strategy to hit fast with a growth vehicle to target children's programming. However, the venture turned highly unprofitable and drained billions. Mattel's management jettisoned its CEO and sold off TLC.

Today, the Barbie software shopper will see Barbie in playful interactive opportunities in Sparkling Ice Show, Pet Rescue, Princess Bride, and the Black Forest tale of Rapunzel, all from Vivendi Universal games. Matchbox Cross Town Heroes and Hot Wheels Velocity and Bash Arena are produced under license by THQ.

Advice from the Pros

"Designing great toys can be easy. However, designing great toys under industry parameters is a challenge. An important part of the toy design process can be summed up as B.P.P.: brainstorming, positioning, and presenting. Each aspect requires due diligence for successful concepts to get off the ground. In toy design, you don't have to 'reinvent the wheel,' but when you do, it's pure gold. Many times it's understanding familiar play patterns and adding a clever new twist."

—Martin Caveza, chair of toy design, Otis College of Art and Design

Fasten Your Seatbelts—This Ride Is Straight Up

Investment banker the Jefferies Company forecasts that the video game market, including PC games, will reach $21.4 billion in North America alone by 2005. If that number is reached, the video game industry will have grown 670 percent since the IDSA began tracking U.S. entertainment software sales in 1995. Then it was $3.2 billion. Only time will tell how much anticipated video growth will come at the expense of traditional toy and game sales.

Sean McGowan, the executive vice president and director of equity research at Gerard, Klauer, Mattison, sees three reasons for this growth potential:

1. Gamers from the old Atari and Coleco systems are still around and playing at 30–35 years old.

2. Segments who didn't play before, such as women, are playing now.

3. People are prepared to buy multiple platforms for their entertainment. If the Atari genre made it to 30 percent of the households then, the current new platforms will ultimately reach 45 percent or more of households.

An IDSA study of 1,500 households released in May 2002 cited specific reasons why video games have connected with a broad range of consumers. The survey found that people who play games do so because computer and video games …

1. Are fun (88 percent).

2. Are challenging (71 percent).

3. Can be played with friends and family (42 percent).

4. Offer a lot of entertainment for the price (36 percent).

5. Offer a way for players to keep up with the latest technology (19 percent).

This major IDSA finding also enumerated characteristics of players' ages, types of games, and number of games owned. Seventy-two percent of the console game players are male. Forty-five percent are under 18, 36 percent are 18 to 35, and 19 percent are over 36. Favorite types of console games are driving/racing games (39 percent), action games (38 percent), sports games (38 percent), and role-playing/adventure games (31 percent). Favorite types of computer games are puzzle/board/card games (35 percent), action games (28 percent), sports games (23 percent), and simulations (23 percent). According to the IDSA study, console gamers own an average of 14 games, while computer gamers own about 13 titles.

Interactive Digital Software
Association (IDSA)
1211 Connecticut Avenue, NW,
Suite 600
Washington, D.C. 20036
Tel: 202-833-4372
Website: www.idsa.com

Kitchen Research Supports the Big Study

Certainly less extensive and more casual than an IDSA survey was "kitchen research" conducted at Glenbrook Middle School in Longmeadow, Massachusetts, a short marble roll from Hasbro Games headquarters. Eighty-six seventh- and eighth-graders confirmed that the future is indeed bright for video games. Of these hip kids, 92 percent had some form of gaming system, the most popular being Game Boy, N-64, and PS2. The majority admitted to owning a range of 10–20 games and playing an average of 5–7 hours a week. Thirteen percent of the kids admitted to an obsessive 15 hours of video games per week.

When asked to identify the most popular titles, the kids listed Mario, Madden Football, and the overwhelming favorite, Grand Theft Auto. After those titles, there was no standout favorite, just a broad array of personal choices.

When asked about traditional games, the group was loyal to the giant game producer—and their neighbor—Hasbro. Monopoly was exceptionally strong with the group who cited Candy Land as their favorite when it was age appropriate. However, only a third reported playing board games with friends as frequently as once a week. When reviewing just the 40 eighth-graders (13-year-olds), only 14 percent acknowledged that they were playing board games with friends once a week. Apparently, as kids get older and more sophisticated, they are more into video games and play traditional games less with family and friends.

This small slice of casual research supports the views of gaming guru Michael Gray of Hasbro Games that there is room in kids' worlds for a diversity of games: "Video games are mostly played alone. Even when two players play a martial arts or car-racing game, the experience is not the same as playing a board game. More people are playing games today than ever: video games, computer games, Internet games, and board games. Board game playing offers a unique social experience and is different from other gaming experiences. There is room for different kinds of games. Board games will never be replaced. We need to keep making fun and compelling games that people enjoy—in cardboard, wood, or plastic—with or without electronics."

Nineteen-year toy-industry veteran Phil Jackson, vice president games and puzzle marketing, worldwide, for Mattel agrees with Gray saying, "We exist comfortably side-by-side with video games. Many consumers today are involved with both formats, choosing video for solo amusement and traditional for social interaction. Traditional games are just that, traditional. They have become part of family traditions, rites of passage, and cross many generational borders. Games are the best entertainment value there is, so they tend to be less affected by the latest trend in recreation."

Advice from the Pros

"In our experience at the Innovation Center, technical issues get lots and lots of attention, while market considerations are often an afterthought. The most successful product developers think about the market right from the start."

—Dr. Debra Malewicki, director of the Wisconsin Innovation Service Center, the University of Wisconsin–Whitewater

Toy Trivia

97. Chutes Away was a 1978 game introduction from _____.

a. Parker Brothers

b. Gabriel

c. Knickerbocker

Video Producers vs. Toy Inventors

In a market expected to sextuple in three to four years, one would think creativity would be welcomed, right? Wrong! In the global community of interactive game developers, cousins from the toy invention business are not widely embraced. The most apparent reason is the talent chasm between what it takes to be a video game developer vs. a toy developer.

Matthew Stibbe, the founder and former CEO of London-based Intelligent Games, observes: "I'm not sure it is possible for a wannabe with no specialized skills to crack the video game market. At IG, I used to get a couple of calls and letters a week from people who thought they could invent a video game but had no design, programming, or art skills at all. They wanted a big advance and a cut of the royalties for an idea on the back of an envelope. I still get one or two e-mails a month off my website asking for advice for people in the same situation."

Marc Segan, who has licensed over 100 toys and created and marketed many successful consumer electronic products, says, "To contribute in these areas may require skill sets that most inventors don't have and often cost a lot. In the video game area, if you're talking the games themselves, chances are, the main skill set in question is deal-making and coordination with studios, game designers/programmers, etc. These are not typical inventor skills."

Noah Falstein, president of The Inspiracy, an interactive design service studio, says, "I speak from my experience, which includes being the main person reviewing external submissions at LucasArts, 3DO, and Dreamworks Interactive. It's just not worth it to send in a concept or design for a video game unless you meet one of two criteria. First, if you have an established track record in the computer/video game industry, with successful titles, and have a team or at least the core of a team that can build the idea you're proposing, then you have a slim chance. Second, if you have a marketable license, like a very successful toy or board game or interactive rights to a successful TV show or movie, you may be able to get some interest."

Though he offers these key criteria for approaching video game producers, Falstein concludes, "In either of these cases, your chances remain very small. The vast majority of games are currently built by major publishers or their favored development groups using internal designers and concepts. Or they are created by independent developers who are self-funding or have a deal with a publisher, in which case they are almost certainly working on their own concept."

Mike Langieri was in charge of video development at Milton Bradley when brands like Scrabble, Operation, and Marble Madness were created for the Nintendo platform. His gaming experiences include association with RARE, Ltd., the Miami-based, high-profile software developer. He says of today's product needs, "I'm not sure video game giants are 100 percent ready to read scripts and pay out money for a clever idea or a theme. There are too many really good development companies set up like small movie studios with in-house artists, animators, game designers, musicians, and managers with experience taking a raw concept all the way to finished code. And in the video game business, it's all about getting the code turned over on time."

Langieri continues, "RARE, for example, has nearly 200 full-time staffers who not only have a track record of success, but also have a consumer following that knows their past games and eagerly await their new ones. Clearly, RARE is a very strong video game developer and knows what can and can't be done with hardware and software. On the other hand, the independent developer might have only a nice story line and no concept of how much RAM or ROM it will take to make the elephant fly, much less how to write code. The 'indie' has as much of a chance of selling a video game to a major producer as he or she has of selling a checker game to Hasbro Games."

Paul Lapidus, a toy agent, shies away from the video business. "Story boards alone aren't going to do it. The video business is after more than just themes. Video games today are so huge that they take multitiered development and complex game play that is beyond the skills of a single person," he observes.

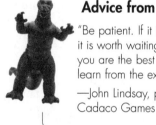

Advice from the Pros

"Be patient. If it is worth doing, it is worth waiting for. Remember, you are the best advocate, but learn from the experts."

—John Lindsay, president, Cadaco Games

Steve Meyer of Chicago-based Meyer/Glass Design recalls an early presentation to Bally-Midway. "I began showing story boards and was interrupted by the comment, 'We are not in the idea business. You have to program these boards to show us how this will work.'" Meyer went on to see the special talents required to create video games when he became vice president of development at Microprose. "You need a staff mix of 3D artists, computer programmers, sound technicians, and a producer to pull everything together. One game can cost $10 million dollars, take as long as 3 years, and involve 50–75 people. Video games can be very costly and very risky."

Playing in the Game

If you want to thrive on the creative side of video games, software engineering, animation programming, 3D rendering, or media and entertainment design are skill prerequisites. If you are starting a career in video or expanding on past creative capabilities, the International Game Developer Association (www.igda.org) is a good information source. For an annual membership fee of $100, IGDA members can immerse in the latest industry news.

The topical industry magazine *Game Developer* (www.gdmag.com) delivers current relevant editorial as well as ads for systems suppliers and educational programs vital to the skills of game developers. In fact, an expanded special issue of *Game Developer* is entitled "2002 Game Career Guide" and includes a directory of game design schools.

Maybe the Twain Shall Meet

Even using all the tips offered in this book to get through the door of a software producer, the viewer is looking for a multimedia extravaganza deliverable from a game console or PC. A prototype must take the medium to a new level and show that the inventor/developer can contribute key skills to the producer. Anything less would be as futile as saying "Hello, Hollywood! Do you want to buy my idea for a movie?"

Dan Klitsner of K.I.D. Group, and the creator of the Keytops line of Tonka Power Tools/Space Station/Construction and Raceway (Hasbro Interactive/Infogrames), says, "You can spend a lot of time searching for a producer who is inventor-friendly. There is no question that Keytops ended up at Hasbro Interactive because of Tom Dusenberry's previous involvement with toy inventors. But many studios are just not comfortable using the toy-inventing community."

Klitsner feels some inventors may be able to contribute to the interactive business with what he calls PC-enhanced toys. "This is a small category which I guess we invented with Keytops. We pitched prototypes complete with full software demos and programmed animation. It was more effort than any toy ever done at K.I.D. And this type of design is very different from console-based games where you have very little chance of selling a concept if you are not a software developer. Maybe when video extends into ancillary products, the interactive industry will be more receptive to inventors."

Matthew Stibbe personally designed LEGO Loco and SimIsle, among many other games for which he was the executive producer. He has seen the complexity of creative projects grow from 2 people working 9 months to as many as 40–50 people developing for 12–18 months or longer for A++ game development. The cost of this expanded commitment of time and staff has impacted risk and has caused producers to be more selective with new projects. The more selective the view is, the harder it has become for developers to place their ideas. Stibbe's highly informative game development views are found on his website, www.stibbe.net.

Though Stibbe sees consumers' continued attraction to the megaproductions, he proposes "a vibrant subculture of small games and teams" to expand developer opportunities. In October 2002, he told *Games Developer* magazine, "I would like so see every console equipped with some type of programming system. Microsoft could offer better support for games development in Visual Basic, and Sun could create a games SDK for Java. In addition, the open source movement could do more to embrace games. This would allow teams of individuals with the proper skill sets to work collaboratively to create large games." Stibbe continued, "My goal is to increase the number of developers making games and to make the work easier in order to increase the number and variety of games in production."

Advice from the Pros

"Don't let the dream of fame and fortune get in the way of good logical thinking and advice from friends and family. Don't be discouraged by failure. Let each lesson enable you to use that knowledge to im-prove your chances of success."

—Lawrence J. Udell, executive director, the California Invention Center

Toy Trivia

98. Which company introduced the Easy-Bake Oven in 1964?

a. Kenner

b. Remco

c. Ideal

Tom Sloper, a designer and producer of video games with major contributions to product lines while at Activision and Atari, offers practical advice to game developers who want to specialize in video games. Among his prerequisites, Sloper advises, "Get a college degree, play lots of games, and, if you want to make games, then where else should you be but in the game industry?"

The Inspiracy's Noah Falstein agrees that getting the skills to do game development is the best way to express video creativity. "There are so many people with good ideas already within the industry that it is quite difficult for someone to break in from the outside. On the other hand, the long and slow but more sure method of getting a job within the computer game industry and working your way up is the way most current successful games get made."

The video game creative community is truly global. The graphics and interactive game designs have become cross-cultural, and producers have made the game experience seamless regardless of the country of development origin. Creative groups are found in England, Scotland, the Czech Republic, Japan, the United States, and other corners of the globe.

Toy Trivia

99. Which toy inventor created the first disposable cell phone?

a. Randice-Lisa Altschul

b. Frank Young

c. Ron Magers

The community has a huge "net-link" that we have attempted to sample for you. No explanation of the video market would be meaningful without the interface with your computer, and we hope that you will check out some suggested websites. Take your own turns and clicks as you explore your interests in the business of game development.

Predictions from the Video Ball

We asked Tom Dusenberry to share his views of where the video side may be in the future. We suspect that these views foretell the future with a high degree of accuracy.

1. Online games will become huge. Players will be able to go head-to-head in real time. We will see tournaments, events, and spectator involvement. Games have always been fundamentally social interactive experiences, and online games will bring this asset to interactive entertainment. Currently, "Middle Age Era"–themed games are popular in massively multiplayer online games. Online games will emerge as a high-growth game market in the next three or four years.

   Authors' Note: In a January 2, 2003, *Dallas Morning News* article on the online playground, market research firm Datamonitor gave the online revenues as $670 million in 2002 growing to $2.9 billion in 2005. Gwen Marker of Sega corporate communications was quoted saying, "We've seen that gamers are very interested in online-console gaming, and if publishers and developers can deliver the right games online, we believe there is great opportunity".

2. Interactive entertainment will grow dramatically over the next five years. We will see online games explode. Wireless telephone games will be as natural to use as Game Boy. Interactive TV could be the biggest breakthrough in industry history. An installed base on interactive entertainment platforms will equal the current number of TV sets. The wireless phone will become the fourth medium after TV, movies, and the PC. This new wireless platform alone will expand content opportunities by way of a new delivery system.

411

On November 7, 2002, Lisa Byron reported in *Develop* magazine, "Nintendo's dominance in the handheld gaming market looks under serious threat following news this week that mobile phone giant Nokia is to roll out a new gaming device early next year. Clearly the greatest attack on the Game Boy format to date, the Nokia N-Gage phone/console looks rather similar to the Nintendo GBA, but features an attractive brushed metal finish and, of course, many more buttons for phone functions. Most significantly, Nokia has adopted the traditional games business model in terms of software for the device. Games titles will be available on solid state memory cards, affording retailers the opportunity to benefit from the introduction of this new format."

Authors' Note: *The Los Angeles Times* reported on January 26, 2003, that the "graying" of the video game market may be underway in Japan; currently a $4 billion market in 2002 but having experienced a downslide the past two years. The loss is reported to be attributed to the segment of kids 12 and under. However, the marketers see upside potential with players in their mid to late 20s where publishers are creating sequels to familiar titles.

3. We will experience technology convergence that will greatly improve the game-play experience. Game players will soon be able to play the same game on the video game machine, transfer the same game to a wireless phone, and then download the game to the PC to continue game play. To the gamer, this will all seem seamless and natural because each platform will have different advantages and disadvantages. This is just another example of multitasking.

4. The adult market will become the largest segment in interactive entertainment. The M mature rating has opened the door to aggressive violence and explicit sex. This will lead to technology advancements that can be applied to nonmature games. Mature games will also expand to consumers that the industry has not yet reached.

Toy Trivia

100. Merle Robbins, an Ohio barbershop owner, loved to play cards. In 1971, he came up with the idea for ____.

a. Phase 10

b. Old Maid

c. UNO

5. The stakes will be sky-high for developers and publishers. Games will cost the same as movies to create and produce. We will see $10–$20 million budgets, and games will take two and a half to three years to produce. The business will be similar to the movie industry; it will involve very franchised and hit-driven games. Games will need to deliver 5 million units to be in the top 10. We will see $500 million game franchises.

That's a Wrap!

So there you have it—some views of the video game segment of the toy and game industry. Ready to join the heat? Here are some tips:

- Buy the magazines, see the screen views, and read the reviews of current video games.
- Browse the producers' websites for glimpses of the sophisticated level of games.
- Want to play? Buy a system and go back to the previous points.
- Want to work? Reread the chapter. If you don't have the skills, get them. Or go back to playing.
- Whichever you choose, you will become interactive. Isn't everyone?

Fun Facts

- The game Battleship is also called Salvo.
- There are some 9,000 species of ants worldwide. Uncle Milton prefers red harvester ants (*pogonomyrmex californicus*) because they are great diggers.
- Before Milton Bradley Co. renamed it Twister, the game was called Pretzel.
- The liquid inside Mattel's Magic 8 Ball is a combination of water, blue dye, and propylene glycol.
- Balsa wood airplanes were very popular in the early 1940s. The world's largest producer of balsa wood is Ecuador. The word *balsa* is Spanish for *raft*.
- Jacks, also called jackstones, was probably derived from Pebble jackstones, a game still played in Europe and Asia. A metal jack has six points.

Appendix A

The Inventor Profiles

The following talents represent 80 of today's active full-time professional inventors. The list is based upon a consensus of senior R&D executives who were polled for their first-tier candidates. Having said this, we knew from the moment we decided to profile inventors that there was a risk of leaving out key people, along with many associates and partners who support the work of the inventors profiled. Indeed, many associates and partners whose names appear as parties to license agreements are not profiled. Nor did we profile creative sources for companies that are not based in the United States. It was hard enough contacting and, in some cases, chasing people to fill out our questionnaires here at home. In addition, we faced page-count limitations imposed by our publisher.

These profiles represent our best efforts to cull from the current aggregate creative body the full-time professionals upon whom the industry depends—inventors on corporate VIP lists and many names on R&D executive speed dialers.

In a few instances, those to whom we e-mailed questionnaires (a.k.a. IQ forms) opted not to participate or to not answer each question. If an inventor did not answer a specific question, we took that element out of the profile. This is why some profiles are shorter than others. Because of space restrictions, we were not able to run every question answered. We wish we had been able to include more, but, as with toys and games, there was a price point to be hit. A few answers were edited to fit space requirements, but, in such cases, we did our best not to change the meaning. It was more important to us that a profile reflect an inventor's personality than conform to an editorial style.

Some inventors not profiled are quoted within the text of the book. Several inventors are also agents. These folks wear two hats. It is not uncommon for inventors who enjoy unrestricted access to decision makers to represent or contribute to concepts brought in from nonprofessionals and, in some cases, other pros. They know no one has a lock on ideas.

Everyone profiled is a highly gifted, dues-paying member of the toy and game inventing community. You can feel it in the air as you read the profiles—an electricity. These people know how to turn ideas into hard cash. Their creative skills, which elude definition, could launch new companies; their creations, indeed, sustain many of today's industry giants.

These inventors are a resilient, dedicated, specialized group representing longevity in a demanding, roller-coaster, all-consuming, highly competitive business—the enterprise of new toy and game ideas. These inventors have been in the business an average of 26 years, of which 20 of those years have been inventing new toys and games. They represent a composite of more than 12 centuries of searching, perceiving, conceiving, and defining new playthings—the activity we have chosen to put under the umbrella of "inventing."

Throughout the responses is a shared view of the inventor as artist-orchestrator—a producer, if you will, more than a pure engineer or scientist/researcher. The pros understand this distinction.

The best toy and game inventors know how to bring talents to bear on their ideas—talents that complement their skills and get the job done. They also know how to bring talents to bear on ideas generated by others. In other words, they get the job done no matter who originates the idea.

These pros respond to unmet needs and ruthlessly apply solutions in very innovative ways. Their inventiveness ignites virtually anytime, anywhere. Clearly, toy and game inventing, like other demanding professions, is not a nine-to-five endeavor. Many inventors admit to creative sparks during a fitful sleep or a refreshing shower, or even while sunbathing *au naturel* on an isolated tropical beach.

We present these profiles as an inspiration to aspiring inventors. They were written by industry professionals who have earned through firsthand experiences their roles as sages and soothsayers. Read their words and discover the keys to their unique powers of creativity and imagination. Read their words and see how these trailblazing elves electrify and transform their profession again and again.

Randi Altschul
Dieceland
Cliffside Park, New Jersey
No. of years in the industry: 18
No. of years as an independent: 18
Approximate number of products licensed: 200+
No. of patents held: 12 (14 pending)
No. of trademarks held: 15

In a typical year:
No. of ideas conceived: 50+
No. of concepts prototyped: 5–10
No. of concepts presented: 50+
No. of concepts licensed: 5–10
No. of products that make it to market: 5–10

Most successful products: Miami Vice: The Game (Pepperlane Industries), Simpson's Game (Cardinal), Turbo Fist and Racing Fist (Tonka), Color Blaster Fast Blast (Kenner). Most anticipated around the world is PHONE-CARD-PHONE (Dieceland Technologies Corp. with North American distribution by General Electric).

What did you do before you were in the industry? Martial arts.

What makes a great toy? Something that stimulates your imagination.

What makes a great game? Something that makes you think and want to get to the next step, like a good book that makes you want to turn the page. When you enjoy it, you always win, no matter who is the overall winner.

An inventor is ... creative, can think out of the box, and figure out what the market is missing and satisfy that need.

Who or what inspired you to become an inventor? I have been inventing things most of my life, but I think the most inspirational aspect of what I do is the freedom to be able to think for a living.

What sparks original ideas? I think most ideas come about from necessity or seeing a gap in the marketplace. In this way, though the idea is original, it really satisfies a need that you may not have thought you had. It could be a creative or imaginative need, or a simple need for entertainment that stimulates.

Advice to would-be inventors: Never let anyone deter you from your dreams. My company motto is and will always be "Conceive It, Believe It, Achieve It!" Just make it happen because no one will do it for you.

Alan Amron
Amron Development, Inc.
Syosset, New York

No. of years in the industry: 30
No. of years as an independent: 30
Approximate number of products licensed: 16
No. of patents held: 28
No. of trademarks held: 2

In a typical year:
No. of ideas conceived: 10
No. of concepts prototyped: 3
No. of concepts presented: 8
No. of concepts licensed: 1
No. of products that make it to market: 1

Most successful products: The battery-operated water guns by Larami, Entertech, LJN, Buddy L, Empire Of Carolina, Coleco and Playtime/Tyco. Air Pressurized One-Pump water guns licensed to Remco and Mattel/Arco Toys. The PhotoWallet CompactFlash digital images pocket-size player to Nikon Camera. Silly Willy Bubbles/sprinkler lawn toy, to Fisher-Price Quick-Fill Air Pressurized STORM water guns, Selective pressurization of utilizing the pressure from your municipal water supply and/or hand pump on board, to Trendmasters Toys.

What did you do before you were in the industry? Hollywood personal manager for Kristy McNichol, Jimmy McNichol, and Robert Guilliame, among others.

What makes a great toy? Low cost, high play value, and novelty and uniqueness.

What makes a great game? Play value and uniqueness.

An inventor is … an innovator and creator.

Who or what inspired you to become an inventor? Satisfaction that I have to come up with things people really love and never saw before. Novelty and unique things.

What sparks original ideas? Needs and wants mostly.

Advice to would-be inventors: Invent-protect-license and do it often.

Hank Atkins
Atkins Associates
West Hartford, Connecticut

No. of years in the industry: 31
No. of years as an independent: 31
Approximate number of products licensed: 23
No. of patents held: 0
No. of trademarks held: 0

In a typical year:
No. of ideas conceived: 40
No. of concepts prototyped: 12
No. of concepts presented: 10
No. of concepts licensed: 1
No. of products that make it to market: 1

Most successful products: Razzle (Parker Brothers), Scrabble Up (Milton Bradley), Roadside Rescue (Binary Arts), Fit to a Tee (Binary Arts), Shove-Off (Ideal).

What did you do before you were in the industry? Invented unrelated products without much success.

What makes a great toy? Sturdy, educational

What makes a great game? Fun! You want to play it again. Not too deep, so it does not embarrass a player.

An inventor is … a person always on the lookout for a new concept; persistent in the search for ideas; excited about the concept he is working on; happy that he's in the business of bringing new ideas to life, even if the odds are against selling them; and confident that sooner or later a company will surprise him and say, "We want to go to contract."

Who or what inspired you to become an inventor? When I was a kid, my parents were aware that I loved to build things. They bought me blocks, Lincoln Logs, an Erector Set, and Tinker Toys. I played with these toys for hours. Luckily in those days, I didn't have the distraction of TV and video and computer games, so I was forced to rely on my own devices to entertain myself.

What sparks original ideas? An original idea can come from many sources, but generally I've had to sit down with idea-generating material and consciously work at it. Those materials can include old and new game catalogs and catalogs of general household items that can spark an idea even though, in the end, there is no relationship to what I started out with.

I've done several animal games that were the result of staring at a set of plastic animals. Puppy Pals from Fisher-Price (2002) came about in this manner. I was trying to think of a game play that would give each player a chance to adopt a dog. I tried different approaches and finally came up with the player having to acquire the cards that showed the items (Frisbie, tennis ball, old shoe, etc.) that a dog required its owner to have before it could be adopted.

Advice to would-be inventors: Do it only because you enjoy the creative process. Do many inventions because, like any kind of selling, it's a "law of average" business. For the same reason, try not to get too emotionally invested in any one idea, but have faith in your ability to create "valid" ideas whether you sell them or not. Keep your day job and try to work on things that don't require a large financial investment.

Ralph Baer
R. H. Baer Consultants
Manchester, New Hampshire
No. of years in the industry: 36
No. of years as an independent: 27
Approximate number of products licensed: 50
No. of patents held: 50 U.S. and 100 worldwide
No. of trademarks held: Zip

In a typical year:
No. of ideas conceived: 50+
No. of concepts prototyped: 30+
No. of concepts presented: 15
No. of concepts licensed: 1 if I am lucky
No. of products that make it to market: 1 if I am lucky

Most successful products: I am the father of the video game business. I invented home video games in 1966 and supported worldwide licensees and litigation, which netted $100 million to Sanders and Magnavox (and the lawyers). I did okay. I was inducted into the American Computer Museum in the fall of 2002 as the Father of Video Games.

Working with Howard Morrison at Marvin Glass and Associates in 1977 in my position as their outside electronics capability, we invented and licensed Electronic Simon to Milton Bradley. It's still on the shelves to this day.

What did you do before you were in the industry? I designed, developed, and put into production (over a period of 30 years) hundreds of millions of dollars' worth of military electronics such as radar test equipment and display systems for NASA. I ran a large division at Sanders Associates, later Lockheed. I was their first Engineering Fellow (1973).

What makes a great toy? One that wakes up the somnambulant wise guys at Hasbro or Mattel who have all the answers but rarely display a little vision.

What makes a great game? Any game you can get by the nay-sayers (our dear customers). But it had better be intuitively playable (like Simon).

An inventor is ... a creative person who had better become a good marketer and negotiator, or he'll wind up getting screwed by his prospective clients.

Who or what inspired you to become an inventor? I'm an EE and an ME (by osmosis), and inventing was handed down to me in my genes by some long-since-dead ancestor. Thank you, whoever you are!

What sparks original ideas? Working on one thing that suggests another. Discussing ideas with associates that lead to unforeseen Eurekas. Looking for an application for some new, low-cost piece of electronic hardware that opens up novel product opportunities.

Advice to would-be inventors: Go get a job! Seriously, if you have that inventing urge real bad, then go for it!

Stephen C. Beck
Berkeley, California

No. of years in the industry: 26
No. of years as an independent: 26
Approximate number of products licensed: 400+
No. of patents held: 12
No. of trademarks held: 10

In a typical year:

No. of ideas conceived: Hundreds
No. of concepts prototyped: 12
No. of concepts presented: 12
No. of concepts licensed: 3–10
No. of products that make it to market: 2–3 (Career: 400+)

Most successful products: My most successful toys and games: Talking Wrinkles (Coleco)*, Pocket Arcade (Sega), Star Wars Electronic Battle Game (Kenner)*, Astrology Computer (Coleco)*, Strobe (Lakeside)*, Melody Madness (GAF)*, VideoShooter (Takara), Nine to 5 Typing (Epyx video game), and Tapper, Up'n'Down, Congo Bongo (Sega video games). (* = in partnership with Eddy Goldfarb)

What did you do before you were in the industry? I invented video synthesizers and created video art for PBS-TV and museums of modern art.

What makes a great toy? Fun to play, sparks imagination in play, makes you smile.

What makes a great game? Fun to play, challenges brain power, keeps you awake, is compelling.

An inventor is ... a person who never gives up, works long hours, enjoys new ideas, sees opportunities where others don't see anything, and is clever and persistent.

Who or what inspired you to become an inventor? My father, who is a structural engineer. My mother, who is innovative. And a partnership with Eddy Goldfarb, who is a gentleman and inventor genius.

What sparks original ideas? Swimming, dreaming, observing, necessity, and lightening striking.

Advice to would-be inventors: Never give up! It takes 100 concepts to get 1 good one.

Sandy Beram
Sandy Beram: Inventor/Writer
Yonkers, New York

No. of years in the industry: 10 (started on April Fool's Day, 1993)
No. of years as an independent: 10
Approximate number of products licensed: 18 (all puzzles)
No. of patents held: 0
No. of trademarks held: 0

In a typical year:
No. of ideas conceived: About 60
No. of concepts prototyped: About 50
No. of concepts presented: All
No. of concepts licensed: 2–3
No. of products that make it to market: 0–3

Most successful products: Search for Small Stuff, Mystery Match (Ceaco); Little People Puppet Puzzles (F-P); Detective Puzzlebee, Smoosh & Squish Puzzles, Clingee Thingee (Hasbro Games).

What did you do before you were in the industry? College professor, author of two books, travel writer.

What makes a great toy? Simple, fun, and encourages repetitive play.

What makes a great game? Easy to learn but challenging to play and master; doesn't become boring.

An inventor is ... someone who is naturally inclined to see what isn't there and fill in the holes in the Swiss cheese. It's someone who is programmed to pounce on possible ideas from anywhere or anything when it "appears."

What sparks original ideas? Anything and everything: museum exhibits, books of all kinds (I once got an idea from the phone book!), conversations, dreams, art work, and so forth.

Advice to would-be inventors: You are bound to have many items rejected, no matter how good you are. After a while, you get used to it. It's part of the game. If you can't handle that, this isn't the business for you. The thrill of every "yes" makes it worth it for me.

Andrew Bergman
Bergman Design Consortium, Inc.
Mountain Lakes, New Jersey
No. of years in the industry: 31
No. of years as an independent: 20
Approximate number of products licensed: 110
No. of patents held: 15
No. of trademarks held: 0

In a typical year:
No. of ideas conceived: 50–100
No. of concepts prototyped: 50
No. of concepts presented: 100
No. of concepts licensed: 12
No. of products that make it to market: 6

Most successful products: Fisher-Price Sesame Street Club House (as F-P in-house designer); PXL-2000 camera (Fisher-Price); Deceptor/Deceiver R/C (Nikko)—Jason Lee, inventor; Super Rebound R/C (Tyco)—Jason Lee, inventor.

What did you do before you were in the industry? I worked for Buckminster Fuller and Goldsmith.

What makes a great toy? Long-term play value and minimal curve.

What makes a great game? Same as above.

An inventor is … a person able to see things in unique way; very knowledgeable as to what has been done, able to communicate ideas visually, aware of child development, and knowledgeable of socioeconomic trends.

Who or what inspired you to become an inventor? The love of work and enjoyable relationships.

What sparks original ideas? Starting with a very regimented and analytical approach, and then letting it go off where it might.

Advice to would-be inventors: View every experience as a learning experience, in terms of both people and products. Don't get hung up on single ideas—keep generating new ones, and do not take rejection as an indication of a bad job on your part. Accept the fact that this is a fashion and fickle business.

Andrew Berton
Excel Development Group
Minneapolis, Minnesota
No. of years in the industry: 17
No. of years as an independent: 17
Approximate number of products licensed: 50
No. of patents held: 2
No. of trademarks held: 12

In a typical year:
No. of ideas conceived: 40
No. of concepts prototyped: 30
No. of concepts presented: 140
No. of concepts licensed: 15
No. of products that make it to market: 15

Most successful products: 1313 Dead End Drive (Hasbro Games), Wacky Water Tunnel (Larami), Battle Cry (Tiger), Up for Grabs (Tyco), Spellbinder (Mattel), Splat!Doh (Hasbro).

What did you do before you were in the industry? Recording executive, CPA.

What makes a great toy? Simplicity. Fun.

What makes a great game? Simplicity. Fun. A short, thought-provoking play pattern.

An inventor is ... the lifeblood of the toy industry.

Who or what inspired you to become an inventor? Having my first game rejected by a major New Zealand company.

What sparks original ideas? Lateral thinking—utilizing clever nontoy mechanisms in a whimsical fashion.

Advice to would-be inventors: Try the licensing route. Don't self-manufacture and leave your current job!

Richard Blank
R&R Licensing, Ltd.
New York, New York

No. of years in the toy industry: 41
No. of years as an independent: 29
Approximate number of products licensed: 100 as inventor and/or agent

In a typical year:

No. of ideas conceived: 10
No. of concepts prototyped: 4
No. of concepts presented: 4–8
No. of concepts licensed: 2
No. of products that make it to market: 0–2

Most successful products: Lightning Strike Balls (Kid Power), Joke Teller (Basic Fun), Funny Face Books (Random House/Blaze), Animal Cracker Books (Simon and Schuster), Pocket Comics (Next 2), The Wedding Game (Avalon Hill).

What did you do before you were in the industry? Grew up in the industry starting as an actor in commercials at age 3.

What makes a good toy? Something that has high play value with novel features.

What makes a good game? Stimulating and fun, with repeat play value.

An inventor is ... someone who recognizes a new creation and extends the perseverance and perspiration to make the creation reality.

Who or what inspired you most to become an inventor? My father, David Blank, owner of an ad agency doing toy advertising.

What sparks an original idea? The inner self connecting with the outside world and environment.

Advice to would-be inventors: Don't try to own 100 percent of nothing. Seek out advice from successful and experienced people, including agents and attorneys.

Judith H. Blau
J. Hope Designs, Ltd.; Judith H. Blau, Inc.
Eastchester, New York
No. of years in the industry: 27
No. of years as an independent: 27
Approximate number of products licensed: 50
No. of patents held: 18
No. of trademarks held: 30

In a typical year:
No. of ideas conceived: 200
No. of concepts prototyped: 15 models, 20 story boards
No. of concepts presented: 100
No. of concepts licensed: 1–3
No. of products that make it to market: 1–3

Most successful products: Sweetie Pops (Hasbro), Foot Lights (Mattel), Baby All Gone (Kenner), Baby Check Up (Kenner), Baby's First Hair Cut (Mattel).

What did you do before you were in the industry? Painted and exhibited art work, wrote and illustrated children's books, designed product for apparel and home-furnishing industries (adult and juvenile products).

What makes a great toy? A toy that is interactive and is the springboard for hours of a child's imaginative play. A toy conceived with the recognition that a child is your partner. A toy that evokes laughter and magic. A toy that can entertain and educate.

What makes a great game? A game that is always a challenge and combines the need for the right balance of luck and strategy.

An inventor is ... a person who has found a way to tap into his or her own "inner child" and creates products that stimulate the imagination using fun, humor, and fantasy as tools.

Who or what inspired you to become an inventor? Although I entered the toy industry due to a fortunate chance meeting with Greg Hyman and Larry Greenberg, I had been creating stories, art, and dolls since childhood. I spent many of my early years isolated and in bed with an illness that caused me to find ways to entertain myself and engage my sister and brothers to play with me. A unique and supportive mom and a story-telling grandfather were my inspirations. Being in business began when I was eight years old; my mom put my bed on the sidewalk outside our house in the Bronx, and I sold my handmade yarn dolls and pastel drawings for a nickel each.

What sparks original ideas? Everything feeds the creative process. Stimulation comes from my own fantasy world, verbal expressions, trends, music, movies, and observation of children at play and their current interests.

Advice to would-be inventors: Respect and try to understand kids, know what's in the marketplace, believe in your concepts, keep your sense of humor, don't take yourself too seriously, be flexible, and never give up. Be able to handle rejection. Work within the context of what's out there, but don't be afraid to create something new and outrageous. Then forget everything and have a good time in the playground of your mind.

Michael Bowling
Pound Puppies, Inc.; Michael Bowling Enterprises
Fernandina Beach, Florida

No. of years in the industry: 21
No. of years as an independent: 16
Approximate number of products licensed: 12
No. of patents held: 12
No. of trademarks held: Hundreds

In a typical year:
No. of ideas conceived: 20
No. of concepts prototyped: 15
No. of concepts presented: 15
No. of concepts licensed: 1
No. of products that make it to market: 1

Most successful products: Pound Puppies (Tonka/Galoob/Jakks Pacific), Lost 'n Founds (Galoob), Bow Wow Boutique (Galoob).

What did you do before you were in the industry? Factory worker.

What makes a great toy? Simple concept with good play pattern.

An inventor is ... someone who knows how to take an idea and see it through to creation.

Who or what inspired you to become an inventor? The desire to do something that I enjoyed doing each day of my life.

What sparks original ideas? Seeing something that sparks an idea to create something to fill a need.

Advice to would-be inventors: You do not have to know how to do everything to create something. As an example, I knew what Pound Puppies should be although I am not an artist or a seamstress. You can hire that talent to create your idea.

Brendan Boyle
IDEO, Skyline Studio
Palo Alto, California

No. of years in the industry: 11
No. of years as an independent: 11
Approximate number of products licensed: 125
No. of patents held: 3
No. of trademarks held: 0

In a typical year:
No. of ideas conceived: Thousands
No. of concepts prototyped: 100–200
No. of concepts presented: Hundreds
No. of concepts licensed: 5–10
No. of products that make it to market: 5–10

Most successful products: Jeep Aftershock (Fisher-Price), Fib Finder (Pressman), Are You for Real? (Hasbro), Max Trax Altitude Rocker (Estes), IntellGear (Meade), Aerobie Football (Superflight), FingerBlaster (Kidpower).

What did you do before you were in the industry? Designed all sorts of things, such as luggage, computer equipment, bike products, and furniture.

What makes a great toy? At the heart of every great toy is the ability to delight kids (and kids at heart).

What makes a great game? The best games keep people laughing. We can calibrate whether it's going to be a great game by what we call the "giggle factor."

An inventor is ... someone who turns observations into inspirations, and then transforms inspirations into ideas.

Who or what inspired you to become and inventor? As a kid, I loved to take things apart (and not put them back together). This is a crazy industry; one sort of discovers it as you're going along. Great feedback from a few really good inventor liaison folks. Other inventors—Paul Rago, David Small, and Elliot Rudell—showed me their operations when I was just starting; that was incredibly inspiring and really generous.

What sparks original ideas? The power of people brainstorming. It's such a great idea maker. Find an awesome group of people and go wild.

Advice to would-be inventors: It's a long road to making a career. Get really good at listening when people say "no" to a concept. The feedback they give can turn the idea into something perfect for someone else.

Jeffrey Breslow
Breslow, Morrision, Terzian & Associates
Chicago, Illinois

No. of years in the industry: 36
No. of years as an independent: 36
Approximate number of products licensed: Hundreds
No. of patents held: Many
No. of trademarks held: Many

In a typical year:

No. of ideas conceived: 800
No. of concepts prototyped: 150
No. of concepts presented: 150
No. of concepts licensed: 40
No. of products that make it to market: 30–40

Most successful products: (since 1990) Trump: The Game, Guesstures, Planet Hollywood: The Game (Hasbro Games); Talkin'Bubba, Barbie's Walking Beauty Horse, Hot Wheels Criss Cross Crash/Volcano Blowout/Fireball, Uno Attack, My Size Barbie (Mattel).

What did you do before you were in the industry? Industrial design student.

An inventor is ... someone who creates something out of something that already exists, who puts together in a new form familiar objects that in this new combination create the "Ahhh" factor—as in, "Ahhh, why didn't I think of that?"

Who or what inspired you to become an inventor? Marvin Glass.

What sparks original ideas? The spark for new ideas always comes from interaction with other people. I never wake up in the middle of the night with an idea. The spark always comes when you are looking for it. You must be ready for opportunity and constantly be alert for ideas.

Advice to would-be inventors: Keep playing with toys and never grow up.

Garry Donner
Random Games & Toys
Ann Arbor, Michigan

No. of years in the industry: 31
No. of years as an independent: 19
Approximate number of products licensed: 100
No. of patents held: 3
No. of trademarks held: 0

In a typical year:
No. of ideas conceived: 50
No. of concepts prototyped: 40
No. of concepts presented: 40
No. of concepts licensed: 4
No. of products that make it to market: 3

Most successful products: Pocket Trivia (Hoyle), Travel Memory (Milton Bradley/Hasbro Games), Phase 10 Dice (Fundex), Don't Go to Jail (Parker/Hasbro Games), Tumblin' Monkeys (Mattel/Tomy UK), Hit The Deck (Fundex), Monster Stomp (Aristoplay).

What did you do before you were in the industry? Data systems supervisor and programmer.

What makes a great toy? It must be engaging, simple, and obvious as to what it does for the child. It must be fun in its repetition.

What makes a great game? It must be engaging, with simple rules but a complexity in play that never allows full mastery. Its basic premise must be understood by the new player in just a few seconds, and it must look like fun and then *be* fun.

An inventor … loves life and curiously explores it, dreams out loud so that others may participate, and strikes a great balance between persistence and practicality.

Who or what inspired you to become an inventor? I always loved to play games as a child; then as an adult I began coming up with my own. There is great satisfaction in making a game or toy work.

What sparks original ideas? Sometimes a trip to the bathroom after a 90-minute brainstorming session. Everything I see in life passes through the game/toy side of my brain.

Advice to would-be inventors: Don't quit your day job until you have serious income. I kept my day job for 12 years, quit with a sizeable toy bankroll, and then barely made it. For ideas, go to the toy and game departments in the stores, and keep going regularly until you are no longer overwhelmed. Pick toy and game areas that interest you; then learn to look at what's on the shelf with an eye to what is missing. Then make what is missing.

Ron Dubren
Ron Dubren & Associates
New York, New York
No. of years in the industry: 23
No. of years as an independent: 23
Approximate number of products licensed: 50–75
No. of patents held: 2
No. of trademarks held: 0

In a typical year:
No. of ideas conceived: 25–50
No. of concepts prototyped: 10–20
No. of concepts presented: 25–50
No. of concepts licensed: 0–8
No. of products that make it to market: 0–5

Most successful products: Tickle Me Elmo (with Greg Hyman).

What did you do before you were in the industry? Research scientist, Ph.D. in psychology.

What makes a great toy? Solitary fun with lots of repeat play value.

What makes a great game? Social fun with lots of repeat play value.

An inventor is … someone who loves the creative process and problem solving.

Who or what inspired you to become an inventor? Scrabble. I realized that someone actually invents toys and games, and I started to noodle around.

What sparks original ideas? An active awareness of the world around me.

Advice to would-be inventors: Have a nest egg and persist.

Julius Ellman (and sons Steven and Fred)
Lernell Company, LLC
New York, New York
No. of years in the industry: Julius, 54; Steven, 44; Fred, 34
No. of years as an independent: Same
Approximate number of products licensed: 100+
In a typical year:
No. of ideas conceived: About 70
No. of concepts prototyped: 20–25
No. of concepts presented: 20–25
No. of concepts licensed: 4–5
No. of products that make it to market: 3–5

Most successful products: Mr. Potato Head (Hasbro); Operation Brain Surgery (Hasbro Games); Tickle Toes (Hasbro Games); Rumblin' Thunder R/C (Tonka); Hush Lil Baby (DSI); Magic Mealtime Baby (Toy Biz); Mouse, Mouse Get Outta My House (Pressman); Hot Foot Racers (Matchbox); Wild Stick Flyers (Galoob); Wild Webber (Parker).

What did you do before you were in the industry? *Steven:* Having grown up in a "toy family," I can't recall a time before toys. I think Julius passed the toy gene on to Fred and me.

What makes a great toy? *Julius:* First, one that gets to market! It should have fresh, exciting, and fun play features. It should be producible at a practical price. It should be easily demonstrable on a commercial and on packaging. *Steven:* Stimulates fantasy, fun, and curiosity. Has one central theme. Keep the intention of the concept clear. Add embellishments only when necessary.

Who or what inspired you to become an inventor? *Steven:* My father and mother inspired me most. Being a child growing up in a house filled with Julie and George's latest creations was exciting, fun, and thought-provoking. My mom, being an excellent artist, inspired me to express myself.

What sparks original ideas? *Julius:* Anything! *Steven:* Using both eyes. That is, one eye on reality, the other on fantasy.

Mary D. Ellroy
GameBird, LLC
Norwalk, Connecticut
No. of years in the industry: 13
No. of years as an independent: 13
Approximate number of products licensed: 14
No. of patents held: 1
No. of trademarks held: 0

In a typical year:
No. of ideas conceived: 30
No. of concepts prototyped: 8–20
No. of concepts presented: 30
No. of concepts licensed: No typical year; 2001–2002 was great, with at least 6 licensed for 2003.
No. of products that make it to market: 90 percent

Most successful products: Great States (International Playthings).

What did you do before you were in the industry? Marketing director at a Fortune 500 company; vice president at a newspaper rep firm startup, media advertising.

What makes a great toy? Something engaging. Maybe you learn while doing it and get better at it the more you play it. Fun! Licenses come and go. A good toy has staying power. Perhaps it also evinces emotion. A doll or a bear that you *have* to hug. I personally prefer mechanical, nonelectronic toys.

What makes a great game? I personally never liked Monopoly, although it has staying power. A good game gets people laughing throughout playing time. It allows creativity (Pictionary). There shouldn't be "dead time" while one player contemplates a move. (I know, people *love* chess ….)

An inventor is … someone who loves to make things up.

Who or what inspired you to become an inventor? I initiated and developed a touch-sensitive interactive video project when I worked for a large telecommunications firm. It got $1 million in funding and international notice. My boss said I was creative. Honestly, I had no clue and had never been called that before. It was as if a light bulb went off in my head.

What sparks original ideas? I've been trying to answer that for years. Usually you see something or hear something in the world around you, and you tweak it to make it a toy idea. Or there is something that already exists, and you figure out how to make it better, cheaper, with more bells and whistles.

Other times you know a certain license is hot or hot-to-be, and you force an idea to the license. Some very strange things can be fitted to a license. (Example—and this is not my idea—Elmer's Glue for Harry Potter. The glue nozzle was the nostril of a gnome. When you squeezed the glue bottle, it looked like mucus coming out his nose.)

Advice to would-be inventors: Get an understanding of the markets you'll be dealing with. Subscribe to the trade journals and join associations. Network. Go to trade shows. Get an agent at first. *Listen* to the toy companies when they critique your ideas. Don't *ever* say "Every kid in the neighborhood said they would buy this if it came out." Understand whom you are inventing for. (*Quiz:* Whom are you inventing for? *Answer:* The retailer.)

Norman Fabricant and Arlene Fabricant
New York, New York

No. of years in the industry: Norman, 33; Arlene, 21
No. of years as an independent: Norman, 33; Arlene, 21
Approximate number of products licensed: 115+

In a typical year:

No. of ideas conceived: 100+
No. of concepts prototyped or rendered: 50
No. of concepts presented: 6–8 per meeting
No. of concepts licensed (in our best year, 1986): 14

No. of products that make it to market (in our career, to date): 70+ (We have licensed at least one item every year. We would always work until that was accomplished.)

Most successful products: Wrist Rattles (Fisher-Price), Foot Jingles (Playskool), Grow to Pro Basketball (Fisher-Price), Dr. Drill 'n' Fill (Playskool), Ready, Steady Ride-On (Fisher-Price).

What did you do before you were in the industry? Norman, engineer; Arlene, teacher.

Steven Fink
Bang Zoom Design, Ltd.
Cincinnati, Ohio

No. of years in the industry: 8
No. of years as an independent: 4
Approximate number of products licensed: 25 (since 2000)
No. of patents held: 17

Most successful products: X-Treme Cycle R/C (Tyco/Mattel), Jacknife R/C (Tyco/Mattel), Super Scooter Shannen (Mattel).

What did you do before you were in the industry? College.

What makes a great toy? A great toy should hold a child's attention for at least two weeks (past the point of no "return" to the store!). Many great toys are fun to watch—even when other kids are playing with them. Most great toys have a magical feature that makes them different from anything else on the market. Oh yeah, I almost forgot—it must be *fun!*

What makes a great game? A great game should have a level of excitement and challenge that will make someone want to play with it over and over. Bop It! is a great example of this. There are also great games that become personalized and unique with each new game—Scrabble is the best example.

An inventor is ... someone who takes into consideration every aspect of the business to create a unique product.

Who or what inspired you to become an inventor? After working on the manufacturing side, I realized that the only way I could contribute to every toy category (dolls, games, vehicles, etc.) was to be an inventor.

What sparks original ideas? First, you should immerse yourself in everything relating to the business—be well versed in old toys, new toys, trends, successes, failures, cartoons, games, etc. Then let your mind be open to anything and everything—but use all of your knowledge as a filter to find that strong, original idea.

Advice to would-be inventors: Get a job on the manufacturing side, and do not leave until you completely understand the product-development process. Once you do this, you can make a better decision whether to become a full-time inventor or keep your day job!

David Fuhrer
Funanuf
Los Angeles, California

No. of years in the industry: 15
No. of years as an independent: 15
Approximate number of products licensed: 150
No. of patents held: 5
No. of trademarks held: 0

In a typical year:
No. of ideas conceived: 80–100
No. of concepts prototyped: 30–35
No. of concepts presented: 80–100
No. of concepts licensed: 12–15
No. of products that make it to market: 8–10

Most successful products: Vortex footballs (Hasbro), Laser FX (Spin Master), BackWords (Random House), Love to Dance Bear (Mattel), Bounce Around Tigger (Mattel), Monkey Dance Boots (Mattel) .

What did you do before you were in the industry? Hollywood talent agent. Part of a group that represented many celebrities, including Bruce Willis, Tina Turner, Brad Pitt, and Christine Lahti.

What makes a great toy? Safe, durable, age-appropriate, and endlessly captures a child's fascination.

What makes a great game? Great interactivity, desire to repeat play, laughter and excitement.

An inventor is … someone who has the ability to execute marketable new ideas by fulfilling the business requirements and the desires of the end consumer.

Who or what inspired you to become an inventor? Growing up in a family that loved to play.

What sparks original ideas? Collaboration with creative people; keeping a heightened awareness of the world around you, such as new trends, technologies, and materials; and frequent communication with client companies.

Advice to would-be inventors: Collaborate with others if they can strengthen your product. Don't be so close to your idea that you can't listen to others. Know when to move on to another idea. Have deep enough pockets to withstand lean years. Stay positive. Be friendly with the Fed Ex and UPS guys/gals.

Robert B. Fuhrer
Nextoy
New York, New York

No. of years in the industry: 26
No. of years as an independent: 22
Approximate number of products licensed: 100+

In a typical year:
No. of ideas conceived: 100+ (includes represented products)
No. of concepts prototyped: 30
No. of concepts presented: 50
No. of concepts licensed: 6–10
No. of products that make it to market: 4–7

Most successful products: Crocodile Dentist (Milton Bradley), Gator Golf (Milton Bradley), Fishin' Around (Hasbro Games), T.H.I.N.G.S. (Milton Bradley), Dragonfly R/C (Toymax), Equalizer R/C Stunt Vehicle (Jakks), Motorized Batcycle (Kenner), Tub Tints (Equity Marketing)

What did you do before you were in the industry? Student. However, I virtually grew up attached to the toy industry because my father, Len Fuhrer, worked for Matchbox, Topper, and Damon, the parent company of Estes Rockets, Hi-Flier kites, and Arrow handicrafts.

What makes a great toy? I prefer simplicity that has a great depth of sustained play value and remains fun through multiple play.

What makes a great game? It is not necessary for a game to be all strategy or all luck, or even to be "fun." The important part of the game is its quality to entertain and amuse the mind consistently.

An inventor is ... an imaginative person who has the ability to be pragmatic in business issues as well as creatively. An inventor should have the capacity to execute the concept or assemble the resources to do so. The successful inventor should ideally be an optimistic forward-thinker with an attitude to react positively to constructive criticism.

Who or what inspired you to become an inventor? I have always had an aptitude for entrepreneurship, with an appreciation for the creative spirit.

What sparks original ideas? Ideas emerge and get triggered from all sorts of places. It could be from a use of language or a play on words that could give an idea for a name of a product first, or simply just combining nouns and allowing the mind to imagine what could be.

Advice to would-be inventors: Educate yourself about the industry. Be patient, tenacious, practical, and determined. Pursue your ideas because you believe in them absolutely, not because you will get rich from them. Persevere!

Derek Gable
West Coast Innovations
Rancho Palos Verdes, California

No. of years in the industry: 36
No. of years as an independent: 19
Approximate number of products licensed: 70
No. of patents held: 50+
No. of trademarks held: 6

In a typical year:

No. of ideas conceived: 60
No. of concepts prototyped: 20
No. of concepts presented: 50
No. of concepts licensed: 3–4
No. of products that make it to market: 2–3

Most successful products: Buzz Saw Masters of the Universe male action figure (Mattel), Computer Warriors male action-figure line (Mattel), Basket Blaster (Cap Toys), Monster Mash Play-Doh (Playskool), Silly Dillies (Milton Bradley), Little Sporties (Tomy America), Robot Play-Doh (Playskool), Sew Easy (Playskool), Go Go Worms (Milton Bradley), Big Top Sort 'n Pop (Mattel).

What did you do before you were in the industry? Development engineer working on spy jet aircraft engines for Rolls-Royce. Worked on mechanical/electrical robots for auto industry. Developed projectors (slide, movie, and overhead). Invented machines to make chocolates for Cadbury.

What makes a great toy? Fun. Absorbing. Wide appeal. Holds your interest. Value. Other factors depend upon target audience.

What makes a great game? Must get players emotionally involved. Satisfying outcome. Uncomplicated rules. Good pace of play.

An inventor is ... somebody who needs a day job. A dreamer. A lucky person who can always stay busy. Someone with a passion for what he or she does.

Who or what inspired you to become an inventor? It has always been in my blood. I have been inventing and building my own toys since the age of eight.

What sparks original ideas? An attitude and perspective on the world around you; seeing beyond the obvious. Looking for ways to improve everything you see. Looking for needs. It's part training, part gift.

Advice to would-be inventors: Don't do it for a living, but rather as a hobby that can make you a lot of money (or not!). Do it for the love of it, not for the money. Think of it as going to Las Vegas with your time. If you go to Vegas to make money, two things happen: First, you don't, and second, you have a lousy time. If you go for the fun of it, you'll have a great time, and once in a while a load of money will come your way (maybe!). Keep it in perspective, and you'll have a lifetime interest that will always keep you interested and happy. Oh yes, and keep your day job.

A. Eddy Goldfarb
Eddy & Martin Goldfarb & Associates
Northridge, California

No. of years in the industry: 56
No. of years as an independent: As long as I can remember
Approximate number of products licensed: About 800
No. of patents held: About 300
No. of trademarks held: Some

In a typical year:
No. of ideas conceived: A lot
No. of concepts prototyped: A lot
No. of concepts presented: A lot
No. of concepts licensed: A little
No. of products that make it to market: Varies

Most successful products: Stompers (Schaper), Yakity-Yak Teeth (H. Fishlove), Busy Biddy (Topic Toys), Quiz Whiz (Coleco), Baby Beans (Mattel), Vacuum Form (Mattel), Kerplunk (Ideal/Mattel), Battling Tops (Ideal), Giant Bubble Gun (Cap Toys).

What did you do before you were in the industry? Inventor, sailor (U.S. Navy).

What makes a great toy? For the inventor, it's a short love affair with an idea. For the manufacturer, it's high volume and no returns. For the consumer, it's children's word of mouth.

What makes a great game? How many millions have played with it and enjoyed the game.

An inventor is ... someone who is in another world.

Who or what inspired you to become an inventor? (I was very young.) My dad, who worked in the clothing industry, proudly brought home an inventor as a dinner guest. I have no idea what he invented—it was long ago. Maybe it was the button.

What sparks original ideas? Bills. These help, but it could be anything we encounter in our daily lives.

Advice to would-be inventors: Do some homework. Even if they are not interested, make a good impression with your presentation. Make them remember you.

Martin Goldfarb
Eddy & Martin Goldfarb and Associates
Northridge, California
No. of years in the industry: 23
No. of years as an independent: 23

Most successful products: Shark Attack (Hasbro), LEGO Creator Game (LEGO), LEGO Racers (LEGO).

What makes a great toy? It's fun!

What makes a great game? You want to play it again and again.

Who or what inspired you to become an inventor? My pop, of course!

Tina Goldkind
Swirl Design
Holbrook, New York
No. of years in the industry: 6
No. of years as an independent: 4
No. of patents held: 2
No. of trademarks held: 4

In a typical year:
No. of ideas conceived: Tons
No. of concepts prototyped: 20–30
No. of concepts presented: Toys, 60; Candy, 20
No. of concepts licensed: 7
No. of products that make it to market: 3

Most successful products: E-baton (Kid Power), Bungee Bunny (Best Sweet), Handcuffs (Best Sweet), Toy Jeans (Toy Jeans), Magna-Pop (Hasbro/Cap).

What did you do before you were in the industry? School. BFA in Toy Design from Fashion Institute of Technology; BA in Biology from SUNY Stony Brook.

What makes a great toy? A great toy causes me to react like, "Oh, my gosh, I have to have that! I have to touch it. I have to play!"

What makes a great game? A challenge.

An inventor is ... anyone who interprets the world through his or her own eyes, and uses the heart and mind to react to it and create new ideas.

Who or what inspired you to become an inventor? Jim Henson—I love the excerpt from his book *The Works* on pages 240–241. My concepts teacher, Maureen Trotto (of Thin Air)—her 10 commandments of toy design is hanging next to my desk. All the other inventors (Cathy Veness, Elliot Rudell, Richard Levy, Robert Fuhrer, Andy Kislevitz, and Betty Morris) who took time out of their busy schedules to be at one time or another a friend and mentor to me and answer all my hundreds of questions!

What sparks original ideas? The world around me, the people with whom I interact, and my family.

Advice to would-be inventors: Go for your dreams. Start and end each day smiling. Laugh hard, cry hard, and at the end of the day, let it all go and start again fresh. Let your experiences re-invent you. Or just do as my father says: Throw enough stuff up against a wall, and something is bound to stick!

Bill Goodman
Bill Goodman Consulting
Portland, Maine
No. of years in the industry: 11
No. of years as an independent: 5.5
Approximate number of products licensed: 10
No. of patents held: 2
No. of trademarks held: 0

In a typical year:
No. of ideas conceived: 10
No. of concepts prototyped: 3
No. of concepts presented: 12
No. of concepts licensed: 2
No. of products that make it to market: 1

Most successful products: Puppy/Kitty Magic (ToyBiz), Baby I Know (ToyBiz).

What did you do before you were in the industry? Industrial electronics products.

What makes a great toy? Fun. Value. Surprise. If you can pack those three things into a product, you have pushed yourself on all levels. Finding ways to create value that allows the end users to afford the product, love using the product, and be surprised by it each time they play with it.

What makes a great game? Challenge. To be challenged every time the game is played.

An inventor is ... a creative businessperson who believes he or she can make life a better, more interesting place through experiences with new products.

Who or what inspired you to become an inventor? My father.

What sparks original ideas? Exposure to new cultures, products, technology, and ways of thinking about a problem give me the boost to develop a solution that fits a market need.

Advice to would-be inventors: Be patient. Pick your partners carefully. Know that everything takes longer than you think. Consume information.

Rick Gurolnick
NeoToy
Chicago, Illinois
(*Note:* Rick Gurolnick is at NeoToy's main office in Chicago. Bob Knetzger—see separate inventor profile—is in Seattle. Although they have been inventing toys together for almost 20 years, they have never worked in the same location.)
No. of years in the industry: 22
No. of years as an independent: 24
Approximate number of products licensed: At least 50
No. of patents held: 2
No. of trademarks held: Several

In a typical year:
No. of ideas conceived: 200
No. of concepts prototyped: 40
No. of concepts presented: 40
No. of concepts licensed: 2
No. of products that make it to market: 1 (Many "fall out of bed" right before Toy Fair.)

Most successful products: Cradlebath (Gerry)—the first sink-mounted baby bathtub; Doctor Dreadful (Tyco)—established the gross food category.

What did you do before you were in the industry? College. I graduated from Arizona State in 1978 as an industrial designer and founded NeoToy with Bob Knetzger in 1982.

What makes a great toy? Cleverness, simplicity, and good execution.

What makes a great game? It engages me and makes me want to play again and again. Gimme "one more potato chip ...."

An inventor is ... tenacious—each a good street fighter in his or her own way.

Who or what inspired you to become an inventor? (1) My father's engineering mind, love of science, and the factories he took me to as a child. (2) Chicago's Museum of Science and Industry. (3) The creative Jack Kirby's drawings for Marvel Comics in the 1960s.

Advice to would-be inventors: Get your real-estate license or learn how to weld.

David Hampton
Sounds Amazing!
Grass Valley, California
No. of years in the industry: 20
No. of years as an independent: 14
Approximate number of products licensed: 6
No. of patents held: 5
No. of trademarks held: 0

In a typical year:
No. of ideas conceived: 8
No. of concepts prototyped: 4
No. of concepts presented: 2
No. of concepts licensed: 2
No. of products that make it to market: 1 (every other year)

Most successful products: Furby (Tiger/Hasbro), Furby Baby (Tiger/Hasbro), Yoda (Tiger/Hasbro), Shelby (Tiger/Hasbro).

What did you do before you were in the industry? Test engineer, software engineer, systems engineer in various electronic industries.

What makes a great toy? First of all, fun. Second, it fills a human need. Nonviolent. Good value, low cost. Allows discovery of "hidden" features, depending on attention of user.

What makes a great game? Logic games: Simple to learn. Quick to learn. Various levels of play, depending upon age group. Difficult to master. Group Games: Quick to learn. Lots of talking, laughing, not too serious. Not too intellectual, so everyone can play. Not too competitive, so you can keep your friends!

An inventor is ... a jack of many trades and a master of at least one. Someone who doesn't take himself or his ideas too seriously. Looks at "failure" as a way of learning what's the next step. Willing to take large risks without getting suicidal. Has an ego big enough to move forward, but not so big as to trip over it.

Who or what inspired you to become an inventor? As a child: 7–14. Tom Swift (fictional 19-year-old inventor), Nicola Tesla (still my hero), and Thomas Edison, although later in life I became disillusioned with him.

What sparks original ideas? Doing something different. (1) Visit Star Trek Experience. (2) Go to a trade show outside your area of expertise. (3) Find water and listen. Go to the beach, river, or, in a pinch, a shower. (4) Watch and listen to a good hard rain with lots of thunder and lightening. (5) Look at common everyday problems all around you; imagine a solution. (6) Play word games.

Advice to would-be inventors: Learn to trust your gut. Love your idea enough to give you energy, but not enough to become blind. Learn to stick to it; you must finish. Be careful of advice from well-meaning friends. If it's not fun, find another job. Ten percent of something is better than 100 percent of nothing.

Clemens V. Hedeen Jr. and Kay Lee Hedeen
Fun City USA
Sturgeon Bay, Wisconsin
No. of years in the industry: 21
No. of years as an independent: 21
Approximate number of products licensed: 100+
No. of patents held: Less than 24
No. of trademarks held: less than 20

In a typical year:
No. of ideas conceived: About 500
No. of concepts prototyped: About 60
No. of concepts presented: About 60
No. of concepts licensed: Up to 15
No. of products that make it to market: Up to 12

Most successful products: MicroMachines (Galoob/Hasbro), Nerf Sharp Shooter (Hasbro).

What did you do before you were in the industry? Trial attorney; district attorney; real-estate developer, including condominiums and five-star time-share properties in Wisconsin.

What makes a great toy? If kids enjoy the time they spend playing with a toy, that's a great toy.

What makes a great game? When people want to play it again and again and get repeat pleasure.

An inventor is ... someone who thinks out of the box, doesn't take "no" for an answer, persists despite repeated rejection, and can see things the average person doesn't see.

Who or what inspired you to become an inventor? Another toy inventor encouraged me to try toy inventing.

What sparks original ideas? Anything and everything.

Advice to would-be inventors: Don't give up.

Brian Hersch
Hersch & Co.
Los Angeles, California
No. of years in the industry: 18
No. of years as an independent: 18
Approximate number of products licensed: 35
No. of patents held: Approx. 6
No. of trademarks held: 20+

In a typical year:
No. of ideas conceived: 4–5
No. of concepts prototyped: 3
No. of concepts presented: 3
No. of concepts licensed: 1–2
No. of products that make it to market: 1–2

Most successful products: Taboo (Milton Bradley); Outburst (Western Publishing, Parker Brothers); Oodles (Milton Bradley); SongBurts (Games Gang); Hilarium (Mattel); Disneyland Game (Parker Brothers); Mad Chatter (Western Publishing); ScrutiEyes (Mattel); Bed Basketball (Cap); Top 10 (Ravensburger); Arguile (Games Gang); LA Law (Galoob); American Monopoly (Milton Bradley); InCahoots (Really

Useful Games); EyeCons (GamePlan); Platinum editions of Taboo, Outburst, and Scattergories (Milton Bradley); Nameburst (Western Publishing); Super Scattergories CD-ROM (Hasbro Interactive); Malarkey (Parker Brothers).

What did you do before you were in the industry? Commercial real-estate development.

What makes a great toy? I won't presume to comment. It is really outside my area.

What makes a great game? I'm too long-winded to give you a short answer. Nonetheless, I will certainly try to respond, but I am going to limit my comments to the specific area of social-interaction games, since that is the primary area in which I work.

Social-interaction games are really lubrication for rusty social skills. They are a facilitator of interpersonal fun. Too many people have forgotten how to access the common bonds they have with the people they spend time with. But whether you are drawing pictures (Pictionary), filling in lists (Outburst), or acting out clues (Guesstures), the result is always a shared experience. And if it is done well, there is laughter and shared recollections as part of the experience. A good game accesses people's commonalities in a convivial manner.

The play experience has to be carefully balanced. Too easy can equate to boring. Too challenging can equate to intimidation. Yet "simple" seems to lie at the core of almost every great game in this arena. Can we provide a simple experience that will bring a smile to those involved for an hour or so? Can we create an entertainment that will work in someone's living room in Des Moines when we are not there to force the fun and smiles personally? Games remain one of the last great participatory entertainments. It isn't about watching; it's about playing.

Beyond the underlying simplicity of theme and compelling play-pattern are all the little details that differentiate a professional inventor from a creative guy with a random cleverness. Everyone looks at the modern painting that is all white with a red circle in the corner (and sold for $4 million) and immediately says, "I could have done that." Same thing with a great game. But the creation of pace, timing, attitude, tactile components, perceived value, cost engineering, and underlying originality are all the hallmarks of great professional inventors.

An inventor is ... (a) a masochist. (b) Someone with the gift of creative spark coupled with a wide field of vision. Writers have that creative spark and narrow their focus into a specific skill area. Same thing with musicians, painters, etc. Similarly, inventors engage themselves in the never-ending quest to see what they can create that is unique and exciting and new.

Who or what inspired you to become an inventor? The opportunity to engage both the right and left sides of my brain in my daily pursuits. As a businessman, I primarily utilized the rational and logical training I had pursued. The opportunity to utilize my natural inclinations toward observation and creation was exciting and fresh. Basically, I recognized a niche, did the correct business exercise and commissioned a market research report about the field, utilized my observational and analytic abilities, and recognized an opportunity. They say, "Opportunity knocks. It's just that most people don't recognize it because it is usually disguised as hard work." I found the opportunity to work hard and prosper in the process. What could be more fulfilling?

What sparks original ideas? As the axiom says, it varies widely from inspiration to perspiration. Sometimes the slightest, most unrelated subject, detail, or passing thought can be harnessed and ridden to completion. Other times it is the concerted effort to "be creative" at will. Almost anything can spark an original idea.

Advice to would-be inventors: This may be the toughest question. Passion is a wonderful thing. It can help you soar with glee. It can also be the death of you. If someone has an absolute passion for toys and games, and has the gift of creativity and inventiveness, then they should not hesitate to be in our business. But, like acting, be prepared to struggle. Stardom is rare, and the riches enjoyed by the luckiest of stars are the exception, not the rule. If your passion outweighs logic and needs, jump in. If you have second thoughts and think of toy and game inventing as a lark, then take a breath and consider whether there are other areas where your passions might be greater and your talents might be equally suited. Oddly, toy and game inventing is not for the weak. Be prepared for insufficiently appreciative licensees, deadlines, failures, idea-creep (theft!), and worse. And if you still are not deterred, well, welcome to the club.

David L. Hoyt
Hoyt & Associates
Chicago, Illinois

No. of years in the industry: 10
No. of years as an independent: 10
Approximate number of products licensed: About 30
No. of patents held: 5
No. of trademarks held: 20

In a typical year:
No. of ideas conceived: 50
No. of concepts prototyped: 20
No. of concepts presented: 20
No. of concepts licensed: 4
No. of products that make it to market: 3

Most successful products: Jumble Plus (Cadaco), Pyramix (Tiger), TV Guide: The Game (Hasbro), NBA Interactive TV Card Game (Mattel), Split (Hasbro), Wild Card (Cadaco), Brainz (Educational Insights), Jumble Crosswords (Tribune Media), Boggle Brain Busters (Hasbro/Tribune Media).

What did you do before you were in the industry? Options trader on floor of Chicago Board Options Exchange.

What makes a great toy? A great toy can create a whole new world in the mind of a child (or adult, for that matter). In my opinion, it's not the actual toy that matters, but rather what's going on in a child's mind as a result of playing with the toy. If a toy creates pure joy in the mind of a child, then it's a good toy. If a toy allows the child to use imagination to create a whole new world in the mind, it's a good toy. If a toy allows a child to feel accomplishment, then it's a good toy.

What makes a great game? In my opinion, a great game is one in which the player truly cares about winning. The more the player wants to win, then usually the better the game is (to the player). Now, of course, all people are different and some people don't care as much about competition as others, but as a whole, most people want to win when they play a game. If they try as hard as they can to win, then they will most likely be playing a game that they truly enjoy and one that would qualify as a good game (to them).

An inventor is ... a person with the desire to play a role in shaping the future. Almost everything we have was "invented." Inventors play a necessary role in converting knowledge into new products. As time goes by, humans learn more and more with each day. Inventors take all that information and knowledge and channel it into the creation of new products and concepts. Not everyone has the ability to do this. Inventors think in a way that allows them to believe that anything is possible.

Who or what inspired you to become an inventor? Actually, no one inspired me to become an inventor—at least, no one I can think of. I can, however, give some credit where credit is due and tell you who inspired me to continue being a game inventor in my early days of inventing. Ron Weingartner of Milton Bradley/Hasbro certainly played an important role in my early career. It was the way in which Ron turned me down that kept me coming back. I showed him things for years before placing a product with Milton Bradley (TV Guide: The Game). Ron saw potential and made it very clear that I was on the right track. I truly believe that had Ron (and a few others) not been as encouraging in the early years of my inventing career, I might have given up on games and toys. He encouraged me in many ways throughout those tough years, and for that he'll always be appreciated.

What sparks an original idea? I'm not sure I have a simple answer for this one. I have gotten good ideas in many different situations, and I'm not 100 percent certain that there was a common spark. The mind of an inventor runs differently, in that his or her mind has a "program" running in the background that, from time to time, will create an original idea.

Advice to would-be inventors: Don't give up. An inventor is most likely going to hear "no" for a long time before even hearing "maybe." It's all a process. An inventor must go through the process of becoming a good inventor. It will take time, and inventors must be patient and not look at "no" as a sign of failure. As long as "no" is accompanied by reasons why the toy or game is being passed on, then the inventor will gain valuable knowledge that can be applied to future inventions. A good inventor should listen very carefully to the reasons why an item is being passed on. Ego must be thrown out during this process. A good inventor should be smart enough to see "no" as an opportunity to improve as an inventor, not as a sign of failure.

Greg Hyman
Greg Hyman Associates
Parkland, Florida
No. of years in the industry: 29
No. of years as an independent: 29
Approximate number of products licensed: 88+
No. of patents held: 17
No. of trademarks held: 2

In a typical year:
No. of ideas conceived: 30–60
No. of concepts prototyped: 10–30
No. of concepts presented: 10–100
No. of concepts licensed: 0–10
No. of products that make it to market: 0–9

Most successful products: Tickle Me Elmo (Tyco/F-P), Electronic Talking Barney (Hasbro), Baby All Gone (Kenner), Alphie the Robot (Playskool), Major Morgan, The Electronic Organ (Playskool).

What did you do before you were in the industry? EE TV production.

What makes a great toy? Me.

What makes a great game? Not me.

An inventor is ... someone who takes Thomas Edison's quote to heart: "Invention is 1 percent inspiration and 99 percent perspiration."

Who or what inspired you to become an inventor? Alexander Graham Bell, Thomas Edison, George Washington Carver, and Guglieimo Marconi.

What sparks original ideas? With me it could be anything ....

Advice to would-be inventors: I would have been a much younger man today if I hadn't gone into this business. But I would not have had as much fun or gained so many good friends as a result of being part of it.

Stephanie Janis
Stephanie Janis, Inc.
New York, New York

No. of years in the industry: 17
No. of years as an independent: 15
Approximate number of products licensed: Never really counted

In a typical year:

No. of ideas conceived: 250
No. of concepts prototyped: 20
No. of concepts presented: 30
No. of concepts licensed: 4
No. of products that make it to market: 1–2 (if lucky)

Most successful products: P. J. Sparkles (Mattel), Water Pets (Playskool), Bundles of Babies (Cap Toys), Topsy Tail (Tyco), Tattoodles (Mattel), Girl Talk (Milton Bradley), Sweet Faith (DSI), Too Cute Twins (DSI).

What did you do before you were in the industry? Display and package design.

What makes a great toy? Play value, long after you retire.

What makes a great game? Wanting to win, repeat play, strategy, and theme.

An inventor is ... a person who dreams.

Who or what inspired you to become an inventor? The challenge beyond just the package the product is in.

What sparks original ideas? It's a ping in your gut (we're talking about an original idea.)

Advice to would-be inventors: Ride the wave.

Bob Jeffway
Robert Jeffway Jr., LLC
South Deerfield, Massachusetts
No. of years in the industry: 26
No. of years as an independent: 21
Approximate number of products licensed: 65
No. of patents held: 12
No. of trademarks held: 1

In a typical year:
No. of ideas conceived: 120
No. of concepts prototyped: 35
No. of concepts presented: 35
No. of concepts licensed: 5
No. of products that make it to market: 3

Most successful products: Baby Loves to Talk (ToyBiz), Tyco Talking Doll House (Tyco), UCSS Speech Technology (Hasbro), Air Trigger (SRM), Kick 'n Splash Cabbage Patch (Mattel), Diva Starz (Mattel).

What did you do before you were in the industry? Worked for a computer company.

What makes a great toy? Simplicity. Something that allows the use of fantasy to emulate a part of real life.

What makes a great game? Don't know. I'm not into playing games.

An inventor is … someone who knows how to connect the dots. Much invention is the clever bringing together of several pre-existing things.

What sparks original ideas? The desire to solve a yet unsolved problem.

Advice to would-be inventors: In order to succeed, you have to wake up every morning with a burning desire to succeed at it. It has to be the sole reason for your existence. If that is the case, then the only way you can fail is to give up too soon.

Larry Jones
California R&D
Westlake Village, California

No. of years in the industry: 42
No. of years as an independent: 34
Approximate number of products licensed: 350+
No. of patents held: 124+
No. of trademarks held: 100+

In a typical year:
No. of ideas conceived: 500+
No. of concepts prototyped: 30+
No. of concepts presented: 300+
No. of concepts licensed: 10–20
No. of products that make it to market: 5–10

Most successful products: Cricket Doll (Playmates), Micronauts (Mego, partners with Takara), Data Race (Mattel/Tyco).

What did you do before you were in the industry? Industrial designer, commercial artist.

What makes a great toy? The creative hook that makes you keep coming back.

What makes a great game? One that lets you "almost" win every time.

An inventor is … someone who creates "novel" items (at least, he thinks they are novel).

Who or what inspired you to become an inventor? Money. Later I learned better.

What sparks original ideas? Attend one of my seminars, and I'll tell you. Actually, it is so simple: relationships. One thought relates to another, all equaling new ideas.

Advice to would-be inventors: Big-time advice is to "play" over 99 percent of the time. Mark Twain used to say that "in all of [his] vast experience, [he has] never seen one shred of evidence anywhere that supports the notion that life is serious!" Live by that one, and you will be extremely successful.

Ed Kaplan
Ed Kaplan Associates
Ft. Lee, New Jersey; Boca Raton, Florida
No. of years in the industry: 46
No. of years as an independent: 22
Approximate number of products licensed: 38
No. of patents held: 2
No. of trademarks held: 8

In a typical year:
No. of ideas conceived: 85–100
No. of concepts prototyped: 28
No. of concepts presented: 50
No. of concepts licensed: 4–6
No. of products that make it to market: 3–5

Most successful products: Doodle Bear (Tyco/Mattel), Puppy (Kitty, Bunny, etc.) Surprise (Hasbro), Crystal Princess (Playskool), Baby's First Doll (Eden).

What did you do before you were in the industry? College, U.S. Army.

What makes a great toy? One that sells itself.

What makes a great game? One that sells itself.

An inventor is ... creative, intuitive, and very independent and courageous.

Who or what inspired you to become an inventor? Wanting to work on what I believed, as opposed to what was assigned to me.

What sparks original ideas? Seeing different things and finding an application to toys; watching and talking to kids.

Advice to would-be inventors: Apprentice first in the industry. Then go out on your own.

Melvin Kennedy and Susan Matsumoto
Kennedy-Matsumoto Design, LLC
Lantana, Florida
No. of years in the industry: About 70 years combined
No. of years as an independent: Mel, 29; Sue, 13
No. of patents held: About 30
No. of trademarks held: 0

Most successful products: Skip It! (Tiger/Hasbro), Maximum Speed (Trendmasters), X-Men Projector Figures (ToyBiz), Bouncin' Babies (Galoob), Zap It! (Panosh), My Pal 2 (Toy Biz), Giggles 'n Go (Tyco), Speed Burners (Mego).

What makes a great toy? The ability of a child (or an adult) to completely get lost in the world the toy creates. In the case of Barbie and Hot Wheels, the toy supplies a springboard for the imagination. What the child brings to the toy in imagination represents the best benefit of that toy. My Pal 2 (like dolls for girls) does something else—it gives the child a playmate that is there all the time.

What makes a great game? The ability to repeatedly challenge players and create a scenario that is totally fun! That's what makes the whole area of video games so strong. Of course, there are traditional games that also do the same thing—like Trivial Pursuit, Boggle, and Pictionary.

An inventor is ... someone who can't or doesn't want to work in a regular corporate environment! Who can't help thinking in terms of what would be better, different, and more exciting—for whom creativity is the most important component of doing something. Who has the intestinal fortitude and bank account to endure the financial lows that go along with the financial highs.

Who or what inspired you to become an inventor? *Mel:* Dietmar Nagel convinced me that what they were accomplishing at Mattel could be replicated on the "outside" as inventors.

What sparks original ideas? Anything—an article in the newspaper, something you see in the stores, the general zeitgeist, etc.

Advice to would-be inventors: If you are thinking of being a full-time inventor, have at least two years of living expenses in your bank account. If you have a good hit, put away most of the income to use between the hits. Keep up with everyone you know in the industry, including other inventors. Other inventors are the source of great information, usually freely given and shared. Never give up on a good concept

Benjamin Kinberg
Benjamin Kinberg & Associates
New York, New York
No. of years in the industry: 35
No. of years as an independent: 31
Approximate number of products licensed: 325
No. of patents held: 26
No. of trademarks held: 6

In a typical year:

No. of ideas conceived: 10–12

No. of concepts prototyped: 6–8

No. of concepts presented: 30 (old and new)

No. of concepts licensed: 4–6

No. of products that make it to market: 4–5

Most successful products: James Bond 007 Attache Case (Multiple Products), Baby Gym (Illco), Luminescent Slate (Tyco).

What did you do before you were in the industry? World traveler.

What makes a great toy? Simplicity, unique play value, gratifying results, and factors that encourage replay.

What makes a great game? Uniqueness, wide age range, hazardous play features, and winning through superior play moves.

An inventor is ... someone who doesn't know any better, is preternaturally lucky, has a good day job or a large bank balance, and has imagination, education, and a tolerance for pain.

Who or what inspired you to become an inventor? It was a textbook case of serendipity. I was a toy factory manager when my boss sold the business, and I needed a job.

What sparks original ideas? It can come from a variety of places, things, or other. For instance, the Bond Attache Case came from seeing the movie *From Russia with Love*.

Advice to would-be inventors: Never quit your day job, and never give up trying.

Adam Kislevitz
The Obb
Englewood, New Jersey

No. of years in the industry: 24

No. of years as an independent: 21

Approximate number of products licensed: Many, many

No. of patents held: Never tracked the number

No. of trademarks held: Never tracked the number

In a typical year:

No. of ideas conceived: Lots and lots and lots

No. of concepts prototyped: Lots

No. of concepts presented: Lots and lots

No. of concepts licensed: Less than lots, but enough to cover payroll and a decent bottle of wine at lunch

No. of products that make it to market: It's not how many make it to market—it is a matter of which ones

Most successful products: DivaStarz (Mattel), Mechanix Hot Wheels (Mattel), Air Rebound R/C (Mattel), Fashion Magic Fun Scrunchie Maker (Mattel/Tyco), Baby Face (Galoob), MicroMachine Double Takes (Galoob).

What did you do before you were in the industry? I was a grunt for Harry Abrams, the book publisher.

What makes a great toy? Depends on the product category, but it still comes down to a compelling and sustainable play pattern.

An inventor is ... independent, creative, and persistent.

Who or what inspired you to become an inventor? My rent.

Advice to would-be inventors: Learn the basics about a company's product needs. If you were a writer, you wouldn't submit to *Hustler* what you would to *Reader's Digest*. Persistence.

Reuben Klamer
ToyLab
San Diego, California
No. of years in the industry: 41
No. of years as an independent: 41
Approximate number of products licensed: Many
No. of patents held: Over 50
No. of trademarks held: Many

In a typical year:
No. of ideas conceived: Difficult to answer
No. of concepts prototyped: Varies
No. of concepts presented: 15–20
No. of concepts licensed: 1–2
No. of products that make it to market: 1–2

Most successful products: The Game of Life (Milton Bradley), Roller Skates (Fisher-Price), Zoo-It-Yourself, Busy Blocks.

What did you do before you were in the industry? I was a regional manager of a transcontinental air cargo company.

What makes a great toy? It keeps the child's attention and has a high level of play value long after the child has acquired the toy.

What makes a great game? When the game is over and the loser wants to play again ("I'll get you next time").

An inventor is ... one who creates something out of nothing.

Who or what inspired you to become an inventor? Elliot Handler, a founder of Mattel. He has a keen mind, great patience, and dedication.

What sparks original ideas? Memories. Seeing children at play. Reading newspapers/magazines; TV/movies; observing nature—without purpose. Going through toy stores regularly. Seeing one thing and visualizing another.

Advice to would-be inventors: Work for a toy/game company or a well-financed independent toy-invention company that needs your talent. Don't mortgage your house to finance an idea.

Dan Klitsner
KID Group, LLC
San Francisco, California
No. of years in the industry: 16
No. of years as an independent: 13
Approximate number of products licensed: 100+
No. of patents held: 60+
No. of trademarks held: 10

In a typical year:
No. of ideas conceived: 100
No. of concepts prototyped: 30
No. of concepts presented: 100–200
No. of concepts licensed: 5–15
No. of products that make it to market: 3–10

Most successful products: Bop It, Bop It Extreme, Top It (Hasbro Games); Tonka Virtual Workshop, Tonka Dig 'n Rigs (the Keytop toy line at Hasbro Interactive); Crash Back R/C (Kenner); Mr. Piano (Mega Bloks); Uno Blitzo (Mattel); Marbleworks Grand Prix (Discovery Toys); Go Go Worms (Milton Bradley).

What did you do before you were in the industry? Product design for consumer products company. Structural packaging and illustration for corporate identity firms.

What makes a great toy? Anything that makes a child or adult laugh, hopefully at the same time. Toys that need no instructions, or that allow the player to make up his own way to play. A good toy engages a child's imagination and creativity, and allows him to express himself uniquely, if played with by himself or with friends.

What makes a great game? I've always thought we need games as an excuse to share a good time with friends and family. The simple process of playing the game should create a bond between the people playing. A good game creates lasting, priceless memories of the experience shared. For kids, the key has been to encourage physical interaction so they can express themselves. A balance between challenge and payoff is important so everyone feels they have a chance to be good at it, even if they don't win. If you can laugh both at your own mistakes or misfortune as well as at your friends, you're playing a good game.

An inventor is … anyone who is crazy enough to try and passionate enough to keep trying.

Who or what inspired you to become an inventor? Playing games with my family as a child.

What sparks original ideas? Lots of little things that catch my eye. Mostly the urge to find the perfect game. How to pick up on new trends, technologies, and materials. Toy company wish lists inspire sparks of ideas simply by asking for concepts that are new. The first spark is very subliminal, pulled from the gut. The rest of the idea evolves during the mockup and play.

Bob Knetzger
NeoToy
Seattle, Washington

(*Note:* Rick Gurolnick—see separate inventor profile—is at NeoToy's main office in Chicago. Bob is in Seattle. Although they have been inventing toys together for almost 20 years, they have never worked in the same location.)

No. of years in the industry: 27
No. of years as an independent: 22
Approximate number of products licensed: At least 50
No. of patents held: 3
No. of trademarks held: Several

In a typical year:
No. of ideas conceived: 200
No. of concepts prototyped: 40
No. of concepts presented: 40
No. of concepts licensed: 2
No. of products that make it to market: 1 (Many "fall out of bed" right before Toy Fair.)

Most successful products: Mine are the ones that later other people enjoy telling *me* about. These include Doctor Dreadful (Tyco), Intellivision (Mattel), Cap'n Crunch cereal premiums, and I hope many more.

What did you do before you were in the industry? I majored in art and design.

What makes a great toy? Inventors "kvetch" when their concepts are compromised due to cost cuts, perceived safety concerns, flubbed production, cheap packaging, weak advertising, bad design, or weak marketing, or are just plain "screwed up." A great toy is one that, even after it has been through the gauntlet, still manages to be profitable for manufacturers and retailers, acceptable to parents, and fun for kids.

An inventor is … anyone who, while solving a problem, has had that "Aha!" feeling.

Who or what inspired you to become an inventor? Charles and Ray Eames, Ed Roth, Leo Fender, and Walt Disney continue to inspire me with their vision, attitude, ingenuity, story-telling, and uniquely American individuality.

What sparks original ideas? When two old things "bump" into each other to make something new.

Advice to would-be inventors: Realize that others' advice does not necessarily apply to you.

Fred Kroll
Uncle Freddie's Fun Factory, Inc.
Boynton Beach, Florida
No. of years in the industry: 66
No. of years as an independent: 28
Approximate number of products licensed: 10
No. of patents held: 20+
No. of trademarks held: 50+

In a typical year:
No. of ideas conceived: 5
No. of concepts prototyped: 5

No. of concepts presented: 5
No. of concepts licensed: I now manufacture my own product.
No. of products that make it to market: 40–50

Most successful products: Trouble (Kohner/Hasbro); Headache (Kohner/Hasbro); Discovered Hungry, Hungry Hippos (Hasbro)

What did you do before you were in the industry? Printing.

What makes a great toy? An idea followed up by good design at a fair price, well packaged and presented.

What makes a great game? A game that can be explained or demonstrated in a very short time. The exception would be a strategy game that's usually for the specialty market.

An inventor is ... anybody who comes up with an idea that is original or that drastically improves an existing item.

Who or what inspired you to become an inventor? The need to have new product to sell as a manufacturer, later as a rep, and then as a manufacturer again.

What sparks original ideas? If I could answer, this I would be the richest inventor in the toy business! I get many ideas just watching real-life situations.

Advice to would-be inventors: Don't give up your day job until you have licensed at least three successful items.

Andy Kunkel
Kunkel & Associates
Westbury, New York
No. of years in the toy industry: 38
No. of years as an independent: 38
Approximate number of products licensed: 17

In a typical year:
No. of ideas conceived: 20–30
No. of concepts prototyped: 10–15
No. of concepts presented: 10–15
No. of concepts licensed: 0–2
No. of products that make it to market: 0–2

What did you do before you were in the industry? Taught school; created and wrote TV game shows.

My most successful products: Slippery Spoons and Chips Are Down (Ideal Toy); Skee Wee (Marx); Jitters, Casino Yahtzee (Milton Bradley); Swing Swang (Milton Bradley); Spring Chicken (Mattel); Special Delivery (Western).

What makes a good toy? Some element that has a fascination function that keeps the child interested and coming back for more play

What makes a good game? Rules of play that give participants choices that impact how well they do in the outcome of the game.

An inventor is ... an individual who truly believes the old saying "Creativity begins with 90 percent perspiration and 10 percent inspiration."

Who or what inspired you most to become an inventor? Julie Cooper, at the time senior vice president R&D at Ideal Toy Company.

What sparks an original idea? One can germinate anytime or anywhere. I usually write it down or sketch it and never let it get away. I put the idea somewhere that my thoughts will be drawn back to it again and again.

Advice to would-be inventors: Never give up, and if it's not fun, don't do it.

Mike Langieri
Toygenius
Longmeadow, Massachusetts
No. of years in the industry: 34
No. of years as an independent: 13
Approximate number of products licensed: 9
No. of patents held: Utility, 12–15; design, 40+
No. of trademarks held: 0

In a typical year:
No. of ideas conceived: Millions
No. of concepts prototyped: 15
No. of concepts presented: 12
No. of concepts licensed: 1
No. of products that make it to market: 1 (maybe)

Most successful products: Play Top Rider (Marx); Stomper Van (Coleco); Play Tote (Playskool); Travel Soccer, Baseball, and Basketball (Hasbro Games); Countin' Cat (Educational Insights).

What did you do before you were in the industry? Industrial design (Lightolier, Aqua-Meter, Zenith, and others).

What makes a great toy? The play (or intended use) should be almost obvious just by looking at it, and it should be something that makes you want to play with it over and over. It needs to be somewhat addictive.

What makes a great game? One that has elements that keep all the players involved for the longest amount of time and that also has a high "repeat play" factor.

An inventor is ... more of a visionary, someone who goes beyond the conception of the basic idea. He has to also understand the market, the consumer, and the business of manufacturing and selling toys and games.

Who or what inspired you to become an inventor? I've been an artist since childhood and have always been fascinated with mechanical gadgets and toys. As an industrial designer, you're taught to focus on design, engineering, and graphics as you work at conceiving new products. I see kids play, and I get ideas about what kids might like even better than what they're playing with. I'm also fortunate because I have the ability to visualize and communicate a new toy or game idea with a variety of media. My senior thesis project at design school was a pull toy.

What sparks original ideas? Watching kids play sparks many ideas. Or, they could come from a million other places. In some respects, no idea is 100 percent original or totally new. Like patents, you can always improve on the state of the art.

Advice to would-be inventors: Learn to communicate in as many different ways as possible, and if you are artistically inclined, you may have the advantage of being able to sketch out an idea on the fly for later refinement. Visit the major toy retailers often and study the products. If you are computer-oriented, learn to use an assortment of software programs that will help you develop and communicate your ideas.

Paul A. Lapidus
NewFuntiers
Palo Cedro, California
No. of years in the industry: 28
No. of years as an independent: 26
Approximate number of products licensed: 25–30
No. of patents held: 18
No. of trademarks held: 2
In a typical year:
No. of ideas conceived: 15–20

No. of concepts prototyped: 5–10
No. of concepts presented: 40–50 (many from years past)
No. of concepts licensed: 1–3
No. of products that make it to market: 1–2

Most successful products: Modifiers (Ertl), Smokin' Shakers (Ertl), Star Wars X-Wing Flight Simulator (Hasbro), Spinner Darts (Placo, and used as a premium by Post Cereals, Denny's, White Castle, Coke, Church's Chicken and at least a dozen fast-food companies).

What did you do before you were in the industry? Director of design for Intercraft Industries, a housewares company.

What makes a great toy? Detail in design. Neat product features (magical mechanical or electronic action). Fantasy play potential. Quality construction. I hate toys that break easily.

What makes a great game? The ability to affect your game-play outcome and that of your opponents.

An inventor is … a creative individual who looks at the world and wonders why things are as they are, and feels there are better (simpler, easier, more convenient, etc.) solutions to the products and tasks he or she sees around them.

Who or what inspired you to become an inventor? As an industrial designer, I looked back over my life, even as a child, and saw that creativity is an integral part of my being. And besides the genes thing, I am rarely satisfied with the world around me; I feel that it can be a lot better and that I can contribute to that in my own small way.

What sparks original ideas? It's funny, I really don't know for sure. I sometimes think I look at the world and the things around me purposely with a "soft focus" and interpret them differently than they really are. Sometimes my interpretation is stronger and more appropriate than the original. Does that make any sense? Somehow it does for me.

Advice to would-be inventors: Don't start unless you have the will, desire, motivation, and fortitude to go on when everyone around you tells you shouldn't. Oh, yeah— truly creative talent, and a broad world view are key if you ever hope to succeed.

Richard C. Levy
Richard C. Levy & Associates
Delray Beach, Florida
No. of years in the industry: 26
No. of years as an independent: 26
Approximate number of products licensed: 125+
No. of patents held: Many
No. of trademarks held: Many

In a typical year:
No. of ideas conceived: About 50
No. of concepts prototyped: About 15
No. of concepts presented: About 25
No. of concepts licensed: 3–5
No. of products that make it to market: 2–4

My most successful products were: Furby/Furby Baby (Tiger/Hasbro); StarBird (Milton Bradley); Hot Lixx (Tyco); *Men Are from Mars, Women Are from Venus* (Mattel/Endless Games); Adver*teasing* (Cadaco); Crest Fluorider (Procter & Gamble).

What did you do before you were in the industry? Feature films—assistant to president at Paramount International Pictures; foreign advertising/publicity executive at Paramount and Avco Embassy Pictures. Producer of 30 + prime-time television documentaries. Appointed to US Government Senior Executive Service—managed U.S. Information Agency Television and Film Service (incl. broadcast television studios); Architect of U.S.I.A.'s global interactive satellite network (Worldnet). Freelance journalist. Author.

What makes a great toy? A great toy stimulates the senses with an echo that awakens the child in us.

What makes a great game? A great game offers levels of challenge, high entertainment, and rewards; requires skill; and, above all, stimulates delightful, enlightening, and even sometimes surprising social interaction between players. Strong marketing tie-in to pop culture.

An inventor is ... a person who has new eras in his (or her) brain; finds comfort and stimulation on the leading edge of uncertainty, experimentation, and exploration; and refuses to trade incentive for security. Inventors resist the usual, introduce change to the skeptical, cross a threshold, and exhibit the "dare to go."

Who or what inspired you to become an inventor? A family comprised of highly creative and successful entrepreneurs and corporate executives taught me, through their actions and words, that America encourages and rewards innovation.

What sparks original ideas? I am stimulated by the actuality and phosphorescence of thought, the past superimposed on the now, and the jolt that happens when I break from the collective framework in which I find myself at any point in time. Time in the sauna does wonders, too.

Advice to would-be inventors: Trust yourself and your instincts. They are anchors in a storm. Realize that what you can accomplish is truly amazing if you keep your feet on the ground and your eyes on the stars. Remember, it is shape that determines whether iron will float or sink. Be honest. And never respond to paracreative sluggards chewing at your toenails.

Bruce Lund
Lund & Company Invention, LLC
Chicago, Illinois

No. of years in the industry: 24
No. of years as an independent: 17
Approximate number of products licensed: 100
No. of patents held: 12
No. of trademarks held: 3

In a typical year:

No. of ideas conceived: 500
No. of concepts prototyped: 100
No. of concepts presented: 100
No. of concepts licensed: 20–25
No. of products that make it to market: 12–18

Most successful products: VacMan (CapToys); Fireball Island (Milton Bradley); Luminator (Kidpower); Baby Sip 'n Slurp (Hasbro); Lickety Treats (Hasbro); Nibbles, Barbie's horse (Mattel); Dizzy Dryer (Mattel).

What did you do before you were in the industry? Biologist, craftsman.

Do you review outside submissions? Rarely—too much time.

What makes a great toy? Inspires and delights; promotes a child's growth and development by exploration of the world through play.

What makes a great game? A game is a machine of human interaction. A good game is an equalizer that allows different ages and abilities to have fun together.

An inventor is ... someone compelled to invent, and nothing else will do.

Who or what inspired you to become an inventor? My father.

What sparks original ideas? Something seen.

Advice to would-be inventors: Do it. If you feel the call, find a way.

Ron Magers
M Design
Essex, Massachusetts

No. of years in the industry: 26
No. of years as an independent: 21
Approximate number of products licensed: 35
No. of patents held: 6
No. of trademarks held: 4

In a typical year:
No. of ideas conceived: 25–30
No. of concepts prototyped: 10–20
No. of concepts presented: 15–20
No. of concepts licensed: 4–5
No. of products that make it to market: 3–4

Most successful products: Attach N' Go (Playskool), Fleas on Fred (Tyco), Puppy Racers (Milton Bradley), Bubble Fire Truck (Tyco), Boppin' Bee (Fisher-Price), Light Wars (Tiger), Silly Willy (Fisher-Price), Sounds Around (Larami), Top Dog (Mattel).

What did you do before you were in the industry? Advertising, package design, product development, graphics.

What makes a great toy? The best toy is one that wears out from so much use, that everyone loves to play with, and that ultimately is handed down to the next generation.

What makes a great game? It may be worn and ragged at the edges, and it can be found on the top shelf in the back of the closet, but you can always count on a "good game" to pull your family together on a rainy evening.

An inventor is ... a person fiercely independent and given to bouts of intense dedication to pursue any minute spark of inspiration with no discernible chances of remuneration. Just a big kid, really!

Who or what inspired you to become an inventor? The wonder of how things work and the ongoing, new innovations that happen around us every day have always been a part of what gives me inspiration.

What sparks original ideas? Looking for the "Wow" in everyday continuous observations of the things around me, and logging them in a book of ideas that I refer to frequently.

Advice to would-be inventors: Don't fall in love and marry a single idea. Work on many products and spread the risk. "SCAN IT"—This is an acronym for producing the perfect product. It stands for: Simple, Clean, and Neat, Inexpensive, and Timely.

Michael Marra and Lynn Marra
Marra Design Associates, Inc.
Chanhassen, Minnesota
No. of years in the industry: 32 (too many!)
No. of years as an independent: 14 (lucky!)
Approximate number of products licensed: 80ish
No. of patents held: 6
No. of trademarks held: 0

In a typical year:
No. of ideas conceived: 4–10
No. of concepts prototyped: 3–6
No. of concepts presented: 25–100
No. of concepts licensed: 3–8
No. of products that make it to market: Typically all licensed items make it to market. It's the amount of money over the advance that makes the difference.

Most successful products: 1313 Dead End Drive (Milton Bradley), 30 Second Candy Machine (General Creations), Tabletop Cotton Candy Machine (General Creations), Simpson's Trivia (Cardinal), WWF Trivia (Cardinal), Old MacDonald Had a Farm (Milton Bradley).

What did you do before you were in the industry? College; machinist.

What makes a great toy? The ability to engage many senses (visual, emotional, creative, and intellectual) and inspire repeat play. A great TV commercial doesn't hurt, either.

What makes a great game? Since there are only four basic game plays, a great game must be innovative enough to attract, stimulate, challenge, captivate, reward, and have tradition without seeming to be old.

An inventor is … someone who thinks beyond what he or she sees and has the ability to create fascination or fill an old need cleverly.

Who or what inspired you to become an inventor? Being unemployed.

What sparks original ideas? A situation. A comment. Seeing someone doing an activity.

Advice to would-be inventors: Do not take rejection personally; it's about the product, not you. Have at least two years of living expenses in the bank. Limit your patent expenses to a patent search, not an actual patent. Your money is better spent on a prototype. Never spend money on a design patent, as they are too easy to get around. Do not quit your day job. There is only one way to measure how much a manufacturer "likes" your idea: You are handed a check and it clears. Find a great toy broker/agent.

Larry Mass
Mass Market Ideas, LLC
Rye Brook, New York
No. of years in the industry: 27
No. of years as an independent: 14
Approximate number of products licensed: 50
No. of patents held: About 15
No. of trademarks held: About 30
In a typical year:
No. of ideas conceived: 65
No. of concepts prototyped: 20
No. of concepts presented: 30 (includes old ideas)
No. of concepts licensed: 4
No. of products that make it to market: 3

Most successful products: Rumblin' Thunder (Tonka), Boglins (Mattel), Hush Lil' Baby (DSI), G. I. Joe Air Commandos (Hasbro), Arch Rival (Parker Brothers), Tickle Toes (Milton Bradley), Operation Brain Surgery (Milton Bradley).

What did you do before you were in the industry? Started right out of college.

What makes a great toy? Repeatability—wanting to play with it over and over again.

What makes a great game? A good mix of fun and drama. A game that facilitates interaction between players is always a good thing.

An inventor is … more than just creative. To be a successful toy/game inventor, you must have an idea that can (a) be mass-produced, (b) excite a manufacturer,

(c) excite a retailer, (d) be profitable when reasonably priced, (e) be communicated and promoted to the consumer (the kid), (f) win moms' approval, and (g) be safe. That aside, you must also be able to easily slip back into the mind-set of the child you once were and be able to tap into what you most remember as being fun. Then apply it with a twist!

Who or what inspired you to become an inventor? I always had toy and game ideas, but I guess I'd have to thank Ben Ordover (president of CBS Toys for a brief period) for serving as my inspiration or catalyst: He fired me, which gave me the perfect opportunity to try out inventing (thanks to Tom Kremer, who hired me for his product-development company).

What sparks original ideas? Many things. Themes; trends; existing products with new, added innovations; music; names; current events—whatever.

Advice to would-be inventors: Keep your day job, but if you must invent, be smart about it. Too many times we see people at Javits who have taken their entire savings to try to launch an item that was ill-fated from the start.

Jim McCafferty
JMP Creative
Santa Ana, California

No. of years in the industry: 14
No. of years as an independent: 14
Approximate number of products licensed: 450
No. of patents held: 4
No. of trademarks held: 30

In a typical year:
No. of ideas conceived: Thousands, in many rough forms
No. of concepts prototyped: 40–60
No. of concepts presented: 400–500
No. of concepts licensed: 100–150
No. of products that make it to market: 70–100

Most successful products: Tekno (Manley), Big Air Shredder (Pepsi, Arco, Conoco), Magic Morphing Cups (7-11, Pepsi), Magic Straw (Pepsi, Takara, Dairy Queen).

What did you do before you were in the industry? Magician.

What makes a great toy? One that can be extended with multiple themes and still seem new fun and fresh with every variation. Strong play value for a child left alone to his or her imagination.

What makes a great game? Simple to learn, difficult to master. Hard to lose pieces. Easy, quick setup and reset. Easy storage. Unique interactive experience

An inventor is ... someone with the most difficult frustrating job you could ever have that you will love to do.

Who or what inspired you to become an inventor? I met Larry Bernstein at MGA and Lester Borden at Sony. They both suggested, after seeing my magic act, that I should use my unique perspective to invent toys. I was always inventing illusions, so toys were not a big leap.

What sparks original ideas? Anything and everything! Travel can be very inspiring.

Advice to would-be inventors: Think through every product as if you were going to manufacture and sell it on your own. What will it take to make it cost-effective? What would a 15- to 30-second commercial look like? Think about it and make sure your idea can be easily communicated in 10–15 seconds and will cost half of what you think you would be willing to pay for it yourself. Most important, pitch it to as many companies as possible, and be open to change and enhance it throughout the process.

Don't have only one idea that you are depending on. Have a 100, and then you will get "lucky."

Bob and Deborah McDarren; Barry Y. Piels
Link Group International
Ridgefield, Connecticut

No. of years in the industry: 37
No. of years as an independent: 25
Approximate number of products licensed: 200
No. of patents held: 5
No. of trademarks held: 20

In a typical year:
No. of ideas conceived: 150
No. of concepts prototyped: 50
No. of concepts presented: 150
No. of concepts licensed: 30
No. of products that make it to market: 25

Most successful products: Lazer Combat (Panosh); Karate Kid (Remco-Azrak Hamway); Creepy Crawlers (Toymax).

What did you do before you were in the industry? Food

What makes a great toy? Play value.

What make a great game? Wanting to play it again.

An inventor is ... necessary.

Who or what inspired you to become an inventor? End to corporate B.S.; independence.

What sparks original ideas? Anything. Observation.

Advice to would-be inventors: Be ready for rejection.

Steve Meyer
Meyer/Glass Design
Chicago, Illinois
No. of years in the industry: 21
No. of years as an independent: 13
Approximate number of products licensed: Lots
No. of patents held: Lots
No. of trademarks held: Lots

In a typical year:
No. of ideas conceived: 500
No. of concepts prototyped: 200
No. of concepts presented: 150
No. of concepts licensed: 10
No. of products that make it to market: 5

Most successful products: Sqwish Ball (Cap), Pretty Pretty Princess (Hasbro Games), The Sticker Factory (Hasbro Toys), Activities to Go (Mattel), Creative Peg Board (F-P), Kitchen Littles (Mattel), Blush Art (Ohio Art), Gooey Louie (Pressman), Catch Phrase (Milton Bradley), Meal Time Magic Baby (Toy Biz), Make-Up Mindy (Hasbro Toys), Silly Six Pins (Hasbro Games), Rain or Sun Barbie (Mattel) (All developed collaboratively by Meyer/Glass Design personnel).

What did you do before you were in the industry? Computer software.

What makes a great toy? One that captures interest quickly and holds it. Provides for repeat play and an experience that has enough depth to provide long-term play value. Of course, it has to be fun, too.

What makes a great game? Same as a great toy, except that now you need to create an experience with competition, in an environment where every player has a chance to win and, win and or lose, wants to play again.

An inventor is … someone who looks for new ways to put ideas together to form product concepts, constantly aware of his or her environment and searching for a new combination of need, novelty, and fun to yield the next hot toy.

Who or what inspired you to become an inventor? My father.

What sparks original ideas? So many things, but most often it is being aware of what is going on around you and putting those things together in different ways.

Advice to would-be inventors: It's a very difficult business, but if you are *absolutely* sure you want to be a toy inventor, stick with it. Today it takes so much for a concept to finally make it to market and be successful. You just have to hang in there. Don't fall in love with one concept. If one doesn't work out, move on to the next. Don't mortgage the house to do it, though. Team up with an invention firm or toy company and see if you have what it takes.

Ron Milner
Applied Design Laboratories, Inc.
Grass Valley, California

No. of years in the industry: 17
No. of years as an independent: 17
Approximate number of products licensed: 15
No. of patents held: 15
No. of trademarks held: 0

In a typical year:
No. of ideas conceived: 100
No. of concepts prototyped: 2
No. of concepts presented: 2
No. of concepts licensed: 0
No. of products that make it to market: 0

Most successful products: Atari 2600 (Atari), AG Bear (Axlon), Hot Lixx (Tyco), Klixx (Klixx).

What did you do before you were in the industry? Went to college.

What makes a great toy? A good toy should be 80 percent imagination—it should enable make-believe, not replace it.

What makes a great game? It needs to have enough elements of luck that you think you have a chance next time, yet enough skill involved that if you win, you know it was because you were brilliant.

An inventor is ... someone who has ideas and doesn't give up even when he or she should.

Who or what inspired you to become an inventor? It just happens. It isn't something you can go to school for or read a book on how to be one.

What sparks original ideas? Usually some kind of need that is not well met by anything I have ever seen.

Advice to would-be inventors: Get a day job!

Betty J. Morris
K&B Innovations, Inc.
North Lake, Wisconsin

No. of years in the industry: 31
No. of years as an independent: 31
Approximate number of products licensed: 200+ Shrinky Dinks items, and 12 others
No. of patents held: 3
No. of trademarks held: 7
No. of concepts licensed: 12
No. of products that make it to market: 12

Note: I spend 100 percent of my time innovating, manufacturing, supplying, and directing Shrinky Dinks worldwide.

Most successful products: Shrinky Dinks.

What did you do before you were in the industry? Housewife, mom.

What makes a great toy? One whose unique concept can be added to and expanded upon to create a line of products, such as LEGO, Shrinky Dinks, and bubbles.

What makes a great game? Visually exciting, plays in 20 minutes, gives all players a chance to win, and is self-storing.

An inventor is ... someone with an alert mind who is always challenging what is. Quickly sees new concepts that might create a new toy or game.

Who or what inspired you to become an inventor? Shrinky Dinks actually exposed me to an industry I never knew existed.

What sparks original ideas? The thought of "Wouldn't it be neat if ..." and then trying to design something that makes it a reality.

Advice to would-be inventors: Read books that have been written to gain pertinent information on how and what to do with any product ideas that you feel are original.

Sean T. Mullaney
Bang Zoom Design, Ltd.
Cincinnati, Ohio
No. of years in the industry: 14
No. of years as an independent: 12
Approximate number of products licensed: 50
No. of patents held: 8
No. of trademarks held: 0

In a typical year:
No. of ideas conceived: 100
No. of concepts prototyped: 25
No. of concepts presented: 300–500
No. of concepts licensed: 12
No. of products that make it to market: 10

Most successful products: Roll 'n Rattle Ball (Playskool), Tantrum R/C (Tyco), Extreme Cycle R/C (Tyco).

What did you do before you were in the industry? I went from design school to BMT.

What makes a great toy? Something that makes you go "Wow!" Sometimes never seen before.

What makes a great game? One without cards and little stubby pencils.

An inventor is ... a pain in the ass. Just kidding. Someone who was dropped on his head as a child. Just kidding. Someone who looks at life a little differently and can process that view into something whimsical and interesting.

Who or what inspired you to become an inventor? My parents instilled a lot of creativity and off-the-wall thinking in me.

What sparks original ideas? You have to keep your mind open to any seemingly silly idea or possibility, and store it away. These things percolate in our subconscious and surface periodically.

Advice to would-be inventors: Somebody once said, "Nothing is more dangerous than an idea when it is the only one you have." Come up with hundreds of ideas— the worse, the better. Boil down the list, and then come up with hundreds more.

Ralph Osterhout
Osterhout Design Group
San Francisco, California

No. of years in the toy industry: 9
No. of years as an independent: 15
Approximate number of products licensed: 50+
No. of patents held: 40+
No. of trademarks held: No idea. I lost track years ago.

In a typical year:
No. of ideas conceived: 20–30
No. of concepts prototyped: 3–4
No. of concepts presented: 10–12
No. of concepts licensed: 5–7
No. of products that make it to market: 4–5

Most successful products: Yak Baks (Yes! Entertainment), Power Penz (Yes! Entertainment), Talk Boy F/X (Tiger Electronics), Talking Nano (Playmates).

What did you do before you were in the industry? Office products, workstations, lighting, military products, sporting goods, and Scuba diving equipment.

What makes a great toy? An overwhelming desire to show it off to another person. It's the ultimate measure of a toy's intrigue.

What makes a great game? Your unwitting desire to demonstrate what you perceive to be your superior skill over another.

An inventor is ... an unconscious problem identifier and solver by nature.

Who or what inspired you to become an inventor? Loneliness as a child and, later, intense curiosity. Curiosity leads to the identification of problems, which, in turn, can lead to the discovery of viable solutions.

What sparks original ideas? Constant exposure to new technology through extensive reading of Tech Magazines and publications. You have to feed the "analog computer" in order to achieve the ultimate state of creativity: spontaneous, unplanned interaction between new thoughts and old memories, whose seemingly random integration can produce meaningful epiphanies.

Advice to would-be inventors: Be absolutely relentless! Be enthusiastic, even in the face of inevitable skepticism from toy companies. Remember, it is neither illegal nor immoral to be enthusiastic. And if you're not, don't expect anyone else to be. Don't give up your day job until you have amassed enough royalties to live off of them for two years, unless reckless gambling is your pastime.

Charles Phillips
New England R&D
Walpole, New Hampshire

No. of years in the industry: 30 (yikes!)
No. of years as an independent: 24
Approximate number of products licensed: 25
No. of patents held: 5+
No. of trademarks held: About 2

In a typical year:
No. of ideas conceived: 200+
No. of concepts prototyped: 10
No. of concepts presented: 30
No. of concepts licensed: 1
No. of products that make it to market: 1

Most successful products: Advance to Boardwalk (Parker), Clue Jr. (Parker).

What did you do before you were in the industry? Mechanical engineer.

What makes a great toy? The capacity to feed fantasy.

What makes a great game? The capacity to evoke player feelings.

An inventor is … anyone who can conceive, design, and relate to others a concept that captures the imagination or satisfies some need, real or imaginary.

Who or what inspired you to become an inventor? As a 2-year-old, I saw my brother make things; parental encouragement.

What sparks original ideas? Anything. An article, an observation, a misunderstanding.

Advice to would-be inventors: Observe a need or a void, create a product to satisfy that condition, go to the right company, see the right person, and give a great pitch. Being lucky, cute, charming, and witty helps.

Steve Rehkemper
Rehkemper Invention & Design
Chicago, Illinois

No. of years in the industry: 23
No. of years as an independent inventor: 20

Approximate number of products licensed: 50+
No. of patents held: Many
No. of trademarks held: Some

In a typical year:
No. of ideas conceived: 1,500–2,000
No. of concepts prototyped: 200–250
No. of concepts presented: 200–250
No. of concepts licensed: 10–15
No. of products that make it to market:10–15

Most successful products: Baby Baseball (Fisher Price), Crocodile Mile (Marchon), Flick Trix, Giga Pets, e-Yo, Travel Skip-It (Tiger), Pixter, Gear Blocks, AlphaBot (Fisher Price), Air Hogs Water Rockets, E-Chargers Airplanes, Air Hogs RC Helicopter (Spinmaster), Let's Pretend Elmo, Thunder Roller Racing, Barbie Fashion Puppy and Kitty, Turbo Cross Cycles, Chat Pals, Pose Me Pets (Mattel), Nerf Gyro Strike, Zudes, Gotta Dance Girls, Tonka Town Construction Site, Play Doh Camera (Hasbro), Shoe Fairies (Blue Box).

What did you do before you were in the industry? Industrial design before joining Marvin Glass & Associates, the University of Toy Inventing.

What makes a great toy? A plaything that needs few words for kids to understand.

What make a great game? A plaything that has a few rules and is played over and over with everyone having a chance to win.

An inventor is: Someone who is a bit crazy and has at least one foot in the twilight zone. Inventors are true magicians who can make something come from nothing; from a thought to 3-D reality is a very nice trick.

What sparks original ideas? Everything in the environment outside the normal operations of conventional businesses. And my reading about Thomas Edison and other inventors where I learned that inventors worked a lot and failed a lot. I thought it would be easier for me and in all likelihood it probably has been easier for me.

Advice to would-be inventors: The biggest challenge an inventor has is to find another person in the world that shares their vision enough to pay money for it. That person will then need to get more people to understand the vision so the product can be made and then ultimatly the consumer has to understand the vision for anybody to make money. Go with the thought that "the best item is yet to come."

Victor G. Reiling
Victor G. Reiling Associates
Kent, Connecticut

No. of years in the industry: 33 (4 at Fisher-Price, 2 at Milton Bradley)
No. of years as an independent: 27
Approximate number of products licensed: 75–80
No. of patents held: About 25
No. of trademarks held: 1

In a typical year:
No. of ideas conceived: 100–150
No. of concepts prototyped: 25–35 (I think more and prototype less these days.)
No. of concepts presented: 25–35 (Pretty much each that reaches prototype stage.)
No. of concepts licensed: 4–6
No. of products that make it to market: 2–5

Most successful products: Hit Stix (Nasta), Hot Potato (Hasbro), Airport, Sesame Street, Castle, Circus Train, Play Desk (all while at Fisher-Price).

What did you do before you were in the industry? Graduate of U.S. Naval Academy. Officer for eight years, commanding a minesweeper in Vietnam theater. Fisher-Price brought me ashore in 1970.

What makes a great toy? Simple concept, no matter how complex the actual toy. Buyers, parents, and kids all have to like it, although there are times when the more parents dislike a product, the more kids like it (for example, Hit Stix noise).

What makes a great game? Straightforward, exciting play with a chance to catch up and the opportunity to nail an opponent.

An inventor is … a concept and element combiner—the right mix of good ideas and practical mechanisms. You bring together the factors that solve a problem that you have identified.

Who or what inspired you to become an inventor? I like engineering, drawing, model making, and working with bright people, both as associates and clients. And I love to solve problems!

What sparks original ideas? Totally different thoughts whizzing by that happen to collide. Someone says something while you are thinking of something else, and, voilà! Identifying a problem or a potential product.

Advice to would-be inventors: How about two years sustenance in the bank? When you know you have a good idea, keep with it—amazing what is new and fresh after 10–12 years.

Catherine Rondeau
Fun & Games
Fairfield, Connecticut
No. of years in the industry: 18
No. of years as an independent: 18
Approximate number of products licensed: 50+
No. of patents held: 1
No. of trademarks held: 5

In a typical year:
No. of ideas conceived: 10
No. of concepts prototyped: 5
No. of concepts presented: 10
No. of concepts licensed: 3–4
No. of products that make it to market: 2

Most successful products: Girl Talk (Western Publishing and Hasbro), Encore (Parker and Endless Games), Dreambuilders (Tyco), Read My Lips (Pressman), Lovies (Applause/Dakin), Are You Afraid of the Dark (Cardinal).

What did you do before you were in the industry? Television production.

What makes a great toy? Lots of things: an appeal to the emotions, a call to laughter and the imagination, longevity/value, whimsy.

What makes a great game? Interaction! Interaction! Interaction! To me, it is important that a game not intimidate the average person, be simple to learn, and provide opportunities for tension, release, spontaneous observations, conversation, and laughter.

An inventor is ... a bit of a maverick at heart. Someone driven by the creative process and a need to explore ideas.

Who or what inspired you to become an inventor? My own toddlers.

What sparks original ideas? Dreams, observation of kids, a funky-sounding word, childhood recollections, constantly asking "What if?"

Advice to would-be inventors: Get an agent. Worry more about producing the best possible prototype and less about getting ripped off. Don't marry your babies—not good for either of you. Personal hygiene—yeah, shower before you go into a presentation. Seriously, do some homework. Try to understand the niche that a particular company occupies and its specific needs. Don't waste time showing Barbie's weed-whacker to a Halloween company.

Elliot Rudell
Rudell Design
Torrance, California
No. of years in the industry: 33
No. of years as an independent: 28
Approximate number of products licensed: Good question
No. of patents held: 60
No. of trademarks held: 25

There is no typical year. Sometimes we will work on one huge, monstrous project for almost a year (like recently), and other times we'll be shooting with a shotgun.

Most successful products: Upwords (Hasbro Games), Weebles (Playskool), Fisher-Price R/C raceways and railroads, GURLZ (Irwin).

What did you do before you were in the industry? College—industrial design.

What makes a great toy? It is fun from the get-go. It is understandable. It is unique in what it does. It wants to be played with again. It evokes emotion. You want to show someone how cool it is. It represents what you are striving for as an inventor.

What makes a great game? It marries chance and skill. It has a level of unpredictability that cannot ever be fully conquered. It plays on more than one level. It continues to challenge. The winner is not always the same person.

An inventor is ... (1) Someone who, due to circumstances beyond his or her control, licensed something early and met with a degree of success and then fell under the misconception that it was either easy or predictable. (2) Someone with the drive and audacity to think he or she can come up with something new and unique, even after so many rocks have already been turned over to discover so many great inventions.

Who or what inspired you to become an inventor? I sort of came into it without much planning, so I give credit to the leading of the Lord, to whom I have committed my life. He determines the boundaries and time frames of a man's life.

What sparks original ideas? (1) Staying in "look-everywhere-at-all-times-for-a-great-idea" mode. (2) Seeing other great ideas, often in other industries, and getting motivated or challenged by its cleverness or technology usage. (3) Necessity. A client is coming out to see product and, dang it, we haven't any!

Advice to would-be inventors: Take your work seriously, but don't take your successes or failures too seriously. Work as humanly hard as you can, and demand the best from yourself. Walk humbly before man and God.

Michael Satten
Michael Satten Design, LLC
Roslyn, New York

No. of years in the industry: 33
No. of years as an independent: 21
No. of concepts prototyped: Varies
No. of concepts presented: Dozens
No. of concepts licensed: The lucky few that defy the odds
No. of products that make it to market: Fewer than above

Most successful products: P. J. Sparkles (Mattel), Sweet Secrets (Galoob), Army Gear (Galoob), Wrestling Buddies (Tonka), Water Pets (Playskool), Bundles of Babies (Cap Toys), Topsy Tail (Tyco), Pretty Crazy Curls (Playmates), Bubble the Pup (Playskool), Tattoodles (Grand Toy), Hot Wheels Car-Go Carrier (Mattel), Battle Trolls (Hasbro).

What did you do before you were in the industry? Corporate design and management positions within the toy industry. I studied industrial design at college. Freelance design. At age 15, I worked for a toy store selling and assembling products.

What makes a great toy? It has to be fun, well executed, and priced sharply. Positive word of mouth helps. Most of all, the stars need to be in alignment, and then you need a dash of luck.

What makes a great game? Fun to play. Minimum rules. Best ask Ron Weingartner—he's the game guy.

An inventor is ... a dreamer, a person who continually sees problems and tries to solve them.

Who or what inspired you to become an inventor? I knew how hard it was, having worked inside a large toy company reviewing outside submissions. But my partner of 20 years convinced me to give it a try against the odds. Eddy Goldfarb also influenced my decision. He always seemed to have the right attitude and values. His license plate read: BIG DAY. When I asked him its meaning, he replied, "Any day could be a big day." I have come to realize that any day, an idea or invention can change your life and the lives of others.

What sparks original ideas? Life experiences. For example, watching my son, as a toddler, trying to manipulate a hard, inflexible baseball glove, led to our developing a soft, fabric baseball glove with features that we licensed to Playskool.

Advice to would-be inventors: Over the past 10 years, I have taught fifth-graders about invention. Here is my message: Dream it. Write it down. Draw it. Built it. Then figure out how to present it. Get help doing what you cannot do yourself. Never give up. Many of the most successful products were turned down by the largest companies before they were finally marketed.

Stephen Schwartz
Stephen Schwartz Design, LLC
Providence, Rhode Island
No. of years in the industry: 31
No. of years as an independent: 13
Approximate number of products licensed: 250
No. of patents held: Many
No. of trademarks held: Many

In a typical year:
No. of ideas conceived: 100
No. of concepts prototyped and/or rendered: 50
No. of concepts presented: 50
No. of concepts licensed: 20
No. of products that make it to market: 10–15

Most successful products: Chicken Limbo (Milton Bradley); Take Care of Me Twins/Triplets (Toy Biz); Sing 'n Snore Ernie (Fisher-Price Brands); Wheels on the Bus (Milton Bradley); Magic Lights Ernie/Elmo (F-P Brands); Fluffy, My Come to Me Puppy (Hasbro); My Pretty Mermaids (Hasbro).

What did you do before you were in the industry? Executive vice president of marketing/R&D at Hasbro; president of Playskool.

What makes a great toy? Fun to play with, innovative.

What makes a great game? Same!

An inventor is ... a little crazy and very immature.

Who or what inspired you to become an inventor? Bernie Loomis, Henry Orenstein.

What sparks original ideas? Everything, anything, and, most times, nothing.

Advice to would-be inventors: Find a new industry.

Robert Schwartzman
Pace Development Group, LLC
New York, New York
No. of years in the industry: 18
No. of years as an independent: 13
Approximate number of products licensed: 85

In a typical year:
No. of ideas conceived: 100
No. of concepts prototyped: 30
No. of concepts presented: 50
No. of concepts licensed: 15
No. of products that make it to market: 7

Most successful products: Barney Banjo and extensions (Hasbro), Dancin' Debbi (Mattel), Hot Wheels Power Launcher (Mattel).

What did you do before you were in the industry? I worked for a nonprofit consulting firm that helps women and minority entrepreneurs start their own businesses in New York City.

Marc Segan
M. H. Segan & Co.
New York, New York
No. of years in the industry: 26
No. of years as an independent: 26
Approximate number of products licensed: 100+
No. of patents held: 25+
No. of trademarks held: Don't know

Most successful products: Santa's Marching Band (Mr. Christmas); Triple Arcade (Fisher-Price); Mickey Mouse Animated Phone, Animated Animations Artwork (M. H. Segan & Co.)

What did you do before you were in the industry? College, music.

What makes a great toy? Clear and instantly understandable, play purpose and theme.

What makes a great game? Not really my area.

An inventor is ... at best, a positive (in attitude), practical, and flexible contributor to good manufacturers.

Who or what inspired you to become an inventor? A reluctance to be normally employed or pigeon-holed.

What sparks original ideas? Anything, but frequently new experiences and travel.

Advice to would-be inventors: (1) Listen. (2) Listen. (3) Do several projects. Don't count on one thing.

Mark Setteducati
New York, New York
No. of years in the industry: 26
No. of years as an independent: 26
Approximate number of products licensed: 60
No. of patents held: 10
No. of trademarks held: 0

In a typical year:
No. of ideas conceived: Many
No. of concepts licensed: 1–2, sometimes more
No. of products that make it to market: 1–2, sometimes more

Most successful products: Magic Works (Milton Bradley), Travel Wheel of Fortune (Pressman), The Magic Show—mechanical book (Workman Publishing), WOW Science (Fantasma Toys).

What did you do before you were in the industry? Attended art school. Worked as the assistant to sculptor Louise Bourgeios. In the beginning, I also supported myself by doing freelance graphic design, and I drove a cab in New York City on the weekends.

What makes a great game? Very few rules and simple to play. Also, a good game must have a good "FY" or "Screw You" factor—and the player who gets "screwed" always has to have some possibility of making a comeback.

Did you ever give up on your dream to become an inventor? Being an inventor was never a dream or a goal. It is what I do.

What sparks original ideas? There are two ways to invent: The first way is to start with a theme such as "a game about the stock market" or "a doll that walks and chews gum." The second way is to start with or look for a principle or an effect that intrigues you, and then try to capture and transfer the essence of the effect or principle in a toy or game product. The second way is how I prefer to work.

Advice to would-be inventors: Never invent something just because you think somebody (a kid, a company) will like it. Your motivation should always be a personal one, that you are intrigued by the idea or find something you will enjoy exploring. Never try to please people or companies by compromising your ideas if you know you are right—even if you never sell it and nobody else likes it, you know that at least one person in the world likes it: you. If you try to please people, it is probable that nobody in the world will like it, including yourself.

Jay Smith
Play It Now
Los Angeles, California
No. of years in the industry: 31
No. of years as an independent: 31
Approximate number of products licensed: 100
No. of patents held: 41
No. of trademarks held: 7

In a typical year:
No. of ideas conceived: 25
No. of concepts prototyped: 4
No. of concepts presented: 6
No. of concepts licensed: 3
No. of products that make it to market: 2

Most successful products: Microvision (Milton Bradley); Vectrex (GCE, then Milton Bradley); Data Race (Aurora); Baby Talk (Galoob); Talk with Me Barbie (Mattel); Starting Lineup Baseball (Parker); Radar (Fisher-Price); over 50 video games, including Spiderman (Sega), X-Men (Sega), Joe Montana Football (Sega), Tiger Woods Golf (EA), Trivial Pursuit (Hasbro), and Ten Pin Alley (THQ).

What did you do before you were in the industry? Aerospace engineer.

What makes a great toy? A sense of fun that stimulates the imagination and gives great value.

What makes a great game? A sense of fun competition, anticipation, and pride of accomplishment if you win.

An inventor is ... a creative problem solver. The biggest obstacle is finding the problem to solve.

Who or what inspired you to become an inventor? I was always a gadget maker, even as a kid.

What sparks original ideas? A lifelong inquisitive mind and no fear of being innovative.

Advice to would-be inventors: Get some experience in the industry first. Next, become independent in a situation where there is income (consultant, development, etc). In parallel, find the needs and come up with the answer to those needs.

Bruce M. Sterten
Sterten & Company
Carmel, California
No. of years in the industry: 13
No. of years as an independent: 26, including TV game shows
Approximate number of products licensed: 3
No. of patents held: 0
No. of trademarks held: 2

In a typical year:
No. of ideas conceived: 12–20
No. of concepts prototyped: 3
No. of concepts presented: 3
No. of concepts licensed: 0–1
No. of products that make it to market: 2

Most successful products: 25 Words or Less (Winning Moves/Hasbro Games), Rapid Recall (Western Publishing).

What did you do before you were in the industry? Television writer/producer.

What makes a great toy? Ease of play.

What makes a great game? Challenging and ease of play.

An inventor is ... the backbone of the industry.

Who or what inspired you to become an inventor? A sense of "looking outside the box."

What sparks original ideas? I'm not telling.

Advice to would-be inventors: Don't steal other people's ideas.

Loren Taylor
Taylored Concepts
Chatam, New Jersey
No. of years in the industry: 21
No. of years as an independent: 9
Approximate number of products licensed: 150
No. of patents held: 4
No. of trademarks held: 7

In a typical year:
No. of ideas conceived: 250
No. of concepts prototyped: 60
No. of concepts presented: 150
No. of concepts licensed: 20
No. of products that make it to market: 7

Most successful products: Lamaze Ocototunes (Learning Curve), Cabbage Patch Kick N' Splash Doll (Mattel), Swim N' Splash Ernie (Tyco Pre-School), EZ Freezy Spin Pop Shop (Cap Toys), Bible Trivia Game (Cadaco), Tweetin' Bath Birdies (Fisher-Price), Baby Learns to Walk Doll (DSI), Baby Learns to Read (Irwin).

What did you do before you were in the industry? Packaged-goods marketing (Close-up Toothpaste and Care*Free Sugarless gum).

What makes a great toy? It keeps a child's interest for a long time, and he or she keeps coming back to it.

What makes a great game? It entertains you again and again.

An inventor is ... one who sees things that no one else sees, and then transforms that vision into something that everyone can see.

Who or what inspired you to become an inventor? I simply like toys. I really do not consider myself an inventor, but a marketer with a creative flair.

What sparks original ideas? An original idea can come from anywhere: watching children play, a movie, an animal, the stars, a machine, a dream, a book, a sporting event, a billboard, or just about anywhere else.

Advice to would-be inventors: Learn as much as you can about your market. Then step back and really ask yourself, "What is missing?" As Casey Stengel said: "Hit 'em where they ain't." Do your homework.

Laureen A. Trotto and Maureen T. Trotto
Thin Air, LLC
Monroe, Connecticut

No. of years in the industry: 19
No. of years as an independent: 19
Approximate number of products licensed: 50
No. of patents held: 2
No. of trademarks held: 0

In a typical year:
No. of ideas conceived: 50+
No. of concepts prototyped: 25–35
No. of concepts presented: 25
No. of concepts licensed: 2–3
No. of products that make it to market: 1–2

Most successful products: Sectars (Coleco), Boglins (Mattel), Bead Blast Barbie (Mattel).

Do you review outside submissions? No. Work only with select professionals in the industry.

Don Ullman
Ulco Toy and Game Co.
Fairfield, Connecticut

No. of years in the toy industry: About 11
No. of years as an independent: 11
Approximate number of products licensed: About 25
No. of patents held: Some pending
No. of trademarks held: 0

In a typical year:
No. of concepts prototyped: 15–20
No. of concepts presented: 20
No. of concepts licensed: 5
No. of products that make it to market: 2–3

My most successful products: Incredible Shrinky Dinks Maker (Spin Master), Clicker Licker, Firestrike Football, Rainbow Riders Puzzle (Ravensburger).

What did you do before toys and games? I was involved in several startups, including a small chain of Italian ice stores.

What makes a good toy? A good toy is anything that can safely, continually keep a kid engaged. There are way too many toys that kids get tired of so quickly.

What makes a good game? I think the interaction between players makes for the best games, although at the preschool level, this doesn't necessarily apply.

An inventor is ... anyone who has ideas and pushes to execute them in whatever form they can. Everyone is an inventor and inventive in everyday life.

What sparks an original idea? Anything can spark a great idea. It's kind of a mystery, and it is different for everyone.

Advice to would-be inventors: Find partners! I work with some really great partners who are far more talented than I. The beautiful thing about it is that everyone can contribute in some very important ways. From practical experience, have a spouse who is gainfully employed and extremely supportive.

David Vogel
Vogel Applied Technologies Corp.
New York, New York
No. of years in the industry: 13
Approximate number of products licensed: 16
No. of patents held: 22
No. of trademarks held: 37

In a typical year:
No. of ideas conceived: 75
No. of concepts prototyped: 25
No. of concepts presented: 50
No. of concepts licensed: 5
No. of products that make it to market: 2

Most successful products: Barbie Holiday Dance Musical (Mr. Christmas), Caroling Kittens (Mr. Christmas), Radical Racers (Yes! Entertainment), Cinemotion Christmas Ornaments (Brainwave Toys), Billboard Santa (Brainwave Toys).

What did you do before you were in the industry? Talent agent.

What makes a good toy? A good toy grows with a child through several successive developmental levels and perhaps even skips a few. Ideally, it expands the child's intellectual horizon, imagination, and skill set. For example, while young children use Erector Sets to create very basic objects, older children use them to construct functional, often complex toys. Some of these kids will grow up to be engineers, scientists, or other creative professionals. Likewise, a young child interacts with Furby in a nurturing fashion; an older one uses its infrared communications capacity to interact with a friend's Furby. The older child's implementation of infrared transmission and reception is a valuable step toward understanding the technology behind it. Here's a noteworthy testament to the capacity of a toy to be "played" with on several levels: In 1999, a Canadian computer consultant named Jeffrey Gibbons "hacked" Furby and reprogrammed it to teach real speech to an autistic child. That's a good toy!

What makes a great game? We did the code for Toymax's Jumpstart and Blaster tabletop electronic games, and they were only so-so. While we were admittedly constrained by time and budget, I believe that we simply missed the mark in terms of fun quotient. The play pattern enabled the child to play one of the built-in arcade games after answering questions correctly and earning a designated number of points. However, our games paled in comparison to anything on Game Boy or Nintendo. The lesson we learned is to more broadly define competitive products (and to pick and choose contract work more carefully).

An inventor is ... somebody who feels that nothing in the world is as satisfying as creating new products. A famous actress once told me that she routinely tells aspiring thespians to pursue acting only if it's the only thing in the world they can do. Inventing is the same way: The competition is vast and the odds are stacked heavily against you, so if you can be happy doing something else, then you probably should.

Who or what inspired you to become an inventor? When I was three years old, my parents took me to the laboratory of Thomas Alva Edison in West Orange, New Jersey. While I was there, I told them that I wanted to be an inventor when I grew up. I've been tinkering with things ever since.

What sparks original ideas? My ideas have been inspired by other toys, movies, paintings, sculpture, Broadway shows—you name it.

Advice to would-be inventors: Get patents and copyrights on everything before presenting it. Document your submissions carefully. Stay away from "invention mills." It's incredibly easy to be ripped off in this business.

Paul J. Von Mohr
Paul J. Von Mohr & Associates
Amelia Island, Florida

No. of years in the industry: 17
No. of years as an independent: 6
Approximate number of products licensed: 42
No. of patents held: 2
No. of trademarks held: 3

In a typical year:
No. of ideas conceived: Hundreds
No. of concepts prototyped: 12–16
No. of concepts presented: 20–30
No. of concepts licensed: 8
No. of products that make it to market: 5

Most successful products: Tubby Buddies (Original San Francisco Toymakers), Lil' Grabber Mat & Leveler (Blueridge), Disgusting Designs (Yes! Entertainment), Pound Puppies extensions (Galoob).

What did you do before you were in the industry? Advertising and creative consultant.

What makes a great toy? That's the million-dollar question we all ponder and strive toward. There are many potential great ones, but it has to have a chance to be sold to the manufacturer and the retailer to prove its worth at the consumer level.

What makes a great game? See above.

An inventor is ... one who has the skill to develop a product that is fresh, exciting, and, most important, marketable.

What sparks original ideas? My children, a movie, a walk along the beach, toy store checks, trend studies in other areas, and applying them to the toy industry.

Joseph J. Wetherell
Wetherell Industrial Design
New York, New York

No. of years in the industry: 43
No. of years as an independent: 39
Approximate number of products licensed: 35
No. of patents held: About 10
No. of trademarks held: 1

In a typical year:
No. of ideas conceived: 42
No. of concepts prototyped: 25
No. of concepts presented: 25
No. of concepts licensed: 2
No. of products that make it to market: 1

Most successful products: Pretty Cut 'n Grow (Gabriel Industries/Hasbro Playskool), Nerf Man (Parker Brothers), Nerf Baseball (Parker Brothers), Dolly Surprise (Hasbro Playskool), Pretty Penny Chatterbox (Remco), WWF Sweating Wrestlers (Jakks Pacific), My First Two-Wheeler (Kenner), Wiggles and Giggles (Tyco), Floam (Mattel/Rose Art), Swim and Splash Ernie (Mattel Fisher-Price).

What did you do before you were in the industry? Industrial design, product development, corporate identity, package design.

What makes a great toy? A great toy is one that has sustained interest after the hype and the peer-group pressure has ended. Any toy that is played with extensively provides an important learning experience. Toys are the tools of a child's development. The best toys and games are the ones that provide social interaction between a child and his or her peers or parents.

What makes a great game? Real fun is the most important characteristic. Social interaction is very important. The lack of frustration, especially in younger games, is also critical. The element of chance should enable a less skilled or younger player to compete successfully.

An inventor is ... someone who can clearly define an area of need and is able to execute a clearly defined solution that will fill the need.

What inspired you to become and inventor? My biggest kick is seeing the realization of an idea, even if it doesn't work. The toy business provides a vehicle for the rapid development of a concept into a working prototype. No other product-development business does this. Imagine trying to develop a space shuttle or a mica-chip by yourself.

What sparks original ideas? An original idea can come from anywhere. Another toy, a movie, a conversation, a relationship, a real-life experience—all can spark the original idea. The way to make that spark into a flame is to work on it. The act of working on a concept will change, direct, and refine the concept, if you are lucky. If you are not, you will learn from the failure. This worked for Edison and Da Vinci. If you can't explain the idea that you have to someone not involved in the concept, then you do not really have an idea. Execution is the name of the game. The real creativity comes in the execution.

Advice to would-be inventors: Have a passion for the process. If you feel fulfilled only if you are successful in selling your concept and making a lot of money, you may be disappointed. Do not be afraid of failure. Each failure, if accompanied by your best efforts, will teach you something and perhaps lead you in a new direction.

Howard Wexler
Howard Wexler, LLC
New York, New York

No. of years in the industry: 33
No. of years as an independent: 31
Approximate number of products licensed: 125
No. of patents held: 12+
No. of trademarks held: 12+

In a typical year:

No. of ideas conceived: 100+ (from the first 20 years of my career)
No. of concepts prototyped: Same
No. of concepts presented: Same
No. of concepts licensed: 10–15 per year in mid-1970s; 0–2 from the 1980s
No. of products that make it to market: 98 percent

Most successful products: Connect Four (Hasbro); Wilson Stuffs (Lewco); Popcorn & Candy Plastic Buckets (Ringling Brothers Circus); 3-D classic comic books, promotional program (Wendy's); Obsession (Mego).

What did you do before you were in the industry? Social worker, educator, psychologist.

What makes a great toy? One that is played with over and over again. I think, for the most part, a toy that the player has to bring something to.

What makes a great game? One that requires little setup time, plays quickly and has repeatability (you want to play it over and over again), requires skill but also a bit of good fortune, and does not intimidate.

An inventor is ... someone who gives the world something brand new or something that is a play on an old concept or theme that, in the end, makes it very different and unique. An inventor sees things in a very special way but can also see the practical aspects of the invention (it is marketable, particularly in our business).

Who or what inspired you to become an inventor? I had just gotten a Ph.D. in 1969 and read an article in the newspaper regarding the psychology of toys. That summer I sat down and invented a bunch of games, not knowing anybody in the industry. But I was able to be seen probably because when I called I said, "This is Dr. Wexler," and they were curious to see who I was. The rest is history.

What sparks original ideas? A misconception by lay people is that the inventor walks around and, like magic, an idea is born. For me, what works is thinking about an area or general plaything that I would like to invent. I believe that subconsciously what I have loaded my mind with eventuates into a specific invention. So, I basically believe you have to be thinking in a particular area to trigger a unique concept.

Advice to would-be inventors: Be aware of how difficult it is, particularly today, to earn some serious money in the game/toy business. I would compare the chances of placing a concept with one of the prime toy companies as tantamount to selling a movie to one of the major film studios.

Adam Wolff
Excel Development Group, Inc.
Minneapolis, Minnesota
No. of years in the industry: 8
No. of years as an independent: 8
Approximate number of products licensed: 24
No. of patents held: 0
No. of trademarks held: 0

In a typical year:
No. of ideas conceived: 50
No. of concepts prototyped: 20
No. of concepts presented: 50+
No. of concepts licensed: 8
No. of products that make it to market: 6

Most successful products: Play-Doh Seaside Playworld (Hasbro), *Parenting Magazine* 1999 Toy of the Year. Now sold as Splat!

What did you do before you were in the industry? Ten years in the restaurant business, followed by a return to school and a brief period in legal support, after which I sort of fell backward into the toy business.

What makes a great toy? A license agreement! The best toys let kids do things they otherwise are not allowed to do or cannot do. Nerf lets you throw a ball indoors, and R/C lets you "drive."

What makes a great game? A license agreement! Great adult games reward two complementary skills: strategy and coordination, knowledge and deduction. Kids' games are best when all the players seem to have an equal shot at winning right up to the very end.

An inventor is ... delusionally optimistic by nature, unwilling to accept second best, and confident that he can do better.

Who or what inspired you to become an inventor? What else could I do?

What sparks original ideas? Lack of sleep. Seriously, if I knew it, I'd bottle it. I know what kills an original idea: conventional concerns for cost, size, difficulty of manufacture, and especially the dreaded Not Invented Here syndrome.

Advice to would-be inventors: Get some professional advice, and recognize that there is a huge gulf from an idea to a product, and another from a product to a paycheck. You'll have to have a lot of help along the way, and you'll have to surrender more control than you'd expect.

David Wyman
David Wyman Associates
Del Mar, California
No. of years in the industry: 23
No. of years as an independent: 19
Approximate number of products licensed: 60
No. of patents held: 1
No. of trademarks held: 0

In a typical year:
No. of ideas conceived: 10
No. of concepts prototyped: 1
No. of concepts presented: 1
No. of concepts licensed: 1
No. of products that make it to market: 1

Most successful product(s): 1313 Dead End Drive (Milton Bradley), Big Wheelie (Empire), Shift Tac Toe (Pressman), Don't Feed the Gators (Waddingtons).

What did you do before you were in the industry? Drank warm beer at college.

What makes a great toy? Any toy that makes a child forget about snack time.

What makes a great game? When the game is over, then you want to play again and again. Of course, it helps if you think that you have a chance to win once in a while. Simple rules, a short playing time, and a judicious balance between luck and skill help.

An inventor is ... the catalyst behind the wonder and excitement of the toy industry. Without inventors, many toy companies would try to foist tired, old brands upon the consumer—luckily, children are smarter then toy companies.

Who or what inspired you to become an inventor? My dad.

What sparks original ideas? I do not believe in the dark room theory of inventing, where one comes up with an idea from thin air. We are products of our environments, and the really clever inventors take a spark from anything or anywhere and then play with it until it catches fire in their imagination.

Advice to would-be inventors: Have a working spouse, a sense of humor, and a wild streak of optimism.

Michael Yurkovic
Yurkovic Designs, LLC
Chicago, Illinois

No. of years in the industry: 7
No. of years as an independent: 7
Approximate number of products licensed: 11
No. of patents held: 6
No. of trademarks held: 0

In a typical year:
No. of ideas conceived: 50–60
No. of concepts prototyped: 50–60
No. of concepts presented: 50–60
No. of concepts licensed: 1–3
No. of products that make it to market: 1–3

Most successful products: Key Charm Cuties (Spinmaster), Chairs Game (Fundex), Bubble Faces (Little Kids).

What did you do before you were in the industry? Designed consumer products, mostly in consumer electronics and home healthcare appliances. Technical illustrations for advertising.

What makes a great toy? Open-ended play that lets you take it in your own direction.

What makes a great game? Simple rules and fast action. Player interaction. Parts you can build or play with, without playing the game.

An inventor is ... someone who is willing to look at the world with a beginner's mind, not affected by what can and can't be done.

Who or what inspired you to become an inventor? My wife, Paula, inspired me the most. I saw what thinking as an inventor did to her as a person.

What sparks original ideas? A clear mind.

Paula Yurkovic
Yurkovic Designs, LLC
Chicago, Illinois
No. of years in the industry: 17
No. of years as an independent: 7
Approximate number of products licensed: 20
No. of patents held: 6
No. of trademarks held: 0

In a typical year:
No. of ideas conceived: 50–60
No. of concepts prototyped: 50–60
No. of concepts presented: 50–60
No. of concepts licensed: 1–3
No. of products that make it to market: 1–3

Most successful products: Key Charm Cuties (Spinmaster), Chairs Game (Fundex), Bubble Faces (Little Kids), Secret Places (Galoob), Pen the Pig (Western Publishing), Wee Wild Things (Mattel).

What did you do before you were in the industry? Registered nurse.

What makes a great toy? It has an aspect that allows a child to bring his or her imagination into play.

What makes a great game? Something about the play that is challenging and fun, and that makes you want to play over and over.

An inventor is ... someone who sees connections and creates something new from it.

Who or what inspired you to become an inventor? I wanted to do something that was challenging—very challenging and very creative.

What sparks original ideas? Just about anything—but shopping inspires me.

Advice to would-be inventors: Don't do it. We don't need more competition.

Appendix B

Companies Seeking Ideas

One thousand toy manufacturers are based in the United States, according to the Toy Industry Association (TIA). But only a fraction actively license outside product from independent inventors.

This is an up-to-date, qualified list that identifies the key acquisition person and preferred submission procedures at more than 50 companies that review outside products. The companies have been selected based upon the writers' personal experiences, recommendations of professional inventors, or interviews with key executives. Some companies contacted did not want to be listed because they handle product development in-house or simply did not have interest in participating in this compilation.

No doubt other companies review outside concepts. We offer this list only as a starting point. New inventor-friendly companies sprout up all the time, so you may expand our list from your own experiences.

The industry is in a constant state of flux. When one door closes, a few others open. Companies that do not welcome outside inventor submissions today may have a change of policy tomorrow, and vice versa. Some companies were in business when we started this list, and belly up when we went to press, e.g. Trendmasters and Irwin.

You can find a complete roster of TIA companies on the trade organization's website, www.toy-tia.org. A handy reference and invaluable tool is the TIA's *Official Toy Fair Directory and Year-Round Resource Guide*. No serious toy or game inventor should be without it.

It is infrequent that a company licenses a product on first sight. But presenting in person is the most effective way to communicate your product. Even if you get a fast "no," at least you can move along to the next target of opportunity.

"There are an infinite number of events that can stand in the way of your idea successfully reaching and penetrating the market. These are not roadblocks, just the nature of the business," says Andrew Bergman, whose credits include the Fisher-Price PXL-2000 camera.

"Toy companies are idea-saturated," says game inventor Mary D. Ellroy, a.k.a. GameBird. "Something really has to pop, and pop right away to get them to notice it. There is no time for 'slow grow.'"

Chicago-based Bruce Lund, inventor of EI's GeoSafari Talking Microscope, says that many inventors fail because of a failure to provide what the company is looking for or to make a compelling argument for our concepts. "In other cases," he adds, "it is the failure of the internal group to fully grasp the value, or being too quick to dismiss a concept."

Companies are always expanding, contracting, and changing product lines and direction. It goes without saying that you need to do your homework before you call a company and arrange for your concept to be reviewed.

As part of your research into a company, its product line, and its capabilities, call the company's inventor contact and see if there is a current wish list defining the kinds of items the company wants to market—or, more important, does not want to market. Do not be timid about showing something that breaks the rules if you believe the company has the capabilities to manufacture and sell it. Quite often these can be the biggest winners.

As you utilize the following list, here are some things to keep in mind.

All numbers provided by companies are merely averages, to give you a sense of their activity with submissions. They are not hard and fast calculations.

It would be impossible to list all products a company markets. The notation of *product* is meant only as a category reference, and that changes. For a current and detailed list of products, ask the company, visit its website, or go visit a large toy retailer.

All companies offer a range of advances (from a few thousand dollars to seven figures) and royalties (from 3 to 8 percent). Every deal is different and must stand on its own merits.

Many companies offer option payments to hold a product during an extended internal review. Specific financial terms and conditions are things you will have to negotiate. Options can run for less than $1,000 for 30 days to tens of thousands of dollars for the same period. Typically options are put against future royalties.

The date of receipt refers to when a company first takes your concept in-house. Do not start the clock the day you show a product to the acquisitions viewer. Furthermore, the companies frequently reply sooner than the times shown. Most companies provide fast turnarounds when a concept is a "pass" or rejection.

Never send in unsolicited submissions. This is a rookie move. *Always* contact the company first and follow the specific advice to make a submission.

Many companies will not open packages that arrive with unknown return addresses and names on them.

Aristoplay

8122 Main St.
Dexter, Michigan 48130
Tel: 734-424-0123
Fax: 734-424-0124
Website: www.aristoplay.com
Products: Award-winning educational board and card games
Number of new products introduced annually: 2–4
Number of inventor submissions reviewed annually: 50
Number of inventor submissions licensed annually: 3
Inventor contact: Laura Seagram, marketing manager
Maximum response time from date of receipt: 1 month

Babies 'n Things

Townsend Square, Suite 201A
Oyster Bay, New York 11771
Tel: 516-624-2690
Fax: 516-624-2691
Products: Infant and toddler products and puzzles
Number of new products introduced annually: 24
Number of inventor submissions reviewed annually: 18
Number of submissions licensed annually: 6
Inventor contact: Harvey Lepselter, senior vice president, R&D/Marketing
Maximum response time from date of receipt: 2 weeks to 30 days

Basic Fun
1080 Industrial Highway
Southampton, Pennsylvania 18966
Tel: 215-364-1665
Fax: 215-364-9676
Website: www.basicfun.com

Products: Impulse items, primarily licensed, miniature, working replicas of popular toys and games
Number of new products introduced annually: 50
Number of inventor submissions reviewed annually: 250
Number of inventor submissions licensed annually: 12
Inventor contact: Arch Beasley, inventor liaison
Maximum response time from date of receipt: 60 days

Big Time Toys
2820 Columbine Place
Nashville, Tennessee 37204
Tel: 615-383-2888
Fax: 615-383-1048

Products: Open to all toy ideas
Number of new products introduced annually: 20
Number of inventor submissions reviewed annually: 400
Number of inventor submissions licensed annually: 3
Inventor contact: Tiffany Cummings, inventor liaison
Maximum response time from date of receipt: 2 weeks

Binary Arts
1321 Cameron St.
Alexandria, Virginia 22314-3449
Tel: 703-549-4999
Fax: 703-549-6210
Website: www.puzzles.com

Products: Brainteaser puzzles, toys, and games
Number of new products introduced annually: 25
Number of inventor submissions reviewed annually: 40
Number of inventor submissions licensed annually: 8
Inventor contact: Attention: Product Submissions
Maximum response time from date of receipt: 60 days

Briarpatch
150 Essex St., Suite 301
Millburn, New Jersey 07041
Tel: 973-376-7002
Fax: 973-376-7003
Website: www.briarpatch.com

Products: Award-winning games and puzzles based upon well-known children's books
Number of new products introduced annually: 15–20
Number of inventor submissions reviewed annually: 50
Number of inventor submissions licensed annually: 1
Inventor contact: George Schimpf, director of marketing
Maximum response time from date of receipt: 3 weeks

Cadaco
4300 W. 47th St.
Chicago, Illinois 60632
Tel: 773-927-1500
Fax: 773-927-0350
Website: www.cadaco.com

Products: Board games, activities, and magic
Number of new products introduced annually: 3–5
Number of inventor submissions reviewed annually: 500
Number of inventor submissions licensed annually: 3–5
Inventor contact: Paul Reidy, marketing manager
Maximum response time from date of receipt: 30–60 days

Ceaco
124 Watertown St.
Watertown, Massachusetts 02472
Tel: 617-926-8080
Fax: 617-924-7554
Website: www.ceaco.com

Products: Puzzles and games
Number of new products introduced annually: 24 new puzzle assortments, 10+ games
Number of inventor submissions reviewed annually: 20+ (many more artist submissions for puzzles)
Number of inventor submissions licensed annually: 1–10+

Inventor Contact: Donna Webster, vice president, marketing

Maximum response time from date of receipt: 4–6 weeks

Craft House

328 N. Westwood Ave.

Toledo, Ohio 43607

Tel: 419-536-8351

Fax: 419-536-4159

Website: www.crafthouse.net

Products: Children and adult craft activities: paint by numbers, sun catchers, magic rocks, plastic model cars, boats and planes, licensed activity kits, chemistry and science kits, candle-making kits, and soap-making kits

Number of new products introduced annually: 100–150

Number of inventor submissions reviewed annually: 30–40

Number of inventor submissions licensed annually: 10

Inventor contact: Karen Thompson, director of marketing and product development

Maximum response time from date of receipt: 2–3 weeks

DSI Toys

1100 W. Sam Houston Parkway (North)

Houston, Texas 77043

Tel: 713-365-9900

Fax: 713-365-9911

Website: www.dsitoys.com

Products: Radio-control vehicles, youth electronics, feature electronics, Kawasaki music feature music, feature dolls, soft dolls, plush items, and girls' activities

Number of new products introduced annually: 100

Number of inventor submissions reviewed annually: 300

Number of inventor submissions licensed annually: 6 major standalone items, 6–12 that plug into existing product or lines

Inventor contact: Jamie Grayson, manager, inventor relations

Maximum response time from date of receipt: 1 month

Duncan Toys

P.O. Box 97

15981 Valplast Road

Middlefield, Ohio 44062

Tel: 440-632-1631

Fax: 440-632-1581

Website: www.duncantoys.com

Products: Yo-yos and spin tops

Number of new products introduced annually: 3–4

Number of inventor submissions reviewed annually: 50

Number of inventor submissions licensed annually: 1

Inventor contact: Robert Hammill

Maximum response time from date of receipt: 45 days

Educational Insights

18730 S. Wilmington Ave., Suite 100

Rancho Dominguez, California 90220

Tel: 310-884-2000

Fax: 310-884-2013

Website: www.educationalinsights.com

Products: Educational toys, games, science kits, and electronic learning aids

Number of new products introduced each year: 100

Number of inventor submissions reviewed annually: 300

Number of inventor submissions licensed annually: 10–20

Inventor contact: Maria Gonzales; submission form available through website

Maximum response time from date of receipt: 30–60 days

Endless Games

22 Hudson Place, Suite One

Hoboken, New Jersey 07030

Tel: 201-386-9465

Fax: 201-386-9471

Website: www.endlessgames.com

Products: Board games

Number of new products introduced annually: 2–3

Number of inventor submissions reviewed annually: 500

Number of inventor submissions licensed annually: 1–2

Inventor contact: Kevin McNulty, vice president

Maximum response time from date of receipt: 2 weeks

Estes-Cox, Inc.
1295 H. St.
Penrose, Colorado 81240
Tel: 719-372-6565
Fax: 719-372-3217
Website: www.estesrockets.com

Products: Flying model rockets and other flying products
Number of new products introduced each year: 8–11
Number of inventor submissions reviewed annually: 25–35
Number of inventor submissions licensed annually: 3–5
Inventor contact: Barry Tunick, president
Maximum response time from date of receipt: 30 days

4Kidz
62 Southfield Ave.
1 Stamford Landing, Suite 128
Stamford, Connecticut 06902
Tel: 203-327-7949
Fax: 203-327-4663
Website: www.4kidzinc.com

Products: Gurglin Goosebumps, based on the books by R. L. Stein; Spalding youth sporting goods; Gurglin Gutz & Gurglin Gutz key chains; and Tubbers bathtub toys
Number of new products introduced annually: 15–20
Number of inventor submissions reviewed annually: 100
Number of inventor submissions licensed annually: 4
Inventor contact: Kenneth B. Lewis, executive vice president
Maximum response time from date of receipt: Less than 30 days

Fun 4 All Corp.
16 W. 19 St., 11th Floor
New York, New York 10010
Tel: 212-647-1000
Fax: 212-647-1000
Website: www.fun-4-all.com

Products: Key chains, licensed plush items, licensed cold cast collectibles, licensed bendables, and various licensed and unlicensed novelties in gift and mass

Number of new products introduced annually: 20+
Number of inventor submissions reviewed annually: 50
Number of inventor submissions licensed annually: 6
Inventor contact: Joseph DiResta, executive vice president, marketing
Maximum response time from date of receipt: Less than 30 days, if possible
Note: Boards are okay for simple concepts, but the more elaborate the concept is, the more important proof of concept becomes.

Funrise Toy
6115 Variel Ave.
Woodland Hills, California 91367
Tel: 818-883-2400
Fax: 818-883-3809
Website: www.funrise.com

Products: Full range of light and sound vehicles, licensed and unlicensed preschool light and sound, micro vehicles and play sets, cosmetics, arts and crafts, collectible animals, spring & bubble toys, and novelty banks
Number of new products introduced annually: 40
Number of inventor submissions reviewed annually: 100
Number of inventor submissions licensed annually: 2
Inventor contact: Dave Schwartz, vice president, marketing
Maximum response time from date of receipt: 2 weeks

Gamewright
(A Division of CEACO)
P.O. Box 120
Newton, Massachusetts 02456-0120
Tel: 617-924-6006
Fax: 617-924-6101
Website: www.gamewright.com

Products: Games
Number of new products introduced annually: 0–15
Number of inventor submissions reviewed annually: 75–100
Number of inventor submissions licensed annually: 5–10
Inventor Contact: Jason Schneider, manager, marketing and product development
Maximum response time from date of receipt: 4–6 weeks

General Creation

601 State St.

First Union Building, Suite 500

Bristol, Virginia 24201

Tel: 540-669-3755

Fax: 540-669-0948

Website: www.generalcreation.com

Products: Preschool educational toys, special feature dolls, and cooking toys

Number of new products introduced annually: 20–25

Number of inventor submissions reviewed annually: 200

Number of inventor submissions licensed annually: 15–20

Inventor contact: Bob Compton, vice president, product development

Maximum response time from date of receipt: 4 weeks

Great American Puzzle Factory

16 S. Main St.

S. Norwalk, Connecticut 06854

Tel: 203-838-4240

Fax: 203-838-2065

Website: www.greatamericanpuzzle.com

Products: Award-winning games and jigsaw puzzles

Number of new products introduced annually: 85

Number of inventor submissions reviewed annually: Games: 25; puzzles 120

Number of inventor submissions licensed annually: Games: 2; puzzles 90

Inventor contact: Tracy Guilford

Maximum response time from date of receipt: 4–6 weeks for games; 2–4 weeks for puzzles

Goldberger Doll

1107 Broadway

Room 402

New York, New York 10010

Tel: 212-924-1194

Fax: 212-691-8153

Website: www.goldbergerdoll.com

Products: Full range of dolls

Number of new products introduced annually: 6

Number of inventor submissions reviewed annually: 10–12

Number of inventor submissions licensed annually: 0–2
Inventor contact: Jeff Holtzman, vice president
Maximum response time from date of receipt: 45 days

Happy Dog Toys
2120 East Raymond St.
Phoenix, Arizona 85040
Tel: 602-243-1771
Fax: 602-243-1999
Website: www.happydogtoys.com

Products: Pet care and pet toy products
Number of new products introduced each year: 20–30
Number of inventor submissions reviewed annually: 50+
Number of inventor submissions licensed annually: 5–15
Inventor contact: Neil Werde, vice president
Maximum response time from date of receipt: 2 weeks

Hasbro Games
443 Shaker Road
East Longmeadow, Massachusetts 01028
Tel: 413-525-6411
Fax: 413-525-8438
Website: www.hasbro.com

Products: World's largest publisher of board games and jigsaw puzzles
Number of new products introduced annually: Varies
Number of outside concepts reviewed annually: 1,600
Number of outside concepts licensed annually: 30
Inventor contact: Mike Hirtle, vice president of R&D, product acquisition, inventor relations
Maximum response time from date of receipt: Under 60 days
Note: The company deals only with professional inventors, designers, and agents known to it. Do not send unsolicited submissions.

Hasbro Toy Group (Kenner, Playskool, and Tonka)
1027 Newport Ave.
Pawtucket, Rhode Island 02861
Tel: 401-431-TOYS
Fax: 401-729-7074
Website: www.hasbro.com

Products: World's second-largest toy company. Wide range of toys, ranging from traditional to high-tech.

Number of new products introduced each year: Hundreds

Number of inventor submissions reviewed annually: 3,000

Number of inventor submissions licensed annually: 30–35

Inventor Contact: Concept Acquisitions Department

Maximum response time from date of receipt: 30–60 days

Note: The company deals only with professional inventors, designers, and agents known to it.

Hedstrom Corporation

710 Orange St.

Ashland, Ohio 44805

P.O. Box 432

Bedford, PA 15522

Website: www.hedscape.com

Products: Ball, bounce, and sports items; backyard and fun items

Number of new products introduced each year: 2–4

Number of inventor submissions reviewed annually: 50

Number of inventor submissions licensed annually: 0–4

Inventor contact: No specific person designated; request a corporate submission agreement by calling 1-800-323-5999.

Maximum response time from date of receipt: 2 weeks

Jakks Pacific

22619 Pacific Coast Highway, Suite 250

Malibu, California 90265

Tel: 310-456-7799

Fax: 310-317-8527

Website: www.jakkspacific.com

Products: Wide range of toys, dolls, activity, and preschool items

Number of new products introduced each year: 150

Number of inventor submissions reviewed annually: 100

Number of inventor submissions licensed annually: 3–5

Inventor contact: Gina Lannen, inventor liaison

Maximum response time from date of receipt: 2 weeks

Learning Resources, Inc.
380 N. Fairway Dr.
Vernon Hills, Illinois 60061
Tel: 847-573-8400
Fax: 847-573-8425
Website: www.learningresources.com

Products: Educational toys and materials, including publications
Number of new products introduced each year: 120–140
Number of inventor submissions reviewed annually: 100
Number of inventor submissions licensed annually: 1–2
Inventor contact: Carol Olson
Maximum response time from date of receipt: 60 days

Little Tikes Company
2180 Barlow Road
Hudson, Ohio 44236
Tel: 330-650-3000
Fax: 330-650-3109
Website: www.littletikes.com

Products: Broad line of basic preschool toys and juvenile furniture
Number of new products introduced annually: 65+
Number of inventor submissions reviewed annually: 75+
Number of inventor submissions licensed annually: 0–3
Inventor contact: Betsy Pasko, inventor relations
Maximum response time from date of receipt: 30 days

Manley Toy Quest
1901 Avenue of the Stars, Suite 1025
Los Angeles, California 90067
Tel: 310-277-7855
Fax: 310-277-6055
Website: www.manleytoyquest.com

Products: Electronic toys
Number of new products introduced each year: 80–100
Number of inventor submissions reviewed annually: 400
Number of inventor submissions licensed annually: 4–5
Inventor contact: Brian Dubinsky, president
Maximum response time from date of receipt: 2 weeks or less

Mattel, Inc.
333 Continental Blvd.
El Segundo, California 90245
Tel: 310-252-2000
Fax: 310-252-2179
Website: www.mattel.com

Products: Three business units with $1.2 billion in sales: Boys, Entertainment, Games and Puzzles; Girls, $2 billion in sales; and Infant and Preschool (Fisher-Price), $1.6 billion in sales
Number of outside concepts reviewed annually: 3,000
Number of outside concepts licensed annually: 50
Inventor contact: Office of Inventor Relations
Note: Mattel works only with professional design houses that it has existing relationships with. First write to request company's product submission form and procedure.

The Ohio Art Company
One Toy St.
Bryan, Ohio 43506
Tel: 419-636-3141
Fax: 419-636-7614
Website: www.ohioart.com

Products: Etch-a-Sketch brand, Betty Spaghetty brand, activity and water toys, and metal lithography
Number of new products introduced annually: 1–8
Number of inventor submissions reviewed annually: 200
Number of inventor submissions licensed annually: 1–3
Inventor contact: Josephine Wood, vice president of R&D
Maximum response time from date of receipt: 2–3 weeks

Panache Place
29883 Santa Margarita Parkway, Suite 700
Rancho Santa Margarita, California 92688
Tel: 949-858-8409
Fax: 949-858-5802
Website: www.unimax.com

Product: Anne Geddes licensed products
Number of new products introduced annually: 10 basic (some private label), 4–6 brands
Number of inventor submissions reviewed annually: 100+

Number of inventor submissions licensed annually: 3–6
Inventor contact: Ryan Slate, vice president
Response time: Immediate or within 30 days

Patch Products
1400 E. Inman Pkwy.
P.O. Box 268
Beloit, Wisconsin 53511
Tel: 608-362-6896
Fax: 608-362-8178
Website: www.patchproducts.com

Products: Games, puzzles, and toys
Number of new products introduced annually: 25
Number of inventor submissions reviewed annually: 500+
Number of inventor submissions licensed annually: Under 10
Inventor contact: Peggy Brown, vice president of product development
Maximum response time from date of receipt: 30 days

Pressman Toy
200 Fifth Ave., Suite 1052.
New York, New York 10010
Tel: 212-675-7910
Fax: 212-645-8512
Website: www.pressmantoy.com

Products: Family games, juvenile games, and adult interactive games
Number of new products introduced annually: 15–20
Number of inventor submissions reviewed annually: 150+
Number of inventor submissions licensed annually: 4–5
Inventor contact: Charlotte Rose
Maximum response time from date of receipt: 30–45 days

Prime Time Toys, Ltd.
Suite 205
Kwong Sang Hong Center
151–153 Hoi Bun Road
Kwun Tong, Hong Kong
Tel: 852 276 39 632
Fax: 852 234 16 130
Website: www.pttoys@netvigator.com

Products: General types of spring and summer toys
Number of new products introduced each year: 15
Number of inventor submissions reviewed annually: 250
Number of inventor submissions licensed annually: 10
Inventor contact: Francis Chia, president
Maximum response time from date of receipt: 1 week

Racing Champions/Ertl

800 Roosevelt Road
Glen Ellyn, Illinois 60137
Tel: 630-790-3507
Fax: 630-790-9474
Website: www.rcertl.com

Products: Die-cast replica toys and collectibles, preschool toys, wooden toys, model kits, and action figures
Number of new products introduced each year: 400–600
Number of inventor submissions reviewed annually: 1,000
Number of inventor submissions licensed annually: 4
Inventor contacts: Jeff Jones, director, new products and technology; Greg Miller, vice president, marketing
Maximum response time from date of receipt: 30 days

Radica USA

13628 A Beta Road
Dallas, Texas 75244
Tel: 972-490-4247
Fax: 972-490-7543
Website: www.radicagames.com

Products: Electronic games and lifestyle products
Number of new products introduced annually: 25
Number of inventor submissions reviewed annually: 400
Number of inventor submissions licensed annually: 12–15+
Inventor contact: Jeff Conrad, vice president, outside development
Maximum response time from date of receipt: 30 days

Rose Art Industries
6 Regent Street
Livingston, New Jersey 07039
Tel: 973-535-1313; 1-800-272-9667
Fax: 973-533-9447

Products: Arts and crafts, stationary, activity kits, compounds, dough, girls' cosmetics, and role playing
Website: www.roseartdirect.com
Number of new products introduced annually: 500
Number of inventor submissions reviewed annually: 150+
Number of inventor submissions licensed annually: 10–20
Inventor contact: Vito Amato, vice president, licensing and marketing
Maximum response time from date of receipt: 30 days

Sandylion
400 Cochrane Dr.
Markham, Ontario, Canada L3R 8E3
Tel: 905-475-0523
Fax: 905-475-1165
Website: www.sandylion.com

Products: Stickers and a myriad of sticker-related items, accessories, and extensions
Number of new products introduced each year: 6–12
Number of inventor submissions reviewed annually: 25+
Number of inventor submissions licensed annually: 0–1
Inventor contact: Ben Zack, inventor liaison
Maximum response time from date of receipt: 30–45 days

Simple Wishes
78-825 Via Malodia
La Quinta, California 92253
Tel: 760-564-4207
Fax: 760-564-6045

Products: Wide variety
Number of new products introduced annually: 15
Number of inventor submissions reviewed annually: 3,000
Number of inventor submissions licensed annually: 5
Inventor contact: Gary Niles; no corporate submission agreement required
Maximum response time from date of receipt: 1–4 days

Spin Master Toys
450 Front St. W.
Toronto, Ontario, Canada M5V 1B6
Tel: 416-364-6002
Fax: 416-364-8005
Website: www.spinmaster.com

Products: Wide range of toys, games, and activity products
Number of new products introduced annually: 60
Number of inventor submissions reviewed annually: 3,000
Number of inventor submissions licensed annually: 30+
Inventor contact: Benjamin Dermer, director, inventor relations
Maximum response time from date of receipt: 30 days

S.R.M. Company
1250 Greenwood Ave.
Suite 5
Jenkintown, Pennsylvania 19046
Tel: 215-572-6200
Fax: 215-884-6525
Website: www.srmentmt.com

Products: Electronic role playing, battery-operated plush items, impulse, and light-up nighttime play products.
Number of new products introduced annually: Varies
Number of outside concepts reviewed annually: 300–400
Number of concepts licensed annually: 8–10
Inventor contact: Thomas J. Wilson, vice president, inventor relations and product innovation
Maximum response time from date of receipt: 30 days

Strombecker Corp.
600 N. Pulaski Rd.
Chicago, Illinois 60624
Tel: 773-638-1000
Fax: 773-638-3679

Products: Hard-body die-cast and plastic vehicles, Mr. Bubbles, and Tootsietoy wooden preschool toys
Number of new products introduced annually: 15–20
Number of inventor submissions reviewed annually: 50+

Number of inventor submissions licensed annually: 0–5
Inventor contact: Ed Watrobka, director of product development
Maximum response time from date of receipt: 2–4 weeks

TDC Games

1456 Norwood
Itasca, Illinois 60143
Tel: 630-860-2500
Fax: 630-860-9977
Website: www.tdcgames.com

Products: Board games and puzzles
Number of new products introduced annually: 2–6
Number of inventor submissions reviewed annually: 50+
Number of inventor submissions licensed annually: 0–6
Inventor contact: Sandy Bergeson, vice president. Offers varied royalties or flat fees. Query first by letter or e-mail with a summary of your idea to give the company the general idea of your product. If TDC responds, you will be instructed how to submit a prototype.
Maximum response time from date of receipt: 1 day to 1 year

Uncle Milton Industries, Inc.

5717 Corsa Ave.
Westlake Village, California 91362
Tel: 818-707-0800
Fax: 818-707-0878
Website: www.unclemilton.com

Products: Ant Farm live ant habitats, Undersea Encounter aquarium, Star Theatre home planetarium, and Surfer Frogs live frog habitat
Number of new products introduced annually: 5–10
Number of inventor submissions reviewed annually: 30–50
Number of inventor submissions licensed annually: 0–3
Inventor contacts: Frank Adler, executive vice president, sales and marketing; Eric Poesch, vice president, R&D
Maximum response time from date of receipt: 2–4 weeks

Uneeda Doll Company

200 Fifth Ave.
New York, New York 10010
Tel: 212-675-3313
Fax: 212-929-6494

Products: Basic soft- and hard-bodied dolls and accessories; and mechanical, interactive, and educational dolls

Number of new products introduced annually: 30–40

Number of inventor submissions reviewed annually: 25

Number of inventor submissions licensed annually: 3–6

Inventor contact: Richard Flaxman, president

Maximum response time from date of receipt: 60 days or less

University Games

2030 Harrison St.

San Francisco, California 94110

Tel: 415-503-1600

Fax: 415-503-0085

Website: www.ugames.com

Products: Games and puzzles, specializing in preschool, family, and adult social interaction games

Number of new products introduced annually: 15–20

Number of inventor submissions reviewed annually: 15–20

Number of inventor submissions licensed annually: 1

Inventor contact: Steve Peek, general manager

Maximum response time from date of receipt: 2 months

USAopoly

565 Westlake St.

Encinitas, California 92024

Tel: 760-634-5910

Fax: 760-634-0450

Website: www.usaopoly.com

Products: Board games and puzzles

Number of new products introduced annually: 15

Number of inventor submissions reviewed annually: 24

Number of inventor submissions licensed annually: 1

Inventor contact: Maggie Matthews, vice president, marketing

Maximum response time from date of receipt: 45 days

Warren Industries

3200 S. St.
Lafayette, Indiana 47904
Tel: 1-800-447-2151, 765-447-2151
Fax: 765-448-1313
Website: www.roseart.com

Products: Games and puzzles
Number of new products introduced annually: Varies
Number of outside concepts reviewed annually: 70-100
Number of outside concepts licensed annually: 5-10
Inventor contact: Jim Bousman, director, new products. *Note:* Faxed or e-mailed proposals will not be considered.
Maximum response time from date of receipt: 45 days

Wild Planet Toys

98 Battery St., Suite 302
San Francisco, California 94111
Tel: 1-800-247-6570, 415-705-8300
Fax: 415-705-8311
Website: www.wildplanet.com

Products: Spy toys, water and outdoor toys, natural exploration toys, and interactive products
Number of products: 50+
Number of new products introduced each year: 25+
Number of inventor submissions reviewed annually: 2,000+
Number of inventor submissions licensed annually: 3–4
Inventor contact: Jennifer Soloway, inventor relations. Submit a board, video, or prototype with a concept name and description via postal mail. Concept review meetings are held regularly. When a concept is received, it will be reviewed within a week or two, depending on the volume of concepts received. Feedback in writing will be returned to the inventor, along with the concept. Concepts sent via e-mail will not be accepted.
Maximum response time from date of receipt: 3 weeks

Winning Moves
100 Conifer Hill Dr.
Suite 102
Danvers, Massachusetts 01923
Tel: 978-777-7464
Fax: 978-739-4847
Website: www.winning-moves.com

Products: Reissues of classic Parker Brothers and Milton Bradley games. A select few new items to fill specific needs, most internally invented. Overall description—"Classic, Retro, Cool & Fun."
Number of new products introduced each year: 8–10
Number of inventor submissions reviewed annually: 20
Number of inventor submissions licensed annually: 1
Inventor contact: Laura Pecci, director of marketing
Maximum response time from date of receipt: 3 weeks

Appendix C

Talk The Talk:
A Glossary of Toy
and Game Jargon

"They're wacky and they're kooky, they're altogether spooky, they're America's incredible toy and game inventors."

—Bob Moog, founder and CEO, University Games

When you step off an airplane onto foreign soil and attempt to speak the language of that country, the nationals pay more attention, warm up a little faster, understand you better, and, in general, want to please you more if you try to communicate in their *lingua franca*.

So it is when your flight (of fancy) arrives in Toy Land. Marketing and R&D executives, the first natives you are most likely to encounter as an outside inventor, have their own idioms. Communication will be a lot smoother if you understand corporate speak.

Knowing appropriate "buzzwords" also ensures exact answers to your queries and helps avoid potentially embarrassing semantic ruptures. For example, if a sales executive complains about "dating" problems, don't try to ingratiate yourself by offering an introduction to a single friend. In toy talk, dating refers to how manufacturers bill customers for merchandise.

If the task is to "cannibalize" a doll, don't grab the next flight to the Amazon. Go to the nearest Toys R Us and bring back an existing doll that they can use for parts.

We hope you will enjoy and make use of this glossary of more than 475 words. You may even find it useful to stump opponents in a game of Scrabble.

A-price   Manufacturer's wholesale price to the trade, as reflected on the company's price sheet.

ABS   Strong, long-wearing, stain-resistant thermoplastic widely used in toy components where extra strength is required. Expensive.

abstract   A brief summary of an invention in the body of a patent application that identifies its key features.

accessory   Companion item, adornment, or other piece developed for use with a toy or game, the number of which usually broadens an inventor's royalty base substantially.

accumulation game   Game in which the object is to be the first player to collect a quantity of objects, like marbles, tokens, or money. Examples include Monopoly and The Game of Life.

acetate   A transparent cellulose sheet typically used as an overlay.

acrylic   A polymer based on synthetic resin; a paint that can be mixed and diluted with water.

action figure   Partially or fully articulated. Examples are G. I. Joe and superheroes in Spandex, whose main purpose is to stimulate the sale of complementary accessories such as clothing, play sets, vehicles, and weapons.

add-on   *See* accessory.

administrivia   Too much paperwork.

advance   Negotiated sum of money given to an inventor against future royalties. It is normally nonrefundable.

age-grading   Labeling of products for the appropriate age level of users.

agency   Marketer's advertising agency that creates all forms of promotion.

agent   Person who represents first-time independent inventors to companies. Also called a broker.

air   1. Large amount of white space in a layout. 2. Wasted space in a package.

airbrush   Atomizer for spraying paint onto models and prototypes; used to achieve soft gradations and merging of tones on original artwork.

animatic   Simple cut-out animation used to demonstrate an idea for a TV commercial.

animatronic   An animated electronic toy with sounds.

archives   1. Collections of product that an inventor has not yet sold. 2. Library of old toy catalogs and discontinued products.

"Are you in a hurry to get this back?"   The company wants to keep your concept for review and not pay an option.

articulated figure   Doll or male action figure with jointed parts, such as legs and arms.

atomic   Refers to a product the likes of Trivial Pursuit that sells way beyond anyone's expectations and jumps suddenly well into the millions of units.

audit   Examination of a company's financial records by an inventor or an appointed representative for the purpose of confirming the veracity of royalty reports.

B-school   Abbreviation for business school, where a new wave of marketing executives get impractical training.

B-sheet   Preliminary sketch.

back to basics   A return to uncomplicated products, usually heard every time the industry has a bad year and wants to support a move away from heavily promoted product.

back wrap   The back label of a game box.

backstory   The storyline developed to set the stage for a toy, action figure, or doll; sometimes the basis for an animated television series.

ball-and-paddle game   A video game format.

bar code   Universal Product Code symbol, or UPC seal. A pattern of lines that identifies details of a product.

BCC   E-mail abbreviation for blind copy. Used only when you want to be sure everyone will read what you've written.

bean counter   1. Person who watches the money and lacks imagination. 2. Non–risk taker.

beauty shot   Product image used on packaging to show what is actually being purchased. It captures the product in its most exciting form.

Big Wheel   Distinctive style of tricycle, made famous by Louis Marx. It has a large, 16-inch front wheel and two smaller back wheels.

bill of materials   List of components used to specify the manufacture of a toy or game.

blank check   What toy companies never give inventors.

blank space   What inventors have to fill with creativity.

bleed   1. What inventors often have to do for companies. 2. Image that extends to the edge of the paper or page.

blister   *See* clam shell.

blister card   Four-color printed card that holds and sells product. Generally displayed hanging on a hook.

blow molding   Manufacturing process consisting of forming a tube and introducing air or gas that causes the heated tube to expand against a mold for forming hollow objects such as bottles or toys.

blow off the shelves   To sell extremely well.

blow up   1. An enlargement. 2. Inventor's reaction when things are not going well.

blue-skying   *See* noodling.

board game   Game played on an illustrated, printed playing field.

boilerplate   Standard language in a license agreement.

bounce back   1. What a professional inventor does after a rejection. 2. An additional offer mailed with a self-liquidator. *See* self-liquidator.

brand equity   Strength of a brand to attract consumers.

breadboard   1. To make an experimental arrangement of a mechanism or electronic circuit on a flat surface. 2. A model that demonstrates to R&D how something will work.

break-even   Point at which a product makes back its initial investment and begins to pull its own weight in the marketplace.

Bridge, The   Ninth-floor passageway that links 200 Fifth Ave. and 1107 Broadway; a favorite meeting place for inventors during the New York Toy Fair.

Bristol board   Fine board used for drawing or printing.

broker   *See* agent.

busy box   Infant activity toy designed for a crib, a playpen, or the floor. Typically incorporates multiple actions, such as clicking dials, squeaking bulbs, spinning wheels, and rattles.

buyer   Decision maker who selects and purchases items that will appear on retail store shelves.

CAD   Abbreviation for computer-aided design.

calendering   1. Manufacturing process that produces thin plastic sheets and films by squeezing melted resin between sets of rollers. It can best be compared to the spreading of butter. 2. Watching the months tick by without a contract while a company holds your item.

camera-ready Artwork ready to be photographed for reproduction.

cannibalize 1. To use parts from an existing product for the purpose of making a prototype. 2. To expand a brand to a point that the extensions erode the market share of the main product.

"Can't wrap my arms around it." Uttered by an executive struggling to understand a submission.

cardware Cards in a board game.

casting Manufacturing process whereby a molten substance (such as zinc for miniature vehicles or pawns) is poured, not squeezed, into a mold and takes shape as it cools. This process is best compared to baking a cake.

category General class to which a particular product belongs, such as hobby, action figure, skill and action, doll, or preschool.

CES Abbreviation for Consumer Electronics Show.

chain Group of three or more retail stores involved in the business of merchandising toys and games.

champion Executive who advocates and defends a product throughout its development process. Recognized by the cuts and bruises around the eyes and mouth. *See* white knight.

chance game Game that requires no skill, strategy, or general knowledge. Player action is entirely dependent on random movement of dice, cards, or a spinner.

character licensing 1. Imprinting of a character, image, logo, signature, design, personality, or property on an existing product to heighten awareness and sales. 2. Reproduction of a character, image, logo, signature, design, or property in and of itself as a viable entity.

child test Formal or informal hands-on testing.

chip 1. Small piece of semiconductor material, typically silicon, on which electronic components are formed. 2. Playing piece in certain games of chance.

chipboard Heavy paper board used for packaging and for appropriate parts of prototypes.

Christmas What it's all about. Ready or not, it's always on December 25.

chromalin Four-color, one-of-a-kind proof on plastic substrate. Used to check artwork before a full press run.

clam shell Packaging in clear plastic that has been molded to an item's physical profile, hinged in the middle, and snapped around the product for point-of-sale display.

classic   Product that has been popular with millions of people for more than 25 years.

closeout   Industry heartbreak. Toy or game that has been a major disappointment and is being reduced in price to get rid of remaining inventory. It causes some inventors to rekindle their full creative powers.

clutch ball   Infant toy.

co-inventor   One or more inventors of a product are referred to as co-inventors.

"Coffee?"   You have someone's undivided attention for an extra five minutes. Take it even if you don't like coffee.

collectible   Assortment of product with a common design or tie-in that encourages multiple purchases. Often consumers think such product will increase in value with age.

commercial shoot   Production of a television spot.

comp   Shortened version of "comprehensive." A drawing or model that shows what a product will look and/or work like when it is finished.

confidential disclosure   Agreement between two or more parties that an idea is being reviewed, with an understanding that information will not be shared.

consumer   Someone who has selected the product at retail with expectations of great entertainment and play value.

consumer research   Studies with consumers to determine their unmet needs, buying patterns, attitudes toward existing products on the market, reactions to packaging and commercials, and other factors related to marketing. Sometimes used as excuse for returning an inventor item. *See* focus group *and* kitchen research.

control drawing   Drawing with specifications, from which model makers can produce working samples.

copyright   Exclusive legal right to reproduce, publish, and sell the matter and form of a literary, musical, or artistic work.

corrugated   Protective paper packaging material used on outer cartons. When decorated with four-color printing, used for individual packaging structures.

CPSC   Abbreviation for Consumer Product Safety Commission, the federal watchdog agency for established safety standards.

crafts   Activity category comprising products that require manual dexterity or artistic skills.

cross-collateralize   Cause synergism between two disparate products or presentations of product, the end result being something stronger than the individual elements alone.

cross-marketing Promotion of one or more products on the back panel of another company product.

cross-sell brochure Insert placed in manufacturer's boxes showing consumers other similar or accessory products available from the same source.

customer Most important person in the business; may refer to a trade buyer or an end user.

cut steel To produce a mold for mass production.

"Cute!" (As in, "That's a cute item!") The kiss of death.

dating Form of billing. The trade receives its merchandise as early in the year as possible, but it doesn't have to pay until after Christmas dollars are received from consumers.

deal breaker 1. A proposed contractual stipulation or condition that one party cannot or will not agree to. 2. A lawyer. 3. Doesn't cost out.

death by tweakage When a product fails because of unnecessary tinkering or too many last-minute revisions.

deco Shorthand for decoration.

deferred Marketing euphemism that means a product has been dropped, but marketing won't tell R&D until next year.

delta hook Opening in the top of a blister card that takes the form of a delta wing.

demo 1. Short for the demonstration of a product to company personnel or trade buyers, which can make or break an item depending upon the quality of the show. 2. Short for demographics. *See* demographics.

demographics Statistical studies relating to human populations, especially with reference to size, density, distribution, and vital statistics.

design patent Protection for the appearance of an item, not its structure or utilitarian features.

designer Person who creates, executes, or builds a product according to artistic skills.

develop further/resubmit Improve a submission at your own expense.

die-cast Metal toy, generally a vehicle or soldier, that is cast from zinc.

die-cut To cut sheet material—whether paper, plastic, or cardboard— into unique forms and shapes using a steel rule die mounted onto heavy press equipment for mass-production purposes.

disclosure form *See* nondisclosure form.

dog   Slang reference to a product that's dead at retail.

dog-and-pony show   Elaborate presentation of a new product by its creator or marketer.

domo aregato   Japanese for "Thank you."

done deal   The start of negotiations.

double tooling   Expanding production output to meet demand. The wish of every inventor.

dough   1. Any of numerous soft modeling compounds. 2. Inventor royalties.

driver   A lead item that can create consumer interest in an entire line.

drop paper   Act of issuing firm purchase orders.

drop shadow   A shadow behind an image or lettering designed to bring the image or letters forward.

dropped item   1. Product that has been withdrawn from consideration. 2. End of an inventor's dream.

dumb it down   Double negative refers to making a product so that the masses can understand it.

dumb it up   Refers to making a product just slightly better for the mass market.

e-mail   1. Electronic mail. 2. Preferred method of communication between companies and inventors because it is fast, flexible, and reliable. *See* I don't have e-mail.

E3   Abbreviation for Electronic Entertainment Expo. Held each June in Los Angeles.

eats like an elephant, s--ts like a sparrow   Refers to larger toymakers who frequently license more than they market.

edutain   To educate through entertainment; usually used for science toys or other discovery products.

eighty-twenty formula   Eighty percent of the volume is done by 20 percent of the products.

ELA   Abbreviation for electronic learning aid.

electronics   Items using microcircuitry in their function instead of mechanical action.

end cap   Best display space a product can get in a toy store; shelves that occupy the ends of aisles.

energy   The vitality of expression an inventor requires to license a toy or game.

engine   Hot product that can pull interest in an entire line. *See* driver.

engineer   Person assigned to transform approved concept, design, and model into specifications and tolerances leading to mass-producible pieces.

engineering drawing   Detailed and accurate drawing of all parts needed to manufacture a new item. These become the blueprints for ultimate tooling and production of parts.

entertainment property   A book, movie, television show, musical talent, sports hero, or other celebrity upon which a toy, game, or line is based.

ergonomics   Science of making buttons and controls fit the product within the limitations of its design.

errata sheet   Message inserted in packages to alert consumers of changes in information affecting game play or assembly.

extension   Independently marketed product that trades on the name and goodwill of another product.

extrusion   Manufacturing process in which solid resin pellets fluidize while being pushed continuously through a heating chamber by a large screw. It can best be compared to the squeezing of a toothpaste tube. Different openings are used to shape the resulting mass.

face panel   The front or main panel of a package that usually faces the aisle on retail shelves.

Fair, The   Shorthand for the annual American International Toy Fair held in New York City each February.

fair use   A court ruling regarding copyright or trademark infringement. It says that under certain conditions a trademark or copyrighted material can be used without a license fee or permission.

fantasy quest   Video game format.

fashion doll   Usually partially or fully articulate. Its main purpose is to stimulate sales of complementary accessories, such as clothing, play sets, and vehicles.

Federal Express   The quickest and most expensive way to get an inventor's prototype to the key marketing and R&D executives just as they leave on vacation.

first-handshake item   Marketing term for a product that captures the attention of a new mother with her first child. A successful first-handshake item will be one that's instrumental in building brand loyalty.

F.I.T.   Abbreviation for Fashion Institute of Technology. Bestows a Bachelor of Fine Arts in Toy Design.

flashing   Excess plastic not trimmed off during the molding process; caused by poor tool match. Easily removed with X-acto blade or pen knife.

FOB   Abbreviation for freight on board, which is generally used to signify a purchase plan whereby the trade can pick up product at its foreign point of manufacture for a lower price than in the United States.

focus group   Formally organized testing of a product by volunteer or paid consumers.

folding carton   Packaging structure (usually of die-cut chipboard) that, when folded into dimension, anchors and displays product.

forecast   Projection of the number of units of a product that will sell within a given period, such as one month or one year; sometimes called a guesstimate.

four fold   Any game board that opens into four sections. Also known as quad fold.

free   No charge, but frequently has strings attached.

free-standing insert   Newspaper supplement in which retailers announce sales for toys and games, usually during the major consumer buying time of Thanksgiving to Christmas. *See* FSI.

front wrap   The front label of a game box.

FSI   Abbreviation for free-standing insert, which refers to Sunday newspaper retailer inserts.

game   Organized play with rules, opposing interests, and goals; sometimes a toy with rules.

gamer   Player of non–mass-market games, such as role-playing formats.

gating authority   Key decision maker, especially over new product submissions.

Glass   Once the industry's leading independent development company; named for founder Marvin Glass. When the organization dissolved, it was called Broken Glass.

glide rate   The downward slide of a product after it has been jump-started; usually occurs in its second year.

glossies   Black-and-white photographic prints used for advertising and publicity.

go south   Inventor's idea dropped by manufacturer.

goodwill   The value of the commercial reputation of a business or of a line of products or services.

grabber   Any visual or verbal element associated with a product that will "grab" executive or consumer attention; may be a special price, name, claim, or payoff.

graphics   Artwork on a toy, game, or package.

green light   The project's a go.

gremlins   1. Obstacles designed into games to create problems for players. 2. In no way related to Furby.

guarantee   1. Minimum sum of money that a manufacturer ensures an inventor he will earn on a product, even if it is dropped or performs poorly. 2. Element desired in life and license agreements.

hair play   Brushable hair, an important and popular feature on some girls' toys.

handhelds   Miniaturized portable games, usually electronic.

hard copy   Paper document.

hard cost   Product's full cost, including materials, labor, and packaging (if offshore, add duty and freight).

hero's powers   What you can do to enemies in video games.

hero's weaknesses   What enemies can do to you in video games.

hitchhiking   The process of one person's idea producing a similar idea or an enhanced idea from another person.

hype   1. Promotion of a product through media events. 2. Product claims. 3. Exaggeration of performance or payoff.

"I don't get it."   Signal that you should pull another idea from your bag of tricks—fast.

"I don't have e-mail."   Signal that you don't want to do business with this individual.

impulse item   A product designed and priced to be bought on impulse by the consumer.

in review process   Often means the secretary hasn't sent out your rejection letter yet.

in stock   Manufacturer's inventory of product ready to ship; a schedule milestone.

in the mail   Inventor's prototype, contract, or check that hasn't yet been sent but that will be now.

in the pipeline   1. Product that is being prepared, processed, or worked on by a company. 2. Product that is being distributed to retail outlets.

in-house   A process or service conducted within a company.

infant   1. Age grading for a variety of toys and activity items. 2. A child under one year of age.

inflatable   Any indoor/outdoor, hollow vinyl toy that requires inflation with air. Primary cause of hyperventilation among parents.

infringement Unauthorized making, using, or selling for practical use, or for profit, of an invention, trademark, trade dress, or copyright, usually announced by a lawyer.

injection molding Manufacturing process in which machines pressure-inject molten plastic granules into relatively cold molds, where they solidify and take the shape of the mold cavity. It can best be compared to making waffles.

insert 1. Packaging element added to a box to anchor the product so it stays in a predetermined position. 2. A clause added to a license agreement.

intellectual property Ideas or concepts that are subject to ownership. *See* IP.

introduction Launch of a new plaything, usually at Toy Fair and hopefully with great fanfare and ballyhoo.

inventing community Catchall for professional inventors. A nice place to be for creative minds.

inventor relations Department at a company that deals with outside developers.

IP Abbreviation for intellectual property, such as patents, trademarks, copyrights, trade secrets, and so forth.

I/R Abbreviation for infrared. A detector sends out modulated infrared light and looks for reflected light coming back. Used to make toys interactive.

ism As in, "That's an ism in the industry." Judgmental declaration delivered to sound like a hard and fast rule. Example: "Clown-theme games don't sell."

item Single product.

j-hook Opening at top of a blister card that takes the form of the letter J. This allows the consumer to remove product from anywhere on the rack without disturbing other blister cards hung in front of and behind it.

j-peg Electronic image that can be e-mailed.

joystick Type of hand control for video games that players use for moving images on the screen.

jump-start a product To throw a lot of television dollars behind an item in hopes of getting strong consumer sell-through.

keeper New product that a manufacturer wants to hold for further review.

key account Major customer determined by number of retail stores and sales history.

kidvid Saturday morning television programs, usually animated.

Kinko it To get something reproduced.

KISS   Abbreviation for Keep It Simple Stupid, usually used when describing a way to approach product design.

kitchen research   Informal research conducted in a casual manner to get reaction to the play of an item.

knock back   *See* screw you factor.

knockoff   1. Stealing of another person or company's product by copying it so closely that it embodies the spirit of the original. 2. Nonpromoted copy of a best-selling product at a lower price.

labor-intensive   Manufacturing requiring large amounts of handwork; usually done offshore.

Law of Unintended Consequences   Whatever can go wrong, will.

lawyers   The only people who consistently turn a profit.

LC   Abbreviation for letter of credit.

LCD   Abbreviation for liquid crystal display; screen that gives scoring or playing fields in a visual form.

LED   Abbreviation for light-emitting diode; a type of light in an electronic toy or game.

legal scrub   To run an agreement by a lawyer.

legals   Corporate shorthand for patent, trademark, and copyright notices that appear on packaging and product.

"Let me show it to my people."   Music to an inventor's ears.

letter of credit   Letter addressed by a banker to a correspondent certifying that the person or company named is entitled to draw a certain amount of money upon the completion of a specific performance—for example, the production of a quantity of toys or games.

licensed property   Unique character, event, or personality that has proven consumer appeal, which companies incorporate into their products for a royalty.

licensee   Term used in licensing agreements to designate the company.

licensing   1. Act of contracting for the rights to manufacture and market an item or concept. 2. Application of an entertainment property to a product at higher than usual royalty rates.

licensing agreement   Authorization to manufacture and market a piece of intellectual property, such as a toy, game, or design.

licensor   Term used in licensing agreements to designate the inventor.

life support   Where an item goes just before it is dropped.

line   1. Family or series of toys or games tied together by a common design or theme; always better than a single item. 2. What an inventor hears when a company drops his item. 3. The full collection of products a company sells.

line art   Drawing made in solid lines as copy for a linecut.

line review   1. Periodic management meeting to review line development. 2. Bloodbath; often catered.

linecut   Letterpress printing plate photoengraved from line art.

living hinge   Flexible joint that is a one-piece molding.

load-'em-up-and-bust game   Players fill something until it overloads and bursts.

lobby lizard   Inventor who hangs out in a lobby waiting to make a pitch.

logged in   Receipt of an inventor item by the inventor relations department, signifying that it is in good hands.

logo   Symbol or identifier for a product or corporation.

looks-like prototype   Three-dimensional model that looks exactly like the production model of an item will look, although it need not be made from the ultimate materials.

looks-like, works-like prototype   Three-dimensional model that looks and performs exactly like a production model, although it need not be made from the ultimate materials.

loss leader   Selling technique used by retailers in pricing a popular item at or below cost to attract consumers in hopes they will buy that item and more.

Majors, The   1. Hasbro and Mattel. 2. Wal-Mart, Toys R Us, and Target.

margin   1. Amount of profit made on an item based upon the difference in manufacturing and other costs versus the manufacturers' selling price. 2. Difference between what a retailer pays and what its customer is charged.

mark-up   Percentage added by the retailer, above what was paid to the manufacturer, to reach a shelf price.

markdown   Reduction in an original selling price.

marker rendering   Illustration done with Magic Marker.

market   1. Price offered for a particular product. 2. Area of demand. 3. Organized coming together of buyers and sellers.

market share   Portion of a particular category "owned" by a particular product. Never big enough.

marketer A person or company masterful in marketing.

marketing 1. Process of selling or offering something for sale based upon a plan. 2. Opening new sales opportunities to maximize and exploit product potential.

marketing plan Business objectives that include merchandising, pricing, distribution channels, personal selling, and advertising.

mass marketer Large chains such as Wal-Mart, Toys R Us, and Target, which have capacity to buy and sell the largest number of SKUs to the greatest number of consumers.

master licensee Company that licenses rights to produce and market the most products for a certain brand.

mature market 1. The major market segment of senior citizens. 2. Market with little growth potential beyond where it is now.

maven Yiddish noun for "expert."

MBA Corporate type whose work is dictated by numbers; usually carries a calculator, an abacus, or worry beads.

me-too product Close copy of another item; usually a knockoff of a successful item. *See* knockoff.

mechanical Art board with layout of typesetting and art placement positioned according to specifications for the production of printed pieces.

media plan Advertising program that delivers effective messages to the greatest number of target consumers at the lowest possible cost.

metalize To give a toy a lustrous metallic veneer.

microcontroller Brain of an electronic game; small integrated circuit that has data entered by the player.

minimum order quantity The number of orders required for a manufacturer to produce a product.

mockup Two- or three-dimensional representation of an idea to translate the verbal into the visual.

model Clear and detailed prototype.

model makers Handcrafters of prototypes/models.

mold 1. Cavity in which a substance is formed. 2. Furry growth on an inventor submission that has been in the company's holding room for too long without light.

momentai (Phonetic spelling). Chinese for "No problem." Heard frequently by Americans on factory visits to China.

MOQ   *See* minimum order quantity.

motion lines   Lines around artwork or lettering that give the impression of movement or speed.

movers   1. Game pawns. 2. Confident execs and inventors.

multicavity mold   Mold with multiple cavities for increased production. Often these cavities produce multiple copies of a single component.

multiple submission   Submission by an inventor of the same concept simultaneously to several companies. Potential survival method used by an inventor to avoid having all his eggs in one basket.

nailed to the shelf   Stiff product; one that doesn't sell.

near-pack   Term used for a direct premium, typically stacked up next to the promoted product.

neophobia   Fear of anything new.

net wholesale price   Manufacturer's billed price to its customers, minus cash and trade discounts and allowances.

new product review   Periodic conference on new submissions.

nice try   Attempt to pay an inventor on a nonroyalty basis. *See* work-for-hire.

NIH   Abbreviation for not invented here; term used to describe companies that do not welcome outside submissions.

NIH syndrome   A corporate state of mind against outside submissions.

"No problem."   Big problem.

no-brainer   A toy or game that is easy to explain or use; something obvious.

nondisclosure form   Agreement between an inventor and a company that makes it possible for both parties to share and review new concepts in confidence. Weighted in the favor of the manufacturer.

nonpromoted item   Toy or game with no advertising or publicity budget.

noodling   Doodling with a purpose, massaging a concept to a more finished form.

novelty   Small, inexpensive manufactured item usually sold on blister cards.

objective   Brief summary of the object of a board game or the storyline of a video game.

OEM   Abbreviation for original equipment manufacturer; used to describe an element in a product that can be purchased ready-made from a source.

on the water   A product that has been made offshore and is en route via sea freighter to the United States.

option   Agreement with financial obligations that lets a company hold a prototype for a period of time.

original   Product that has been done before, but in a different way.

overpackaged   1. Far too little product for the size of the box. 2. Too much air.

paddle controls   Type of hand controller for video games that players use to move the images on the screen.

paper   Customer order to purchase merchandise.

parallel development   Similar products from two different inventing sources.

patent   Grant of property right by the government to the inventor; it confers the right to exclude others from making, using, or selling the invention throughout the United States for 17 years from the date of issue, subject to the payment of maintenance fees. *See also* infringement.

patent attorney   Lawyer who specializes in writing patent applications.

patent infringement   *See* infringement.

patent pending   Notice to the public that an application for patent on a particular item is on file in the USPTO.

pawn   Playing piece or token used in games to represent individual players.

payoff   1. Reward at the end of a game. 2. A physical action of a toy that delights the user.

perceived value   Worth of a product, as reflected in its components, packaging, and ad campaign.

pips   Markings on each side of a die cube, from one to six.

plan-o-gram   Diagram of a store shelf layout that a mass-market retailer plans to devote to a category or a specific manufacturer's product line.

plastic   Synthetic material produced from chemicals that can be molded into almost any form. It may be any color or colorless. Some have the hardness of steel; others have the softness of silk.

plastic by the pound   Basic, inexpensive playthings sold primarily by mass-market retailers, often unpackaged, as in balls and beach and tub toys.

play environment   1. Line of accessories that complement toys, such as houses, forts, and garages. 2. Setting in which toys and games are enjoyed.

461

play pattern   The way in which children use a toy.

play value   Lasting fun inherent in a toy or game.

playthings   1. Toys. 2. Leading trade magazine. *(Playthings)*

plush   Stuffed animals or toys.

P.O.   Abbreviation for purchase order.

polyethylene   Lightweight, flexible thermoplastic that has a waxlike feel—for example, a beach bucket and shovel.

polypropylene   Lightweight, strong, heat-resistant moldable thermoplastic that bends but does not break.

pond   1. The Atlantic Ocean. 2. Pacific Ocean.

POP   Abbreviation for point of purchase; advertising displays positioned near the product on the shelf.

preliminary design   1. R&D department, a think tank charged with taking concepts to earliest definition. 2. The breadboard stage of a product under development. 3. Conversion of a concept into 3D form.

prepricing   Price printed on a product by the manufacturer to designate a suggested retail cost.

preschool   In age grading for a variety of toys and games, children under five years of age.

presell   To sell a product to the trade before its introduction at Toy Fair.

presentation   1. Meeting to show product. 2. The belief that if an inventor spends $1,000 on a plane ticket, rental car, and hotel room, a concept will sell itself.

press proof   Litho sheet that shows preproduction artwork off a printing press.

price point   Price at which a product is offered for sale to the trade.

print campaign   Advertising schedule of ad placement in magazines or newspapers versus other media, such as radio and TV.

prior art   Usually refers to patents in a certain field of invention that exist (or do not exist) when a patent search is conducted.

product description   The only verbiage that is read less often than assembly instructions.

product manager   Marketing person charged with seeing a product through from its initial stages to completion, positioning, packaging, and promotional campaign. Responsible for bottom line. His or her word has become law in many companies.

profit   Dollar return over and above all expenses to develop, produce, and market a product.

progression game   Game whose object is to be the first player to reach a goal, such as the end of a path. Moves are typically determined by dice or a spinner.

promoted item   A major toy or game that has an advertising and publicity budget. An inventor's dream.

promotion   1. Product hype, usually involving a combined campaign of print, television, trade displays, and public relations. 2. Reward to an executive for doing a great job.

proof   Test applied to articles or substances to determine whether they are of standard or satisfactory quality.

prototype   1. Original model on which something is patterned. 2. To create an original model.

PTDL   Abbreviation for Patent and Trademark Depository Library.

PTO   Abbreviation for Patent and Trademark Office in Washington, D.C. *See* USPTO.

purchase intent   Indication by consumers during product testing that if a product is available in a particular form at a specific price, then, in all likelihood, they would buy it.

push 'n pull   1. Type of preschool toy. 2. Play pattern.

PVC   Abbreviation for polyvinyl chloride.

QA   Abbreviation for quality assurance.

QC   Abbreviation for quality control.

quad fold   *See* four fold.

quarterly reports   1. Statements from manufacturers to inventors that tell how many of any particular licensed item have been sold. Inventors hope that royalty checks also accompany such reports. 2. Financial report to stockholders on the condition of business during the previous three-month period.

R&D   Abbreviation for research and development.

rack jobbers   Wholesalers specializing in carded toys.

random generator   Dice, spinner, or other device for randomizing moves in a game.

randomizer   *See* random generator.

rapid prototyping   Technologies that additively "grow" a design layer by layer through a process driven by 3D CAD data. Stereolithography (SLA) and selective laser sintering (SLA) are two of the leading technologies, and objet is the latest. In a design process, early development of a small-scale prototype used to test certain key features of a design.

R/C   Abbreviation for radio-controlled toys, such as cars, boats, and aircraft, that are either gas- or battery-powered and steered by means of handheld transceivers.

receptionist   1. The first stop. 2. Key inventor contact.

red light   1. New product that stops traffic. 2. Corporate speak for "Don't spend any more of our money on that prototype."

reject   Conflicts with internal development. "Thanks for your idea; we can now develop it as an internal item." Often used when a company does not want to pay a royalty.

rejection letter   A regular happening; standard communication between manufacturer and inventor.

research and development   1. Careful and diligent investigation that companies conduct on products they contemplate manufacturing. 2. The process of creating new products.

returns   Products that have been on sale at retail, have not sold through, and are being shipped back to the manufacturer by the retailer.

reusable compound   Type of activity toy, such as Play-Doh.

ride-on   Pedal, foot-to-floor, or battery-operated vehicle.

role play   A category of toys that encourages kids to act out characters.

roller ball   Type of hand controller for video games that players use to move images on the screen.

rotational molding   The heating of finely ground vinyl plastisols in a rotating mold until melting or fusion occurs. When the mold is cooled, a hollow part is removed. This is a relatively cheap, scrap-free process that is especially popular for the production of large plastic items.

rotos   *See* FSI.

royalty   1. Payment made to an inventor by a manufacturer for each piece sold. 2. Toy and game inventors.

sand timer   Instrument for measuring the time of game play, consisting of a plastic hourglass in which sand runs from the top into the lower section.

schematic   Diagram of an electronic circuit.

screw you factor   Method to set back an opponent in a game.

sculptor   Artist capable of producing three-dimensional forms from verbal, sketch, or photographic guidelines.

second line copy   *See* tag line.

secret   Something everybody is talking about.

secretary   The second stop. A good person to know on a first-name basis.

selective laser sintering   Form of rapid prototyping that uses 3D CAD geometry to create models. The software slices the 3D CAD model into thin cross-sections or layers; the laser sinters/fuses layers of materials together to form solid 3D objects from the original 3D CAD model.

self-liquidator   Consumer premium offered (usually by mail) for proof of purchase and a cash amount to cover merchandise cost, postage, and handling.

sell panel   Any panel on a package that communicates features and benefits of a product; usually the front panel.

sell sheet   A promotional flyer that hypes a product.

sell-in   Purchase of product by the trade.

sell-through   Purchase of product by the end user.

sellitus   A disease that overtakes inventors, amateurs, and professionals who have not sold a product for a while and need the victory (or an advance).

semiconductors   Conductors of electricity (typically made from silicon) that allow the design and manufacturing of very small, very complicated, yet very inexpensive electric circuits.

separations   Lithographic process by which printers "separate" colors of artwork in preparation for making printing plates; most often four-color.

setup box   Common packaging structure in which there is a box top and a box bottom.

shakers and rollers   Entrepreneurs and intrapreneurs. Both make toys and games happen. *See* movers.

shelf space   Linear footage in a store that manufacturers can never get enough of and that retailers monitor for product movement.

shelf talker   Audio device that calls consumer attention to a product at retail.

ship air   1. To pack a product improperly so that the package is oversized for the dimensions of the contents, thereby capturing excess space (that is, air). 2. Often referred to as slack packaging.

shoot   Session for still photography or video/film production, as in a commercial shoot.

shrink-wrapping   Tight plastic protective covering used to seal packaging.

shtikmeister   Root: Yiddish, for "showman."

shut-up toy   Plaything given to a child to keep him or her quiet and occupied.

skill-and-action game   Fast-paced, three-dimensional game in which two to four players race to complete the collection of certain pieces.

SKU   *See* stock-keeping unit. Sometimes written "skew."

SLA   Abbreviation for stereolithography. *See* stereolithography.

slicensing   Slicing a licensed property too thin; having too many licensees in the same category.

slot car   Electric toy racing vehicle that has an arm underneath that fits into a groove for guidance and metal strips alongside the groove for power.

SLS   Abbreviation for selective laser sintering. *See* selective laser sintering.

small entity status   Status of an independent inventor that qualifies the inventor for a 50 percent discount on USPTO patent fees.

soft goods   *See* plush.

soft sales   Rate of sale below company expectations.

soft sculpture   Umbrella term that refers to stuffed animals or toys.

soft-toy designer   Person experienced in soft sculpture, pattern making, and prototype construction.

"Sorry, I gotta take this call."   Take a deep breath and be prepared to wow 'em. You've got two more minutes.

sourcing   Locating a supplier or manufacturer of component parts required to produce a particular toy or game.

specifications   1. Description of an invention for which a patent is sought. 2. Detailed dimensions or list of components or processes for something to be manufactured.

spinner   Movable arrow spun on a dial to indicate the number or kind of moves a player may make in a board game.

split royalty   Situation whereby two or more inventors or licensors divide a royalty.

splurge ad   Full-page print advertisement.

spot   Television commercial. Most common increments are 15, 30, and 60 seconds.

stacking rings   Infant toy comprised of colorful rings of various sizes.

stand   A trade show exhibition booth (British term).

staple   Product that sells year in and year out, considered indispensable by the manufacturer.

stereolithography   System and materials that enable you to create durable, metal, plastic, or rubberlike parts directly from any solid CAD model in as little as one day and without dependence on costly tooling or skilled labor.

stiff   Product that does not sell through at retail.

stock-keeping unit (SKU)   Single toy or game inventoried by a retailer that occupies shelf space.

storyboards   Sketches of pictures and their related narration or dialogue; used to plan a television commercial or animated program.

strategy game   Game won through mental superiority. Formats include whodunits, war games, and games of alignment.

sublicensing   Licensing product to one or more third parties by the primary licensee, usually for the purpose of manufacturing and distributing in another territory.

submission form   *See* nondisclosure form.

suggested list price   Retail price suggested by the manufacturer.

suggestion box   Management tool used when trying to get a read on internal issues that no one wants to face directly.

tag line   Slogan, usually printed under the trademark.

take 'n shake toy   Infant toy with interesting sounds.

tasteless cake, beautiful frosting   A product that has great form but little substance.

telegenics   Characteristics necessary for a product to deliver a message via television.

think box   Human brain.

thumbnails   Rough pencil or charcoal sketches. *See* tissues.

thunderbolt thinking   Flashes of insight.

TIA   Abbreviation for Toy Industry Association.

time line   Schedule showing a planned order or sequence of a product's development and introduction.

tissues   Rough pencil sketches of a concept.

titanium dioxide   Contents of Magna Doodle that allow an image to be drawn on the surface of the toy.

TM   Abbreviation for trademark.

tooling   Steel molds with which to manufacture plastic components for an item.

T.O.T.Y. Awards   Toy of the Year, an honor bestowed by the TIA on best-selling products.

touch points   Where a company and its products and services come in contact with the customer, hopefully at retail and not through returns.

Toy Center   *See* Two Hundred Fifth Ave.

toy doctor   Model maker who repairs prototypes for manufacturers during Toy Fair or sales meeting.

toyetics   Play values that make up a good toy.

Toy Fair   Largest American trade event, which takes place every February in New York City.

tracking number   The method through which inventors can follow their submissions to and from toy companies.

trade buyer   *See* buyer.

trade dress   Product packaging and presentation.

trademark   Any word, name, symbol, or device used in trade with goods to indicate the source or origin of the goods and to distinguish them from the goods of others.

trades   Specialized magazines and newspapers dedicated to the industry, *such as Playthings.*

travel games   Games designed for portability.

triple tooling   Expanding production output to meet strongest trade demand. The dream of every inventor.

truncated cylinder   Device used to simulate the throat passage in children three years and under, for the purpose of measuring the safety of small parts.

try-me   Design that permits the consumer to activate a product at a retail site without removing it from its package.

TV item   Product that the company will promote through television ads.

Two Hundred Fifth Avenue   200 Fifth Avenue, a.k.a. The Toy Center, site of the annual American International Toy Fair (February in New York City).

under active consideration   An item in the review process that is somewhere between costing engineering, design, sourcing, and marketing.

under consideration   Response to an inventor who is checking on the status of a submission that has not been put into costing engineering, design, sourcing, and marketing.

USPTO   Abbreviation for the U.S. Patent and Trademark Office.

utility patent   Protection for the novel utilitarian features of an item.

vac-forming   Manufacturing process in which a heated sheet of plastic is drawn into or over a mold via vacuum; used for prototyping and blisters.

value-add   Extra features on a product that give the consumer more for the money.

vampire project   Project capable of sucking the blood out of anyone associated with it.

vendor   Supplier of products or services required by a manufacturer in the production and preparation of a toy or game for market.

video game   Game played through a monitor on a gaming system with dedicated software.

virtual prototype   A prototype created by computer and animated on a computer screen.

visual punctuation   Decoration.

wannabe   1. Product that is not fully or accurately defined—it wants to be something else. 2. An amateur inventor, usually part-time, who wants to play in the big leagues.

"We've already done that."   1. No interest. 2. Take a lower royalty.

"Whatever you say."   You have too much control over the company's project. Get ready to take the fall.

"Whathaveyougotforme?"   Opening words from exec to inventor when a company needs a product.

wheeled goods   Bicycles, tricycles, wagons, and scooters.

white knight   Product champion prepared to do battle on behalf of an inventor submission.

"Who has seen this?"   "Which of our competitors has passed on this, and why?"

win/win   A way of approaching business as a relationship, not just a transaction.

word game   Game dependent on the players' understanding of words, spelling, or definitions.

word-of-mouth   Best form of advertising, bar none; one consumer tells another about product satisfaction.

work-for-hire   Flat fee. No royalty. *See* nice try.

works-like prototype   Model that works exactly like the production model of an item will, although it need not be made from the ultimate materials.

worm-eaten   Product seen and passed by many companies.

WOW factor   Strongest and most promotable feature of a new toy or game; a remarkable and exciting point of difference.

X-acto   Cutting instruments that hold a variety of blades designed for different purposes.

XOXOX's   Abbreviation for hugs and kisses. The way highly creative inventors sign off e-mails and other communiqués to colleagues and friends.

Yachtie   A nut for Yahtzee.

yawn   Boring product.

"You're kidding, right?"   It's downhill from here. Start pitching the next product.

"You're the genius."   All the pressure is on you.

yum-yum   Tasty, delightful new product. Hold for review.

zookeeper   Inventor relations executive.

Appendix D

Toy Trivia Scoring and Answers

Toy Trivia Scoring Chart

If you got 90-100 answers correct, you are SANTA CLAUS.

If you got 80-89 answers correct, you are PROFESSIONAL TOY INVENTOR.

If you got 60-79 answers correct, you are CEO.

If you got 40-59 answers correct, you are a VP of R&D.

If you got 30-39 answers correct, you are a MARKETING MBA.

If you got 20-29 answers correct, you are a SALES REP.

If you got 19 or less answers correct, you are a TRADE BUYER.

Toy Trivia Answers

1. C	26. A	51. A	76. B
2. A	27. A	52. B	77. B
3. B	28. C	53. C	78. A
4. A	29. A	54. A	79. B
5. B	30. A	55. B	80. A
6. C	31. A	56. A	81. A
(est. 1876)	32. B	57. A	82. B
7. A	33. C	58. B	83. A
8. A	34. B	59. A	84. C
9. B	35. B	60. C	85. A
10. B	36. A	61. A	86. A
11. A	37. B	62. B	87. B
12. C	38. A	63. C	88. A
13. B	39. B	64. A	89. B
14. B	40. B	65. A	90. A
15. C (John)	41. C	66. B	91. B
16. B	42. B	67. A	92. A
17. A	43. A	68. B	93. B
18. A	44. B	69. A	94. C
19. B	45. A	70. B	95. B
20. A	46. A	71. A	96. A
21. A	47. B	72. C	97. B
22. B	48. A	73. A	98. A
23. A	49. A	74. B	99. A
24. B	50. B	75. A	100. C
25. C			

Appendix E

Bibliography

Books

Ancient Inventions, Peter James and Nick Thorpe (Ballantine Books, 1994).

A Toy Is Born, Marvin Kaye (Stein & Day, 1973).

Bad Fads, Mark A. Long (ECW Press, 2002).

Dr. Toy's Smart Play, Stevanne Auerbach, Ph.D. (St. Martin's Griffin, 1998).

Furby Trainer's Guide, J. Douglas Arnold (Sandwich Islands Publishing Co., Ltd. 1999).

GI Joe, John Michlig (Chronicle Books, 1998).

Guiness World Records 2002, (Guiness, 2002).

I Had One of Those Toys of Our Generation, Robin Langley Sommer (Crescent, 1992).

Inside Santa's Workshop, Richard C. Levy, Ronald O. Weingartner (Henry Holt, 1990).

Inventing the 20th Century, Stephen Van Dulken (New York University Press, 2000).

It's All in the Game, James J. Shea as told to Charles Mercer (G.P. Putnam's Sons, 1960).

Kid Stuff, David Hoffman (Chronicle Books, 1996).

Microcomputer Controlled Toys & Games & How They Work, Van Waterford (TAB, 1983).

Model Collectibe Dolls, Patsy Moyer (Collector Books, 1999).

99% Inspiration, Bryan W. Mattimore (AMA Com, 1993).

100 Greatest Baby Boomer Toys, Mark Rich (Krause, 2000).

POGS: The Milkcap Guide, Tommi Lewis (Andrews & McMeel, 1994).

Secrets of Selling Inventions, Richard C. Levy (RicSher Publishing, 1984).

The Complete Idiot's Guide To Cashing In on Your Inventions, Richard C. Levy (Alpha Books, 2002).

The Evolution of Useful Things, Henry Petroski (Alfred A. Knopf, 1993).

The Game Inventor's Handbook, Steve Peek (Better Way Books, 1993).

The Game of Words, Willard R. Espy (Grosset & Dunlap, 1972).

The Greatest Inventions, John Brockman (Simon & Schuster, 2000).

The Inventing & Patenting Sourcebook, Richard C. Levy (Gale Research, 1992).

The Inventor's Desktop Companion, Richard C. Levy (Visible Ink Press, 1995).

The Monopoly Companion, Phil Orbanes (Bob Adams, 1988).

The Playful World, Mark Pesce (Ballantine Books, 2000).

The Top, D.W. Gould (Bailey Bros. & Swinfen, 1973).

Toyland, Sydney Ladensohn Stern and Ted Schoenhaus (Contemporary Books, 1990).

Toys for a Lifetime, Stevanne Auerbach, Ph.D. (Universe, 1999).

Toy Wars, G. Wayne Miller (Times Books, 1998).

Turning Your Great Idea into Great Success, Judy Ryder (Peterson's/Pacesetter Books, 1995).

Magazines

100th Annual American International Toy Fair Official Directory, (Toy Industry Association, 2003).

2003 Playthings Buyers Guide, (Reed Business Information, 2003).

Index

J–K

L

P

Q–R